SECOND EDITION

THE STRUCTURE OF ARGUMENT

Annette T. Rottenberg

BEDFORD BOOKS   *BOSTON*

For Alex and Anna

For Bedford Books
President and Publisher: Charles H. Christensen
General Manager and Associate Publisher: Joan E. Feinberg
Managing Editor: Elizabeth M. Schaaf
Developmental Editor: Stephen A. Scipione
Editorial Assistants: Rebecca Jerman, Kate O'Sullivan
Production Editor: Karen S. Baart
Production Assistant: Stasia Zomkowski
Copyeditor: Cynthia Benn
Text Design: Claire Seng-Niemoeller
Cover Design: Night and Day Design
Cover Painting: David Park, *Two Heads,* gouache on paper. Collection of Whitney Museum of American Art. Gift of Mrs. Volney F. Righter. Photograph Copyright © 1996: Whitney Museum of American Art, New York.

Library of Congress Catalog Card Number: 96–84941

Manufactured in the United States of America.

1   0   9   8   7
f   e   d   c   b

For information, write: Bedford Books, 75 Arlington Street, Boston, MA 02116
(617–426–7440)

ISBN: 0–312–13412–6

ACKNOWLEDGMENTS

Gordon Allport, "The Nature of Prejudice." From the 17th Claremont Reading Conference Yearbook, 1952. Reprinted by permission of the Claremont Reading Conference.

Amtrak® advertisement, "There's something about a train that's magic." Reprinted by permission of Amtrak®. Amtrak® is a registered service mark of the National Railroad Passenger Corporation.

Mike Barnicle, "Heroes on Our Doorstep." From the *Boston Globe,* June 21, 1994. Reprinted courtesy of The Boston Globe.

Bostongas advertisement, "Perhaps the most beautiful thing about using energy more efficiently isn't the fuel it can save." Illustrator: Suzanne Barnes. Reprinted by permission of Bostongas and the illustrator.

Acknowledgments and copyrights are continued at the back of the book on pages 397–99, which constitute an extension of the copyright page. It is a violation of the law to reproduce these selections by any means whatsoever without the written permission of the copyright holder.

Preface
for Instructors

PURPOSE

Argumentation as the basis of a composition course should need no defense, especially at a time of renewed pedagogical interest in critical thinking. A course in argumentation encourages practice in close analysis, use of supporting materials, and logical organization. It encompasses all the modes of development around which composition courses are often built. It teaches students to read and to listen with more than ordinary care. Not least, argument can engage the interest of students who have been indifferent or even hostile to required writing courses. Because the subject matter of argument can be found in every human activity, from the most trivial to the most elevated, both students and teachers can choose the materials that appeal to them.

Composition courses using the materials of argument are, of course, not new. But the traditional methods of teaching argument through mastery of the formal processes of reasoning cannot account for the complexity of arguments in practice. Even more relevant to our purposes as teachers of composition is the tenuous relationship between learning about induction and deduction, however helpful in analysis, and the actual process of student composition. The challenge has been to find a method of teaching argument that assists students in defending their claims as directly and efficiently as possible, a method that reflects the way people actually go about organizing and developing claims outside the classroom.

One such method, first adapted to classroom instruction by teachers of rhetoric and speech, uses a model of argument advanced by Stephen Toulmin in *The Uses of Argument.* Toulmin was interested in producing a description of the real *process* of argument. His model was the law. "Arguments," he said, "can be compared with lawsuits, and the claims we make and argue for in extra-legal contexts with claims made in the courts."[1] Toulmin's model of argument was based on three principal elements: claim, evidence, and warrant. These elements answered the questions, "What are you trying to prove?" "What have you got to go on?" "How did you get from evidence to claim?" Needless to say, Toulmin's model of argument does not guarantee a classroom of skilled arguers, but his questions about the parts of an argument and their relationship are precisely the ones that students must ask and answer in writing their own essays and analyzing those of others. They lead students naturally into the formulation and development of their claims.

In this text I have adapted — and greatly simplified — some of Toulmin's concepts and terminology for first-year students. I have also introduced two elements of argument with which Toulmin is not directly concerned. Most rhetoricians consider them indispensable, however, to discussion of what actually happens in the defense or rejection of a claim. One is motivational appeals — warrants based on appeals to the needs and values of an audience, designed to evoke emotional responses. A distinction between logic and emotion may be useful as an analytical tool, but in producing or attacking arguments human beings find it difficult, if not impossible, to make such a separation. In this text, therefore, persuasion through appeals to needs and values is treated as a legitimate element in the argumentative process.

I have also stressed the significance of audience as a practical matter. In the rhetorical or audience-centered approach to argument, to which I subscribe in this text, success is defined as acceptance of the claim by an audience. Arguers in the real world recognize intuitively that their primary goal is not to demonstrate the purity of their logic, but to win the adherence of their audiences. To gain this adherence, students need to be reminded of the necessity for establishing themselves as credible sources for their readers.

I hope *The Structure of Argument* will lead students to discover not only the practical and intellectual rewards of learning how to argue but the real excitement of engaging in civilized debate.

---

[1] *The Uses of Argument* (Cambridge: Cambridge University Press, 1958), p. 7.

ORGANIZATION

In Part One, after two introductory chapters, a chapter each is devoted to the chief elements of argument — the claims that students make in their arguments, the definitions and support they must supply for their claims, the warrants that underlie their arguments, the language that they use. Popular fallacies, as well as induction and deduction, are treated in Chapter 8; because fallacies represent errors of reasoning, a knowledge of induction and deduction can make clear how and why fallacies occur. Each chapter ends with an advertisement illustrating the element of argument treated in that chapter.

I have provided examples, readings, discussion questions, and writing suggestions that are, I hope, both practical and stimulating. With the exception of several student dialogues, the examples are real, not invented; they have been taken from speeches, editorial opinions, letters to the editor, advertisements, interviews, and news reports. They reflect the liveliness and complexity that invented examples often suppress.

The forty-eight selections in Part One support the discussions in several important ways. First, they illustrate the elements of argument; in each chapter, one or more essays have been analyzed to emphasize the chapter's principles of argument. Second, they are drawn from current publications and cover as many different subjects as possible to convince students that argument is a pervasive force in the world they read about and live in. Third, some of the essays are obviously flawed and thus enable students to identify the kinds of weaknesses they should avoid in their own essays.

Part Two takes up the process of writing and researching. Chapter 9 explains how to find a topic, define the issues that it embraces, organize the information, and draft and revise an argument. Chapter 10 introduces students to the business of finding sources and using these sources effectively in research papers. The chapter concludes with two annotated student research papers, one of which employs the materials of literature and the Modern Language Association (MLA) documentation system, the other of which represents research in the social and natural sciences and uses a modified American Psychological Association (APA) documentation style.

The instructor's manual, *Resources for Teaching* The Structure of Argument, provides additional suggestions for using the book, as well as for finding and using the enormous variety of materials available in a course on argument.

A longer version, *Elements of Argument,* Fifth Edition, is available for instructors who prefer more readings. It presents not only Parts One and Two and the appendix, Arguing about Literature, but also two anthologies: Opposing Viewpoints, which includes seventy selections on eight currently controversial topics, and a chronologically arranged selection of eleven classic arguments, such as Jonathan Swift's "A Modest Proposal" and Martin Luther King, Jr.'s "Letter from Birmingham Jail."

NEW TO THIS EDITION

This edition is substantially larger and richer than the previous edition. Revising a successful textbook presents both a challenge and an opportunity. The challenge is to avoid undoing features that have been well received in the earlier editions. The opportunity is to tap into the experiences of instructors and students who have used the earlier editions and to make use of their insights to improve what needs improvement. In Part One, for example, a simplified warrants chapter responds to instructors' suggestions by focusing on only three types of warrants. Other warrants — and a chart of types — are now discussed in the instructor's manual.

The principles and concerns of the book have not changed. Rather, I have included a greater breadth of material to increase the book's usefulness as a teaching tool. Several important new features have been added: in Part One, a chapter on responding to argument, and a short debate at the end of each chapter; in Part Two, a discussion on finding the middle ground, and a revised and expanded research chapter that now includes instructions for research using the computer; and an appendix on arguing about literature.

Chapter 2 demonstrates how students can respond to arguments as readers who annotate texts critically, writers who analyze rhetoric effectively, and listeners who think carefully about the astonishing proliferation of oral arguments that confront us daily, especially via the electronic media, on talk shows and political programs. Many students have had little education in critical listening, and even a short introduction can produce significant improvement, not only in response to oral argument but in treatment of written argument as well. In this chapter students will also find a useful guide for civil discourse in the networked classroom and on the Internet.

The short debates at the end of each chapter bring into sharp focus six familiar and timely subjects: legalization of drugs, teenage pregnancy, animal rights, capital punishment, smoking, and alien abduction. Debate on all these subjects can, of course, be enlarged with further research.

In addition to explaining the stock issues of debate, Writing an Argumentative Paper in Part Two recognizes the virtues of trying to find a middle ground between opposing viewpoints. The chapter offers examples from writers who suggest compromises in the heated abortion and pornography debates. Chapter 10, Researching an Argumentative Paper, addresses the changes in library facilities, the biggest change being the replacement of the card catalog by a computerized catalog in many schools, and the increasing use by students of computers for academic research.

Finally, the appendix, Arguing about Literature, is a helpful adjunct to courses in the humanities that require analytical papers. For this section I have summarized the principal elements of fiction, drama, and poetry and added a student essay analyzing a short story.

The number of selections in the second edition has grown to fifty-two — thirty-three of them new, with a corresponding increase in the number of debatable issues and teaching options. Taken as a whole, the changes in the second edition should enhance the versatility of the book, deepen students' awareness of how pervasive argument is, and increase their ability to think critically and communicate persuasively.

This book has profited by the critiques and suggestions of reviewers and instructors who responded to a questionnaire. I appreciate the thoughtful consideration given to the first edition by Kathryn Murphy Anderson, Kathryn Benander, Bill Bolin, John Bradford, Kristina D. Busse, Alice Cleveland, Martha Goodman, Jean E. Graham, Paul D. Knoke, David A. Kossy, Rebecca Lartigne, Madeleine Marchaterre, Judith Mikesch, Theresa R. Mooney, John D. Musselman, Karen L. Regal, Diane Schlegel, and Elaine C. Theismeyer. The instructor's manual is the better for the contribution of Gail Stygall of the University of Washington. Fred Kemp of Texas Tech University drafted the section on responding on-line in Chapter 2, and Debra Canale of the University of Akron revised Chapter 10's discussion of information technologies; I am grateful to both of them.

I would also like to thank those who have reviewed and responded to questionnaires about the longer text from which this one developed, *Elements of Argument,* through its several editions: Nancy E. Adams, Timothy C. Alderman, Yvonne Alexander, John V. Andersen, William Arfin, Alison K. Armstrong, Karen Arnold, Mark Edward Askren, David B. Axelrod, Peter Banland, Carol A. Barnes, Marilyn Barry, Marci Bartolotta, Dr. Bonnie C. Bedford, Frank Beesley, Don Beggs, Martine Bellen, Bruce Bennett, Chester Benson, Robert H. Bentley, Scott Bentley, Patricia Bizzell, Don Black, Kathleen Black, Stanley S. Blair, Laurel Boyd, Mary Virginia Brackett, Robert J. Branda, Dianne Brehmer, Alan Brown, Paul L. Brown, Bill Buck, W. K. Buckley, Alison A. Bulsterbaum, Clarence Bussinger, Deborah N. Byrd, Gary T. Cage, Ruth A. Cameron, Dr. Rita Carey, Barbara R. Carlson, Eric W. Cash, Donna R. Chaney, Gail Chapman, Linda D. Chinn, Roland Christian, Gina Claywell, Dr. John O. Clemons, Dr. Thomas S. Costello, David J. Cranmer, Edward

Crothers, Sara Cutting, Jo Ann Dadisman, Sandra Dahlberg, Mimi Dane, Judy Davidson, Dr. Cynthia C. Davis, Philip E. Davis, Stephanie Demma, Julia Dietrich, Marcia B. Dinnech, Jane T. Dodge, Ellen Donovan, L. Leon Duke, P. Dunsmore, Bernard Earley, Carolyn L. Engdahl, David Estes, Kristina Faber, Lester Faigley, Faridoun Farroth, B. R. Fein, Delia Fisher, Catherine Fitzgerald, Evelyn Flores, David D. Fong, Donald Forand, Mary A. Fortner, Alice R. France, Leslye Friedberg, Sondra Frisch, Richard Fulkerson, Maureen Furniss, Diane Gabbard, Donald J. Gadow, Eric Gardner, Frieda Gardner, Gail Garloch, Darcey Garretson, Victoria Gaydosik, E. R. Gelber-Beechler, Scott Giantralley, Michael Patrick Gillespie, Paula Gillespie, Wallace Gober, Sara Gogol, Stuart Goodman, Joseph Gredler, Lucie Greenberg, Mildred Buza Gronek, Marilyn Hagans, Linda L. Hagge, Lee T. Hamilton, Carolyn Han, Phillip J. Hanse, Pat Hardré, Susan Harland, A. Leslie Harris, Carolyn G. Hartz, Theresia A. Hartz, Fredrik Hausmann, Michael Havens, William Hayes, Ursula K. Heise, Anne Helms, Peter C. Herman, Diane Price Herndl, Heidi Hobbs, William S. Hochman, Sharon E. Hockensmith, Andrew Hoffman, Joyce Hooker, Richard S. Hootman, Clarence Hundley, Patrick Hunter, Richard Ice, Mary Griffith Jackson, Ann S. Jagoe, Katherine James, Ruth Jeffries, Owen Jenkins, Ruth Y. Jenkins, Iris Jennings, Linda Johnson, Janet Jubnke, E. C. Juckett, Catherine Kaikowska, George T. Karnezis, Richard Katula, Mary Jane Kearny, Joanne Keel, Patricia Kellogg-Dennis, N. Kesinger, Susan Kincaid, Joanne Kirkland, Judith Kirscht, Nancy Klug, John H. Knight, Paul D. Knoke, Frances Kritzer, George W. Kuntzman, Barbara Ladd, M. Beardsley Land, Marlene J. Lang, Lisa Lebduska, Sara R. Lee, William Levine, Mary Levitt, Diana M. Liddle, Jack Longmale, Cynthia Lowenthal, Marjorie Lynn, Marcia MacLennan, Nancy McGee, Patrick McGuire, Ray McKerrow, Michael McKoski, Pamela J. McLagen, Suzanne McLaughlin, Dennis McMillan, Donald McQuade, Christina M. McVay, D'Ann Madewell, Beth Madison, Susan Maloney, Dan M. Manolescu, Barbara A. Manrigue, Joyce Marks, Quentin E. Martin, Michael Matzinger, Charles May, Jean-Pierre Meterean, Ekra Miezan, Carolyn R. Miller, Lisa K. Miller, Logan D. Moon, Dennis D. Moore, Dan Morgan, Karen L. Morris, Curt Mortenson, Philip A. Mottola, Thomas Mullen, Charlotte A. Myers, Michael B. Naas, Joseph Nassar, Byron Nelson, Elizabeth A. Nist, Jody Noerdlinger, Paralee F. Norman, Dr. Mary Jean Northcutt, Thomas O'Brien, James F. O'Neil, Mary O'Riordan, Arlene Okerland, Renee Olander, Amy Olsen, Richard D. Olson, Steven Olson, Lori Jo Oswald, Sushil K. Oswald, Gary Pak, Linda J. Palumbo, Jo Patterson, Laurine Paule, Leland S. Person, Betty Peters, Nancy L. Peterson, Susan T. Peterson, Steve Phelan, Gail W. Pieper, Gloria Platzner, Mildred Postar, Ralph David Powell, Jr., Teresa Marie Purvis, Barbara E. Rees, Karen L. Regal, Pat Regel, Charles Reinhart, Thomas C. Renzi, Janice M. Reynolds, Douglas

F. Rice, G. A. Richardson, Katherine M. Rogers, Marilyn Mathias Root, Judith Klinger Rose, Cathy Rosenfeld, Robert A. Rubin, Norma L. Rudinsky, Lori Ruediger, Cheryl W. Ruggiero, Richard Ruppel, Victoria Anne Sager, Joseph L. Sanders, Suzette Schlapkohl, Sybil Schlesinger, Richard Schneider, Eileen Schwartz, Esther L. Schwartz, Eugene Senff, Jeffrey Seyall, Ron Severson, Lucy Sheehey, William E. Sheidley, Sallye J. Sheppeard, Sally Bishop Shigley, John Shout, Dr. Barbara L. Siek, Thomas Simmons, Michael Simms, Jacqueline Simon, Richard Singletary, Roger L. Slakey, Thomas S. Sloane, Beth Slusser, Denzell Smith, Rebecca Smith, Margaret Smolik, Katherine Sotol, Donald L. Soucy, Minoo Southgate, Linda Spain, Richard Spilman, Sarah J. Stafford, Martha L. Stephens, Arlo Stoltenberg, Elissa L. Stuchlik, Judy Szaho, Andrew Tadie, Fernanda G. Tate-Owens, R. Terhorst, Marguerite B. Thompson, Arline R. Thorn, Mary Ann Trevathan, Sandia Tuttle, Whitney G. Vanderwerff, Jennie Ver-Steeg, David L. Wagner, Jeanne Walker, Linda D. Warwick, Carol Adams Watson, Roger D. Watson, Karen Webb, Raymond E. Whelan, Betty E. White, Julia Whitsitt, Toby Widdicombe, Mary Louise Willey, Heywood Williams, Matthew C. Wolfe, Alfred Wong, Bonnie B. Zitz, and Laura Zlogar.

I am grateful to freelancers Cynthia Benn and Meg Hyre, and to the people at Bedford Books whose efforts have made the progress of the fifth edition a pleasure as well as a business: Charles Christensen, Joan Feinberg, Elizabeth Schaaf, Kate O'Sullivan, Rebecca Jerman, and Stasia Zomkowski. I especially thank Karen Baart, whose gentle but compelling arguments helped me to reach sound conclusions on many occasions, and, as always, Steve Scipione, who remains the ideal editor for all seasons.

Contents

PART ONE

The Structure of Argument

CHAPTER ONE

Understanding Argument

THE NATURE OF ARGUMENT

A conversation overheard in the school cafeteria:

"Hey, how come you didn't order the meat loaf special? It's pretty good today."

"Well, I read this book about vegetarianism, and I've decided to give up meat. The book says meat's unhealthy and vegetarians live longer."

"Don't be silly. Americans eat lots of meat, and we're living longer and longer."

"Listen, this book tells how much healthier the Danes were during World War II because they couldn't get meat."

"I don't believe it. A lot of these health books are written by quacks. It's pretty dumb to change your diet after reading one book."

These people are having what most of us would call an argument, one that sounds dangerously close to a quarrel. There are, however, significant differences between the colloquial meaning of argument as a quarrel and its definition as a process of reasoning and advancing proof, although even the exchange reported above exhibits some of the characteristics of formal argument. The kinds of arguments we deal with in this text are not quarrels. They often resemble ordinary discourse about controversial issues. You may, for example, overhear a conversation like this one:

"This morning while I was trying to eat breakfast I heard an announcer describing the execution of that guy in Texas who raped

and murdered a teenaged couple. They gave him an injection, and it took him ten minutes to die. I almost lost my breakfast listening to it."

"Well, he deserved it. He didn't show much pity for his victims, did he?"

"Okay, but no matter what he did, capital punishment is really awful, barbaric. It's murder, even if the state does it."

"No, I'd call it justice. I don't know what else we can do to show how we feel about a cruel, pointless murder of innocent people. The punishment ought to be as terrible as we can make it."

Each speaker is defending a value judgment about an issue that tests ideas of good and evil, right and wrong, and that cannot be decided by facts.

In another kind of argument the speaker or writer proposes a solution for a specific problem. Two men, both under twenty, are engaged in a conversation.

"I'm going to be broke this week after I pay my car insurance. I don't think it's fair for males under twenty to pay such high rates. I'm a good driver, much better that my older sister. Why not consider driving experience instead of age or sex?"

"But I always thought that guys our age had the most accidents. How do you know that driving experience is the right standard to apply?"

"Well, I read a report by the Highway Commission that said it's really driving experience that counts. So I think it's unfair for us to be discriminated against. The law's behind the times. They ought to change the insurance laws."

In this case someone advocates a policy that appears to fulfill a desirable goal — making it impossible to discriminate against drivers just because they are young and male. Objections arise that the arguer must attempt to answer.

In these three dialogues, as well as in all the other arguments you will read in this book, human beings are engaged in explaining and defending their own actions and beliefs and opposing those of others. They do this for at least two reasons: to justify what they do and think both to themselves and to their opponents and, in the process, to solve problems and make decisions, especially those dependent on a consensus between conflicting views.

Unlike the examples cited so far, the arguments you will read and write will not usually take the form of dialogues, but arguments are implicit dialogues. Even when our audience is unknown, we write to persuade the unconvinced, to acquaint them with good reasons for changing their minds. As one definition has it, "Argumentation is the art of influencing others, through the medium of reasoned discourse, to believe or act as we wish them to believe or act."[1] This process is inherently dramatic; a good argument can create the kinds of tensions generated at sporting events. Who will win? What are the factors that enable a winner to emerge? One of the most popular and enduring situations on television is the courtroom debate, in which two lawyers (one, the defense attorney, the hero, unusually knowledgeable and persuasive; the other, the prosecuting attorney, bumbling and corrupt) confront each other before an audience of judge and jury that must render a heart-stopping verdict. Tensions are high because a life is in the balance. In the classroom the stakes are neither so intimidating nor so melodramatic, but even here a well-conducted argument can throw off sparks.

Of course, not all arguments end in clear victories for one side or another. Nor should they. The French philosopher Joseph Joubert said, "It is better to debate a question without settling it than to settle a question without debating it." In a democratic society of competing interests and values, a compromise between two or more extreme points of view may be the only viable solution to a vexing problem. Although formal debates under the auspices of a debating society, such as take place on many college campuses, usually end in winners and losers, real-life problems, both public and private, are often resolved through negotiation. Courtroom battles may result in compromise, and the law itself allows for exemptions and extenuating circumstances. Elsewhere in this book we speak of the importance of "trade-offs" in social and political transactions, giving up one thing in return for another.

Keep in mind, however, that some compromises will not be morally defensible. In searching for a middle ground, the thoughtful arguer must determine that the consequences of a negotiated solution will contribute to "the common good," not, in the words of one essayist, merely the good of "the sovereign self." (In Chapter 9 you will find a detailed guide for writing arguments in which you look for common ground.)

Most of the arguments in this book will deal with matters of public controversy, an area traditionally associated with the study of argument. As the word *public* suggests, these matters concern us as members of a community. "They are," according to one rhetorician, "the problems of war and peace, race and creed, poverty, wealth, and population, of democracy and communism. . . . Specific issues arise on which we must take decision from time to time. One day it is Suez, another Cuba. One week it is the Congo, another it is the plight of the American farmer or the railroads. . . . On these subjects

[1]J. M. O'Neill, C. Laycock, and R. L. Scale, *Argumentation and Debate* (New York: Macmillan, 1925), p. 1.

the experts as well as the many take sides."[2] Today the issues are different from the issues that writers confronted more than twenty years ago. Today we are concerned about unemployment, illegal immigration, bilingual education, gun control, gay rights, drug abuse, prayer in school, to name only a few,

Clearly, if all of us agreed about everything, if harmony prevailed everywhere, the need for argument would disappear. But given what we know about the restless, seeking, contentious nature of human beings and their conflicting interests, we should not be surprised that many controversial questions, some of them as old as human civilization itself, will not be settled nor will they vanish despite the energy we devote to settling them. Unresolved, they are submerged for a while and then reappear, sometimes in another form, sometimes virtually unchanged. Capital punishment is one such stubborn problem; abortion is another. Nevertheless, we value the argumentative process because it is indispensable to the preservation of a free society. In *Areopagitica,* his great defense of free speech, John Milton, the seventeenth-century poet, wrote, "I cannot praise a fugitive and cloistered virtue, unexercised and unbreathed, that never sallies out and sees her adversary." How can we know the truth, he asked, unless there is a "free and open encounter" between all ideas? "Give me liberty to know, to utter, and to argue freely according to conscience, above all liberties."

WHY STUDY ARGUMENT?

Perhaps the question has already occurred to you: Why *study* argument? Since you've engaged in some form of the argumentative process all your life, is there anything to be learned that experience hasn't taught you? We think there is. If you've ever felt frustration in trying to decide what is wrong with an argument, either your own or someone else's, you might have wondered if there were rules to help in the analysis. If you've ever been dissatisfied with your attempt to prove a case, you might have wondered how good arguers, the ones who succeed in persuading people, construct their cases. Good arguers do, in fact, know and follow rules. Studying and practicing these rules can provide you with some of the same skills.

You will find yourself using these skills in a variety of situations, not only in arguing important public issues. You will use them, for example, in your academic career. Whatever your major field of study — the humanities, the social sciences, the physical sciences,

---

[2]Karl R. Wallace, "Toward a Rationale for Teachers of Writing and Speaking," *English Journal,* September 1961, p. 386.

business — you will be required to defend views about materials you have read and studied.

Humanities. Why have some of the greatest novels resisted translation into great films?

Social Science. What is the evidence that upward social mobility continues to be a positive force in American life?

Physical Science. What will happen to the world climate as the amount of carbon dioxide in the atmosphere increases?

Business. Are the new tax laws beneficial or disadvantageous to the real estate investor?

For all these assignments, different as they may be, you would use the same kinds of analysis, research techniques, and evaluation. The conventions or rules for reporting results might differ from one field of study to another, but for the most part the rules for defining terms, evaluating evidence, and arriving at conclusions cross disciplinary lines. Many employers, not surprisingly, are aware of this. One sheriff in Arizona advertised for an assistant with a degree in philosophy. He had discovered, he said, that the methods used by philosophers to solve problems were remarkably similar to the methods used in law enforcement.

Whether or not you are interested in serving as sheriff's assistant, you will encounter situations in the workplace that call for the same analytical and argumentative skills employed by philosophers and law enforcement personnel. Almost everywhere — in the smallest businesses as well as the largest corporations — a worker who can articulate his or her views clearly and forcefully has an important advantage in gaining access to positions of greater interest and challenge. Even when they are primarily informative, the memorandums, reports, instructions, questions, and explanations that issue from offices and factories obey the rules of argumentative discourse.

You may not anticipate doing the kind of writing or speaking at your job that you will practice in your academic work. It is probably true that in some careers, writing constitutes a negligible part of a person's duties. But outside the office, the studio, and the salesroom, you will be called on to exhibit argumentative skills as a citizen, as a member of a community, and as a consumer of leisure. In these capacities you can contribute to decision making if you are knowledgeable and prepared. By writing or speaking to the appropriate authorities, you can argue for a change in the meal ticket plan at your school or the release of pornographic films at the neighborhood theater or against a change in automobile insurance rates. Most of us are painfully aware of opportunities we lost because we were uncertain of how to proceed, even in matters that affected us deeply.

A course in argumentation offers another invaluable dividend: It can help you to cope with the bewildering confusion of voices in the world around you. It can give you tools for distinguishing between what is true and what is false, what is valid and what is invalid, in the claims of politicians, promoters of causes, newscasters, advertisers, salespeople, teachers, parents and siblings, employers and employees, neighbors, friends, and lovers, any of whom may be engaged at some time in attempting to persuade you to accept a belief or adopt a course of action. It can even offer strategies for arguing with yourself about a personal dilemma.

So far we have treated argument as an essentially pragmatic activity that benefits the individual. But choosing argument over force or evasion has clear moral benefits for society as well. We can, in fact, defend the study of argumentation for the same reasons that we defend universal education despite its high cost and sometimes controversial results. In a democracy, widespread literacy ultimately benefits all members of society, not only those who are the immediate beneficiaries of education, because only an informed citizenry can make responsible choices. One distinguished writer explains that "democracy depends on a citizenry that can reason for themselves, on men who know whether a case has been proved, or at least made probable."[3]

It is not too much to say that argument is a civilizing influence, the very basis of democratic order. In repressive regimes, coercion, which may express itself in a number of reprehensible forms — censorship, imprisonment, exile, torture, or execution — is a favored means of removing opposition to establishment "truth." In free societies, argument and debate remain the preeminent means of arriving at consensus.

Of course, rational discourse in a democracy can and does break down. Confrontations with police at abortion clinics, shouting and heckling at a meeting to prevent a speaker from being heard, student protests against university policies — such actions have become common in recent years. The demands of the demonstrators are often passionately and sincerely held, and the protesters sometimes succeed through force or intimidation in influencing policy changes. When this happens, however, we cannot be sure that the changes are justified. History and experience teach us that reason, to a far greater degree than other methods of persuasion, ultimately determines the rightness or wrongness of our actions.

A piece of folk wisdom sums up the superiority of reasoned argument as a vehicle of persuasion: "A man convinced against his will

---

[3]Wayne C. Booth, "Boring from Within: The Art of the Freshman Essay," adapted from a speech delivered to the Illinois Council of College Teachers of English in May 1963.

is of the same opinion still." Those who accept a position after engaging in a dialogue offering good reasons on both sides will think and act with greater willingness and conviction than those who have been coerced or denied the privilege of participating in the decision.

WHY WRITE?

If we agree that studying argumentation provides important critical tools, one last question remains: Why *write*? Isn't it possible to learn the rules by reading and talking about the qualities of good and bad arguments? Not quite. All writers, both experienced and inexperienced, will probably confess that looking at what they have written, even after long thought, can produce a startled disclaimer: But that isn't what I meant to say! They know that more analysis and more hard thinking are in order. Writers are also aware that words on paper have an authority and a permanency that invite more than casual deliberation. It is one thing to make an assertion, to express an idea or a strong feeling in conversation, and perhaps even to deny it later; it is quite another to write out an extended defense of your own position or an attack on someone else's that will be read and perhaps criticized by people unsympathetic to your views.

Students are often told that they must become better thinkers if they are to become better writers. It works the other way, too. In the effort to produce a clear and convincing argument, a writer matures as a thinker and a critic. The very process of writing calls for skills that make us better thinkers. Writing argumentative essays tests and enlarges important mental skills — developing and organizing ideas, evaluating evidence, observing logical consistency, expressing ourselves clearly and economically — that we need to exercise all our lives in our various social roles, whether or not we continue to write after college.

THE TERMS OF ARGUMENT

One definition of argument, emphasizing audience, has been given earlier: "Argumentation is the art of influencing others, through the medium of reasoned discourse, to believe or act as we wish them to believe or act." A distinction is sometimes made between argument and persuasion. Argument, according to most authorities, gives primary importance to logical appeals. Persuasion introduces the element of ethical and emotional appeals. The difference is one of emphasis. In real-life arguments about social policy, the distinction is hard to measure. In this book we use the term *argument* to represent forms of discourse that attempt to persuade readers or listeners to accept a claim, whether acceptance is based on logical or on emotional appeals or, as is usually the case, on both. The following brief definition includes other elements: *An argument is a statement or statements offering support for a claim.*

An argument is composed of at least three parts: the claim, the support, and the warrant.[4]

The Claim

The claim (also called a *proposition*) answers the question "What are you trying to prove?" It may appear as the thesis statement of your essay, although in some arguments it may not be stated directly. There are three principal kinds of claim (discussed more fully in Chapter 3): claims of fact, of value, and of policy. (The three dialogues at the beginning of this chapter represent these three kinds of claim respectively.) *Claims of fact* assert that a condition has existed, exists, or will exist and are based on facts or data that the audience will accept as being objectively verifiable:

> The present cocaine epidemic is not unique. From 1885 to the 1920s, cocaine was as widely used as it is today.

> Horse racing is the most dangerous sport.

> California will experience colder, stormier weather for the next ten years.

All these claims must be supported by data. Although the last example is an inference or an educated guess about the future, a reader will probably find the prediction credible if the data seem authoritative.

Claims of value attempt to prove that some things are more or less desirable than others. They express approval or disapproval of standards of taste and morality. Advertisements and reviews of cultural events are one common source of value claims, but such claims emerge whenever people argue about what is good or bad, beautiful or ugly.

> The opera *Tannhäuser* provides a splendid viewing as well as listening experience.

> Football is one of the most dehumanizing experiences a person can face. — Dave Meggyesy

> Ending a patient's life intentionally is absolutely forbidden on moral grounds. — Presidential Commission on Medical Ethics, 1983

---

[4]Some of the terms and analyses used in this text are adapted from Stephen Toulmin's *The Uses of Argument* (Cambridge: Cambridge University Press, 1958).

Claims of policy assert that specific policies should be instituted as solutions to problems. The expression *should, must,* or *ought to* usually appears in the statement.

> Prisons should be abolished because they are crime-manufacturing concerns.

> Our first step must be to immediately establish and advertise drastic policies designed to bring our own population under control. — Paul Ehrlich, biologist

> The New York City Board of Education should make sure that qualified women appear on any new list [of candidates for Chancellor of Education].

Policy claims call for analysis of both fact and value. (A full discussion of claims follows in Chapter 3.)

The Support

Support consists of the materials used by the arguer to convince an audience that his or her claim is sound. These materials include *evidence* and *motivational appeals.* The evidence or data consist of facts, statistics, and testimony from experts. The motivational appeals are the ones that the arguer makes to the values and attitudes of the audience to win support for the claim. The word *motivational* points out that these appeals are the reasons that move an audience to accept a belief or adopt a course of action. For example, in his argument advocating population control, Ehrlich first offered statistical evidence to prove the magnitude of the population explosion. But he also made a strong appeal to the generosity of his audience to persuade them to sacrifice their own immediate interests to those of future generations. (See Chapter 5 for detailed discussion of support.)

The Warrant

The warrant is an inference or an assumption, a belief or principle that is taken for granted. A warrant is a guarantee of reliability; in argument it guarantees the soundness of the relationship between the support and the claim. It allows the reader to make the connection between the support and the claim.

Warrants or assumptions underlie all the claims we make. They may be stated or unstated. If the arguer believes that the audience shares his assumption, he may feel it unnecessary to express it. But if he thinks that the audience is doubtful or hostile, he may decide to state the assumption in order to emphasize its importance or argue for its validity.

This is how the warrant works. In the dialogue beginning this chapter, one speaker made the claim that vegetarianism was more healthful than a diet containing meat. As support he offered the evidence that the authors of a book he had read recommended vegetarianism for greater health and longer life. He did not state his warrant — that the authors of the book were trustworthy guides to theories of healthful diet. In outline form the argument looks like this:

CLAIM: Adoption of a vegetarian diet leads to healthier and longer life.

SUPPORT: The authors of *Becoming a Vegetarian Family* say so.

WARRANT: The authors of *Becoming a Vegetarian Family* are reliable sources of information on diet.

A writer or speaker may also need to offer support for the warrant. In the case cited above, the second speaker is reluctant to accept the unstated warrant, suggesting that the authors may be quacks. The first speaker will need to provide support for the assumption that the authors are trustworthy, perhaps by introducing proof of their credentials in science and medicine. Notice that although the second speaker accepts the evidence, he cannot agree that the claim has been proved unless he also accepts the warrant. If he fails to accept the warrant — that is, if he refuses to believe that the authors are credible sources of information about diet — then the evidence cannot support the claim.

The following example demonstrates how a different kind of warrant, based on values, can also lead an audience to accept a claim.

CLAIM: Laws making marijuana illegal should be repealed.

SUPPORT: People should have the right to use any substance they wish.

WARRANT: No laws should prevent citizens from exercising their rights.

Support for repeal of the marijuana laws often consists of medical evidence that marijuana is harmless. Here, however, the arguer contends that an important ethical principle is at work: Nothing should prevent people from exercising their rights, including the right to use any substance, no matter how harmful. Let us suppose that the reader agrees with the supporting statement, that individuals should have the right to use any substance. But in order to accept the claim, the reader must also agree with the principle expressed in the warrant, that government should not interfere with the individual's right. He or she can then agree that laws making marijuana illegal should be repealed. Notice that this warrant, like all warrants, certifies that the relationship between the support and the claim is sound. (For more on warrants, see Chapter 6.)

Definition, Language, Logic

In addition to the claim, the support, and the warrant, several other elements of clear, persuasive prose are crucial to good argument. For this reason we have devoted separate chapters to each of them.

One of the most important is definition. In fact, many of the controversial questions you will read or write about are primarily arguments of definition. Such terms as *abortion, pornography, racism, poverty, addiction,* and *mental illness* must be defined before useful solutions to the problems they represent can be formulated. (Chapter 4 deals with definition.)

Another important resource is the careful use of language, not only to define terms and express personal style but also to reflect clarity of thought and avoid the clichés and outworn slogans that frequently substitute for fresh ideas. (See Chapter 7 for more on language.)

Last, we have included an examination of induction and deduction, the classic elements of logic. Understanding the way in which these reasoning processes work can help you to determine the truth and validity of your own and other arguments and to identify faulty reasoning. (Induction and deduction are covered in Chapter 8.)

THE AUDIENCE

All arguments are composed with an audience in mind. We have already pointed out that an argument is an implicit dialogue or exchange. Often the writer of an argument about a public issue is responding to another writer or speaker who has made a claim that needs to be supported or opposed. In writing your own arguments, you should assume that there is a reader who may not agree with you. Throughout this book, we will continue to refer to ways of reaching such a reader.

Speechmakers are usually better informed than writers about their audience. Some writers, however, are familiar with the specific persons or groups who will read their arguments; advertising copywriters are a conspicuous example. They discover their audiences through sophisticated polling and marketing techniques and direct their messages to a well-targeted group of prospective buyers. Other professionals may be required to submit reports to persuade a specific and clearly defined audience of certain beliefs or courses of action: An engineer may be asked by an environmental interest group to defend his plans for the building of a sewage treatment plant; or a town planner may be called on to tell the town council why she believes that rent control may not work; or a sales manager may find it necessary to explain to his superior why a new product should be launched in the Midwest rather than the South.

In such cases the writer asks some or all of the following questions about the audience:

Why has this audience requested this report? What do they want to get out of it?

How much do they already know about the subject?

Are they divided or agreed on the subject?

What is their emotional involvement with the issues?

Assessing Credibility

Providing abundant evidence and making logical connections between the parts of an argument may not be enough to win agreement from an audience. In fact, success in convincing an audience is almost always inseparable from the writer's credibility, or the audience's belief in the writer's trustworthiness. Aristotle, the Greek philosopher who wrote a treatise on argument that has influenced its study and practice for more than two thousand years, considered credibility — what he called *ethos* — the most important element in the arguer's ability to persuade the audience to accept his or her claim.

Aristotle named "intelligence, character, and goodwill" as the attributes that produce credibility. Today we might describe these qualities somewhat differently, but the criteria for judging a writer's credibility remain essentially the same. First, the writer must convince the audience that he is knowledgeable, that he is as well informed as possible about the subject. Second, he must persuade his audience that he is not only truthful in the presentation of his evidence but also morally upright and dependable. Third, he must show that, as an arguer with good intentions, he has considered the interests and needs of others as well as his own.

As an example in which the credibility of the arguer is at stake, consider a wealthy Sierra Club member who lives on ten acres of a magnificent oceanside estate and who appears before a community planning board to argue against future development of the area. His claim is that more building will destroy the delicate ecological balance of the area. The board, acting in the interests of all the citizens of the community, will ask themselves: Has the arguer proved that his information about environmental impact is complete and accurate? Has he demonstrated that he sincerely desires to preserve the wilderness, not merely his own privacy and space? And has he also made clear that he has considered the needs and desires of those who might want to live in a housing development by the ocean? If the answers to all these questions are yes, then the board will hear the arguer with respect, and the arguer will have begun to establish his credibility.

A reputation for intelligence, character, and goodwill is not often won overnight. And it can be lost more quickly than it is won. Once a writer or speaker has betrayed an audience's belief in her character or judgment, she may find it difficult to persuade an audience to accept subsequent claims, no matter how sound her data and reasoning are. "We give no credit to a liar," said Cicero, "even when he speaks the truth."

Political life is full of examples of lost and squandered credibility. After it was discovered that President Lyndon Johnson had deceived the American public about U.S. conduct in the Vietnam War, he could not regain his popularity. After President Gerald Ford pardoned former President Richard Nixon for his complicity in the Watergate scandal, Ford was no longer a serious candidate for reelection. After asserting in a presidential debate that he would not raise taxes, President George Bush lost the favor of many voters — and possibly reelection — when he did.

We can see the practical consequences when an audience realizes that an arguer has been guilty of a deception — misusing facts and authority, suppressing evidence, distorting statistics, violating the rules of logic. But suppose the arguer is successful in concealing his or her manipulation of the data and can persuade an uninformed audience to take the action or adopt the idea that he or she recommends. Even supposing that the argument promotes a "good" cause, is the arguer justified in using evasive or misleading tactics?

The answer is no. To encourage another person to make a decision on the basis of incomplete or dishonestly used data is profoundly unethical. It indicates lack of respect for the rights of others — their right to know at least as much as you do about the subject, to be allowed to judge and compare, to disagree with you if they challenge your own interests. If the moral implications are still not clear, try to imagine yourself not as the perpetrator of the lie but as the victim.

There is also a danger in measuring success wholly by the degree to which audiences accept our arguments. Both as writers and readers, we must be able to respect the claim, or proposition, and what it tries to demonstrate. Toulmin has said: "To conclude that a proposition is true, it is not enough to know that this [person] or that finds it 'credible': the proposition itself must be *worthy* of credence."[5]

---

[5]*An Examination of the Place of Reason in Ethics* (Cambridge: Cambridge University Press, 1964), p. 71.

Acquiring Credibility

You may wonder how you can acquire credibility. You are not yet an expert in many of the subjects you will deal with in assignments, although you are knowledgeable about many other things, including your cultural and social activities. But there are several ways in which you can create confidence by your treatment of topics derived from academic disciplines, such as political science, psychology, economics, sociology, and art, on which most assignments will be based.

First, you can submit evidence of careful research, demonstrating that you have been conscientious in finding the best authorities, giving credit, and attempting to arrive at the truth. Second, you can adopt a thoughtful and judicious tone that reflects a desire to be fair in your conclusion. Tone expresses the attitude of the writer toward his or her subject. When the writer feels strongly about the subject and adopts a belligerent or complaining tone, for example, he or she forgets that readers who feel differently may find the tone disagreeable and unconvincing. In the following excerpt a student expresses his feelings about standard grading, that is, grading by letter or number on a scale that applies to a whole group.

> You go to school to learn, not to earn grades. To be educated, that's what they tell you. "He's educated, he graduated Magna Cum Laude." What makes a Magna Cum Laude man so much better than a man that graduates with a C? They are both still educated, aren't they? No one has a right to call someone less educated because they got a C instead of an A. Let's take both men and put them in front of a car. Each car has something wrong with it. Each man must fix his broken car. Our C man goes right to work while our Magna Cum Laude man hasn't got the slightest idea where to begin. Who's more educated now?

Probably a reader who disagreed with the claim — that standard grading should not be used — would find the tone, if not the evidence itself, unpersuasive. The writer sounds as if he is defending his own ability to do something that an honors graduate can't do, while ignoring the acknowledged purposes of standard grading in academic subjects. He sounds, moreover, as if he's angry because someone has done him an injury. Compare the preceding passage to the following one, written by a student on the same subject.

> Grades are the play money in a university Monopoly game. As long as the tokens are offered, the temptation will be largely irresistible to play for them. Students are so busy taking notes, doing tests, and getting tokens that they have forgotten to ask: Of what worth is all this? Or perhaps they ask and the grade is their answer.
>
> One certainly learns something in the passive lecture-note-read-note-test process: how to do it all more efficiently next time (in the

hope of eventually owning Boardwalk and Park Place). As Marshall McLuhan has said, we learn what we do. In this process most students come to view learning as studying and remembering what other people have learned. They assume that knowledge is logically and for practical reasons divided up into discrete pieces called "disciplines" and that the highest knowledge is achieved by specializing in a discipline. By getting good grades in a lot of disciplines they conclude they have learned a lot. They have indeed, and it is too bad.[6]

Most readers would consider this writer more credible, in part because he has adopted a tone that seems moderate and impersonal. That is, he does not convey the impression that he is interested only in defending his own grades. Notice also that the language of this passage suggests a higher level of learning and research.

Sometimes, of course, an expression of anger or even outrage is appropriate and morally justified. But if readers do not share your sense of outrage, you must try to reach them through a more moderate approach. In his autobiography, Benjamin Franklin recounted his attempts to acquire the habit of temperate language in argument:

> Retaining . . . the habit of expressing myself in terms of modest diffidence, never using when I advance anything that may possibly be disputed, the words *certainly, undoubtedly,* or any others that give the air of positiveness to an opinion; but rather say, *I conceive,* or *I apprehend* a thing to be so or so; *it appears to me,* or *I should think it so or so for such and such reasons,* or *I imagine* it to be so, or *it is so if I am not mistaken.* — This habit I believe has been of great advantage to me, when I have had occasion to inculcate my opinions and persuade men into measures that I have been from time to time engaged in promoting.[7]

This is not to say that the writer must hedge his or her opinions or confess uncertainty at every point. Franklin suggests that the writer must recognize that other opinions may also have validity and that, although the writer may disagree, he or she respects the other opinions. Such an attitude will also dispose the reader to be more generous in evaluating the writer's argument.

A final method of establishing credibility is to produce a clean, literate, well-organized paper, with evidence of care in writing and proofreading. Such a paper will help persuade the reader to take your efforts seriously.

Now let us turn to one of the most famous arguments in American history and examine its elements.

---

[6]Roy E. Terry in "Does Standard Grading Encourage Excessive Competitiveness?" *Change,* September 1974, p. 45.

[7]*The Autobiography of Benjamin Franklin,* ed. Louis P. Masur (Boston: Bedford Books, 1993), pp. 39–40. Italics are Franklin's.

The Declaration of Independence

THOMAS JEFFERSON

When in the course of human events, it becomes necessary for one people to dissolve the political bands which have connected them with another, and to assume among the Powers of the earth, the separate and equal station to which the Laws of Nature and Nature's God entitle them, a decent respect to the opinions of mankind requires that they should declare the causes which impel them to the separation.

We hold these truths to be self-evident, that all men are created equal, that they are endowed by their Creator with certain unalienable Rights, that among these are Life, Liberty and the pursuit of Happiness.

That to secure these rights, Governments are instituted among Men, deriving their just powers from the consent of the governed.

That whenever any Form of Government becomes destructive of these ends, it is the Right of the People to alter or to abolish it, and to institute a new Government laying its foundation on such principles and organizing its powers in such form, as to them shall seem most likely to effect their Safety and Happiness. Prudence, indeed, will dictate that Governments long established should not be changed for light and transient causes; and accordingly all experience hath shown that mankind are more disposed to suffer, while evils are sufferable, than to right themselves by abolishing the forms to which they are accustomed. But when a long train of abuses and usurpations pursuing invariably the same Object evinces a design to reduce them under absolute Despotism, it is their right, it is their duty, to throw off such government, and to provide new Guards for their future security.

Such has been the patient sufferance of these Colonies; and such 5 is now the necessity which constrains them to alter their former Systems of Government. The history of the present King of Great Britain is a history of repeated injuries and usurpations, all having in direct object the establishment of an absolute Tyranny over these States. To prove this, let Facts be submitted to a candid world.

He has refused his Assent to Laws, the most wholesome and necessary for the public good.

He has forbidden his Governors to pass Laws of immediate and pressing importance, unless suspended in their operation till his Assent should be obtained; and when so suspended, he has utterly neglected to attend to them.

He has refused to pass other Laws for the accommodation of large districts of people, unless those people would relinquish the right of Representation in the Legislature, a right inestimable to them and formidable to tyrants only.

He has called together legislative bodies at places unusual, uncomfortable, and distant from the depository of their Public Records, for the sole purpose of fatiguing them into compliance with his measures.

He has dissolved Representative Houses repeatedly, for oppos- 10 ing with manly firmness his invasions on the rights of the people.

He has refused for a long time, after such dissolutions, to cause others to be elected; whereby the Legislative Powers, incapable of Annihilation, have returned to the People at large for their exercise; the State remaining in the mean time exposed to all the danger of invasion from without, and convulsions within.

He has endeavored to prevent the population of these States; for that purpose obstructing the Laws of Naturalization of Foreigners; refusing to pass others to encourage their migration hither, and raising the conditions of new Appropriations of Lands.

He has obstructed the Administration of Justice, by refusing his Assent to Laws for establishing Judiciary Powers.

He has made Judges dependent on his Will alone, for the tenure of their offices, and the amount and payment of their salaries.

He has erected a multitude of New Offices, and sent hither 15 swarms of Officers to harass our People, and eat out their substance.

He has kept among us, in time of peace, Standing Armies without the consent of our Legislature.

He has affected to render the Military independent of and superior to the Civil Power.

He has combined with others to subject us to jurisdictions foreign to our constitution, and unacknowledged by our laws; giving his Assent to their acts of pretended Legislation:

For quartering large bodies of armed troops among us:

For protecting them, by a mock Trial, from Punishment for any 20 Murders which they should commit on the Inhabitants of these States:

For cutting off our Trade with all parts of the world:

For imposing Taxes on us without our Consent:

For depriving us in many cases, of the benefits of Trial by Jury:

For transporting us beyond Seas to be tried for pretended offenses:

For abolishing the free System of English Laws in a Neighbouring 25 Province, establishing therein an Arbitrary government, and enlarging its boundaries so as to render it at once an example and fit instrument for introducing the same absolute rule into these Colonies:

For taking away our Charters, abolishing our most valuable Laws, and altering fundamentally the Forms of our Governments:

For suspending our own legislatures, and declaring themselves invested with Power to legislate for us in all cases whatsoever.

He has abdicated Government here, by declaring us out of his Protection and waging War against us.

He has plundered our seas, ravaged our Coasts, burnt our towns and destroyed the Lives of our people.

He is at this time transporting large Armies of foreign Mercenar- 30
ies to compleat the works of death, desolation and tyranny, already begun with circumstances of Cruelty & perfidy scarcely paralleled in the most barbarous ages, and totally unworthy the Head of a civilized nation.

He has constrained our fellow Citizens taken Captive on the high Seas to bear Arms against their Country, to become the executioners of their friends and Brethren, or to fall themselves by their Hands.

He has excited domestic insurrections amongst us, and has endeavored to bring on the inhabitants of our frontiers, the merciless Indian Savages, whose known rule of warfare is an undistinguished destruction of all ages, sexes, and conditions.

In every stage of these Oppressions We Have Petitioned for Redress in the most humble terms. Our repeated petitions have been answered only by repeated injury. A Prince, whose character is thus marked by every act which may define a Tyrant, is unfit to be the ruler of a free People.

Not have We been wanting in attention to our British brethren. We have warned them from time to time of attempts by their legislature to extend an unwarrantable jurisdiction over us. We have reminded them of the circumstances of our emigration and settlement here. We have appealed to their native justice and magnanimity and we have conjured them by the ties of our common kindred to disavow these usurpations, which would inevitably interrupt our connections and correspondence. They too have been deaf to the voice of justice and of consanguinity. We must, therefore, acquiesce in the necessity, which denounces our Separation, and hold them, as we hold the rest of mankind, Enemies in War, in Peace Friends.

We, therefore, the Representatives of the United States of Amer- 35
ica, in General Congress, Assembled, appealing to the Supreme Judge of the world for the rectitude of our intentions, do, in the Name, and by Authority of the good People of these Colonies, solemnly publish and declare, That these United Colonies are, and of Right ought to be, Free and Independent States; that they are Absolved from all Allegiance to the British Crown, and that all political connection between them and the State of Great Britain, is and ought to be totally dissolved; and that as Free and Independent States, they have full power to levy War, conclude Peace, contract

Alliances, establish Commerce, and to do all other Acts and Things which Independent States may of right do. And for the support of this Declaration, with a firm reliance on the protection of Divine Providence, we mutually pledge to each other our lives, our Fortunes and our sacred Honor.

Analysis

Claim: What is Jefferson trying to prove? *The American colonies are justified in declaring their independence from British rule.* Jefferson and his fellow signers might have issued a simple statement such as appears in the last paragraph, announcing the freedom and independence of these United Colonies. Instead, however, they chose to justify their right to do so.

Support: What does Jefferson have to go on? The Declaration of Independence bases its claim on two kinds of support: *factual evidence* and *motivational appeals* or appeals to the values of the audience.

Factual Evidence: Jefferson presents a long list of specific acts of tyranny by George III, beginning with "He has refused his Assent to Laws, the most wholesome and necessary for the public good." This list constitutes more than half the text. Notice how Jefferson introduces these grievances: "The history of the present King of Great Britain is a history of repeated injuries and usurpations, all having in direct object the establishment of an absolute Tyranny over these States. *To prove this, let Facts be submitted to a candid world*" (italics for emphasis added). Jefferson hopes that a recital of these specific acts will convince an honest audience that the United Colonies have indeed been the victims of an intolerable tyranny.

Appeal to Values: Jefferson also invokes the moral values underlying the formation of a democratic state. These values are referred to throughout. In the second and third paragraphs he speaks of equality, "Life, Liberty and the pursuit of Happiness," "just powers," "consent of the governed," and in the fourth paragraph, safety. In the last paragraph he refers to freedom and independence. Jefferson believes that the people who read his appeal will, or should, share these fundamental values. Audience acceptance of these values constitutes the most important part of the support. Some historians have called the specific acts of oppression cited by Jefferson trivial, inconsequential, or distorted. Clearly, however, Jefferson felt that the list of specific grievances was vital to definition of the abstract terms in which values are always expressed.

Warrant: How does Jefferson get from support to claim? *People have a right to revolution in order to free themselves from oppression.* This warrant is explicit: "But when a long train of abuses and usurpations pursuing invariably the same Object evinces a design to reduce them under absolute Despotism, it is their right, it is their duty, to throw off such government, and to provide new Guards for their future security." Some members of Jefferson's audience, especially those whom he accuses of oppressive acts, will reject the principle that any subject people have earned the right to revolt. But Jefferson believes that the decent opinion of mankind will accept this assumption. Many of his readers will also be aware that the warrant is supported by seventeenth-century political philosophy, which defines government as a social compact between the government and the governed.

If Jefferson's readers do, in fact, accept the warrant and if they also believe in the accuracy of the factual evidence and share his moral values, then they will conclude that his claim has been proved, that Jefferson has justified the right of the colonies to separate themselves from Great Britain.

Audience: The Declaration of Independence is addressed to several audiences: to the American colonists; to the British people; to the British Parliament; to the British king, George III; and to mankind or a universal audience.

Not all the American colonists were convinced by Jefferson's argument. Large numbers remained loyal to the king and for various reasons opposed an independent nation. In the next-to-the-last paragraph, Jefferson refers to previous addresses to the British people. Not surprisingly, most of the British citizenry as well as the king also rejected the claims of the Declaration. But the universal audience, the decent opinion of mankind, found Jefferson's argument overwhelmingly persuasive. Many of the liberal reform movements of the eighteenth and nineteenth centuries were inspired by the Declaration. In basing his claim on universal principles of justice and equality, Jefferson was certainly aware that he was addressing future generations.

Definition: Several significant terms are not defined. Modern readers will ask for further definition of "all men are created equal," "Life, Liberty and the pursuit of Happiness," "Laws of Nature and Nature's God," among others. We must assume that the failure to explain these terms more strictly was deliberate, in part because Jefferson thought that his readers would understand the references — for example, to the eighteenth-century belief in freedom as the birthright of all human beings — and in part because he wished the terms to be understood as universal principles of justice, applicable in all struggles, not merely those of the colonies against the king of England. But a failure to narrow the terms of argument can have unpredictable consequences. In later years the Declaration of Independence would be used to justify other rebellions, including the secession of the South from the Union in 1861.

Language: Although some stylistic conventions of eighteenth-century writing would not be observed today, Jefferson's clear, elegant, formal prose — "a surprising mixture of simplicity and majesty," in the words of one writer — remains a masterpiece of English prose and persuades us that we are reading an important document. Several devices are worth noting:

1. *Parallelism* or balance of sentence construction gives both emphasis and rhythm to the statements in the introduction (first four paragraphs) and the list of grievances.
2. *Diction* (choice of words) supports and underlines the meaning: nouns that have positive connotations — *safety, happiness, prudence, right, duty, Supreme Judge, justice;* verbs and verbals that suggest negative actions (taken by the king) *refused, forbidden, dissolved, obstructed, plundered, depriving, abolishing.*
3. The *tone* suggests reason and patience on the part of the author or authors (especially paragraphs 5, 33, 34).

Logic: As a logical pattern of argument, the Declaration of Independence is largely *deductive*. Deduction usually consists of certain broad general statements which we know or believe to be true and which to lead us to other statements that follow from the ones already laid down. The Declaration begins with such general statements, summarizing a philosophy of government based on the equality of men, the inalienable rights derived from the Creator, and the powers of the governed. These statements are held to be "self-evident," that is, not needing proof, and if we accept them, then it follows that a revolution is necessary to remove the oppressors and secure the safety and happiness to which the governed are entitled. The particular grievances against the king are proof that the king has oppressed the colonies, but they are not the basis for revolution.

The fact that Jefferson emphasized the universal principles underlying the right of revolution meant that the Declaration of Independence could appeal to all people everywhere, whether or not they had suffered the particular grievances in Jefferson's list.

EXERCISES

1. From the following list of claims, select the ones you consider most controversial. Tell why they are difficult to resolve. Are the underlying assumptions controversial? Is support hard to find or disputed? Can

you think of circumstances under which some of these claims might be resolved?

a. Congress should endorse the right-to-life amendment.

b. Solar power can supply 20 percent of the energy needs now satisfied by fossil and nuclear power.

c. Homosexuals should have the same job rights as heterosexuals.

d. Rapists should be treated as mentally ill rather than depraved.

e. Whale hunting should be banned by international law.

f. Violence on television produces violent behavior in children who watch more than four hours a day.

g. Both creationism and evolutionary theory should be taught in the public schools.

h. Mentally defective men and women should be sterilized or otherwise prevented from producing children.

i. History will pronounce Reggie Jackson a greater all-round baseball player than Joe DiMaggio.

j. Bilingual instruction should not be permitted in the public schools.

k. Some forms of cancer are caused by a virus.

l. Dogs are smarter than horses.

m. Curfews for teenagers will reduce the abuse of alcohol and drugs.

n. The federal government should impose a drinking age of twenty-one.

o. The United States should proceed with unilateral disarmament.

p. Security precautions at airports are out of proportion to the dangers of terrorism.

q. Bodybuilding cannot be defined as a sport; it is a form of exhibitionism.

2. Report on an argument you have heard recently. Identify the parts of that argument — claim, support, warrant — as they are defined in this chapter. What were the strengths and weaknesses in the argument you heard?

3. Choose one of the more controversial claims in the previous list and explain the reasons it is controversial. Is support lacking or in doubt? Are the warrants unacceptable to many people? Try to go as deeply as you can, exploring, if possible, systems of belief, traditions, societal customs. You may confine your discussion to personal experience with the problem in your community or group. If there has been a change over the years in the public attitude toward the claim, offer what you think may be an explanation for the change.

4. Write your own argument for or against the value of standard grading in college.

5. Discuss an occasion when a controversy arose that the opponents could not settle. Describe the problem and tell why you think the disagreement was not settled.

CHAPTER TWO

Responding to Argument

Most of us learn how to read, to listen, and to write arguments by attending critically to the arguments of those who have already mastered the important elements as well as those who have not. As we acquire skill in reading, we learn to uncover the clues that reveal meaning and to become sensitive to the kinds of organization, support, and language that experienced writers use in persuading their audiences. Listening, too, is a skill, often underrated, but increasingly important in an era when the spoken voice can be transmitted worldwide with astonishing speed. In becoming more expert listeners, we can engage in discussions with a wide and varied audience and gain proficiency in distinguishing between responsible and irresponsible speech.

A full response to any argument means more than understanding the message. It also means evaluating, deciding whether or not the message is successful and, then, determining *how* it succeeds or fails in persuading us. In making these judgments about the written and spoken arguments of others, we learn how to deliver our own. We try to avoid what we perceive to be flaws in another's arguments, and we adapt the strategies that produce clear, honest, forceful arguments.

RESPONDING AS A CRITICAL READER

You already know how essential critical reading can be to mastery of most college subjects, but its importance for reading and writing about argument, where meaning is often complex and multilayered, can hardly be overestimated. Critical, or close, reading of

25

arguments leads to greater comprehension and more thorough evaluation. The first step is comprehension — understanding what the author is trying to prove. Then comes evaluation — careful judgment of the extent to which the author has succeeded.

Good readers are never merely passive recipients of the material. They engage in active dialogue with the author, as if he or she were present, asking questions, offering objections, expressing approval. They often write comments in the margins of the book as they read or in a notebook they reserve for this purpose. Clearly, the more information they have about the author and the subject as well as the circumstances surrounding it — an event in the news, for example — the easier and more productive their reading of any material will be. But whatever their level of preparation, they have learned to extract meaning by attending to clues both in the material itself and in their knowledge of the world around them.

Here are a few strategies for close reading of an argument.

1. Pay attention to the title — and the subtitle. They can provide a good deal of information.
   a. The title can tell you what the essay is about. It may even state the purpose of the argument in specific terms, as in "Cocaine is Even Deadlier Than We Thought," the title of one of the essays in this book.
   b. It can make reference to other writing that you will recognize. The title of the article that follows, "The Pursuit of Whining," brings to mind the phrase in the Declaration of Independence, "the pursuit of Happiness." The subtitle clinches the connection: "Affirmative Action circa 1776."
   c. It can express the author's attitude toward the subject. In the title quoted above, we realize that "whining," because it has negative connotations, will probably be attacked as a means of achieving happiness. The subtitle adds the rather surprising suggestion that the author is unfriendly to some aspects of the American Revolution.
2. As you read the essay for the first time, look for the main idea and the structure of the whole essay. Make a skeleton outline in your mind or on paper. Remember that your purpose in reading an argument is to learn what the author wants to prove and how he or she proves it, and to frame a response to it as you read. At this stage, avoid concentrating on details. Reading is a complex mental operation, and you cannot do everything at once.

   In a well-written essay, even a long one, the main idea and the organization should emerge clearly from a careful reading. Every argument, however long and complicated, has a beginning, a middle, and an end. It will offer a claim and several parts devoted to support. (Development of an important point may take two or more paragraphs.)

3. You will probably find the main idea or *thesis statement* in one of the first two or three paragraphs. Remember, however, that the beginning of an argument often has other purposes; it may lay out not the author's position but the position that the author will oppose, or background for the whole argument.

4. Pay attention to topic sentences. The topic sentence is usually but not always the first sentence of a paragraph. It is the general statement that controls the details and examples in the paragraph.

5. Don't overlook the language signposts, especially the transitional words and phrases that tell you whether the writer will change direction or offer support for a previous point — words and phrases like *but, however, nevertheless, yet, moreover, for example, at first glance, more important, the first reason,* etc.

6. Select the method for vocabulary search that suits you best: either guessing the meaning of an unfamiliar word from the context and going on or else looking it up immediately. It's true that the first method makes for more rapid reading and is sometimes recommended by teachers of reading, but guessing can be risky. Keep a good dictionary handy. If you are at all in doubt about a word that seems crucial to meaning, check your guess before you go too far in what may be the wrong direction.

7. If you use a colored marker to highlight main points, use it sparingly. Marking passages in color is meant to direct you to the major ideas and reduce the necessity for rereading the whole passage when you review.

8. Don't be timid about asking questions of the text. No author is infallible. Some authors are not always clear. Ask any questions whose answers are necessary to improve your comprehension. Disagree with the author if you feel confident of the support for your view. After you have read the whole argument, you may discover that most of your early questions have been answered. If not, this may be a signal to read the article again. Be cautious about concluding that the author hasn't proved his point.

9. Reading an assigned work is usually a solitary activity, but what follows a reading should be shared. Talk about the material with classmates or others who have read it. You probably know that discussion of a book or a movie strengthens both your memory of details and your understanding of the whole. And defending or modifying your evaluation will mean going back to the text and finding clues that you may have overlooked. Not least, it can be fun to discuss even something you didn't enjoy.

The following essay is annotated by a student as he reads. He is already familiar, as you are, with the Declaration of Independence. After reading and commenting on the essay, he adds a brief summary for his own review.

The Pursuit of Whining: Affirmative Action circa 1776

JOHN PATRICK DIGGINS

Anything to do with "the pursuit of happiness"? Who's doing the whining in 1776?

Is this about affirmative action or the Revolution? Or both?

Usually means that a second glance will show the opposite

Means it's not what it seems

So he's against aff. action because it violates the D of I?

Seems to be his thesis; is group opportunity bad?

All politics, we are now told, will not be local but universal, a struggle over values. In these "culture wars," a candidate who can touch the core nerve of American values will be sure to be elected. How will affirmative action stand up to such a contest?

At first glance, affirmative action appears to be consistent with America's commitment to egalitarianism, which derives from the Declaration of Independence and its ringing pronouncement that "all men are created equal" and are "endowed by their creator with certain unalienable rights." Actually affirmative action, as carried out, has little to do with equality and is so dependent on biology, ancestry, and history that it subverts the individualist spirit of the Declaration.

But the second part of the Declaration, which no one remembers, may affirm affirmative action as the politics of group opportunity.

The Declaration held rights to be equal and unalienable because in the state of nature, before social conventions had been formed, "Nature and Nature's God" (Jefferson's phrase) gave no person or class the authority to dominate over others. Aristocracy became such a class, and the idea of equality was not so much

---

John Patrick Diggins teaches history at the Graduate Center of the City University of New York. This column appeared in the *New York Times* on September 25, 1995.

Reason for the Revolution

{ an accurate description of the human species as it was a protest against artificial privilege and hereditary right.

Today we have a new identity politics 5 of entitlement, and who one is depends on ethnic categories and descriptions based on either ancestry or sex. This return to a pseudo-aristocratic politics of privilege based on inherited rights by reason of birth means that equality has been replaced by diversity as the criteri[on] of governmental decisions.

Interesting point—today's affirmative action is like yesterday's aristocracy (both claim privileges of birth).

The founding fathers were against inherited privileges.

Jefferson loved diversity, but he and Thomas Paine trusted the many and suspected the few who saw themselves entitled to preferential treatment as an accident of birth. Paine was unsparing in his critique of aristocracy as a parasitic "no-ability." Speaking for the colonists, many of whom had worked their way out of conditions of indentured servitude, he insisted that hereditary privilege was "as absurd as an hereditary mathematician, or an hereditary wise man; and as ridiculous as an hereditary poet-laureate."

So far, he's proved that first part of D of I argues against affirmative action.

But the second part, listing grievances, is consistent with it.

But if America's egalitarian critique of aristocratic privilege could be in conflict with affirmative action, the second part of the Declaration may be perfectly consistent with it. Here begins the art of protest as the Declaration turns to the colonists' grievances, and we are asked to listen to a long tale of woe. Instead of admitting that they simply had no desire to cough up taxes, even to pay for a war that drove the French out of North America and thus made possible a situation where settlers were now secure enough to demand self-government, the colonists blamed King George for every outrage conceivable.

Thinks the colonists are cry-babies!

"He has erected . . . swarms of offices to harass our people and eat out their substance." Because the King, in response to the colonists' refusal to pay for the cost of protection, withdrew such protection, he is charged with abdicating "his *strong language*

Even Jefferson gets a few lumps!

Help! I can't find it in the D of I! (Look it up?)

Wow!

Were any of their complaints justified?

"Paranoia" seems a bit much

He's talking about blacks and women. Is he saying, "no justification for complaints against whites and males?" No way!

Explain a bit further

Our choices

allegiance and protection: he has plundered our seas, ravaged our coasts, burnt our towns, destroyed the lives of our people." Even Edmund Burke, the British parliamentarian and orator who supported the colonists, saw them as almost paranoid, "protestants" who protest so much that they would "snuff the approach of tyranny in every tainted breeze."

The ultimate hypocrisy comes when Jefferson accuses the King of once tolerating the slave trade, only "he is now exciting those very people to rise up in arms among us, and to purchase their liberty of which he has deprived them, by murdering the people upon whom he has obtruded them." The notion that slavery was forced upon the innocent colonists, who in turn only sought to be free of "tyranny," suggests the extent to which the sentiment of the Revolution grumbles with spurious charges.

The Declaration voiced America's first 10 proclamation of victimology. Whatever the theoretical complexities embedded in the doctrine of equality, the Declaration demonstrated that any politics that has its own interests uppermost is best put forward in the language of victimization and paranoia.

The very vocabulary of the document ("harass," "oppress," and so on) is consistent with affirmative action, where white racists and male chauvinists have replaced King George as the specter of complaint.

Seeing themselves as sufferers to whom awful things happen, the colonists blamed their alleged oppressors and never acknowledged that they had any responsibility for the situation in which they found themselves.

What then is America's core value? Is it equality and civic virtue? Or is it the struggle for power that legitimizes itself in

An ending that's all questions.   the more successful, and least demand-
I like it. But they're fake ques-   ing, shameless politics of whining?
tions. He knows the answers
and wants us to agree with
him.

Summary: Is affirmative action consistent with the Declaration of Independence? On that subject the two parts of the Declaration contradict each other. The first part says that equality and individual rights are the principles of the American Revolution. Because the founding fathers opposed privileges awarded on account of ancestry and history, they would be against affirmative action. But in the second part of the Declaration, the grievances of the colonists sound like the complaints of groups today that claim they are victims of oppression and want special privileges because of their ancestry and history. Today America must choose between equality and privileges for special groups. Note: From The Declaration of Independence, a book by Carl Becker, I found out that the excerpts in paragraph 9 come from an earlier draft of the Declaration. This argument about slavery was omitted from the final draft because Jefferson thought that it was weaker than the others. So was it fair to include it here?

RESPONDING AS A WRITER

The following essay is a claim of policy; that is, it offers a solution to a problem. The solution is summarized in the title. Such an expression of the main idea of an essay is frequently used in newspaper and magazine articles as a means of capturing attention. Although the solution is baldly stated, it is controversial, and you will see that the conclusion suggests a more limited resolution of the problem.

Keep in mind that an essay of this length can never do justice to a complicated and highly debatable subject. It will probably lack sufficient evidence, as this one does, to answer all the questions and objections of a reader opposed to orphanages. What it can do is provoke thought and initiate an intelligent discussion.

Bring Back the Orphanage

JAMES Q. WILSON

Orphanages are almost extinct in the United States, but orphans are not. More than 400,000 children now live in foster homes, and unknown thousands more live nominally at home but actually as latch-key children surviving on the mean streets of America with no fathers, crack-abusing mothers, and drug-dealers as role models.

America once provided orphanages for many children. In 1910, about 123,000 lived in such places, or about 3 out of every 1,000 persons under the age of twenty-one. Today these institutions have almost disappeared. Most people think — wrongly, as we shall see — that they vanished because they had failed. Mention "orphanage" to someone and the image that springs to mind is of Oliver Twist begging for another bowl of gruel in a bleak prison.

The negative view of orphanages has been reinforced by historians who, writing in the late 1960s, and early 1970s, reinterpreted the late nineteenth-century impulse to help children as a form of class-conscious "social control." What previously had been seen as a public-spirited effort to impart decent values was now seen as effort to impose suspect (that is, "middle-class") values.

An especially sharp-edged version of the social-control theory was set forth in Anthony Platt's 1974 book, *The Child Savers*. A more nuanced but even more influential variant on the same theory was David Rothman's 1971 *The Discovery of the Asylum*. These writings helped to convince a generation of scholars and activists that prisons, asylums, and orphanages were institutions designed by the privileged classes to ensure control over poor people.

Decent Places

Today, however, a new group of historians has produced evidence that casts great doubt on the social-control view. A particularly good example by Nurith Zmora was published this year under the title *Orphanages Reconsidered* (Temple University Press). It examines three such institutions in Baltimore (one Catholic, one Jewish, and one Protestant) out of the twenty-eight, all privately run, that existed there in 1910.

5

James Q. Wilson is professor of management and public policy at the University of California, Los Angeles. This article is from the August 22, 1994, edition of the *Wall Street Journal*.

Ms. Zmora's conclusions can be simply stated: The orphanages were decent places run by caring professionals who maintained close ties to the community. The children were housed in adequate physical facilities, offered good food and hygiene, and supplied a better education than they would have received elsewhere. Though problems existed, they were grappled with by public and private agencies that shared the view that helping children was not the same thing as indoctrinating them. Ms. Zmora was able to trace the later lives of forty-five graduates. Most did quite well, finding jobs and becoming self-supporting.

Most of the youngsters in these institutions were not literally orphans. They were, instead, children whose parents, owing to poverty or disorganization, could not adequately care for them and who were enrolled voluntarily. Half entered before they were nine years old, and several before they were six; the average stay was about five years, though a few stayed for more than ten. The orphanages did not take incorrigible children. In a sense, these institutions were not orphanages but boarding schools that charged no tuition.

Consider, for example, the Samuel Ready School, founded in the early 1870s to help orphaned girls of any religion, although most were Protestant. The school was used by impoverished single mothers as either a temporary shelter or a boarding school for their daughters.

The Ready School was a pleasant place in a parklike setting that provided its students with better surroundings than they had enjoyed at home. The food was adequate, but probably no more appealing than any institutional fare. Of the first forty girls to enter Ready, twenty-nine completed their education there and eleven were expelled or withdrawn by relatives. Of those finishing, most studied dressmaking or secretarial skills. The school devoted great efforts to finding jobs for their graduates, mostly as clerks, dressmakers, and teachers. It was not easy, because growing up in an orphanage carried a stigma. Nevertheless, Ms. Zmora reports that of twenty-six girls who entered between 1887 and 1889 and finished their vocational training, twenty-three got jobs in their fields.

Other orphanages were less devoted to vocational training. At 10 the Dolan School for Irish youngsters, some children eventually returned to their families while others were "placed out" in foster families. It was hard to be sure that the foster parents took adequate care of their charges, and so some of the latter ran away — sometimes back to Dolan.

Some scholars, such as Michael Sherraden, have suggested that these institutions were a way of coping with an important change in the labor market. Before 1870, children, even very young ones, worked; after the 1870s, there was less demand for and much opposition to child labor, and the orphanages were an alternative to living on the street or with parents who were unable to support them. The so-called orphanages were a way for children to get the benefits of middle-class life despite having parents who had not entered that status.

These institutions did not disappear because an enlightened public was shocked by stories of abuse and neglect within their walls. On the contrary, they were destroyed by their success and the ideology of their rivals. So popular did they become, so great was the demand for places in them, that private charities could no longer afford them and public agencies refused to make up the difference. Social workers opposed them because they "broke up the family," liberal reformers because they involved "social control," fiscal conservatives because they were too expensive.

Orphanages (or free boarding schools) still exist, but in reduced numbers. Boys Town is one that has not only survived but prospered. Mary-Lou Weisman recently gave a vivid account of its successes in an *Atlantic Monthly* article. But everywhere the idea is in retreat because critics think that such places just "warehouse" children (that was never true) and that a better alternative is to provide money that will enable parents to take care of their own children (that may have been true once, but it isn't now).

Incompetent or abusive parents existed when boarding schools flourished; they exist today. But today, unlike a century ago, the ideology of "family preservation" has intervened with its plausible but overly broad message that a child is invariably better off with his parents. It is an appealing idea and an inexpensive one to boot, since supporting the child in his family or in a foster family is cheaper than caring for him in an institution.

But not all families are worth preserving. Indeed, the dramatic increase in single-parent families suggests that there is a declining number of true families worth preserving. And the main current alternative to the biological parent — namely, foster-family care — has its own problems. Many foster families simply cannot handle the kind of children they are now getting. And all foster families are hard to oversee to ensure that the best interests of the child are being served. 15

Need to Know More

We don't know as much as we should about how well institutional care might function under contemporary conditions. Such evidence as exists suggests that troubled teenagers may do well while in boarding schools but do poorly when returned to their families and communities. On the other hand, very young children placed in such schools before they become troubled may (no one knows for certain) do as well today as their predecessors did in turn-of-the-century Baltimore. Careful studies can answer these questions.

Foster care has an important role to play — for some children. But for others institutional care is necessary. At least the research of writers such as Nurith Zmora, Michael Sherraden, and Mary-Lou Weisman is making it harder to argue that boarding schools and orphanages are discredited alternatives.

Organization

While there are numerous conventional patterns of organization (see Chapter 9), it is worth pointing out that most essays of more than 750 words are rarely perfect examples of such patterns. Authors mix structures wherever it seems necessary to make a stronger case. The pattern of organization in this essay is primarily a *defense of the main idea* — that orphanages should be reestablished to take care of children who would otherwise be abused or homeless. But because the claim is highly controversial, the author must also try to *refute the opposing views* that will prevent realization of his proposal.

Having stated his claim in the title, the author can move directly to the evidence that supports it. He has divided his essay into two parts. The first part attempts to prove that orphanages have worked in the past and that views of orphanages as a form of social control are false. The second part supports the idea that such institutions can work and refutes the theory and practice of "family preservation" which governs social welfare policy today.

The essay is perfectly unified — that is, all parts of the essay contribute to the development of the main idea. But in at least one place the author has made a choice with which a reader might disagree. Another writer might have moved paragraph 11 elsewhere in the essay, perhaps after the first sentence in paragraph 5, where the author begins to discuss the favorable reports on orphanages. But its position in the essay reflects the author's decision to use it as a summary of these reports rather than an introduction to them.

You may have noticed other small departures from strict rules of organization which, nevertheless, make good sense. Paragraph 2, for example, only five sentences long, contains at least three different ideas, not the one idea that a paragraph is commonly meant to develop. In the author's mind there was no need for a conventional topic sentence. The transitions within the paragraph are smooth, and the meaning is entirely clear.

Support

The author tries to provide an answer to a question you will ask as soon as you read the title: "How are you going to prove that this is a good idea? Aren't orphanages terrible places that harmed children in the past?" As support, the author offers examples, assumptions about social theory (or ideology), and an appeal to values. Real examples are taken from history, and rejection of a prevailing theory is based on the author's knowledge of the social environment and assumptions about its impact on children.

The response to this evidence will probably be mixed. Half the essay is devoted to the historical record as it appears in three recent studies, with descriptions of the orphans and their lives both in and out of the institutions. Because these details are interesting and unfamiliar to many readers, they have a strong, immediate appeal. But the bulk of the evidence comes from research about orphanages of seventy or eighty years ago. Critics will want more evidence than examples from the work of only three authors (although a short essay can hardly provide more) and more attention to present-day institutions. (There is one reference to Boys Town.) The theory (or ideology) — that "family preservation" doesn't work for many children — is more difficult to defend or refute, especially regarding predictions of the future. The author cites data to support his own theory (paragraph 15); in addition, he brings to his argument his reputation as a widely known and respected social scientist. But critics will say that his evidence is too selective and that other theorists can effectively refute him.

The appeal to values will probably go unchallenged. It is indirect, but it pervades the essay, and all readers are likely to share with the author a concern for the welfare of children.

Style

The clear, direct prose of this essay is writing of a kind that you can aspire to as a student writer. The author makes effective use of tone, diction, transitions, sentence variety, and parenthetical insertions. Throughout he writes for an audience that he perceives as generally well-informed, interested in evidence, and socially concerned. He is also aware that some readers will disagree with his proposal and that the style, therefore, must reflect a conciliatory approach. He must give neutral or hostile readers confidence in his willingness to compromise.

The author's tone, the expression of his attitude toward his material and his audience is serious, modest, and reasonable. He gives an unemotional explanation of the opposing views, and his language makes clear that he doesn't presume to know all the answers. A number of expressions show this: "We don't know," "No one knows for certain," Such evidence as exists," "Careful studies can answer these questions."

His diction, or choice of words, is appropriate to his audience, among others, people who read the *Wall Street Journal*. It is the standard English of an educated layman, which avoids the specialized vocabulary of the academic social scientist. The choice of words is broad but accessible. The author even employs contractions here and there to reduce formality.

Transitions are the words and phrases that occur between sentences and between paragraphs to promote greater coherence or connections between ideas. It isn't necessarily true that shorter sentences without transitions make for easier reading; they may, in fact, make understanding more difficult. Transitional words and phrases help us to follow the movement of the author's thinking — words and phrases like *but, at least, indeed, on the contrary, in a sense, on the other hand, however, for example*. These expressions should not be used indiscriminately. This author limits them to what seems necessary and no more.

Varying the sentence structure is still another way to make reading and comprehension easier. For example, using complex sentences — sentences with dependent clauses — allows you to subordinate some ideas within the sentence. Compound sentences using two or more independent clauses tell the reader that the main ideas are equally important. In other words, the structure of the sentence can create emphasis. The author of this essay uses long and short sentences, simple, compound, and complex sentences, and a variety of sentence beginnings. Look at paragraphs 2 and 13 for a combination of long and short sentences; at paragraphs 6 and 9 for different kinds of sentences; at paragraphs 12 and 15 for different sentence beginnings.

Finally, there are the parenthetical insertions. They are a very small part of good style, and many writers don't use them. Student writers seldom do, but such interruptions, carefully placed, can sound like part of a thoughtful conversation.

You will find it helpful to look back over the essay to see how the examples we've cited and others work to fulfill the writer's purpose.

RESPONDING AS A CRITICAL LISTENER

Of course, not all public arguments are written. Oral arguments on radio and television now enjoy widespread popularity and influence. In fact, their proliferation means that we listen far more than we talk, read, or write. Today the art of listening has become an indispensable tool for learning about the world we live in. One informed critic predicts that the dissemination of information and opinions through the electronic media will "enable more and more Americans to participate directly in making the laws and policies by which they are governed."[1]

Because we are interested primarily in arguments about public issues — those that involve democratic decision making — we will not be concerned with the afternoon TV talk shows that are largely devoted to personal problems. (Occasionally, however, *Oprah* and *Sally Jessy Raphael* introduce topics of broad social significance.) More relevant to the kinds of written arguments you will read and write about in this course are the television and radio shows that also examine social and political problems. The most intelligent and responsible programs usually consist of a panel of experts — politicians, journalists, scholars — led by a neutral moderator (or one who, at least, allows guests to express their views). Some of these programs are decades old; others are more recent — *Meet the Press, Face the Nation, Firing Line, The McLaughlin Group, The Monday Group, The NewsHour with Jim Lehrer.* An outstanding radio show, *Talk of the Nation* on National Public Radio, invites listeners, who are generally informed and articulate, to call in and ask questions of, or comment on remarks by, experts on the topic of the day.

Several enormously popular radio talk shows are hosted by people with strong, sometimes extreme ideological positions. They may use offensive language and insult their listeners in a crude form of theater. Among the most influential shows are those of Rush Limbaugh and Howard Stern. In addition, elections and political crises bring speeches and debates on radio and TV by representatives of a variety of views. Some are long and formal, written texts that are simply read aloud, but others are short and impromptu.

Whatever the merits or shortcomings of individual programs, significant general differences exist between arguments on radio and television and arguments in the print media. These differences include the degree of organization and development and the risk of personal attacks.

First (excluding for the moment the long, prepared speeches), contributions to a panel discussion must be delivered in fragments, usually no longer than a single paragraph, weakened by time constraints, interruptions, overlapping speech, memory gaps, and real or feigned displays of derision, impatience, and disbelief by critical panelists. Even on the best programs, the result is a lack of both coherence — or connections between ideas — and solid evidence that requires development. Too often we are treated to conclusions with little indication of how they were arrived at.

---

[1] Lawrence K. Grossman, *The Electronic Republic: Reshaping Democracy in the Information Age* (New York: Viking, 1995).

The following brief passage appeared in a newspaper review of "Resolved: The flat tax is better than the income tax," a debate on *Firing Line* by an impressive array of experts. It illustrates some of the difficulties that accompany programs attempting to capture the truth of a complicated issue on TV or radio.

> "It is absolutely true," says a proponent. "It is factually untrue," counters an opponent. "It's factually correct," responds a proponent. "I did my math right," says a proponent. "You didn't do your math right," says an opponent. At one point in a discussion of interest income, one of the experts says, "Oh, excuse me, I think I got it backward."

No wonder the TV critic called the exchange "disjointed and at times perplexing."[2]

In the sensational talk shows the participants rely on personal experience and vivid anecdotes which may not be sufficiently typical to prove anything.

Second, listeners and viewers of all spoken arguments are in danger of evaluating them according to criteria that are largely absent from evaluation of written texts. It is true that writers may adopt a *persona* or a literary disguise which the tone of the essay will reflect. But many readers will not be able to identify it or recognize their own response to it. Listeners and viewers, however, can hardly avoid being affected by characteristics that are clearly definable: a speaker's voice, delivery, bodily mannerisms, dress, and physical appearance. In addition, listeners may be adversely influenced by clumsy speech containing more slang, colloquialisms, and grammar and usage errors than written texts that have had the benefit of revision.

But if listeners allow consideration of physical attributes to influence their judgment of what the speaker is trying to prove, they are guilty of an *ad hominem* fallacy, that is, an evaluation of the speaker rather than the argument. This is true whether the evaluation is favorable or unfavorable. (See pp. 267–68 for a discussion of this fallacy.)

Talk shows may indeed be disjointed and perplexing, but millions of us find them both instructive and entertaining. Over time we are exposed to an astonishing variety of opinions from every corner of American life, and we also acquire information from experts who might not otherwise be available to us. Then there is the appeal of hearing the voices, seeing the faces of people engaged in earnest, sometimes passionate, discourse — a short, unrehearsed drama in which we also play a part as active listeners in a far-flung audience.

---

[2] Walter Goodman, "The Joys of the Flat Tax, Excluding the Equations," *New York Times*, December 21, 1995, Sec. C, p. 14.

Guidelines to Critical Listening

Listening is hearing with attention, a natural and immensely important human activity which, unfortunately, many people don't do very well. The good news is that listening is a skill that can be learned and, unlike some other skills, practiced every day without big investments of money and effort.

Here are some of the characteristics of critical listening most appropriate to understanding arguments.

1. Above all, listening to arguments requires concentration. If you are distracted, you cannot go back as you do with the written word to clarify a point or recover a connection. Devices such as flow sheets and outlines can be useful aids to concentration. In following a debate, for example, judges and other listeners often use flow sheets — distant cousins of baseball scorecards — to record the major points on each side and their rebuttals. For roundtable discussions or debates you can make your own simple flow chart to fill out as you listen, with columns for claims, different kinds of support, and warrants. Leave spaces in the margin for your questions and comments about the soundness of the proof. An outline is more useful for longer presentations, such as lectures. As you listen, try to avoid being distracted by facts alone. Look for the overall pattern of the speech.

2. Listeners often concentrate on the wrong things in the spoken argument. We have already noted the distractions of appearance and delivery. Research shows that listeners are likely to give greater attention to the dramatic elements of speeches than to the logical ones. But you can enjoy the sound, the appearance, and the drama of a spoken argument without allowing these elements to overwhelm what is essential to the development of a claim.

3. Good listeners try not to allow their prejudices to prevent careful evaluation of the argument. This doesn't mean accepting everything or even most of what you hear. It means trying to avoid premature judgments about what is actually said. This precaution is especially relevant when the speakers and their views are well known and the listener has already formed an opinion about them, favorable or unfavorable.

RESPONDING ON-LINE

You have learned that writers need the responses of readers and other writers to improve their writing. As the influence of computers increases in our society and more people begin using local and wide-area computer networks such as the Internet to send electronic mail ("e-mail"), it will become ever easier for writers to distribute their writing and for readers to respond to it. Only a few years ago, if you wanted feedback for your writing, you had to either read it aloud to others or copy and distribute it by hand or postal mail. Both methods were cumbersome and time-consuming, even expensive. Electronic networks now allow your writing to be distributed almost instantaneously to dozens or even thousands of readers with virtually no copying or mailing costs. Readers can respond to you just as quickly and cheaply. Even though there can be pitfalls and problems with communicating on-line, the overall ease of use can only encourage writers to seek, and readers to provide, editorial feedback.

Reading and Revising on a Word Processor

Reading text on a computer screen for the first time can be bewildering. It is difficult to get a sense of the "page," since most computer screens do not correspond to the typical fifty-line, 8½ by 11-inch typewriter page. As a reader of books and magazines, you are accustomed to taking in a whole page at a glance; as a writer, you are used to being able to spread out the pages of a draft and edit directly on them. A reader can, of course, use a *scroll bar* to scroll text up and down the screen, exposing all text in a document section by section, but even the strongest advocates of computers acknowledge that the smaller "page" of most computer monitors challenges ingrained reading practices. Still, as you grow accustomed to the screen, your difficulties in reading and editing should diminish, and you will come to appreciate the advantages of "digital text" — text that can be cut, pasted, and moved around your document far more easily than scissors, tape, liquid paper, or typewriter correction tape will allow. As one student put it, "I never realized how important it was to be able to change words and move them around so easily until I began using a word processor. It was hard at first using the mouse and scrolling, but you forget all about that once you see how easy it is to revise."

On-screen you can manipulate text in ways impossible with printed materials. By pressing a key you can increase the size of the print (the "point size") and alter the type style (the "font"; for example, Times Roman). Such options help you to focus on individual words or phrases. You can also separate out individual sentences and even clauses and phrases by using double "carriage returns" (press the <enter> or <return> key twice or click the mouse twice) at the end of each word group. (This is like hitting a return bar on a typewriter twice to double-space.) Double-spacing allows you to "spread the page" and visually isolate elements. Important words or phrases can be put in boldface or capital letters, a tactic almost certain to reveal conceptual and stylistic elements otherwise lost in a word-dense paragraph.

Most word-processing programs provide a *global search and replace* feature that allows you automatically to replace a word or term with another word or term throughout the document. This option is useful for exposing specific stylistic strengths or weaknesses in the draft you are reading. A particularly important word or phrase, for instance, or one that is habitually overused, can be globally boldfaced or capitalized, calling attention to it so that you can decide where to substitute a synonym. Globally highlighting a punctuation mark, such as an exclamation mark or colon, can graphically reveal the problem of repetitiveness of punctuation style in your own writing or that of the person whose draft you are reading on-screen.

From Word Processing to E-Mail Networks

You can anticipate that sometime during your college career — maybe even in your writing course — instructors will ask you to send drafts and comments via e-mail. On some systems this will be easy to do and on others not so easy. You may have difficulty either writing your text directly into the e-mail text editor or copying it from a word processor into an e-mail program. For example, if you are accustomed to the way word processors manipulate type size and format, you may be surprised to discover that most e-mail text editing programs do not permit text formatting. They exclude such features as underlining, boldface, and different font sizes and styles. But because the goal of most on-line responding is to improve a text's focus, development, and writing style rather than its appearance on the page, the lack of formatting is not a drawback in your drafting stage.

Some network software designed for classrooms combines a word processor with a special e-mail feature. These programs make it easy to transmit a draft, but they often limit where the e-mail can be sent — sometimes no farther than a single room or building, the limits of the local area network. (Whether or not this is a disadvantage depends mainly upon your instructor's ambitions for distributing student writing.)

Since there are so many different types of e-mail programs and text editors, specific technical information on how to use them is well beyond the scope of this discussion. The best advice is to be patient, read the instructions for your own system carefully, ask questions of your instructor and classmates, do not be afraid to experiment, and practice, practice, practice. Your patience will be rewarded once you become adept on your system.

Editing and Commenting On-Line

Before word processors, responding to a text usually meant writing comments directly on a page, squeezing suggestions into the margins or between the double-spaced lines of a draft. Such hand-editing often made a manuscript difficult to read. Electronic text, however, allows you to create as much room as necessary for a comment, simply by placing the cursor at the end of a line and pressing the return (or by clicking the mouse) several times. There are numerous typographical ways to distinguish your comments as a peer editor from the type of the original text. For example, if your response is to be delivered through e-mail, you can highlight your response by typing it in capital letters. The ease of such unrestricted interlinear note-making tends to encourage a reader to respond more fully and specifically (and legibly) than ever before.

Another instance of the handy manipulability of e-mail text (*e-text*) is the *responding template*. A responding template is a series of questions, or *prompts*, prepared by an instructor or other expert, that can be pasted close to the text being commented on in order to guide a peer responder through a critical reading session. Examples of such prompts are "Evaluate the clarity and significance of the thesis statement," or "What improvements could be made in the use of sources?" The elements of the document the instructor wishes to emphasize can be distilled into prompts and circulated to the responders as a word-processing file or e-mail message.

Guidelines for Responding On-Line

You know that in face-to-face conversation the words themselves constitute only a part of your message. Much of what you say is communicated through your body language and tone of voice. Written words provide a much narrower channel of communication, which is why you must be more careful when you write to someone than when you speak directly to them. Electronic writing, however, especially through e-mail, fosters a casualness and immediacy that often fools writers into assuming they are talking privately rather than writing publicly. On-line you may find yourself writing quickly, carelessly, and intimately; without the help of your tone and body language, you may end up being seriously misunderstood. Words written hastily are often read much differently than intended; this is especially true when the writer attempts an ironic or sarcastic tone. For example, if a classmate walks up to you with a critical comment about one of your sentences and you respond by saying "I didn't realize you were so smart," the words, if unaccompanied by a placating smile and a pleasant, jocular tone, may come across as sarcastic or hostile. In e-writing, the same words appear without the mitigating body language and may be perceived as harsh, possibly insulting. You must keep this danger in mind as you respond on-line, or risk alienating your reader.

Keep in mind, too, that electronic mail may be read not only by your addressee, but also by anyone with whom the addressee chooses to share your message. An intemperate or indiscreet message may be forwarded to other classmates or your instructor, or, depending on the limits of the system, to many other readers whom you do not know.

Experienced on-line communicators advocate a set of network etiquette guidelines called "netiquette." Here are some generally accepted netiquette rules:

- Keep your sentences short and uncomplicated.

- Separate blocks of text — which should be no more than four or five lines long — by blank lines. For those rare occasions when a comment requires more than ten or fifteen consecutive lines of text, use subheadings on separate lines to guide your reader.

- Refer specifically to the text to which you are responding. You may want to quote directly from it, cutting and pasting phrases or sentences from the document to help show exactly what you are responding to.

- Greet the person(s) to whom you are writing politely and by name.

- Be wary about attempting to be funny. Humor, as just explained, often requires a context, tone of voice, and body language to emphasize that it is not to be taken seriously. Writing witty comments that are sure to be taken humorously calls for skill and care, and e-mail messages usually are written too quickly for either.

- Avoid profanity or invective, and be wary of brusque or abrupt statements. Consider how you would feel if someone wrote to you that way.

- Avoid discussion of politics or religion unless that is the specific topic of your message.

- Do not ridicule public figures. Your reader may not share your opinions of, say, Senator Edward Kennedy or radio talk show host Rush Limbaugh.

- Frame all comments in a helpful, not critical, tone. For instance, rather than beginning a critique with "I found a number of problems in your text," you may want to start out more like this: "You have some good ideas in this paper and with a few changes, I think it will do well."

EXERCISES

Pre-Reading

1. If you haven't read "Kids in the Mall: Growing Up Controlled" (p. 57), do the following: Take note of the title of the book in which this excerpt appears. Now, write down briefly what you guess the attitude of the author will be toward his subject. Tell which words in the titles of the excerpt and the book suggest his approach. Next, read the quotation that heads the essay and the first paragraph. If you think there are further clues here, explain briefly how you interpreted them. (For example, did your own experience with malls enter into your thinking as you read?)

   Keep your notes. Refer to them after you have read the whole article (and perhaps discussed it in class). How well did your preparation help you to find the main point and understand the examples that supported it? Are there other things you might do to improve your pre-reading?

Annotating

2. Choose an editorial of at least two paragraphs in a newspaper or your school paper on a controversial subject that interests you. The title will probably reveal the subject. Annotate the editorial as you read, questioning, agreeing, objecting, offering additional ideas. (The annotation of the "The Pursuit of Whining" will suggest ways of doing this, although your personal responses are what make the annotation useful.) Then, read the editorial again. You should discover that annotating the article caused you to read more carefully, more critically, with greater comprehension and a more focused response.

Evaluating

3. Summarize the claim of the editorial in one sentence. Omit the supporting data and concentrate on the thesis. Then explain briefly your reaction to it. Has the author proved his or her point? Your annotation will show you where you expressed doubt or approval. If you already know a good deal about the subject, perhaps you will be reasonably confident of your judgment. If not, you may find that your response is tentative, that you need to read further for more information about the subject and to consult guidelines for making evaluations about the elements of argument.

Listening

4. People sometimes object to lectures as an educational tool. Think about some of the specific lectures you have listened to recently and analyze the reasons that you liked or disliked them (or liked some

aspects and disliked others). Do you think that you learned everything that the lecturer intended you to learn? If the results were doubtful, how much did your listening skills, good or bad, contribute to the result? Should the lecturer have done something differently to improve your response?

5. Watch (and *listen* to) one of the afternoon talk shows like *Oprah Winfrey* in which audiences discuss a controversial social problem. (The *TV Guide* and daily newspapers often list the subject. Recent topics on *Oprah* include the responsibility of parents for crimes committed by their children and the value of school integration.) Write a critical review of the discussion, mentioning as completely as you can the major claims, the most important evidence, and the declared or hidden warrants. (Unspoken warrants or assumptions may be easier to identify in arguments on talk shows where visual and auditory clues can reveal what participants try to hide.) How much did the oral format contribute to success or failure of the argument(s)?

6. Listen to one of the TV talk shows that feature invited experts. Write a review, telling how much you learned about the subject(s) of discussion. Be specific about the elements of the show that were either helpful or unhelpful to your understanding.

7. Listen with a friend or friends to a talk show discussion. Take notes as you listen. Then compare notes to discover if you agree on the outstanding points, the degree to which claims have been supported, and the part that seeing and/or hearing the discussion played in your evaluation. If there is disagreement about any of the elements, how do you account for it?

On-Line

8. If you are working in a networked classroom, with three or four of your classmates select an argumentative essay in this book that all of you agree to read. Each of you should draft a response to the essay, either agreeing or disagreeing with the author's position, citing evidence to support your position. Then each of you prepare a letter soliciting a response to your draft from the members of your group. For example, you may want to state what your objective was, suggest what you think are the strengths and weaknesses of the draft, and ask what sort of revisions seem appropriate. E-mail the letter and the draft to each of your peer responders. Be prepared to revise based on their comments, which should either be given to you handwritten on a printed-out copy of your draft or in an e-mailed response.

CHAPTER THREE

Claims

Claims, or propositions, represent answers to the question: "What are you trying to prove?" Although they are the conclusions of your arguments, they often appear as thesis statements. Claims can be classified as *claims of fact, claims of value,* and *claims of policy.*

CLAIMS OF FACT

Claims of fact assert that a condition has existed, exists, or will exist and their support consists of factual information — that is, information such as statistics, examples, and testimony that most responsible observers assume can be verified.

Many facts are not matters for argument: Our own senses can confirm them, and other observers will agree about them. We can agree that a certain number of students were in the classroom at a particular time, that lions make a louder sound than kittens, and that apples are sweeter than potatoes.

We can also agree about information that most of us can rarely confirm for ourselves — information in reference books, such as atlases, almanacs, and telephone directories; data from scientific resources about the physical world; and happenings reported in the media. We can agree on the reliability of such information because we trust the observers who report it.

However, the factual map is constantly being redrawn by new data in such fields as history and science that cause us to reevaluate our conclusions. For example, the discovery of the Dead Sea Scrolls in 1947 revealed that some books of the Bible — *Isaiah,* for one — were far older than we had thought. Researchers at New York Hospital–Cornell Medical Center say that many symptoms previously thought inevitable in the aging process are now believed to be treatable and reversible symptoms of depression.[1]

In your conversations with other students you probably generate claims of fact every day, some of which can be verified without much effort, others of which are more difficult to substantiate.

> CLAIM: Most of the students in this class come from towns within fifty miles of Boston.

To prove this the arguer would need only to ask the students in the class where they come from.

> CLAIM: Students who take their courses Pass/Fail make lower grades than those who take them for specific grades.

In this case the arguer would need to have access to student records showing the specific grades given by instructors. (In most schools the instructor awards a letter grade, which is then recorded as a Pass or a Fail if the student has elected this option.)

> CLAIM: The Red Sox will win the pennant this year.

This claim is different from the others because it is an opinion about what will happen in the future. But it can be verified (in the future) and is therefore classified as a claim of fact.

More complex factual claims about political and scientific matters remain controversial because proof on which all or most observers will agree is difficult or impossible to obtain.

> CLAIM: Bilingual programs are less effective than English-only programs in preparing students for higher education.

> CLAIM: The only life in the universe exists on this planet.

Not all claims are so neatly stated or make such unambiguous assertions. Because we recognize that there are exceptions to most generalizations, we often qualify our claims with words such as *generally, usually, probably, as a rule.* It would not be true to state flatly, for example, "College graduates earn more than high school graduates." This statement is generally true, but we know that some high school graduates who are electricians or city bus drivers or sanitation workers earn more than college graduates who are schoolteachers or nurses or social workers. In making such a claim, therefore, the writer should qualify it with a word that limits the claim.

To support a claim of fact, the writer needs to produce sufficient and appropriate data, that is, examples, statistics, and testimony

---

[1]*New York Times,* February 20, 1983, Sec. 22, p. 4.

from reliable sources. Provided this requirement is met, the task of establishing a factual claim would seem to be relatively straightforward. But as you have probably already discovered in ordinary conversation, finding convincing support for factual claims can pose a number of problems. Whenever you try to establish a claim of fact, you will need to ask at least three questions about the material you plan to use: *What are sufficient and appropriate data? Who are the reliable authorities?* and *Have I made clear whether my statements are facts or inferences?*

Sufficient and Appropriate Data

The amount and kind of data for a particular argument depend on the importance and complexity of the subject. The more controversial the subject, the more facts and testimony you will need to supply. Consider the claim "The murder rate in New York City is lower this year than last year." If you want to prove the truth of this claim, obviously you will have to provide a larger quantity of data than for a claim that says, "By following three steps, you can train your dog to sit and heel in fifteen minutes." In examining your facts and opinions, an alert reader will want to know if they are accurate, current, and typical of other facts and opinions that you have not mentioned.

The reader will also look for testimony from more than one authority, although there may be cases where only one or two experts, because they have achieved a unique breakthrough in their field, will be sufficient. These cases would probably occur most frequently in the physical sciences. The Nobel Prize winners James Watson and Francis Crick, who first discovered the structure of the DNA molecule, are an example of such experts. However, in the case of the so-called Hitler diaries that surfaced in 1983, at least a dozen experts — journalists, historians, bibliographers who could verify the age of the paper and the ink — were needed to establish that they were forgeries.

Reliable Authorities

Not all those who pronounce themselves experts are trustworthy. Your own experience has probably taught you that you cannot always believe the reports of an event by a single witness. The witness may be poorly trained to make accurate observations — about the size of a crowd, the speed of a vehicle, his distance from an object. Or his own physical conditions — illness, intoxication, disability — may prevent him from seeing or hearing or smelling accurately. The circumstances under which he observes the event — darkness, confusion, noise — may also impair his observation. In addition, the witness may be biased for or against the outcome of the event, as in a hotly contested baseball game, where the observer sees the play that he wants to see. You will find the problems associated with the biases of witnesses to be relevant to your work as a reader and writer of argumentative essays.

You will undoubtedly want to quote authors in some of your arguments. In most cases you will not be familiar with the authors. But there are guidelines for determining their reliability: the rank or title of the experts, the acceptance of their publications by other experts, their association with reputable universities, research centers, or think tanks. For example, for a paper on euthanasia, you might decide to quote from an article by Paul Ramsey, identified as the Harrington Spear Paine Professor of Religion at Princeton University. For a paper on prison reform you might want to use material supplied by Tom Murton, a professional penologist, formerly superintendent in the Arkansas prison system, now professor of criminology at the University of Minnesota. Most readers of your arguments would agree that these authors have impressive credentials in their fields.

What if several respectable sources are in conflict? What if the experts disagree? After a preliminary investigation of a controversial subject, you may decide that you have sufficient material to support your claim. But if you read further, you may discover that other material presented by equally qualified experts contradicts your original claim. In such circumstances you will find it impossible to make a definitive claim. (On pp. 152–54, in the treatment of support of a claim by evidence, you will find a more elaborate discussion of this vexing problem.)

Facts or Inferences

We have defined a fact as a statement that can be verified. An inference is "a statement about the unknown on the basis of the known."[2] The difference between facts and inferences is important to you as the writer of an argument because an inference is an *interpretation,* or an opinion reached after informed evaluation of evidence. As you and your classmates wait in your classroom on the first day of the semester, a middle-aged woman wearing a tweed jacket and a corduroy skirt appears and stands in the front of the room. You don't know who this woman is. However, based on what you do know about the appearance of many college teachers and the fact that teachers usually stand in front of the classroom, you may

---

[2]S. I. Hayakawa, *Language in Thought and Action* (New York: Harcourt, Brace, Jovanovich, 1978), p. 35.

infer that this woman is your teacher. You will probably be right. But you cannot be certain until you have more information. Perhaps you will find out that this woman has come from the department office to tell you that your teacher is sick and cannot meet the class today.

You have probably come across a statement such as the following in a newspaper or magazine: "Excessive television viewing has caused the steady decline in the reading ability of children and teenagers." Presented this way, the statement is clearly intended to be read as a factual claim that has been or can be proved. But it is an inference. The facts, which can be, and have been, verified, are (1) the reading ability of children and teenagers has declined and (2) the average child views television for six or more hours a day. (Whether this amount of time is "excessive" is also an opinion.) The cause-effect relation between the two facts is an interpretation of the investigator who has examined both the reading scores and the amount of time spent in front of the television set and *inferred* that one is the cause of the other. The causes of the decline in reading scores are probably more complex than the original statement indicates. Since we can seldom or never create laboratory conditions for testing the influence of television separate from other influences in the family and the community, any statement about the connection between reading scores and television viewing can only be a guess.

By definition, no inference can ever do more than suggest probabilities. Of course, some inferences are much more reliable than others and afford a high degree of probability. Almost all claims in science are based on inferences, interpretations of data on which most scientists agree. Paleontologists find a few ancient bones from which they make inferences about an animal that might have been alive millions of years ago. We can never be absolutely certain that the reconstruction of the dinosaur in the museum is an exact copy of the animal it is supposed to represent, but the probability is fairly high because no other interpretation works so well to explain all the observable data — the existence of the bones in a particular place, their age, their relation to other fossils, and their resemblance to the bones of existing animals with which the paleontologist is familiar.

Inferences are profoundly important, and most arguments could not proceed very far without them. But an inference is not a fact. The writer of an argument must make it clear when he or she offers an inference, an interpretation, or an opinion that it is not a fact.

Defending a Claim of Fact

Here is a summary of the guidelines that should help you to defend a factual claim. (We'll say more about support of factual claims in Chapter 5.)

1. Be sure that the claim — what you are trying to prove — is clearly stated, preferably at the beginning of your paper.
2. Define terms that may be controversial or ambiguous. For example, in trying to prove that "radicals" had captured the student government, you would have to define "radicals," distinguishing them from "liberals" or members of other ideological groups, so that your readers would understand exactly what you meant.
3. As far as possible, make sure that your evidence — facts and opinions, or interpretations of the facts — fulfills the appropriate criteria. The data should be sufficient, accurate, recent, typical; the authorities should be reliable.
4. Make clear when conclusions about the data are inferences or interpretations, not facts. For example, you might write, "The series of lectures, 'Modern Architecture,' sponsored by our fraternity, was poorly attended because the students at this college aren't interested in discussions of art." What proof could you offer that this *was* the reason, that your statement was a *fact*? Perhaps there were other reasons that you hadn't considered.
5. Arrange your evidence in order to emphasize what is most important. Place it at the beginning or the end, the most emphatic positions in an essay, and devote more space to it.

SAMPLE ANALYSIS: CLAIM OF FACT

Cocaine Is Even Deadlier Than We Thought

LOUIS L. CREGLER and HERBERT MARK

To the Editor:

In his July 3 letter about recreational cocaine use, Dr. Carl C. Pfeiffer notes that some of the toxic effects of cocaine on the heart have long been known to those versed in pharmacology. We wish to point out that cardiologists and neurologists are seeing additional complications not previously known. Indeed, little information on the cardiovascular effects of cocaine appeared until recently.

As Dr. Pfeiffer says, cocaine sensitizes the heart to the normal stimulant effects of the body's adrenaline. This ordinarily makes the

Louis L. Cregler, M.D., is assistant chief of medicine, and Herbert Mark, M.D., is chief of medicine at the Bronx Veterans Administration Medical Center. This article appeared in the *New York Times* on July 30, 1986.

heart beat much faster and increases blood pressure significantly. Cocaine abuse has also been associated with strokes, heart attacks (acute myocardial infarctions), and sudden deaths. Individuals with weak blood vessels (aneurysms or arteriovenous malformations) in the head are at greatest risk of having a stroke. With the sudden surge in blood pressure, a blood vessel can burst. Cocaine can also cause blood vessels supplying the heart muscle itself to undergo vasoconstriction (coronary spasm), and this can produce a heart attack.

Deaths have been reported after administration of cocaine by all routes. Most such deaths are attributed to cocaine intoxication, leading to generalized convulsions, respiratory failure, and cardiac arrhythmias, minutes to hours after administration. Much of this information is so new that it has not found its way into the medical literature or standard textbooks.

Cocaine abuse continues to escalate in American society. It is estimated that 30 million Americans have used it, and some 5 million use it regularly. As cocaine has become less expensive, its availability and purity are increasing. It has evolved from a minor problem into a major threat to public health. And as use has increased, greater numbers of emergency-room visits, cocaine-related heart problems, and sudden deaths have been reported. With so many people using cocaine, it is not unexpected that more strokes, heart attacks, and sudden cardiac deaths will be taking place.

Louis L. Cregler, M.D.
Herbert Mark, M.D.

Analysis

The authors of this letter supply data to prove that the deadly effects of cocaine exceed those that are already well known in medicine and pharmacology. Four aspects of this factual claim are noteworthy. First, it is a response to a letter that, according to the authors, ignored significant new evidence. Many factual claims originate in just this way — as answers to previous claims. Second, the authors, both physicians at a large medical center, apparently have expert knowledge of the scientific data they report. Third, the effects of cocaine use are precisely and vividly described. It is, in fact, these specific references to the damage done to heart and blood vessels that make the claim particularly convincing. Finally, the authors make this claim in order to promote a change in our attitudes toward the use of cocaine; they do not call on their readers to abstain from cocaine. This use of a factual claim as a first step in calling for changes in attitude and behavior is a familiar and often effective argumentative strategy.

CLAIMS OF VALUE

Unlike claims of fact, which attempt to prove that something is true and which can be validated by reference to the data, claims of value make a judgment. They express approval or disapproval. They attempt to prove that some action, belief, or condition is right or wrong, good or bad, beautiful or ugly, worthwhile or undesirable.

CLAIM: Democracy is superior to any other form of government.

CLAIM: Killing animals for sport is wrong.

CLAIM: The Sam Rayburn Building in Washington is an aesthetic failure.

Some claims of value are simply expressions of tastes, likes and dislikes, or preferences and prejudices. The Latin proverb "De gustibus non est disputandum" states that we cannot dispute about tastes. Suppose you express a preference for chocolate over vanilla. If your listener should ask why you prefer this flavor, you cannot refer to an outside authority or produce data or appeal to her moral sense to convince her that your preference is justified.

Many claims of value, however, can be defended or attacked on the basis of standards that measure the worth of an action, a belief, or an object. As far as possible, our personal likes and dislikes should be supported by reference to these standards. Value judgments occur in any area of human experience, but whatever the area, the analysis will be the same. We ask the arguer who is defending a claim of value: *What are the standards or criteria for deciding that this action, this belief, or this object is good or bad, beautiful or ugly, desirable or undesirable? Does the thing you are defending fulfill these criteria?*

There are two general areas in which people often disagree about matters of value: aesthetics and morality. They are also the areas that offer the greatest challenge to the writer. What follows is a discussion of some of the elements of analysis that you should consider in defending a claim of value in these areas.

Aesthetics is the study of beauty and the fine arts. Controversies over works of art — the aesthetic value of books, paintings, sculpture, architecture, dance, drama, and movies — rage fiercely among experts and laypeople alike. They may disagree on the standards for judging or, even if they agree, may disagree about how successfully the art object under discussion has met these standards.

Consider a discussion about popular music. Hearing someone praise the singing of a well-known vocalist, Sheila Jordan, you might ask why she is so highly regarded. You expect Jordan's fan to say more than "I like her" or "Man, she's great." You expect the fan to give reasons to support his claim. "She's unique," he says. He shows you a short review from a widely read newspaper that says, "Her singing is filled with fascinating phrasings, twists, and turns, and she's been compared with Billie Holiday for her emotional intensity. . . . She can be so heart-wrenching that conversations stop cold." Her fan agrees with the criteria for judging a singer given by the author of the review: uniqueness, fascinating phrasings, emotional intensity.

You may not agree that these are the only standards or even the significant ones for judging a singer. But the establishment of standards itself offers material for a discussion or an argument. You may argue about the relevance of the criteria, or, agreeing on the criteria, you may argue about the success of the singer in meeting them. Perhaps you prefer cool singers to intense ones. Or, even if you choose intensity over coolness, you may not think Sheila Jordan can be described as "expressive." Moreover, in any arguments about criteria, differences in experience and preparation acquire importance. You would probably take for granted that a writer with formal musical training who has listened carefully to dozens of singers over a period of years, who has read a good deal of musical criticism and discussed musical matters with other knowledgeable people would be a more reliable critic than someone who lacked these qualifications.

It is probably not surprising then, that, despite wide differences in taste, professional critics more often than not agree on criteria and whether an art object has met the criteria. For example, almost all movie critics agreed that *Citizen Kane* and *Gone with the Wind* were superior films. They also agreed that *Plan 9 from Outer Space*, a horror film, was terrible.

Value claims about morality express judgments about the rightness or wrongness of conduct or belief. Here disagreements are as wide and deep as in the arts. The first two examples on page 54 reveal how controversial such claims can be. Although you and your reader may share many values, among them a belief in democracy, a respect for learning, and a desire for peace, you may also disagree, even profoundly, about other values. The subject of divorce, for example, despite its prevalence in our society, can produce a conflict between differing moral standards. Some people may insist on adherence to absolute standards, arguing that the values they hold are based on immutable religious precepts derived from God and Scripture. Since marriage is sacred, divorce is always wrong, they say, whether or not the conditions of society change. Other people may argue that values are relative, based on the changing needs of societies in different places and at different times. Since marriage is an institution created by human beings at a particular time in history to serve particular social needs, they may say, it can also be dissolved when other social needs arise. The same conflicts between moral values might occur in discussions of abortion or suicide.

As a writer you cannot always know what system of values is held by your reader. Yet it might be possible to find a rule on which almost all readers agree. One such rule was expressed by the eighteenth-century German philosopher Immanuel Kant: "Man and, in general, every rational being exists as an end in itself and not merely as a means to be arbitrarily used by this or that will." Kant's prescription urges us not to subject any creature to a condition that it has not freely chosen. In other words, we cannot use other creatures, as in slavery, for our own purposes. (Some philosophers would extend this rule to the treatment of animals by human beings.) This standard of judgment has, in fact, been invoked in recent years against medical experimentation on human beings in prisons and hospitals without their consent and against the sterilization of poor or mentally defective women without their knowledge of the decision.

Nevertheless, even where there is agreement about standards for measuring behavior, you should be aware that a majority preference is not enough to confer moral value. If in a certain neighborhood a majority of heterosexual men decide to harass a few gay men and lesbians, that consensus does not make their action right. In formulating value claims, you should be prepared to ask and answer questions about the way in which your value claims and those of others have been arrived at. Lionel Ruby, an American philosopher, sums it up in these words: "The law of rationality tells us that we ought to justify our beliefs by evidence and reasons, instead of asserting them dogmatically."[3]

Of course, you will not always be able to persuade those with whom you argue that your values are superior to theirs and that they should therefore change their attitudes. Nor, on the other hand, would you want to compromise your values or pretend that they were different in order to win an argument. What you can and should do, however, as Lionel Ruby advises, is give *good reasons* why you think one thing is better than another. If as a child you asked why it was wrong to take your brother's toys, you might have been told by an exasperated parent, "Because I say so." Some adults still give such answers in defending their judgments, but such answers are not arguments and do nothing to win the agreement of others.

Defending a Claim of Value

The following suggestions are a preliminary guide to the defense of a value claim. (We discuss value claims further in Chapter 5.)

1. Try to make clear that the values or principles you are defending should have priority on any scale of values. Keep in mind that you and your readers may differ about their relative importance. For example, although your readers may agree with you that

---

[3]*The Art of Making Sense* (New York: Lippincott, 1968), p. 271.

brilliant photography is important in a film, they may think that a well-written script is even more crucial to its success. And although they may agree that freedom of the press is a mainstay of democracy, they may regard the right to privacy as even more fundamental.

2. Suggest that adherence to the values you are defending will bring about good results in some specific situation or bad results if respect for the values is ignored. You might argue, for example, that a belief in freedom of the press will make citizens better informed and the country stronger while a failure to protect this freedom will strengthen the forces of authoritarianism.

3. Since value terms are abstract, use examples and illustrations to clarify meanings and make distinctions. Comparisons and contrasts are especially helpful. If you are using the term *heroism,* can you provide examples to differentiate between *heroism* and *foolhardiness* or *exhibitionism?*

4. Use testimony of others to prove that knowledgeable or highly regarded people share your values.

SAMPLE ANALYSIS: CLAIM OF VALUE

Kids in the Mall: Growing Up Controlled
WILLIAM SEVERINI KOWINSKI

> Butch heaved himself up and loomed over the group. "Like it was different for me," he piped. "My folks used to drop me off at the shopping mall every morning and leave me all day. It was like a big free baby-sitter, you know? One night they never came back for me. Maybe they moved away. Maybe there's some kind of a Bureau of Missing Parents I could check with."
>
> — Richard Peck
> *Secrets of the Shopping Mall,*
> a novel for teenagers

From his sister at Swarthmore, I'd heard about a kid in Florida whose mother picked him up after school every day, drove him straight to the mall, and left him there until it closed — all at his in-

---

William Severini Kowinski is a free-lance writer who has been the book review editor and managing arts editor of the *Boston Phoenix.* This excerpt is from his book *The Malling of America: An Inside Look at the Great Consumer Paradise* (1985).

sistence. I'd heard about a boy in Washington who, when his family moved from one suburb to another, pedaled his bicycle five miles every day to get back to his old mall, where he once belonged.

These stories aren't unusual. The mall is a common experience for the majority of American youth; they have probably been going there all their lives. Some ran within their first large open space, saw their first fountain, bought their first toy, and read their first book in a mall. They may have smoked their first cigarette or first joint, or turned them down, had their first kiss or lost their virginity in the mall parking lot. Teenagers in America now spend more time in the mall than anywhere else but home and school. Mostly it is their choice, but some of that mall time is put in as the result of two-paycheck and single-parent households, and the lack of other viable alternatives. But are these kids being harmed by the mall?

I wondered first of all what difference it makes for adolescents to experience so many important moments in the mall. They are, after all, at play in the fields of its little world and they learn its ways; they adapt to it and make it adapt to them. It's here that these kids get their street sense, only it's mall sense. They are learning the ways of a large-scale, artificial environment; its subtleties and flexibilities, its particular pleasures and resonances, and the attitudes it fosters.

The presence of so many teenagers for so much time was not something mall developers planned on. In fact, it came as a big surprise. But kids became a fact of mall life very easily, and the International Council of Shopping Centers found it necessary to commission a study, which they published along with a guide to mall managers on how to handle the teenage incursion.

The study found that "teenagers in suburban centers are bored   5 and come to the shopping centers mainly as a place to go. Teenagers in suburban centers spent more time fighting, drinking, littering and walking than did their urban counterparts, but presented fewer overall problems." The report observed that "adolescents congregated in groups of two to four and predominantly at locations selected by them rather than management." This probably had something to do with the decision to install game arcades, which allow management to channel these restless adolescents into naturally contained areas away from major traffic points of adult shoppers.

The guide concluded that mall management should tolerate and even encourage the teenage presence because, in the words of the report, "The vast majority support the same set of values as does shopping center management." *The same set of values* means simply that mall kids are already preprogrammed to be consumers and that the mall can put the finishing touches to them as hard-core, lifelong shoppers just like everybody else. That, after all, is what the mall is about. So it shouldn't be surprising that in spending a lot of time there, adolescents find little that challenges the assumption that the goal of life is to make money and buy products, or that just about everything else in life is to be used to serve those ends.

Growing up in a high-consumption society already adds inestimable pressure to kids' lives. Clothes consciousness has invaded the grade schools, and popularity is linked with having the best, newest clothes in the currently acceptable styles. Even what they read has been affected. "Miss [Nancy] Drew wasn't obsessed with her wardrobe," noted the *Wall Street Journal.* "But today the mystery in teen fiction for girls is what outfit the heroine will wear next." Shopping has become a survival skill and there is certainly no better place to learn it than the mall, where its importance is powerfully reinforced and certainly never questioned.

The mall as a university of suburban materialism, where Valley Girls and Boys from coast to coast are educated in consumption, has its other lessons in this era of change in family life and sexual mores and their economic and social ramifications. The plethora of products in the mall, plus the pressure on teens to buy them, may contribute to the phenomenon that psychologist David Elkind calls "the hurried child": kids who are exposed to too much of the adult world too quickly and must respond with a sophistication that belies their still-tender emotional development. Certainly the adult products marketed for children — form-fitting designer jeans, sexy tops for preteen girls — add to the social pressure to look like an adult, along with the home-grown need to understand adult finances (why mothers must work) and adult emotions (when parents divorce).

Kids spend so much time at the mall partly because their parents allow it and even encourage it. The mall is safe, doesn't seem to harbor any unsavory activities, and there is adult supervision; it is, after all, a controlled environment. So the temptation, especially for working parents, is to let the mall be their baby-sitter. At least the kids aren't watching TV. But the mall's role as a surrogate mother may be more extensive and more profound.

Karen Lansky, a writer living in Los Angeles, has looked into the 10 subject, and she told me some of her conclusions about the effects on its teenaged denizens of the mall's controlled and controlling environment. "Structure is the dominant idea, since true 'mall rats' lack just that in their home lives," she said, "and adolescents about to make the big leap into growing up crave more structure than our modern society cares to acknowledge." Karen pointed out some of the elements malls supply that kids used to get from their families, like warmth (Strawberry Shortcake dolls and similar cute and cuddly merchandise), old-fashioned mothering ("We do it all for you," the fast-food slogan), and even home cooking (the "homemade" treats at the food court).

The problem in all this, as Karen Lansky sees it, is that while families nurture children by encouraging growth through the assumption of responsibility and then by letting them rest in the bosom of the family from the rigors of growing up, the mall as a structural mother encourages passivity and consumption, as long as the kid doesn't make trouble. Therefore all they learn about becoming adults is how to act and how to consume.

Kids are in the mall not only in the passive role of shoppers — they also work there, especially as fast-food outlets infiltrate the mall's enclosure. There they learn how to hold a job and take responsibility, but still within the same value context. When *CBS Reports* went to Oak Park Mall in suburban Kansas City, Kansas, to tape part of their hour-long consideration of malls, "After the Dream Comes True," they interviewed a teenaged girl who worked in a fast-food outlet there. In a sequence that didn't make the final program, she described the major goal of her present life, which was to perfect the curl on top of the ice-cream cones that were her store's specialty. If she could do that, she would be moved from the lowly soft-drink dispenser to the more prestigious ice-cream division, the curl on top of the status ladder at her restaurant. These are the achievements that are important at the mall.

Other benefits of such jobs may also be overrated, according to Laurence D. Steinberg of the University of California at Irvine's social ecology department, who did a study on teenage employment. Their jobs, he found, are generally simple, mindlessly repetitive and boring. They don't really learn anything, and the jobs don't lead anywhere. Teenagers also work primarily with other teenagers; even their supervisors are often just a little older than they are. "Kids need to spend time with adults," Steinberg told me. "Although they get benefits from peer relationships, without parents and other adults it's one-side socialization. They hang out with each other, have age-segregated jobs, and watch TV."

Perhaps much of this is not so terrible or even so terribly different. Now that they have so much more to contend with in their lives, adolescents probably need more time to spend with other adolescents without adult impositions, just to sort things out. Though it is more concentrated in the mall (and therefore perhaps a clearer target), the value system there is really the dominant one of the whole society. Attitudes about curiosity, initiative, self-expression, empathy, and disinterested learning aren't necessarily made in the mall; they are mirrored there, perhaps a bit more intensely — as through a glass brightly.

Besides, the mall is not without its educational opportunities. 15 There are bookstores, where there is at least a short shelf of classics at great prices, and other books from which it is possible to learn more than how to do sit-ups. There are tools, from hammers to

VCRs, and products, from clothes to records, that can help the young find and express themselves. There are older people with stories, and places to be alone or to talk one-on-one with a kindred spirit. And there is always the passing show.

The mall itself may very well be an education about the future. I was struck with the realization, as early as my first forays into Greengate, that the mall is only one of a number of enclosed and controlled environments that are part of the lives of today's young. The mall is just an extension, say, of those large suburban schools — only there's Karmelkorn instead of chem lab, the ice rink instead of the gym: It's high school without the impertinence of classes.

Growing up, moving from home to school to the mall — from enclosure to enclosure, transported in cars — is a curiously continuous process, without much in the way of contrast or contact with unenclosed reality. Places must tend to blur into one another. But whatever differences and dangers there are in this, the skills these adolescents are learning may turn out to be useful in their later lives. For we seem to be moving inexorably into an age of preplanned and regulated environments, and this is the world they will inherit.

Still, it might be better if they had more of a choice. One teenaged girl confessed to *CBS Reports* that she sometimes felt she was missing something by hanging out at the mall so much. "But I'm here," she said, "and this is what I have."

Analysis

Kowinski has chosen to evaluate one aspect of an extraordinarily successful economic and cultural phenomenon — the commercial mall. He asks whether the influence of the mall on adolescents is good or bad. The answer seems to be a little of both. The good values may be described as exposure to a variety of experiences, a protective structure for adolescents who often live in unstable environments, and immersion in a world that may well serve as an introduction to adulthood. But the bad values, which Kowinski thinks are more influential (as the title suggests) are those of the shoppers' paradise, a society that believes in acquisition and consumption of goods as ultimate goals, and too much control over the choices available to adolescents. The tone of the judgment, however, is moderate and reflects a balanced, even scholarly, attitude. More than other arguments, the treatment of values requires such a voice, one which respects differences of opinion among readers. But serious doesn't mean heavy. His style is formal but highly readable, brightened by interesting examples and precise details. The opening paragraph is a strikingly effective lead.

Some of his observations are personal, but others are derived from studies by professional researchers, from *CBS Reports* to a well-known writer on childhood. These studies give weight and authority to his conclusions. Here and there we detect an appealing sympathy for the adolescents in their controlled environment.

Like any thoughtful social commentator, Kowinski casts a wide net. He sees the mall not only as a hangout for teens but as a good deal more, an institution that offers insights into family life and work, the changing urban culture, the nature of contemporary entertainment, even glimpses of a somewhat forbidding future.

CLAIMS OF POLICY

Claims of policy argue that certain conditions should exist. As the name suggests, they advocate adoption of policies or courses of action because problems have arisen that call for solution. Almost always *should* or *ought to* or *must* is expressed or implied in the claim.

> CLAIM: Voluntary prayer should be permitted in public schools.
>
> CLAIM: A dress code should be introduced for all public high schools.
>
> CLAIM: A law should permit sixteen-year-olds and parents to "divorce" each other in cases of extreme incompatibility.
>
> CLAIM: Mandatory jail terms should be imposed for drunk driving violations.

In defending such claims of policy you may find that you must first convince your audience that a problem exists. This will require that, as part of your longer argument, you make a factual claim, offering data to prove that present conditions are unsatisfactory. You may also find it necessary to refer to the values that support your claim. Then you will be ready to introduce your policy, to persuade your audience that the solution you propose will solve the problem.

We will examine a policy claim in which all these parts are at work. The claim can be stated as follows: "The time required for an undergraduate degree should be extended to five years." Immediate agreement with this policy among student readers would certainly not be universal. Some students would not recognize a problem. They would say, "The college curriculum we have now is fine. There's no need for a change. Besides, we don't want to spend more time in school." First, then, the arguer would have to persuade a skeptical audience that there is a problem, that four years of college are no longer enough because the stock of knowledge in almost all fields of study continues to increase. The arguer would provide data to show how many more choices in history, literature, and science students have now compared to the choices in the those fields a generation ago. She would also find it necessary to emphasize the value of greater knowledge and more schooling compared to the value of other goods the audience cherishes, such as earlier independence. Finally, the arguer would offer a plan for putting her policy into effect. Her plan would have to take into consideration initial psychological resistance, revision of the curriculum, the costs of more instruction, and the costs of lost production in the work force. Most important, she would point out the benefits for both individuals and society if this policy were adopted.

In this example, we assumed that the reader would disagree that a problem existed. In many cases, however, the reader may agree that there is a problem but disagree with the arguer about the way of solving it. Most of us, no doubt, will agree that we want to reduce or eliminate the following problems: misbehavior and vandalism in schools, drunk driving, crime on the streets, child abuse, pornography, pollution. But how shall we go about solving those problems? What public policy will give us well-behaved, diligent students who never destroy school property? Safe streets where no one is ever robbed or assaulted? Loving homes where no child is ever mistreated? Some members of society would choose to introduce rules or laws that punish infractions so severely that wrongdoers would be unwilling or unable to repeat their offenses. Other members of society would prefer policies that attempt to rehabilitate or reeducate offenders through training, therapy, counseling, and new opportunities.

Defending a Claim of Policy

The following steps will help you organize arguments for a claim of policy.

1. Make your proposal clear. The terms in the proposal should be precisely defined.
2. If necessary, establish that there is a need for a change. If changes have been ignored or resisted, there may be good or at least understandable reasons why this is so. (It is often wrongly assumed that people cling to cultural practices long after their significance and necessity have eroded. But rational human beings do not continue to observe practices unless those practices serve a purpose. The fact that you and I may see no value or purpose in the activities of another is irrelevant.)
3. Consider the opposing arguments. You may want to state the opposing arguments in a brief paragraph in order to answer them in the body of your argument.

4. Devote the major part of your essay to proving that your proposal is an answer to the opposing arguments and that there are distinct benefits for your readers in adopting your proposal.
5. Support your proposal with solid data, but don't neglect the moral considerations and the common-sense reasons, which may be even more persuasive.

SAMPLE ANALYSIS: CLAIM OF POLICY

The Real Victims
ALBERT SHANKER

It's increasingly clear that the biggest roadblock to improving the achievement of U.S. students is violence and disorder in our schools. Education reformers say we must set high standards for student achievement and create curriculums and assessments embodying these standards — and I agree with them. But high standards and excellent curriculums and assessments are not enough. Indeed, they will be worthless if students cannot learn because they are constantly afraid of being hit by a stray bullet or because their classes are dominated by disruptive students. This is just common sense.

A couple of weeks ago, *Washington Post* columnist Courtland Milloy told the story of a girl who had seen some classmates stab another student and was so terrified by the possibility of reprisals that she quit school ("An Education in Self-Help," January 29, 1995). This story has a relatively happy ending: The girl went on to earn a GED and is now attending college. But for every one who is motivated to continue her education the way this girl did, there are thousands and tens of thousands who are intimidated and distracted and are lost to school and learning.

Classroom disruption is more pervasive than school violence and just as fatal to learning. If there is one student in a class who constantly yells, curses out the teacher, and picks on other students who are trying to listen or participate in class, you can be sure that most of the teacher's time will not be devoted to helping the other youngsters learn math or science or English; it will be spent figuring out how to contain this student. And it does not take many

---

Albert Shanker is president of the American Federation of Teachers. His weekly column, "Where We Stand," has appeared in the *New York Times* Week in Review section for twenty-five years. This column is from February 19, 1995.

such students to ruin the learning of the great majority of youngsters in a school.

School officials seem generally to be at a loss. In Washington,
D.C., and elsewhere, students who have been caught bringing guns
or drugs to school or who have hurt other students may simply be
transferred to another school or suspended for a little while. There
seems to be a high level of tolerance for this kind of behavior where
there should be none. And when it comes to chronically disruptive
students, we are even more tolerant. Little happens to kids who
merely keep others from learning.

Parents are painfully aware of these problems. That's why both   5
African American and white parents put safe and orderly schools at
the top of their list of things that would improve student achievement. And that is undoubtedly why vouchers and tuition tax credits
are so popular — especially among many parents of kids in inner-
city schools. These parents are saying, "If your schools are so violent and disorderly that our children can't learn — and are not even
safe — let us put them in schools that won't tolerate kids who behave that way."

Many education experts insist that our first responsibility is to
the few violent and disruptive kids. They say these kids have the
"right" to an education, and we need to keep them in class and in
school so we can help them overcome their problems. But what
about the "rights" of the twenty-five or thirty kids in every class who
come to school ready to work? Why are we willing to threaten their
safety and learning? I'm not advocating putting violent or disruptive
kids out on the streets. We need alternative programs for these
youngsters, but we also need to change a system that sacrifices the
overwhelming majority of children for a handful — without even
doing the handful any good.

Most children come to school believing that doing right matters,
but they soon learn to question that belief. Say a youngster in kinder-
garten does something that is way out of line — he knocks another
kid down and kicks him. The other five-year-olds are sure something
terrible is going to happen to this child, and they are very glad
they're not in his place. Well, what happens? Probably the teacher
gets in trouble for reporting the child. So the children's sense of justice — their belief that acting naughty has consequences — begins
to be eroded. The youngster who defied the teacher becomes the de
facto leader of the class, and peer pressure now encourages the
other children to ignore what the teacher tells them to do. At a very
early age, kids are taught a bad lesson — nothing will happen if they
break the rules — and whatever else they learn in English or math
or science, this lesson remains consistent throughout school.

We have an irrational system, and it's no wonder that angry parents are calling for vouchers, tuition tax credits — anything that would allow them to get their kids out of schools where a few violent and disruptive kids call the shots. What this means, though, is that 98 percent of students would be leaving public schools to get away from the 2 percent. Wouldn't it make a lot more sense just to move the 2 percent?

Analysis

Shanker argues that disruptive students should be removed from their classes, but in only two places does he make the policy explicit, referring to "alternative programs" and moving "the 2 percent." Instead, he devotes almost the whole of his essay to proving that a policy to remove disruptive students is absolutely necessary. Even the title reveals the emphasis of the essay. The real victims are children who are prevented from learning by violence in the classroom, and it is their needs that must be addressed.

A reader can guess why Shanker adopts such a rhetorical strategy. Many policy claims require the arguer to first prove that a problem exists — in effect, establishing a claim of fact — and often this is the most important task. Since a policy that expels or removes students from a regular classroom, while not new, is still hotly debated, the advocate of such a policy must make a strong case for it. Shanker acknowledges the objections to his policy in paragraph 6 and answers them.

Shanker emphasizes two unfortunate consequences of a failure to adopt his policy recommendation. One is the cost imposed on children who want to learn and are prevented from doing so. Development of this idea begins in the second paragraph and occupies most of the essay. Its strength lies in its appeal to our sense of fairness. There is also an implicit appeal to fear. The withdrawal of children to safer, often private schools weakens the public school system. Shanker obviously believes that his readers will agree that public schools are worth saving.

The second consequence is more difficult to measure. It is the wrong moral lesson absorbed by children when they see that hurtful behavior goes unpunished. Although a psychological effect cannot easily be proved by numbers, unlike the exodus of children to private schools, most readers will recognize it as one common to their experience.

Despite the fact that we know little or nothing about the details of a removal policy, Shanker's argument suggests that, if the necessity for a change of policy is made sufficiently strong, the way for its adoption has been prepared.

The Landfill Excavations

WILLIAM L. RATHJE and CULLEN MURPHY

The Garbage Project began excavating landfills primarily for two reasons, both of them essentially archaeological in nature. One was to see if the data being gleaned from garbage fresh off the truck could be cross-validated by data from garbage in municipal landfills. The second, which derived from the Garbage Project's origins as an exercise in the study of formation processes, was to look into what happens to garbage after it has been interred. As it happens, the first landfill excavation got under way, in 1987, just as it was becoming clear — from persistent reports about garbage in the press that were at variance with some of the things the Garbage Project had been learning — that an adequate knowledge base about landfills and their contents did not exist. It was during this period that news of a mounting garbage crisis broke into the national consciousness. And it was during this period that two assertions were given wide currency and achieved a status as accepted fact from which they have yet to be dislodged. One is that accelerating rates of garbage generation are responsible for the rapid depletion and present shortage of landfills. The other is that, nationwide, there are few good places left to put new landfills. Whether these propositions are true or false — they happen, for the most part, to be exaggerations — it was certainly the case that however quickly landfills were being filled, the public, the press, and even most specialists had only the vaguest idea (at best) of what they were being filled up *with*. Yes, think tanks and consulting firms have done some calculations and come up with estimates of garbage quantities by commodity, based on national production figures and assumptions about rates of discard. But until 1987, when the Garbage Project's archaeologists began systematically sorting through the evidence from bucket-auger wells, no one had ever deliberately dug into landfills with a view to recording the inner reality in minute detail. . . .

One key aim of the landfill excavations was to get some idea of the volume occupied by various kinds of garbage in landfills. Although many Garbage Project studies have relied on garbage weight for comparative purposes, volume is the critical variable when it

---

William L. Rathje is a professor of anthropology at the University of Arizona, where he heads the Garbage Project. Cullen Murphy is managing editor of the *Atlantic Monthly*. This excerpt is from their book *Rubbish! The Archeology of Garbage* (1992).

comes to landfill management: Landfills close not because they are too heavy but because they are too full. And yet reliable data on the volume taken up by plastics, paper, organic material, and other kinds of garbage once it has been deposited in a landfill did not exist in 1987. The Garbage Project set out to fill the gap, applying its usual sorting and weighing procedures to excavated garbage, and then adding a final step: a volume measurement. Measuring volume was not a completely straightforward process. Because most garbage tends to puff up with air once it has been extracted from deep inside a landfill, all of the garbage exhumed was subjected to compaction, so that the data on garbage volume would reflect the volume that garbage occupies when it is squashed and under pressure inside a landfill. The compactor used by the Garbage Project is a thirty-gallon cannister with a hydraulic piston that squeezes out air from plastic bags, newspapers, cereal boxes, mowed grass, hot dogs, and everything else at a relatively gentle pressure of 0.9 pounds per square inch. The data on garbage volume that emerged from the Garbage Project's landfill excavations were the first such data in existence.

What do the numbers reveal? Briefly, that the kinds of garbage that loom largest in the popular imagination as the chief villains in the filling up and closing down of landfills — fast-food packaging, expanded polystyrene foam (the material that coffee cups are made from), and disposable diapers, to name three on many people's most-unwanted list — do not deserve the blame they have received. They may be highly visible as litter, but they are not responsible for an inordinate contribution to landfill garbage. The same goes for plastics. But one kind of garbage whose reputation has thus far been largely unbesmirched — plain old paper — merits increased attention.

Over the years, Garbage Project representatives have asked a variety of people who have never seen the inside of a landfill to estimate what percentage of a landfill's contents is made up of fast-food packaging, expanded polystyrene foam, and disposable diapers. In September of 1989, for example, this very question was asked of a group attending the biennial meeting of the National Audubon Society, and the results were generally consistent with those obtained from surveys conducted at universities, at business meetings, and at conferences of state and local government officials: Estimates at the Audubon meeting of the volume of fast-food packaging fell mainly between 20 and 30 percent of a typical landfill's contents; of expanded polystyrene foam, between 25 and 40 percent; and of disposable diapers, between 25 and 45 percent. The overall estimate, then, of the proportion of a landfill's volume that is taken up by fast-food packaging, foam in general, and disposable diapers ranged from a suspiciously high 70 percent to an obviously impossible 125 percent.

Needless to say, fast-food packaging has few friends. It is de- 5
signed to be bright, those bold reds and yellows being among the
most attention-getting colors on a marketer's palette; this, coupled
with the propensity of human beings to litter, means that fast-food
packaging gets noticed. It is also greasy and smelly, and on some
level it seems to symbolize, as do fast-food restaurants themselves,
certain attributes of modern America to which modern Americans
remain imperfectly reconciled. But is there really all that much
fast-food packaging? Is it "straining" the capacity of America's landfills, as a 1988 editorial in the *New York Times* contended?

The physical reality inside a landfill is, in fact, quite different
from the picture painted by many commentators. Of the more than
fourteen tons of garbage from landfills that the Garbage Project has
sorted, fewer than a hundred pounds was found to consist of
fast-food packaging of any kind — that is, containers or wrappers
for hamburgers, pizzas, chicken, fish, and convenience-store sand-
wiches, plus all the accessories, such as cups, lids, straws, sauce
containers, and so on, plus all the boxes and bags used to deliver
food and other raw materials to the fast-food restaurant. In other
words, less than one-half of 1 percent of the weight of the materials
excavated from nine municipal landfills over a period of five years
(1985–89) consisted of fast-food packaging. As for the amount of
space that fast-food packaging takes up in landfills — a more important indicator than weight — the Garbage Project estimate after
sorting is that it accounts for no more than one-third of 1 percent of
the total volume of a landfill's contents.

What about expanded polystyrene foam — the substance that
most people are referring to when they say Styrofoam (which is a
registered trademark of the Dow Chemical Corporation, and is baby
blue in color and used chiefly to insulate buildings)? Expanding polystyrene foam is, of course, used for many things. Only about 10 percent of all foam plastics that were manufactured in the period
1980–83 were used for fast-food packaging. Most foam was (and is)
blown into egg cartons, meat trays, coffee cups (the fast-food kind,
yes, but mainly the plain kind that sit stacked upside down beside
the office coffee pot), "peanuts" for packing, and the molded forms
that protect electronic appliances in their shipping cases. All the expanded polystyrene foam that is thrown away in America every
year, from the lowliest packing peanut to the most sophisticated
molded carton, accounts for no more than 1 percent of the volume
of garbage landfilled between 1980 and 1989.

Expanded polystyrene foam has been the focus of many vocal
campaigns around the country to ban it outright. It is worth remembering that if foam were banned, the relatively small amount of space
that it takes up in landfills would not be saved. Eggs, hamburgers, coffee, and stereos must still be put in *something*. The most likely re-

placement for foam is some form of coated cardboard, which can be difficult to recycle and takes up almost as much room as foam in a landfill. Indeed, in cases where cardboard replaced foam, it could often happen that a larger volume of cardboard would be needed to fulfill the same function fulfilled by a smaller volume of foam. No one burns fingers holding a foam cup filled with coffee, because the foam's insulating qualities are so effective. But people burn their fingers so frequently with plastic- or wax-coated cardboard coffee cups (and all cardboard hot-drink cups are coated) that they often put one such cup inside another for the added protection.

As for disposable diapers, the debate over their potential impact on the environment is sufficiently vociferous and complex to warrant its own chapter. . . . Suffice it to say for present purposes, though, that the pattern displayed by fast-food packaging and expanded polystyrene foam is apparent with respect to diapers, too. People *think* that disposable diapers are a big part of the garbage problem; they are not a very significant factor at all.

The three garbage categories that, as we saw, the Audubon respondents believed accounted for 70 to 125 percent of all garbage actually account, together, for only about 3 percent. The survey responses would probably have been even more skewed if respondents had also been asked to guess the proportion of a typical landfill's contents that is made up of plastic. Plastic is surrounded by a maelstrom of mythology; into the very word Americans seem to have distilled all of their guilt over the environmental degradation they have wrought and the culture of consumption they invented and inhabit. Plastic has become an object of scorn — who can forget the famous scene in *The Graduate* (or quote it properly)? — no doubt in large measure because its development corresponded chronologically with, and then powerfully reinforced, the emergence of the very consumerist ethic that is now despised. (What Mr. McGuire, a neighbor, says to Benjamin Braddock is: "I just want to say one word to you. Just one word. Are you listening? . . . Plastics. There is a great future in plastics. Think about it.") Plastic is the Great Satan of garbage. It is the apotheosis of the cheap, the inauthentic; even the attempts to replace or transform plastic — such as the recent ill-fated experiments with "biodegradable" plastic . . . — seem somehow inauthentic. . . .

[But] in landfill after landfill the volume of all plastics — foam, film, and rigid; toys, utensils, and packages — from the 1980s amounted to between 20 and 24 percent of all garbage, as sorted; when compacted along with everything else, in order to replicate actual conditions inside a landfill, the volume of plastics was reduced to under 16 percent.

Even if its share of total garbage is, at the moment, relatively low, is it not the case that plastics take up a larger proportion of landfill space with every passing year? Unquestionably a larger number of physical objects are made of plastic today than were in 1970 or 1950. But a curious phenomenon becomes apparent when garbage deposits from our own time are compared with those from strata characteristic of, say, the 1970s. While the number of individual plastic objects to be found in a deposit of garbage of a constant size has increased considerably in the course of a decade and a half — more than doubling — the proportion of landfill space taken up by these plastics has not changed; at some landfills, the proportion of space taken up by plastics was actually a little less in the 1980s than it was in the 1970s.

The explanation appears to be a strategy that is known in the plastics industry as "light-weighting" — making objects in such a way that the objects retain all the necessary functional characteristics but require the use of less resin. The concept of light-weighting is not limited to the making of plastics; the makers of glass bottles have been light-weighting their wares for decades, with the result that bottles today are 25 percent lighter than they were in 1984. (That is why bottles in landfills are likely to show up broken in the upper, more-recent, strata, whereas lower strata, holding garbage from many years ago, contain many more whole bottles.) Environmentalists might hail light-weighting as an example of source reduction. Businessmen embrace it for a different reason: sheer profit. Using fewer raw materials for a product that is lighter and therefore cheaper to transport usually translates into a competitive edge, and companies that rely heavily on plastics have been light-weighting ever since plastics were introduced. PET soda bottles had a weight of 67 grams in 1974; the weight today is 48 grams, for a reduction of 30 percent. High-density polyethylene (HDPE) milk jugs in the mid-1960s had a weight of 120 grams; the weight today is about 65 grams, for reduction of more than 45 percent. Plastic grocery bags had a thickness of 30 microns in 1976; the thickness today is at most 18 microns, for a reduction of 40 percent. Even the plastic in disposable diapers has been light-weighted, although the superabsorbent material that was added at the same time (1986) ensures that even if diapers enter the house lighter they will leave it heavier than ever. When plastic gets lighter, in most cases it also gets thinner and more crushable. The result, of course, is that many more plastic items can be squeezed into a given volume of landfill space today than could have been squeezed into it ten or twenty years ago.

This fact has frequently been met with skepticism. In 1989, Robert Krulwich, of the CBS network's *Saturday Night with Connie Chung* program, conducted a tour of the Garbage Project's operations in Tucson, and he expressed surprise when told about the light-weighting of plastics. He asked for a crushed PET soda bottle from 1989 and tried to blow it up. The light plastic container inflated easily. He was then given a crushed PET soda bottle found in a stratum dating back to 1981 — a bottle whose plastic would be considerably thicker and stiffer. Try as he might, Krulwich could not make the flattened container inflate.

Reading and Discussion Questions

1. The paragraphs in this excerpt are rather long, but while some can be divided into two or more paragraphs, others cannot. Paragraph 1, for example, can be divided. Where might it be appropriate to make a cut without violating coherence? Paragraph 2, on the other hand, seems to resist cutting. Why? Can you divide paragraph 13? Why or why not?
2. What reasons do the authors give for the importance of the Garbage Project? Do their findings seem to justify their "archeological" research?
3. Some factual claims imply a need for changes in behavior. (See the analysis of "Cocaine Is Even Deadlier Than We Thought," p. 52.) Is there any evidence that Rathje and Murphy are interested in influencing behavior?
4. How do they account for the erroneous information held by the public? Does this information reflect certain values or prejudices? Were some of your own views overturned by the authors' conclusions?

Writing Suggestions

5. Describe any changes you or your family might make in your purchases and methods of disposal as a result of reading "The Landfill Excavations." Explain how these changes would affect your life. Would they impose a hardship? If you are not persuaded to make any changes, explain why.
6. Choose another garbage or litter "problem" — one from your own experience or one you have read about — and provide the data to prove that it is or is not a problem. Newspapers and news magazines are one source of information, but remember that expert minority views may be overlooked and unreported. Like the authors of "The Landfill Excavations," select relevant statistics and examples with human interest, wherever possible.

Starving Children

FRANCINE DU PLESSIX GRAY

In the movie *Kids*, a band of teenagers forages for sex, drugs, and booze on New York City streets. The cruelty of these adolescents who taunt gay men and beat up random passersby, the callousness with which they call their girlfriends "bitches" as they paw them into submission, the subhuman grunts and epithets of their speech make the mind reel. I'm still haunted by the shot at the end of the film of their bodies sprawled over one another, like youths brought in for a Roman emperor's debauch, on the floor of a spacious Manhattan apartment. I keep recalling the remains of their daily fodder — liquor bottles and discarded joints, tacos, burritos drenched in pools of salsa — that litter the site of their orgy. It is that last detail, suggesting their feral, boorishly gulped diet, that somehow comes to mind when one of the film's characters wakes up from his all-night bender in a Manhattan apartment filled with leather furniture and abstract art, looks straight at the camera, and asks, "What happened?"

What has happened to the American family — the fraying effect of harassed working parents, the stranglehold of the media, the pressures of peer culture — is a theme much ranted about. Yet one aspect of what has happened has been overlooked: Kids like those we see in *Kids* — they come from all over the social spectrum — never seem to sit down to a proper meal at home anymore. This is not another pious harangue on "spiritual starvation"; this is about the fact that we may be witnessing the first generation in history that has not been required to participate in that primal rite of socialization, the family meal. The family meal is not only the core curriculum in the school of civilized discourse; it is also a set of protocols that curb our natural savagery and our animal greed, and cultivate a capacity for sharing and thoughtfulness.

Dinner rituals have nothing to do with class, or working women's busy lives, or any particular family structure. I've had dinners of boiled potatoes with families in Siberia, suppers of deli cold cuts with single welfare mothers in Chicago, bowls of watery gruel in the Sahara — all made memorable by the grace with which they were offered and by the sight of youngsters learning through experience the art of human companionship. The teenagers on display in *Kids* are not only physically starved — devitaminized, made hyper-

---

This essay by Francine du Plessix Gray, a journalist and novelist, appeared in *The New Yorker* on October 16, 1995.

active — by the junk food they consume as they slouch in front of the TV or lope toward their next bacchanal. Far worse, they are deprived of the main course of civilized life — the practice of sitting down at the dinner table and observing the attendant conventions. Like the Passover seder or the Communion bread, the ritual of nutrition helps to imbue families, and societies at large, with greater empathy and fellowship. However, all rituals involve, to some degree, a sacrifice, and the home meal requires genuine sacrifices of time and energy, large expenditures of those very traits it nurtures — patience, compassion, self-discipline.

Many of the teenagers in *Kids* — the more affluent ones — are the offspring of the "me generation," members of what Christopher Lasch called "the culture of narcissism." And those parents may be the most at fault. Might it be that they have stinted on the socializing of their children by focusing on their own rituals of self-improvement — enjoying their workout highs at health clubs or their learning highs in evening classes? How much more fun it is, how much less tiring, for us to enjoy a fine, quiet dinner by ourselves, or with our buddies, without the litany of questions and corrections that youngsters' company entails. But the family meal should continue to be a ceremonial, sacred time. If we don't hold on to it, we risk rearing yet more kids who wake up asking "What happened?"

Reading and Discussion Questions

1. Contrary to what Gray seems to suggest, the movie *Kids* is a fiction film, not a documentary, and the characters are actors. Does knowledge of this fact influence your appreciation of the author's argument?
2. The essay is only four paragraphs long, although it tackles a big subject. If you were asked to make this essay longer, what parts would you choose to develop?
3. In paragraphs 1 and 3, Gray offers details and examples to support her larger points. Should the essay have more of this kind of evidence?
4. How does Gray define "socialization"? Does she emphasize particular aspects of the definition?
5. Gray is a novelist and a splendid stylist. Point out places where she uses transitions, sentence variety, and other devices to embellish her prose and clarify ideas.

Writing Suggestions

6. Do the family meals you're familiar with resemble rituals that "imbue families . . . with greater empathy and fellowship"? Explain what the family meal means to you. If it has changed over time, explain why and how it has affected you. Or discuss a holiday meal — at Thanksgiving or Christmas — and what it means or should mean for you and your family.

7. One criticism of this essay might be that Gray imputes far too much importance to the family meal. Can you suggest other remedies for the alienation of these kids? Given the length of the essay you will write, the remedies should be modest. Perhaps you know of children who have been rescued from nightmarish lives. How did it happen?

Green Eggs & Ham
THE WALL STREET JOURNAL

To paraphrase Dr. Seuss, "I do like gambling, Sam-I-Am, I really like it, and I can. For I can do it in a plane, on a boat, at the track, and in the rain. I can do it in a casino, with the lottery, or with Keno." In a plane? Not quite yet, but the latest proposal is to equip airline seats with a video terminal that can eat credit cards and bankrupt you while you're still belted in, which is in many ways the opposite of what happens to a Strasbourg goose.

Some estimates suggest that gambling revenues are higher than the defense budget, and they are now poised to take a leap to the next energy level as technology threatens to bring casinos to every home and conveyance. Mayor Daley of Chicago is backing "gaming executives" who want to build a 100-acre $2 billion palace of sin in what the AP [Associated Press] calls "downtown" Chicago: Finding a 100-acre site in downtown Chicago will be only the first problem. Riverboat gambling is back on the Mississippi, and Indians are opening casinos all over the West. Thirty-three states have fallen to the lottery and more are on the way. And then there are pull-tabs; blackjack; OTB [off-track betting]; bingo; numbers; video poker; horse, dog, and insect racing (in bars); Reno; Las Vegas; Atlantic City; and Ed McMahon, the classic figure of trust, who periodically announces to every household in America that if it has won $10 million it has won $10 million. (Thank you, Ed.)

Other than littering the desert with immense, metastasized replicas of Port Said bordellos, gambling creates nothing. It reallocates resources from the desperate and the needful to the unspeakable and the inane. It, like the British royal family, is the worst possible model for the poor, being the polar opposite of thrift, discipline, hard work, and ingenuity. It violates every standard, all common sense, and every sensible equation, from ancient religious edicts to the laws of thermodynamics (at least figuratively), and it runs with almost every other form of crime and corruption.

This editorial is from the April 27, 1992, edition of the *Wall Street Journal*.

Are we for it because we favor free markets? No, in the same way that we do not favor a free market for recreational drugs, legalized prostitution, or, for that matter, the unrestricted sale of nuclear weapons. The West long ago identified gambling as a sin not because it violates some mystical equilibrium, although it does, but because it, like drunkenness or (as one might now say) spouse-beating, is destructive to society. Among other things, it is the Arnold Schwarzenegger of regressive taxation. And lotteries don't actually pay much to education, which has little to do with money anyway.

In America we once dealt wisely with gambling by isolating it in   5
the middle of a desert surrounded by unexploded practice munitions. This allowed the hardest cases to get to the roulette wheels and served as a safety valve for the ill-effects of absolutism. Now, however, the thing is spreading, and government is the sponsor. But when government substitutes gambling for taxation it relinquishes its moral authority. To the argument that if government does not play, others will, we say, in that case why not have [then New York state governor] Mario Cuomo rob jewelry stores?

Although you'd hardly know it from observing our elected officials, government's job is to resist and suppress that which is immoral and destructive, not to form a partnership with it. We would like to hear from the presidential candidates on this subject, for gambling is now almost everywhere, and has achieved a terrible hold on a people raised to think that lunch can be free.

Reading and Discussion Questions

1. Did you find any of the references to people, places, and activities unfamiliar? If so, did they prevent you from following the argument? Explain how you would go about finding out what these references mean.
2. At what point in the essay did you recognize the attitude of the writer toward gambling? Explain.
3. Why is gambling authorized or sponsored by the government more pernicious than gambling by private enterprise?
4. In the last paragraph the author summarizes his or her objections to gambling as "immoral and destructive." What is immoral about gambling? Why is it destructive?
5. The author at one point seems to advocate a solution to the gambling problem. Would that solution be workable today? Why or why not?

Writing Suggestions

6. Because gambling is widespread among all classes in the United States — and in many other societies — its appeal must be strong and universal. Some observers think it is an addiction. What is the appeal? Use your own experience as a gambler or your acquaintance with gam-

blers as well as the opinions of psychologists and other experts to explain it.

7. Find evidence from advocates of gambling to justify government spon-
   sorship, especially in state lotteries.

8. Gambling is said to be common on college campuses. What kinds of
   gambling do college students engage in? Does gambling serve a useful
   purpose? Is it harmful in any way?

A Liberalism of Heart and Spine

HENRY LOUIS GATES, JR.

Gunmen burst into a Bahai church in a South African township,
line up the few white (Iranian) members of the congregation and
shoot them dead. The Bahai religion holds that all races are one,
and the Azanian People's Liberation Army, which apparently dispatched the killers, explained that it wanted to send a clear message
against the mixing of races.

In fact, the Azanian movement has been profoundly shaped by
European racial thinking, as you might expect of a group that borrows its name from an invented place of barbarism in Evelyn
Waugh's satiric novel *Black Mischief.* The truth is, the Azanians' ab-
juration of "race mixing" has nothing to do with indigenous local traditions and everything to do with the logic of apartheid.

"One million Arabs are not worth a Jewish fingernail," Rabbi Yaa-
cov Perrin said in a funeral eulogy for Dr. Baruch Goldstein before a
thousand sympathizers. The phrase reflects a perverse misreading
of a passage from Exodus. But we have heard this voice before. It is
the voice of messianic hatred. We hear it from the Balkans to the
Bantustans; we hear it from Hezbollah and from Kach. We hear it in
the streets of Bensonhurst.

And, of course, we hear it from some who profess to be addressing the misery of black America. "Never will I say I am not an anti-
Semite," said Khalid Abdul Muhammad of the Nation of Islam. "I pray
that God will kill my enemy and take him off the face of the planet
Earth." He is peddling tape recordings of his speeches under the
suggestive title "No Love for the Other Side."

And so it goes, with the victimized bidding to be victimizers. 5
That suffering ennobles is a lie, an old lie that has been exposed
countless times, yet has proved surprisingly durable.

Henry Louis Gates, Jr., is chairman of the Afro-American Studies Department at
Harvard University. This article appeared in the *New York Times* on March 27, 1994.

Messianic hatred is scarcely the province of the privileged classes. David Duke draws his support from the least affluent and most anxious of white Southerners. Similarly, if calculating demagogues find inviting prey in black America, our immediate circumstances make this unsurprising. That nearly half of African American children live in poverty is one scandal; another is simply that this fact has become an acceptable feature of our social landscape, as unremarkable as crab grass. No love for the other side?

Yet if profoundly antimodern creeds like these continue to grow, perhaps liberalism — that political tradition of individual liberty that harks back at least to the Enlightenment — must shoulder some blame.

For too long, liberalism has grown accustomed to recusing itself from other people's problems. Genital mutilation in Africa? Don't ask us to arbitrate among the mores of other cultures. Human rights abuses in China? Are we really in a position to judge? Deference to the autonomy of other beliefs, other values, other cultures has become an easy alibi for moral isolationism. When we need action, we get hand-wringing. When we need forthrightness, we get equivocation.

What we have is a rhetoric of relativism. But let's call such "moral relativism" by its real name: moral indifference. And let's admit how finite are our vaunted moral sympathies, here in the comfortable West.

According to recent reports, perhaps 100,000 people have died 10 in recent ethnic conflicts that have raged through tiny Burundi. Could any type of intervention have helped? Maybe not. But that isn't the point. The point is that nobody is asking. Not enough love for the other side. Meanwhile, the tragedy of Bosnia took on the look of the Kitty Genovese syndrome on a global scale.

We need a liberalism that has confidence in its own insights, a liberalism possessed of clarity as well as compassion. To creeds that prate of sacred fingernails, as the rabbi did, of "no love for the other side," of the sins of mixing ethnic or racial categories, we must juxtapose a muscular humanism. A humanism that is without arrogance and is unafraid to assert itself, its hard-won moral knowledge. One that neither shuns religious devotion nor mistakes itself for a religion. One that has courage as well as conviction.

There is something of a paradox here. The most heinous of deeds have always been committed in the name of future generations, of an awaiting utopia. The nature of these evils could not be concealed if they were committed in the name of our own interests in the here and now, but utopianism wraps them in the garb of virtuous "sacrifice." Accordingly, it is its stoutly anti-utopian aspect — its capacity for self-doubt — that liberalism has claimed as a moral advantage.

But the capacity to entertain uncertainly needn't entail Hamlet-like paralysis. It merely promotes a willingness to revise our beliefs in the light of experience, to extend respect to those we do not agree with. Is it, after all, unreasonable to be suspicious of Westerners who are exercised over female circumcision but whose eyes glaze over when the same women are merely facing starvation?

The Azanian, the West Bank fanatic, the American demagogue march to a single drum. There has been much talk about the politics of identity — a politics that has a collective identity as its core. One is to assert oneself in the political arena as a woman, a homosexual, a Jew, a person of color.

But while the conversation about it may seem recent, the phe- 15 nomenon itself is age-old. The politics of identity starts with the assertion of a collective allegiance. It says: This is who we are, make room for us, accommodate our special needs, confer recognition upon what is distinctive about us. It is about the priority of difference, and while it is not, by itself, undesirable, it is — by itself — dangerously inadequate.

By contrast, what I'm calling humanism starts not with the possession of identity, but with the capacity to *identify with*. It asks what we have in common with others, while acknowledging the diversity among ourselves. It is about the promise of a shared humanity.

In short, the challenge is to move from a politics of identity to a politics of identification. It was this conversion that Malcolm X underwent toward the end of his life. If Minister Farrakhan, a brilliant, charismatic man, undergoes a similar conversion, he will earn a place in the annals of our time. If not, he will just be another in a long line of racial demagogues, joining Father Coughlin, Gerald L. K. Smith, and the like.

A politics of identification doesn't enjoin us to ignore or devalue our collective identities. For it's only by exploring the multiplicity of human life in culture that we can come to terms with the commonalities that cement communitas. It is only by this route that we can move a little closer to what the poet Robert Hayden, himself a Bahai, conjured up when he urged us to "renew the vision of a human world where godliness / is possible and man / is neither god, nigger, honky, wop, nor kike / but man / permitted to be man." We may be anti-utopian, but we have dreams, too.

Reading and Discussion Questions

1. Make sure that you understand several terms in this essay that carry important ideas: relativism, messianic, humanism, liberalism, utopianism, Hamlet-like paralysis, Kitty Genovese syndrome. Were any of these terms clear from the context, or was it necessary to look them up?

   There are also references to people, groups, and places in the news: Hezbollah, Bantustans, Burundi, Bosnia, Nation of Islam, Malcolm X,

Louis Farrakhan, Father Coughlin, Gerald L. K. Smith. While it isn't necessary to know a great deal about these persons and places in order to
understand what Gates is trying to prove, knowing *something* about
them will deepen your understanding of his essay and other articles
and essays that refer to the same things.

2. Most of us can probably guess what "a liberalism of heart" means, but
   what is "a liberalism of spine"? Where does Gates explain it?
3. How can utopianism promote evil deeds? If you can, find examples from
   history to explain your answer.
4. What is the difference between the politics of identity and the politics
   of identification? Tell why Gates favors one over another.

Writing Suggestions

5. Gates denounces moral indifference. (See paragraphs 8 and 9.) Do you
   think that you are justified in condemning a custom practiced by members of another culture? You have read about such cases in the news.
   Cock-fighting is one example. Another more serious example is child
   marriage and pregnancy. (Such a case surfaced recently in Texas, concerning a couple who were living together. The male, an adult, and the
   female, a thirteen-year-old who was pregnant, were separated by the
   court, and the male was charged with violation of Texas laws. The
   couple was from a rural community in Mexico which sanctioned their
   relationship.) Choose a practice that you disapprove of and tell why
   you would or would not move to have it abolished. Make clear what
   principles would govern your decision.
6. How does religion serve either to include or to exclude other people?
   Notice that Gates makes reference to religions and religious leaders.
   This is a very large subject. Restrict your argument to development of
   one or two ideas in a religion you are familiar with.

The Right to Bear Arms
WARREN E. BURGER

Our metropolitan centers, and some suburban communities of
America, are setting new records for homicides by handguns. Many
of our large centers have up to ten times the murder rate of all of
Western Europe. In 1988, there were 9,000 handgun murders in
America. Last year, Washington, D.C., alone had more than 400
homicides — setting a new record for our capital.

The Constitution of the United States, in its Second Amendment,
guarantees a "right of the people to keep and bear arms." However,

Warren E. Burger (1907–1995) was chief justice of the United States from 1969 to
1986. This article is from the January 14, 1990, issue of *Parade* magazine.

the meaning of this clause cannot be understood except by looking to the purpose, the setting, and the objectives of the draftsmen. The first ten amendments — the Bill of Rights — were not drafted at Philadelphia in 1787; that document came two years later than the Constitution. Most of the states already had bills of rights, but the Constitution might not have been ratified in 1788 if the states had not had assurances that a national Bill of Rights would soon be added.

People of that day were apprehensive about the new "monster" national government presented to them, and this helps explain the language and purpose of the Second Amendment. A few lines after the First Amendment's guarantees — against "establishment of religion," "free exercise" of religion, free speech and free press — came a guarantee that grew out of the deep-seated fear of a "national" or "standing" army. The same First Congress that approved the right to keep and bear arms also limited the national army to 840 men; Congress in the Second Amendment then provided:

Connotation

> A well regulated Militia, being necessary to the security of a free State, the right of the people to keep and bear Arms, shall not be infringed.

In the 1789 debate in Congress on James Madison's proposed Bill of Rights, Elbridge Gerry argued that a state militia was necessary:

> to prevent the establishment of a standing army, the bane of liberty. . . . Whenever governments mean to invade the rights and liberties of the people, they always attempt to destroy the militia in order to raise an army upon their ruins.

We see that the need for a state militia was the predicate of the   5
"right" guaranteed; in short, it was declared "necessary" in order to have a state military force to protect the security of the state. That Second Amendment clause must be read as though the word "because" was the opening word of the guarantee. Today, of course, the "state militia" serves a very different purpose. A huge national defense establishment has taken over the role of the militia of 200 years ago.

Some have exploited these ancient concerns, blurring sporting guns — rifles, shotguns, and even machine pistols — with all firearms, including what are now called "Saturday night specials." There is, of course, a great difference between sporting guns and handguns. Some regulation of handguns has long been accepted as imperative; laws relating to "concealed weapons" are common. That we may be "overregulated" in some areas of life has never held us back from more regulation of automobiles, airplanes, motorboats, and "concealed weapons."

Let's look at the history.

examples

First, many of the 3.5 million people living in the thirteen original Colonies depended on wild game for food, and a good many of them required firearms for their defense from marauding Indians — and later from the French and English. Underlying all these needs was an important concept that each able-bodied man in each of the thirteen independent states had to help or defend his state.

The early opposition to the idea of national or standing armies was maintained under the Articles of Confederation; that confederation had no standing army and wanted none. The state militia — essentially a part-time citizen army, as in Switzerland today — was the only kind of "army" they wanted. From the time of the Declaration of Independence through the victory at Yorktown in 1781, George Washington, as the commander in chief of these volunteer-militia armies, had to depend upon the states to send those volunteers.

When a company of New Jersey militia volunteers reported for   10 duty to Washington at Valley Forge, the men initially declined to take an oath to "the United States," maintaining, "Our country is New Jersey." Massachusetts Bay men, Virginians, and others felt the same way. To the American of the eighteenth century, his state was his country, and his freedom was defended by his militia.

The victory at Yorktown — and the ratification of the Bill of Rights a decade later — did not change people's attitudes about a national army. They had lived for years under the notion that each state would maintain its own military establishment, and the seaboard states had their own navies as well. These people, and their fathers and grandfathers before them, remembered how monarchs had used standing armies to oppress their ancestors in Europe. Americans wanted no part of this. A state militia, like a rifle and powder horn, was as much a part of life as the automobile is today; pistols were largely for officers, aristocrats — and dueling.

Against this background, it was not surprising that the provision concerning firearms emerged in very simple terms with the significant predicate — basing the right on the *necessity* for a "well regulated militia," a state army.

In the two centuries since then — with two world wars and some lesser ones — it has become clear, sadly, that we have no choice but to maintain a standing national army while still maintaining a "militia" by way of the National Guard, which can be swiftly integrated into the national defense forces.

Americans also have a right to defend their homes, and we need not challenge that. Nor does anyone seriously question that the Constitution protects the right of hunters to own and keep sporting guns for hunting game any more than anyone would challenge the right to own and keep fishing rods and other equipment for fishing — or to own automobiles. To "keep and bear arms" for hunting today is essentially a recreational activity and not an imperative of survival, as it was 200 years ago; "Saturday night specials" and machine guns are not recreational weapons and surely are as much in need of regulation as motor vehicles.

Americans should ask themselves a few questions. The Constitu- 15 tion does not mention automobiles or motorboats, but the right to keep and own an automobile is beyond question; equally beyond question is the power of the state to regulate the purchase or the transfer of such vehicle and the right to license the vehicle and the driver with reasonable standards. In some places, even a bicycle must be registered, as must some household dogs.

If we are to stop this mindless homicidal carnage, is it unreasonable:

accomodate

1. to provide that, to acquire a firearm, an application be made reciting age, residence, employment, and any prior criminal convictions?
2. to require that this application lie on the table for ten days (absent a showing for urgent need) before the license would be issued?
3. that the transfer of a firearm be made essentially as that of a motor vehicle?
4. to have a "ballistic fingerprint" of the firearm made by the manufacturer and filed with the license record so that, if a bullet is found in a victim's body, law enforcement might be helped in finding the culprit?

These are the kinds of questions the American people must answer if we are to preserve the "domestic tranquility" promised in the Constitution.

Reading and Discussion Questions

1. This essay can be divided into three or four parts. Provide headings for these parts.
2. Which part of the essay is most fully developed? What explains the author's emphasis?
3. Why does Burger recount the history of the Second Amendment so fully? Explain his reason for arguing that the Second Amendment does not guarantee the right of individuals to "bear arms."
4. Burger also uses history to argue that there is a difference between legislation against sporting guns and legislation against handguns. Summarize his argument.
5. How effective is his analogy between licensing vehicles and licensing handguns?

Writing Suggestions

6. Other people interpret "the right to bear arms" differently. Look at some of their arguments and write an essay summarizing their interpretations and defending them.

7. Burger outlines a policy for registration of handguns that would prevent criminal use. But at least one sociologist has pointed out that most guns used by criminals are obtained illegally. Examine and evaluate some of the arguments claiming that registration is generally ineffective.

8. Analyze arguments of the National Rifle Association, the nation's largest gun lobby. Do they answer Burger's claims?

Discussion Questions

1. Notice the headline. The advertiser has supplied lots of numbers. What claim are these numbers meant to support?
2. Did you find the ad interesting to read? Do you think the advertiser was correct in thinking that people would read seven paragraphs about numbers? Explain your answer.
3. What specific aspects of the language might induce people to continue reading even if they find numbers tedious?

The initials of a friend

You will find these letters on many tools by which electricity works. They are on great generators used by electric light and power companies; and on lamps that light millions of homes.

They are on big motors that pull railway trains; and on tiny motors that make hard housework easy.

By such tools electricity dispels the dark and lifts heavy burdens from human shoulders. Hence the letters G-E are more than a trademark. They are an emblem of service—the initials of a friend.

GENERAL ELECTRIC

This advertisement first appeared in 1923. Today, you'll find our initials on many more things — from appliances, plastics, motors and lighting to financial services and medical equipment. Wherever you see our initials, we want them to mean the same thing to you — the initials of a friend.

We bring good things to life.

Discussion Questions

1. To what need does the ad make an appeal?
2. What devices in the ad — both objects and the choice of objects to discuss — contribute to the effectiveness of the message?
3. How does the company's present-day slogan compare?

A gun in the home is much more likely to
kill a family member than to kill an intruder.

CEASE 🏠 FIRE

Think about your family before you think about getting a handgun.

Cease Fire, Inc. P.O. Box 33424, Washington, D.C. 20033-0424.

Discussion Questions

1. Would this claim of policy be just as successful if the note were excluded? Would additional facts about guns contribute to its effectiveness?
2. Why is the gun so much larger than the printed message?
3. What is the basis of the emotional appeal? Is there more than one? Does the note go too far in exploiting our emotions?

The Case for Medicalizing Heroin

ALAN DERSHOWITZ

When *Time* magazine has a cover story on the legalization of drugs, and when Oprah Winfrey devotes an entire show to that "unthinkable" proposition, you can be sure that this is an issue whose time has come — at least for serious discussion.

But it is difficult to get politicians to *have* a serious discussion about alternatives to our currently bankrupt approach to drug abuse. Even thinking out loud about the possibility of decriminalization is seen as being soft on drugs. And no elected official can afford to be viewed as less than ferocious and uncompromising on this issue.

Any doubts about that truism were surely allayed when Vice President Bush openly broke with his president and most important supporter over whether to try to make a deal with Panamanian strongman Manuel Noriega, whom the United States has charged with drug-trafficking.

I was one of the guests on the recent Oprah Winfrey show that debated drug decriminalization. The rhetoric and emotions ran high, as politicians and audience members competed over who could be tougher in the war against drugs.

"Call out the marines," "Bomb the poppy fields," "Execute the 5 drug dealers" — these are among the "constructive" suggestions being offered to supplement the administration's simpleminded "just say no" slogan.

Proposals to medicalize, regulate, or in another way decriminalize any currently illegal drug — whether it be marijuana, cocaine, or heroin — were greeted by derision and cries of "surrender." Even politicians who *in private* recognize the virtues of decriminalization must continue to oppose it when the cameras are rolling.

That is why it is so important to outline here the politically unpopular case for an alternative approach.

Ironically, the case is easiest for the hardest drug — heroin. There can be no doubt that heroin is a horrible drug: It is highly ad-

---

Alan Dershowitz is a professor at the law school of Harvard University. This essay, originally published in 1988, is reprinted in his book *Contrary to Popular Opinion* (1992).

dictive and debilitating; taken in high, or unregulated, doses, it can kill; when administered by means of shared needles, it spreads AIDS; because of its high price and addictive quality, it makes acquisitive criminals out of desperate addicts. Few would disagree that if we could rid it from the planet through the passage of a law or the invention of a plant-specific herbicide, we should do so.

But since we can neither eliminate heroin nor the demand for it, there is a powerful case for medicalizing as much of the problem as is feasible. Under this proposal, or one of its many variants, the hard-core addict would receive the option of getting his fix in a medical setting, administered by medical personnel.

The setting could be a mobile hospital van or some other facility 10 close to where the addicts live. A doctor would determine the dosage for each addict — a maintenance dosage designed to prevent withdrawal without risking overdose. And the fix would be injected in the medical facility so the addict could not sell or barter the drug or prescription.

This will by no means solve all the problems associated with heroin addiction, but it would ameliorate some of the most serious ones. The maintained heroin addict will not immediately become a model citizen. But much of the desperation that today accounts for the victimization of innocent home-dwellers, store employees, and pedestrians — primarily in urban centers — would be eliminated, and drug-related crime would be significantly reduced.

Today's addict is simply not deterred by the law. He will get his fix by hook or by crook, or by knife or by gun, regardless of the risk. That is what heroin addiction means. Giving the desperate addict a twenty-four-hour medical alternative will save the lives of countless innocent victims of both crime and AIDS.

It will also save the lives of thousands of addicts who now kill themselves in drug shooting galleries by injecting impure street mixtures through AIDS-infected needles.

There will, of course, always be a black market for heroin, even if it were medicalized. Not every addict will accept a medically administered injection, and even some of those who do will supplement their maintenance doses with street drugs. But much of the desperate quality of the constant quest for the fix will be reduced for at least some heroin addicts. And this will have a profound impact on both the quantity and violence of inner-city crime.

Nor would new addicts be created by this medical approach. 15 Only long-term adult addicts would be eligible for the program. And the expenses would be more than offset by the extraordinary savings to our society in reduced crime.

If this program proved successful in the context of heroin addiction, variants could be considered for other illegal drugs such as cocaine and marijuana. There is no assurance that an approach which is successful for one drug will necessarily work for others. Many of the problems are different.

We have already decriminalized two of the most dangerous drugs known to humankind — nicotine and alcohol. Decriminalization of these killers, which destroy more lives than all other drugs combined, has not totally eliminated the problems associated with them.

But we have come to realize that criminalization of nicotine and alcohol causes even more problems than it solves. The time has come to consider whether that is also true of heroin and perhaps of other drugs as well.

Selling Syringes:
The Swiss Experiment
RACHEL EHRENFELD

As U.S. communities continue to experiment with programs to cut drug addiction and HIV infection spread by drug users, some have cited European experiments with the decriminalization of drug use. But before venturing further in this direction, policymakers should acquaint themselves with an elaborate new "scientific" program set in motion in 1992 in Switzerland, which has the highest per-capita rate of drug addiction and HIV infection in Europe.

Seven hundred of the 30,000 to 40,000 opiate addicts in Switzerland were targeted; nine cities participate. The experiment — in which heroin, morphine, and methadone are administered intravenously, orally, and by smoking — is scheduled to end in December 1996. Previously, the Swiss addicts were concentrated in central parts of major cities, such as "Needle Park" in Zurich. But the result was increased drug use, crime, violence, and prostitution, which quickly became intolerable. So the addicts are now in government-sponsored centers and "shooting galleries."

In analyzing this "scientific" project, I met with its administrators and evaluators and visited the major heroin distribution center, Arbeitsgemeinschaft für risikoarmen Umgang mit Drogen (ARUD), in Zurich, which currently treats seventy to eighty heroin addicts. Most have a criminal record, are unemployed, and are on social welfare. Nearly half are HIV positive. A majority of the patients are multidrug users, and many use cocaine in addition to the heroin they're

Rachel Ehrenfeld, author of *Narco-Terrorism* (1992), is preparing a book on the movement to legalize drugs. This article appeared in the *Wall Street Journal* on September 16, 1995.

given at the center. Their outside drug use, however, does not prohibit their participation in the program. Urine analysis to monitor drug consumption is conducted once a month on a set day because "the treatment in our center is based on trust," said Andre Seidenberg, director of ARUD.

The center is easily accessible and anyone can enter. A half-dozen people sit in the waiting room smoking specially developed cigarettes containing 100 milligrams of heroin, which are distributed by the receptionist behind the window. She also provides syringes with heroin up to nine times a day and a maximum of 300 milligrams. Each addict is listed in a computer system that monitors his consumption. The injecting room, off the entrance, contains a large mirror used to provide the addicts with a better view of their veins, so they can inject more efficiently, explained the director. Why feed heroin to the addicts? "Because the addicts prefer heroin [to methadone]," responded Dr. Seidenberg, "and we should give them what they want without conditions."

The design of the project calls for supervision of the injecting 5
process, to make sure the addicts don't save the drugs to sell them later on the street, but I saw none. Although the addicts return the syringe after the injection, they could easily inject the heroin into a small container to be sold later. Moreover, in addition to the injectable heroin, they are given twenty-six heroin cigarettes to be used at home overnight. The heroin costs the addicts about $12.50 a day, covered by health insurance, the City Council, the canton (state), or the federal government. The design of the project also calls for support services — especially psychiatric and medical treatment, job training, occupational therapy, etc. But none of these are available at the center.

In an emergency, the addict is sent either to a psychiatric hospital or to an emergency room. As for therapy: "There is no proof that there is long-term effect to therapy — therapy doesn't make a difference," Dr. Seidenberg said. And as for work, "you go when you feel like it — you really don't have to [work]," according to Ueli Locher, the deputy director of the Department of Social Services of Zurich.

The Swiss experiment originated from a desire to reduce HIV infection among the population. Complementing this experiment are information programs and pamphlets supplied to teenagers, young adults and adults. This information equates homosexuality and drug addiction and describes both as "alternative lifestyles." Both sexual activity and drug use are described in detail with illustrations and the motto that "if you want to experiment — do it well."

Currently, according to Mr. Locher, "cocaine is not given [to addicts] because of political reasons." But he and his comrades in drug liberalization hope that this will change and that all drugs will be available to those who need them. Drug supply by the government is supposed to reduce the number of addicts, but so far there is no indication that fewer people are taking illegal drugs in Switzerland. There are no signs that crime and violence have gone down. And the Swiss taxpayer is footing the bill for a growing number of AIDS patients, more welfare recipients, and a growing police force.

Discussion Questions

1. What are the bases for Dershowitz's claim that drugs should be legalized?
2. His support consists in part of hypothetical examples of the way that legalized heroin would work. What are the strengths and weaknesses of such evidence?
3. What kinds of evidence does Ehrenfeld supply? How relevant is her argument to drug control in the United States?
4. Does Ehrenfeld's article constitute a response to Dershowitz? Explain why or why not.

EXERCISES

1. Look for personal advertisements (in which men and women advertise for various kinds of companionship) in a local or national paper or magazine. (The *Village Voice,* a New York paper, is an outstanding source.) What inferences can you draw about the people who place these particular ads? About the "facts" they choose to provide? How did you come to these conclusions? You might also try to infer the reasons that more men than women place ads and why this might be changing.
2. "I like Colonel Sanders" is the title of an article that praises ugly architecture, shopping malls, laundromats, and other symbols of "plastic" America. The author claims that these aspects of the American scene have unique and positive values. Defend or refute his claim by pointing out what the values of these things might be, giving reasons for your own assessments.
3. A psychiatrist says that in pro football personality traits determine the positions of the players. Write an essay developing this idea and providing adequate evidence for your claim. Or make inferences about the relationship between the personalities of the players and another sport that you know well.
4. At least one city in the world — Reykjavik, the capital of Iceland — bans dogs from the city. Defend or attack this policy by using both facts and values to support your claim.
5. Write a review of a movie, play, television program, concert, restaurant, or book. Make clear your criteria for judgment and their order of importance.
6. The controversy concerning seat belts and air bags in automobiles has generated a variety of proposals, one of which is mandatory use of seat belts in all the states. Make your own policy claim regarding laws about safety devices (the wearing of motorcycle helmets is another thorny

subject), and defend it by using both facts and values — facts about safety, values concerning individual freedom and responsibility.

7. Select a ritual with which you are familiar and argue for or against the value it represents. *Examples:* the high school prom, Christmas gift-giving, a fraternity initiation, a wedding, a confirmation or bar mitzvah, a funeral ceremony, a Fourth of July celebration.

8. Choose a recommended policy — from the school newspaper or elsewhere — and argue that it will or will not work to produce beneficial changes. *Examples:* expansion of core requirements, comprehensive tests as a graduation requirement, reinstitution of a physical education requirement, removal of junk food from vending machines.

Critical Listening

9. Have you ever been a member of a group which tried but failed to solve a problem through discussion? Communication theorists talk about "interference," defined by one writer as "anything that hinders or lessens the efficiency of communication."[4] Some of the elements of interference in the delivery of oral messages are fatigue, anger, inattention, vague language, personality conflict, political bias. You will probably be able to think of others. Did any of these elements prevent the group from arriving at an agreement? Describe the situation and the kinds of interference that you were aware of.

---

[4]Richard E. Crable, *One to Another* (New York: Harper and Row, 1981), p. 18.

CHAPTER FOUR

Definition

THE PURPOSES OF DEFINITION

Before we examine the other elements of argument, we need to consider definition, a component you may have to deal with early in writing an essay. Definition may be used in two ways: to clarify the meanings of vague or ambiguous terms or as a method of development for the whole essay. In some arguments your claims will contain words that need explanation before you can proceed with any discussion. But you may also want to devote an entire essay to the elaboration of a broad concept or experience that cannot be adequately defined in a shorter space.

The Roman statesman Cicero said, "Every rational discussion of anything whatsoever should begin with a definition in order to make clear what is the subject of dispute." You have probably already discovered the importance of definition in argument. If you have ever had a disagreement with your parents about using the car or drinking or dyeing your hair or going away for a weekend or staying out till three in the morning, you know that you were really arguing about the meaning of the term "adolescent freedom."

Arguments often revolve around definitions of crucial terms. For example, how does one define *democracy*? Does a democracy guarantee freedom of the press, freedom of worship, freedom of assembly, freedom of movement? In the United States, we would argue that such freedoms are essential to any definition of *democracy*. But countries in which these freedoms are nonexistent also represent themselves as democracies or governments of the people. In the words of Senator Daniel P. Moynihan, "For years now the most brutal totalitarian regimes have called themselves 'people's' or 'democratic' republics." Rulers in such governments are aware that defining their regimes as democratic may win the approval of people who would otherwise condemn them. In his formidable attack on totalitarianism, *Nineteen Eighty-Four,* George Orwell coined the slogans "War Is Peace" and "Slavery Is Freedom," phrases that represent the corrupt use of definition to distort reality.

But even where there is no intention to deceive, the snares of definition are difficult to avoid. How do you define *abortion*? Is it "termination of pregnancy"? Or is it "murder of an unborn child"? During a celebrated trial in 1975 of a physician who performed an abortion and was accused of manslaughter, the prosecution often used the word *baby* to refer to the fetus, but the defense referred to "the products of conception." These definitions of *fetus* reflected the differing judgments of those on opposite sides. Not only do judgments create definitions; definitions influence judgments. In the abortion trial, the definitions of *fetus* used by both sides were meant to promote either approval or disapproval of the doctor's action.

Definitions can indeed change the nature of an event or a "fact." How many farms are there in the state of New York? The answer to the question depends on the definition of *farm*. In 1979 the *New York Times* reported:

> Because of a change in the official definition of the word "farm," New York lost 20 percent of its farms on January 1, with numbers dropping from 56,000 to 45,000. . . .
> Before the change, a farm was defined as "any place from which $250 or more of agricultural products is sold" yearly or "any place of 10 acres or more from which $50 or more of agricultural products is sold" yearly. Now a farm is "any place from which $1,000 or more of agricultural products is sold" in a year.[1]

A change in the definition of poverty can have similar results. An article in the *New York Times,* whose headline reads, "A Revised Definition of Poverty May Raise Number of U.S. Poor," makes this clear.

> The official definition of poverty used by the Federal Government for three decades is based simply on cash income before taxes. But in a report to be issued on Wednesday, a panel of experts convened by the [National] Academy of Sciences three years ago at the behest of Congress says the Government should move toward a concept of poverty based on disposable income, the amount left after a family pays taxes and essential expenses.[2]

The differences are wholly a matter of definition. But such differences can have serious consequences for those being defined, most of all in the disposition of billions of federal dollars in aid of various

---

[1]*New York Times,* March 4, 1979, Sec. 1, p. 40.
[2]*New York Times,* April 10, 1995, Sec. A, p. 1.

kinds. In 1992 the Census Bureau classified 14.5 percent of Americans as poor. Under the new guidelines, at least 15 or 16 percent would be poor and, under some measures recommended by a government panel, 18 percent would be so defined.

In fact, local and federal courts almost every day redefine traditional concepts that can have a direct impact on our everyday lives. The definition of the family, for example, has undergone significant changes that acknowledge the existence of new relationships. In January 1990 the New Jersey Supreme Court ruled that a family may be defined as "one or more persons occupying a dwelling unit as a single nonprofit housekeeping unit, who are living together as a stable and permanent living unit, being a traditional family unit or the *functional equivalent* thereof" (italics for emphasis added). This meant that ten Glassboro State College students, unrelated by blood, could continue to occupy a single-family house despite the objection of the borough of Glassboro.[3] Even the legal definition of maternity has shifted. Who is the mother — the woman who contributes the egg or the woman (the surrogate) who bears the child? Several states, acknowledging the changes brought by medical technology, now recognize a difference between the "birth mother" and the "legal mother."

DEFINING THE TERMS IN YOUR ARGUMENT

In some of your arguments you will introduce terms that require definition. We've pointed out that a definition of poverty is crucial to any debate on the existence of poverty in the United States. The same may be true in a debate about the legality of euthanasia, or mercy killing. Are the arguers referring to passive euthanasia, that is, the withdrawal of life-support systems, or to active euthanasia, in which death is hastened through the direct administration of drugs?

It is not uncommon, in fact, for arguments about controversial questions to turn into arguments about the definition of terms. If, for example, you wanted to argue in favor of the regulation of religious cults, you would first have to define *cult.* In so doing, you might discover that it is not easy to distinguish clearly between conventional religions and cults. Then you would have to define *regulation,* spelling out the legal restrictions you favored so as to make them apply only to cults, not to established religions. An argument on the subject might end almost before it began if writer and reader could not agree on definitions of these terms. While clear definitions do not guarantee agreement, they do ensure that all parties understand the nature of the argument.

---

[3]*New York Times,* February 1, 1990, Sec. B, p. 5.

Defining Vague and Ambiguous Terms

You will need to define other terms in addition to those in your claim. If you use words and phrases that have two or more meanings, they may appear vague and ambiguous to your reader. In arguments of value and policy abstract terms such as *freedom, justice, patriotism,* and *equality* require clarification. Despite their vagueness, however, they are among the most important in the language because they represent the ideals that shape our laws. When conflicts arise, the courts must define these terms to establish the legality of certain practices. Is the Ku Klux Klan permitted to make disparaging public statements about ethnic and racial groups? That depends on the court's definition of "free speech." Can execution for some crimes be considered "cruel and unusual punishment"? That, too, depends on the court's definition of "cruel and unusual punishment." In addition, such terms as *happiness, mental health, success,* and *creativity* often defy precise definition because they reflect the differing values within a society or a culture.

The definition of *success,* for example, varies not only among social groups but also among individuals within the group. One scientist has postulated five signs by which to judge the measure of success: wealth (including health), security (confidence in retaining the wealth), reputation, performance, and contentment.[4] Consider whether all of these are necessary to your own definition of *success.* If not, which may be omitted? Do you think others should be added? Notice that one of the signs — reputation — depends on definition by the community; another — contentment — can be measured only by the individual. The assessment of performance probably owes something to both the group and the individual.

Christopher Atkins, an actor, gave an interviewer an example of an externalized definition of success, that is, a definition based on the standards imposed by other people:

> Success to me is judged through the eyes of others. I mean, if you're walking around saying, "I own a green Porsche," you might meet somebody who says, "Hey, that's no big deal, I own a green Porsche and a house." So all of a sudden, you don't feel so successful. Really, it's in the eyes of others.[5]

So difficult is the formulation of a universally accepted measure for success that some scholars regard the concept as meaningless. Nevertheless, we continue to use the word as if it represented a definable concept because the idea of success, however defined, is im-

---

[4]Gwynn Nettler, *Social Concerns* (New York: McGraw-Hill, 1976), pp. 196–197.
[5]*New York Times,* August 6, 1982, Sec. III, p. 8.

portant for the identity and development of the individual and the group. It is clear, however, that when crossing subcultural boundaries, even within a small group, we need to be aware of differences in the úse of the word. If "contentment" — that is, the satisfaction of achieving a small personal goal — is enough, then a person lying under a palm tree subsisting on handouts from picnickers may be a success. But you should not expect all your readers to agree that these criteria are enough to define *success.*

In arguing about aesthetic matters, whose vocabulary is almost always abstract, the criteria for judgment must be revealed, either directly or indirectly, and then the abstract terms that represent the criteria must be defined. If you want to say that a film is distinguished by great acting, have you made clear what you mean by *great*? That we do not always understand or agree on the definition of *great* is apparent, say, on the morning after the Oscar winners have been announced.

Even subjects that you feel sure you can identify may offer surprising insights when you rethink them for an extended definition. One critic, defining rock music, argued that the distinguishing characteristic of rock music was *noise* — not the beat, not the harmonies, not the lyrics, not the vocal style, but noise, "nasty, discordant irritating noise — or, to its practitioners, unfettered, liberating, expressive noise."[6] In producing this definition, the author had to give a number of examples to prove that he was justified in rejecting the most familiar criteria.

Consider the definition of race, around which so much of American history has revolved, often with tragic consequences. Currently the only categories listed in the census are white, black, Asian-Pacific, and Native American, "with the Hispanic population straddling them all." But rapidly increasing intermarriage and ethnic identity have caused a number of political and ethnic groups to demand changes in the classifications of the Census Bureau. Some Arab Americans, for example, prefer to be counted as "Middle Eastern" rather than white. Children of black-white unions are defined as black 60 percent of the time, while children of Asian-white unions are described as Asian 42 percent of the time. Research is now being conducted to discover how people feel about the terms being used to define them. As one anthropologist pointed out, "Socially and politically assigned attributes have a lot to do with access to economic resources."[7]

---

[6]Jon Pareles, "Noise Evokes Modern Chaos for a Band," *New York Times,* March 9, 1986, Sec. H, p. 26.

[7]*Wall Street Journal,* September 9, 1995, Sec. B, p. 1.

METHODS FOR DEFINING TERMS

The following strategies for defining terms in an argument are by no means mutually exclusive. You may use all of them in a single argumentative essay.

Dictionary Definition

Giving a dictionary definition is the simplest and most obvious way to define a term. An unabridged dictionary is the best source because it usually gives examples of the way a word can be used in a sentence; that is, it furnishes the proper context.

In many cases, the dictionary definition alone is not sufficient. It may be too broad or too narrow for your purpose. Suppose, in an argument about pornography, you wanted to define the word *obscene*. *Webster's New International Dictionary* (third edition, unabridged) gives the definition of *obscene* as "offensive to taste; foul; loathsome; disgusting." But these synonyms do not tell you what qualities make an object or an event or an action "foul," "loathsome," and "disgusting." In 1973 the Supreme Court, attempting to narrow the definition of *obscenity,* ruled that obscenity was to be determined by the community in accordance with local standards. One person's obscenity, as numerous cases have demonstrated, may be another person's art. The celebrated trials in the early twentieth century about the distribution of novels regarded as pornographic — D. H. Lawrence's *Lady Chatterley's Lover* and James Joyce's *Ulysses* — emphasized the problems of defining obscenity.

Another dictionary definition may strike you as too narrow. *Patriotism,* for example, is defined in one dictionary as "love and loyal or zealous support of one's country, especially in all matters involving other countries." Some readers may want to include an unwillingness to support government policies they consider wrong.

Stipulation

In stipulating the meaning of a term, the writer asks the reader to accept a definition that may be different from the conventional one. He or she does this in order to limit or control the argument. Someone has said, "Part of the task of keeping definitions in our civilization clear and pure is to keep a firm democratic rein on those with the power, or craving the power, to stipulate meaning." Perhaps this writer was thinking of a term like *national security,* which can be defined by a nation's leaders in such a way as to sanction persecution of citizens and reckless military adventures. Likewise, a term such as *liberation* can be appropriated by terrorist groups whose activities often lead to oppression rather than liberation.

Religion is usually defined as a belief in a supernatural power to be obeyed and worshiped. But in an article entitled "Civil Religion in America," a sociologist offers a different meaning.

> While some have argued that Christianity is the national faith, and others that church and synagogue celebrate only the generalized religion of "the American way of life," few have realized that there actually exists alongside of and rather clearly differentiated from the churches an elaborate and well-institutionalized civil religion in America. This article argues not only that there is such a thing, but also that this religion . . . has its own seriousness and integrity and requires the same care in understanding that any other religion does.[8]

When the author adds, "This religion — there seems no other word for it — was neither sectarian nor in any specific sense Christian," he emphasizes that he is distinguishing his definition of religion from definitions that associate religion and church.

Even the word *violence,* which the dictionary defines as "physical force used so as to injure or damage" and whose meaning seems so clear and uncompromising, can be manipulated to produce a definition different from the one normally understood by most people. Some pacifists refer to conditions in which "people are deprived of choices in a systematic way" as "institutionalized quiet violence." Even where no physical force is employed, this lack of choice in schools, in the workplace, in the black ghettos is defined as violence.[9]

In *Through the Looking-Glass* Alice asked Humpty Dumpty "whether you can make words mean so many different things."

"When I use a word," Humpty Dumpty said scornfully, "it means just what I choose it to mean, neither more nor less."[10]

A writer, however, is not free to invent definitions that no one will recognize or that create rather than solve problems between writer and reader.

Negation

To avoid confusion it is sometimes helpful to tell the reader what a term is *not.* In discussing euthanasia, a writer might say, "By euthanasia I do not mean active intervention to hasten the death of the patient."

---

[8]Robert N. Bellah, "Civil Religion in America," *Daedalus,* Winter 1967, p. 1.

[9]Newton Garver, "What Violence Is," in *Moral Choices,* edited by James Rachels (New York: Harper and Row, 1971), pp. 248–249.

[10]Lewis Carroll, *Alice in Wonderland and Through the Looking-Glass* (New York: Grosset and Dunlap, 1948), p. 238.

A negative definition may be more extensive, depending on the complexity of the term and the writer's ingenuity. The critic of rock music quoted earlier in this chapter arrived at his definition by rejecting attributes that seemed misleading. The ex-Communist Whittaker Chambers, in a foreword to a book on the spy trial of Alger Hiss, defined communism this way:

> First, let me try to say what Communism is not. It is not simply a vicious plot hatched by wicked men in a subcellar. It is not just the writings of Marx and Lenin, dialectical materialism, the Politburo, the labor theory of value, the theory of the general strike, the Red Army secret police, labor camps, underground conspiracy, the dictatorship of the proletariat, the technique of the coup d'état. It is not even those chanting, bannered millions that stream periodically, like disorganized armies, through the heart of the world's capitals: Moscow, New York, Tokyo, Paris, Rome. These are expressions, but they are not what Communism is about.[11]

This, of course, is only part of the definition. Any writer beginning a definition in the negative must go on to define what the term *is*.

Examples

One of the most effective ways of defining terms in an argument is the use of examples. Both real and hypothetical examples can bring life to abstract and ambiguous terms. The writer in the following passage defines *preferred categories* (classes of people who are meant to benefit from affirmative action policies) by invoking specific cases:

> The absence of definitions points up one of the problems with preferred categories. . . . These preferred categories take no account of family wealth or educational advantages. A black whose father is a judge or physician deserves preferential treatment over any nonminority applicant. The latter might have fought his way out of the grinding poverty of Appalachia, or might be the first member of an Italian American or a Polish American family to complete high school. But no matter.[12]

Insanity is a word that has been used and misused to describe a variety of conditions. Even psychiatrists are in dispute about its meaning. In the following anecdote, examples narrow and refine the definition.

> Dr. Zilboorg says that present-day psychiatry does not possess any satisfactory definition of mental illness or neurosis. To illustrate, he

---

[11]*Witness* (New York: Random House, 1952), p. 8.

[12]Anthony Lombardo, "Quotas Work Both Ways," *U.S. Catholic,* February 1974, p. 39.

told a story: A psychiatrist was recently asked for a definition of a "well-adjusted person" (not even slightly peculiar). The definition: "A person who feels in harmony with himself and who is not in conflict with his environment." It sounded fine, but up popped a heckler. "Would you then consider an anti-Nazi working in the underground against Hitler a maladjusted person?" "Well," the psychiatrist hemmed, "I withdraw the latter part of my definition." Dr. Zilboorg withdrew the first half for him. Many persons in perfect harmony with themselves, he pointed out, are in "distinctly pathological states."[13]

Extended Definition

When we speak of an extended definition, we usually refer not only to length but also to the variety of methods for developing the definition. Let's take the word *materialism*. A dictionary entry offers the following sentence fragments as definitions: "1. the doctrine that comfort, pleasure, and wealth are the only or highest goals or values. 2. the tendency to be more concerned with material than the spiritual goals or values." But the term *materialism* has acquired so many additional meanings, especially emotional ones, that an extended definition serves a useful purpose in clarifying the many different ideas surrounding our understanding of the term.

Below is a much longer definition of *materialism,* which appears at the beginning of an essay entitled, "People and Things: Reflections on Materialism."[14]

There are two contemporary usages of the term, materialism, and it is important to distinguish between them. On the one hand we can talk about *instrumental materialism,* or the use of material objects to make life longer, safer, more enjoyable. By instrumental, we mean that objects act as essential means for discovering and furthering personal values and goals of life, so that the objects are instruments used to realize and further those goals. There is little negative connotation attached to this meaning of the word, since one would think that it is perfectly sensible to use things for such purposes. While it is true that the United States is the epitome of materialism in this sense, it is also true that most people in every society aspire to reach our level of instrumental materialism.

On the other hand the term has a more negative connotation, which might be conveyed by the phrase *terminal materialism.* This is the sense critics use when they apply the term to Americans. What they mean is that we not only use our material resources as instruments to make life more manageable, but that we reduce our ultimate goals to the possession of things. They believe that we don't just use our cars to

---

[13]Quoted in *The Art of Making Sense,* p. 48.
[14]Mihaly Csikszentmihalyi and Eugene Rochberg-Halton, "People and Things: Reflections on Materialism," *University of Chicago Magazine,* Spring 1978, pp. 7–8.

get from place to place, but that we consider the ownership of expensive cars one of the central values in life. Terminal materialism means that the object is valued only because it indicates an end in itself, a possession. In instrumental materialism there is a sense of directionality, in which a person's goals may be furthered through the interactions with the object. A book, for example, can reveal new possibilities or widen a person's view of the world, or an old photograph can be cherished because it embodies a relationship. But in terminal materialism, there is no sense of reciprocal interaction in the relation between the object and the end. The end is valued as final, not as itself a means to further ends. And quite often it is only the status label or image associated with the object that is valued, rather than the actual object.

In the essay from which this passage is taken, the authors distinguish between two kinds of materialism and provide an extended explanation, using contrast and examples as methods of development. They are aware that the common perception of materialism, the love of things for their own sake, is a negative one. But this view, according to the authors, doesn't fully account for the attitudes of many Americans toward the things they own. There is, in fact, another more positive meaning that the authors call *instrumental materialism.* You will recognize that the authors are *stipulating* a meaning with which their readers might not be familiar. In their essay they distinguish between *terminal materialism,* in which "the object is valued only because it indicates an end in itself" and *instrumental materialism,* "the use of material objects to make life longer, safer, more enjoyable." Since *instrumental materialism* is the less familiar definition, the essay provides a great number of examples that show how people of three different generations value photographs, furniture, musical instruments, plants, and other objects for their memories and personal associations rather than as proof of the owners' ability to acquire the objects or win the approval of others.

THE DEFINITION ESSAY

The argumentative essay can take the form of an extended definition. An example of such an essay is the one from which we've just quoted, as well as the three essays at the end of this chapter. The definition essay is appropriate when the idea under consideration is so controversial or so heavy with historical connotations that even a paragraph or two cannot make clear exactly what the arguer wants his or her readers to understand. For example, if you were preparing a definition of patriotism, you would want to answer some or all of the following questions. You would probably use a number of methods to develop your definition: personal narrative, examples, stipulation, comparison and contrast, and cause and effect analysis.

1. *Dictionary Definition.*   Is the dictionary definition the one I will elaborate on? Do I need to stipulate other meanings?
2. *Personal History.*   Where did I first acquire my notions of patriotism? What was taught? How and by whom was it taught?
3. *Cultural Context.*   Has my patriotic feeling changed in the last few years? Why or why not? Does my own patriotism reflect the mood of the country or the group to which I belong?
4. *Values.*   What is the value of patriotism? Does it make me more humane, more civilized? Is patriotism consistent with tolerance of other systems and cultures? Is patriotism the highest duty of a citizen? Do any other values take precedence? What was the meaning of President Kennedy's injunction: "Ask not what your country can do for you; ask rather what you can do for your country"?
5. *Behavior.*   How do I express my patriotism (or lack of it)? Can it be expressed through dissent? What sacrifice, if any, would I make for my country?

WRITING AN ESSAY OF DEFINITION

The following list suggests several important steps to be taken in writing an essay of definition.

1. Choose a term that needs definition because it is controversial or ambiguous, or because you want to offer a personal definition that differs from the accepted interpretation. Explain why an extended definition is necessary. Or choose an experience that lends itself to treatment in an extended definition. One student defined "culture shock" as she had experienced it while studying abroad in Hawaii among students of a different ethnic background.
2. Decide on the thesis — the point of view you wish to develop about the term you are defining. If you want to define "heroism," for example, you may choose to develop the idea that this quality depends on motivation and awareness of danger rather than on the specific act performed by the hero.
3. Begin by consulting the dictionary for the conventional definition, the one with which most readers will be familiar. Make clear whether you want to elaborate on the dictionary definition or take issue with it because you think it is misleading or inadequate.
4. Distinguish wherever possible between the term you are defining and other terms with which it might be confused. If you are defining "love," can you make a clear distinction between the different kinds of emotional attachments contained in the word?
5. Try to think of several methods of developing the definition — using examples, comparison and contrast, analogy, cause and ef-

fect analysis. However, you may discover that one method alone — say, use of examples — will suffice to narrow and refine your definition. See the sample essay "The Nature of Prejudice" on page 116 for an example of such a development.

6. Arrange your supporting material in an order that gives emphasis to the most important ideas.

SAMPLE ANALYSIS

Addiction Is Not a Disease
STANTON PEELE

Why Addiction Is Not a Disease

Medical schools are finally teaching about alcoholism; Johns Hopkins will require basic training for all students and clinicians. . . . Alcoholism, as a chronic disease, offers "a fantastic vehicle to teach other concepts," says Jean Kinney [of Dartmouth's Cork Institute]. . . . William Osler, Kinney remarks, coined the aphorism that "to know syphilis is to know medicine," . . . Now, she says, the same can be said of alcoholism.
— "The Neglected Disease in Medical Education," *Science*[1]

OCD (obsessive-compulsive disorder) is apparently rare in the general population.
— American Psychiatric Association, 1980[2]

The evidence is strong OCD is a common mental disorder that, like other stigmatized and hidden disorders in the past, may be ready for discovery and demands for treatment on a large scale.
— National Institute of Mental Health, 1988[3]

In America today, we are bombarded with news about drug and alcohol problems. We may ask ourselves, "How did we get here?" Alternatively, we may wonder if these problems are really worse now

---

Stanton Peele, who receive his Ph.D. in social psychology from the University of Michigan, has taught at Harvard and Columbia Universities, the University of California, and is coauthor of the bestselling *Love and Addiction* (1975). This excerpt is from *Diseasing of America* (Boston: Houghton Mifflin, 1989).

[1]C. Holden, "The Neglected Disease in Medical Education," *Science* 229 (1985), pp. 741–742.

[2]*Diagnostic and Statistical Manual of Mental Disorders,* 3rd ed. (Washington, D.C.: American Psychiatric Association, 1980).

[3]M. Karno et al., "The Epidemiology of Obsessive-Compulsive Disorder in Five US Communities," *Archives of General Psychiatry* 45 (1988), pp. 1094–1099.

than they were five or ten years ago, or fifty or one hundred. Actually, in many cases the answer is no. Estimates of the number of alcoholics requiring treatment are wildly overblown, and reputable epidemiological researchers find that as little as 1 percent of the population fits the clinical definition of alcoholism — as opposed to the 10 percent figure regularly used by the alcoholism industry. Meanwhile, cocaine use is down. All indicators are that very few young people who try drugs ever become regular users, and fewer still get "hooked."

Of course, we have real problems. The nightly news carries story after story of inner-city violence between crack gangs and of totally desolate urban environments where drugs reign supreme. The cocaine problem has resolved itself — not exclusively, but very largely — into a ghetto problem, like many that face America. A *New York Times* front-page story based on an eight-year study of young drug users showed that those who abuse drugs have a number of serious background problems, and *that these problems don't disappear from their lives when they stop using drugs.*[4] In other words, the sources — and solutions — for what is going on in our ghettos are only very secondarily a matter of drug availability and use.

America is a society broken into two worlds. The reality of the crack epidemic and of inner cities and poor environments sometimes explodes and impinges unpleasantly on our consciousness. For the most part, however, our reality is that of the middle class, which fills our magazines with health stories and warnings about family problems and the strivings of young professionals to find satisfaction. And for some time now, this other world has also focused on addiction. But this new addiction marketplace is only sometimes linked to alcohol and drugs. Even when it is, we have to redefine alcoholism as the new Betty Ford kind, which is marked by a general dull malaise, a sense that one is drinking too much, and — for many, like Betty Ford and Kitty Dukakis — relying on prescribed drugs to make life bearable.

However we define loss-of-control drinking, Betty Ford didn't experience it. But treating problems like hers and those of so many media stars is far more rewarding and profitable than trying to deal with street derelicts or ghetto addicts. At the same time, *everything can be an addiction.* This remarkable truth — which I first described in *Love and Addiction* in 1975 — has so overwhelmed us as a society that we have gone haywire. We want to pass laws to excuse compulsive gamblers when they embezzle money to gamble and to force insurance companies to pay to treat them. We want to treat people

---

[4]S. Blakeslee, "8-Year Study Finds 2 Sides to Teen-Age Drug Use," *New York Times,* July 21, 1988, p. 1, Sec. A, p. 23.

who can't find love and who instead (when they are women) go after dopey, superficial men or (when they are men) pursue endless sexual liaisons without finding true happiness. And we want to call all these things — and many, many more — addictions.

Since I was part of the movement to label non-drug-related behaviors as addictions, what am I complaining about? My entire purpose in writing *Love and Addiction* was to explain addictions as part of a larger description of people's lives. Addiction is an experience that people can get caught up in but that still expresses their values, skills at living, and personal resolve — or lack of it. The label *addiction* does not obviate either the meaning of the addictive involvement within people's lives, or their responsibility for their misbehavior or for their choices in continuing the addiction. Forty million Americans have quit smoking. What, then, are we to think about the people who do not quit but who sue a tobacco company for addicting them to cigarettes after they learn they are going to die from a smoking-related ailment?

This discrepancy between understanding addiction within the larger context of a person's life and regarding it as an *explanation* of that life underlies my opposition to the "disease theory" of addiction, which I contest throughout this book. My view of addiction explicitly refutes this theory's contentions that (1) the addiction exists *independently* of the rest of a person's life and *drives* all of his or her choices; (2) it is progressive and irreversible, so that the addiction *inevitably worsens* unless the person seeks medical treatment or joins an AA-type support group; (3) addiction means the person is incapable of controlling his or her behavior, either in relation to the addictive object itself or — when the person is intoxicated or in pursuit of the addiction — in relation to the person's dealings with the rest of the world. Everything I oppose in the disease view is represented in the passive, *1984*-ish phrase, *alcohol abuse victim,* to replace *alcohol abuser.* On the contrary, this book maintains that people are *active agents* in — not passive victims of — their addictions.

While I do believe that a host of human habits and compulsions can be understood as addictions, I think the disease version of addiction does *at least* as much harm as good. An addiction does not mean that God in heaven decided which people are alcoholics and addicts. There is no biological urge to form addictions, one that we will someday find under a microscope and that will finally make sense of all these different cravings and idiocies (such as exercising to the point of injury or having sex with people who are bad for you). No medical treatment will ever be created to excise addictions from people's lives, and support groups that convince people that they are helpless and will forever be incapable of controlling an activity are better examples of self-fulfilling prophecies than of therapy.

What is this new addiction industry meant to accomplish? More and more addictions are being discovered, and new addicts are being identified, until all of us will be locked into our own little addictive worlds with other addicts like ourselves, defined by the special interests of our neuroses. What a repugnant world to imagine, as well as a hopeless one. Meanwhile, *all of the addictions we define are increasing.* In the first place, we tell people they can never get better from their "diseases." In the second, we constantly find new addicts, looking for them in all sorts of new areas of behavior and labeling them at earlier ages on the basis of more casual or typical behaviors, such as getting drunk at holiday celebrations ("chemical-dependency disease") or checking to see whether they locked their car door ("obsessive-compulsive disorder").

We must oppose this nonsense by understanding its sources and contradicting disease ideology. . . . Our society is going wrong in excusing crime, compelling people to undergo treatment, and wildly mixing up moral responsibility with disease diagnoses. Indeed, understanding the confusion and self-defeating behavior we display in this regard is perhaps the best way to analyze the failure of many of our contemporary social policies. . . . [We must] confront the actual social, psychological, and moral issues that we face as individuals and as a society — the ones we are constantly repressing and mislabeling through widening our disease nets. It is as though we were creating distorted microscopes that actually muddy our vision and that make our problems harder to resolve into components we can reasonably hope to deal with.

What are real diseases? If we are to distinguish between addiction 10 and other diseases, then we first need to understand what have been called diseases historically and how these differ from what are being called diseases today. To do so, let us review three generations of diseases — physical ailments, mental disorders, and addictions.

The *first* generation of diseases consists of disorders known through their physical manifestations, like malaria, tuberculosis, cancer, and AIDS. The era of medical understanding that these diseases ushered in began with the discovery of specific microbes that cause particular diseases and for which preventive inoculations — and eventually antibodies — were developed. These maladies are the ones we can unreservedly call diseases without clouding the issue. This first generation of diseases differs fundamentally from what were later called diseases in that the former are *defined by their measurable physical effects.* They are clearly connected to the functioning of the body, and our concern is with the damage the disease does to the body.

The *second* generation of diseases are the so-called mental illnesses (now referred to as emotional disorders). They are not defined in the same way as the first generation. Emotional disorders are apparent to us not because of what we measure in people's bodies but because of the feelings, thoughts, and behaviors that they produce in people, which we can only know from what the sufferers say and do. We do not diagnose emotional disorders from a brain scan; if a person cannot tell reality from fantasy, we call the person mentally ill, no matter what the person's EEG says.

The *third* generation of diseases — addictions — strays still farther from the model of physical disorder to which the name *disease* was first applied by modern medicine. That is, unlike a mental illness such as schizophrenia, which is indicated by disordered thinking, addictive disorders *are known by the goal-directed behaviors they describe.* We call a person a drug addict who consumes drugs compulsively or excessively and whose life is devoted to seeking out these substances. If an addicted smoker gives up smoking or if a habituated coffee drinker decides to drink coffee only after Sunday dinner, then each ceases to be addicted. We cannot tell whether a person is addicted or will be addicted in the absence of the ongoing behavior — the person with a hypothetical alcoholic predisposition (say, one who has an alcoholic parent or whose face flushes when drinking) but who drinks occasionally and moderately is not an alcoholic.

In order to clarify the differences between third-generation and first-generation diseases, we often have to overcome shifting definitions that have been changed solely for the purpose of obscuring crucial differences between problems like cancer and addiction. After a time, we seem not to recognize how our views have been manipulated by such gerrymandered disease criteria. For example, by claiming that alcoholics are alcoholics even if they haven't drunk for fifteen years, alcoholism is made to seem less tied to drinking behavior and more like cancer. Sometimes it seems necessary to remind ourselves of the obvious: that a person does not get over cancer by stopping a single behavior or even by changing a whole life-style, but the sole and essential indicator for successful remission of alcoholism is that the person ceases to drink.

Addictions involve appetites and behaviors. While a connection 15 can be traced between individual and cultural beliefs and first- and second-generation diseases, this connection is most pronounced for addictions. Behaviors and appetites are addictions only in particular cultural contexts — obviously, obesity matters only where people have enough to eat and think it is important to be thin. Symptoms like loss-of-control drinking depend *completely* on cultural and personal meanings, and cultural groups that don't understand how people can lose control of their drinking are almost immune to alcoholism. What is most important, however, is not how cultural beliefs affect addictions but how our defining of addictions as diseases affects our views of ourselves as individuals and as a society. . . .

What Is Addiction, and How Do People Get It?

While individual practitioners and recovering addicts — and the whole addiction movement — may believe they are helping people, they succeed principally at expanding their industry by finding more addicts and new types of addictions to treat. I too have argued — in books from *Love and Addiction* to *The Meaning of Addiction* — that addiction *can* take place with any human activity. Addiction is *not,* however, something people are born with. Nor is it a biological imperative, one that means the addicted individual is not able to consider or choose alternatives. The disease view of addiction is equally untrue when applied to gambling, compulsive sex, and everything else that it has been used to explain. Indeed, the fact that people become addicted to all these things *proves* that addiction is not *caused* by chemical or biological forces and that it is not a special disease state.

The nature of addiction. People seek specific, essential human experiences from their addictive involvement, no matter whether it is drinking, eating, smoking, loving, shopping, or gambling. People can come to depend on such an involvement for these experiences until — in the extreme — the involvement is totally consuming and potentially destructive. Addiction can occasionally veer into total abandonment, as well as periodic excesses and loss of control. Nonetheless, even in cases where addicts die from their excesses, an addiction must be understood as a human response that is motivated by the addict's desires and principles. All addictions *accomplish something for the addict.* They are ways of coping with feelings and situations with which addicts cannot otherwise cope. What is wrong with disease theories as science is that they are *tautologies;* they avoid the work of understanding *why* people drink or smoke in favor of simply declaring these activities to be addictions, as in the statement "He drinks so much because he's an alcoholic."

Addicts seek experiences that satisfy needs they cannot otherwise fulfill. Any addiction involves three components — the person, the situation or environment, and the addictive involvement or experience (see Table 1). In addition to the individual, the situation, and the experience, we also need to consider the overall cultural and social factors that affect addiction in our society.

The social and cultural milieu. We must also consider the enormous social-class differences in addiction rates. That is, the farther down the social and economic scale a person is, the more likely the person is to become addicted to alcohol, drugs, or cigarettes, to be obese, or to be a victim or perpetrator of family or sexual abuse. How does it come to be that addiction is a "disease" rooted in certain social experiences, and why in particular are drug addiction and alcoholism associated primarily with certain groups? A smaller

TABLE 1

The Person	The Situation	The Addictive Experience
Unable to fulfill essential needs	Barren and deprived: disadvantaged social groups, war zones	Creates powerful and immediate sensations; focuses and absorbs attention
Values that support or do not counteract addiction: e.g., lack of achievement motivation	Antisocial peer groups	Provides artificial or temporary sense of self-worth, power, control, security, intimacy, accomplishment
Lack of restraint and inhibition	Absence of supportive social groups; disturbed family structure	
Lack of self-efficacy; sense of powerlessness vis-à-vis the addiction	Life situations: adolescence, temporary isolation, deprivation, or stress	Eliminates pain, uncertainty, and other negative sensations

range of addiction and behavioral problems are associated with the middle and upper social classes. These associations must also be explained. Some addictions, like shopping, are obviously connected with the middle class. Bulimia and exercise addiction are also primarily middle-class addictions.

Finally, we must explore why addictions of one kind or another 20 appear on our social landscape all of sudden, almost as though floodgates were released. For example, alcoholism was unknown to most colonial Americans and to most Americans earlier in this century; now it dominates public attention. This is not due to greater consumption, since we are actually drinking *less* alcohol than the colonists did. Bulimia, PMS, shopping addiction, and exercise addiction are wholly new inventions. Not that it isn't possible to go back in time to find examples of things that appear to conform to these new diseases. Yet their widespread — almost commonplace — presence in today's society must be explained, especially when the disease — like alcoholism — is supposedly biologically inbred. . . .

Are addicts disease victims? The development of an addictive life-style is an accumulation of patterns in people's lives of which drug use is neither a result nor a cause but another example. Sid Vicious was the consummate drug addict, an exception even among heroin users. Nonetheless, we need to understand the extremes to gain a sense of the shape of the entire phenomenon of addiction. Vicious, rather than being a passive victim of drugs, seemed intent on being and remaining addicted. He avoided opportunities to escape and turned every aspect of his life toward his addictions — booze,

Nancy, drugs — while sacrificing anything that might have rescued him — music, business interests, family, friendships, survival instincts. Vicious was pathetic; in a sense, he was a victim of his own life. But his addiction, like his life, was more an active expression of his pathos than a passive victimization.

Addiction theories have been created because it stuns us that people would hurt — perhaps destroy — themselves through drugs, drinking, sex, gambling, and so on. While people get caught up in an addictive dynamic over which they do not have full control, it is at least as accurate to say that people consciously select an addiction as it is to say an addiction has a person under its control. And this is why addiction is so hard to ferret out of the person's life — because it fits the person. The bulimic woman who has found that self-induced vomiting helps her to control her weight and who feels more attractive after throwing up is a hard person to persuade to give up her habit voluntarily. Consider the homeless man who refused to go to one of Mayor Koch's New York City shelters because he couldn't easily drink there and who said, "I don't want to give up drinking; it's the only thing I've got."

The researcher who has done the most to explore the personalities of alcoholics and drug addicts is psychologist Craig MacAndrew. MacAndrew developed the MAC scale, selected from items on the MMPI (a personality scale) that distinguish clinical alcoholics and drug abusers from normal subjects and from other psychiatric patients. This scale identifies antisocial impulsiveness and acting out: "an assertive, aggressive, pleasure-seeking character," in terms of which alcoholics and drug abusers closely "resemble criminals and delinquents."[5] These characteristics are not the *results* of substance abuse. Several studies have measured these traits in young men *prior* to [their] becoming alcoholics and in young drug and alcohol abusers.[6] This same kind of antisocial thrill-seeking characterizes most women who become alcoholic. Such women more often have disciplinary problems at school, react to boredom by "stirring up some kind of excitement," engage in more disapproved sexual practices, and have more trouble with the law.[7]

---

[5]C. MacAndrew, "What the MAC Scale Tells Us about Men Alcoholics," *Journal of Studies on Alcohol* 42 (1981), p. 617.

[6]H. Hoffman, R. G. Loper, and M. L. Kammeier, "Identifying Future Alcoholics with MMPI Alcoholism Scores," *Quarterly Journal of Studies on Alcohol* 35 (1974), pp. 490–498; M. C. Jones, "Personality Correlates and Antecedents of Drinking Patterns in Adult Males," *Journal of Consulting and Clinical Psychology* 32 (1968), pp. 2–12; R. G. Loper, M. L. Kammeier, and H. Hoffman, "MMPI Characteristics of College Freshman Males Who Later Become Alcoholics," *Journal of Abnormal Psychology* 82 (1973), pp. 159–162; C. MacAndrew, "Toward the Psychometric Detection of Substance Misuse in Young Men," *Journal of Studies on Alcohol* 47 (1986), pp. 161–166.

[7]C. MacAndrew, "Similarities in the Self-Depictions of Female Alcoholics and Psychiatric Outpatients," *Journal of Studies on Alcohol* 47 (1986), pp. 478–484.

The typical alcoholic, then, fulfills antisocial drives and pursues immediate, sensual, and aggressive rewards while having underdeveloped inhibitions. MacAndrew also found that another, smaller group comprising both men and women alcoholics — but more often women — drank to alleviate internal conflicts and feelings like depression. This group of alcoholics viewed the world, in MacAndrew's words, "primarily in terms of its potentially punishing character." For them, "alcohol functions as a palliation for a chronically fearful, distressful internal state of affairs." While these drinkers also sought specific rewards in drinking, these rewards were defined more by internal states than by external behaviors. Nonetheless, we can see that this group too did not consider normal social strictures in pursuing feelings they desperately desired.

MacAndrew's approach in this research was to identify particu- 25
lar personality types identified by the experiences they looked to alcohol to provide. But even for alcoholics or addicts without such distinct personalities, the purposeful dynamic is at play. For example, in *The Lives of John Lennon,* Albert Goldman describes how Lennon — who was addicted over his career to a host of drugs — would get drunk when he went out to dinner with Yoko Ono so that he could spill out his resentments of her. In many families, drinking allows alcoholics to express emotions that they are otherwise unable to express. The entire panoply of feelings and behaviors that alcohol may bring about for individual drinkers thus can be motivations for chronic intoxication. While some desire power from drinking, others seek to escape in alcohol; for some drinking is the route to excitement, while others welcome its calming effects.

Alcoholics or addicts may have more emotional problems or more deprived backgrounds than others, but probably they are best characterized as feeling powerless to bring about the feelings they want or to accomplish their goals without drugs, alcohol, or some other involvement. Their sense of powerlessness then translates into the belief that the drug or alcohol is extremely powerful. They see in the substance the ability to accomplish what they need or want but can't do on their own. The double edge to this sword is that the person is easily convinced that he or she cannot function without the substance or addiction, that he or she requires it to survive. This sense of personal powerlessness, on the one hand, and of the extreme power of an involvement or substance, on the other, readily translates into addiction.[8]

---

[8]G. A. Marlatt, "Alcohol, the Magic Elixir," in *Stress and Addiction,* ed. E. Gottheil et al. (New York: Brunner/Mazel, 1987); D. J. Rohsenow, "Alcoholics' Perceptions of Control," in *Identifying and Measuring Alcoholic Personality Characteristics,* ed. W. M. Cox (San Francisco: Jossey-Bass, 1983).

People don't manage to become alcoholics over years of drinking simply because their bodies are playing tricks on them — say, by allowing them to imbibe more than is good for them without realizing it until they become dependent on booze. Alcoholics' long drinking careers are motivated by their search for essential experiences they cannot gain in other ways. The odd thing is that — despite a constant parade of newspaper and magazine articles and TV programs trying to convince us otherwise — most people recognize that alcoholics drink for specific purposes. Even alcoholics, however much they spout the party line, know this about themselves. Consider, for example, . . . Monica Wright, the head of a New York City treatment center, [who] describes how she drank over the twenty years of her alcoholic marriage to cope with her insecurity and with her inability to deal with her husband and children. It is impossible to find an alcoholic who does not express similar reasons for his or her drinking, once the disease dogma is peeled away. . . .

Analysis

Peele is not the only writer to take issue with the popular practice of defining all kinds of mental and social problems as addictions. (A recent satirical newspaper article is entitled, "It's Not Me That's Guilty. My Addiction Just Took Over.") Peele's definition will be disputed by many doctors, psychologists, and a powerful industry of self-appointed healers. But definitions that attack popular opinions are often the liveliest and most interesting both to read and to write. In addition, they may serve a useful purpose, even if they are misguided, in encouraging new thinking about apparently intractable problems.

In defense of a controversial definition, an author must do at least two things: (1) make clear why a new definition is needed, that is, why the old definition does not work to explain certain conditions, and (2) argue that the new definition offers a better explanation and may even lead to more effective solutions of a problem.

The first part of Peele's argument is definition by negation. (Notice the title of this section.) Peele insists that the number of drug and alcohol addicts among both the poor and the well-to-do is not nearly so large as practitioners would have it. Next, he points out that addiction is not an explanation of a person's life, as some have insisted, nor does it mean that the addict is a victim to be absolved of responsibility for the consequences of his actions. Last, he provides the reasons that addiction is not a disease, basing his argument on the historic definition of disease as a bodily ailment whose physical effects are measurable. Defining mental illness and addiction as diseases is, Peele thinks, an evasion of the truth.

Some readers will question the narrowness of Peele's stipulation. Since the term *disease* has come to signify almost everywhere (including the dictionary) a disorder that need not be biological in origin, these readers may feel that Peele is attacking a nonexistent problem. But in the next section — "What Is Addiction?" — he elaborates on his major point: Addicts are not passive victims. Addiction is a choice, derived from the addict's desires and principles. Because this is the heart of the controversy, Peele devotes the rest of his essay to its development. In "The Nature of Addiction" he gives an overview of the motives that lead addicts to alcohol or drugs. Later, in "Are Addicts Disease Victims?" he enlarges on the descriptions of their behavior and identifies specific reasons for their actions. One of the strengths of his argument is the breadth of the analysis. In a few pages he touches on all the relevant causes of the addict's choices: the individual, the situation, the addictive experience, the social and cultural milieu.

The support for his claim is not exhaustive, but it offers a variety of evidence: examples of familiar individuals and types (Sid Vicious, John Lennon, the bulimic, the homeless man, the head of a treatment center), clear explanations of different kinds of addictive behavior, and a detailed summary of expert opinion.

All this evidence, if it is to work, must make an appeal to the common sense and experience of the reader. As Peele says, "The odd thing is that — despite a constant parade of newspaper and magazine articles and TV programs trying to convince us otherwise — most people recognize that alcoholics drink for specific purposes." Most readers, of course, will not be experts, but if they find the evidence consistent with their knowledge of and experience with addiction, they will find Peele's definition deserving of additional study.

The Nature of Prejudice

GORDON ALLPORT

Before I attempt to define prejudice, let us have in mind four instances that I think we all would agree are prejudice.

The first is the case of the Cambridge University student who said, "I despise all Americans. But," he added, a bit puzzled, "I've never met one that I didn't like."

The second is the case of another Englishman, who said to an American, "I think you're awfully unfair in your treatment to Negroes. How *do* Americans feel about Negroes?" The American replied, "Well, I suppose some Americans feel about Negroes just the way you feel about the Irish." The Englishman said, "Oh, come now. The Negroes are human beings."

Then there's the incident that occasionally takes place in various parts of the world (in the West Indies, for example, I'm told). When an American walks down the street the natives conspicuously hold their noses till the American goes by. The case of odor is always interesting. Odor gets mixed up with prejudice because odor has great associative power. We know that some Chinese deplore the odor of Americans. Some white people think Negroes have a distinctive smell and vice versa. An intrepid psychologist recently did an experiment; it went as follows. He brought to a gymnasium an equal number of white and colored students and had them take shower baths. When they were nice and clean he had them exercise vigorously for fifteen minutes. Then he brought his judges in, and each went to the sheeted figures and sniffed. They were to say "white" or "black," guessing at the identity of the subject. The experiment seemed to prove that when we are sweaty we all smell the same way. It's good to have experimental demonstration of the fact.

The fourth example I'd like to bring before you is a piece of writing that I quote. Please ask yourselves who, in your judgment, wrote it. It's a passage about the Jews. 5

> The synagogue is worse than a brothel. It's a den of scoundrels. It's a criminal assembly of Jews, a place of meeting for the assassins of

---

Gordon Allport (1897–1967) was a psychologist who taught at Harvard University from 1924 until his death. He was author of numerous books, among them *Personality: A Psychological Interpretation* (1937). Allport delivered "The Nature of Prejudice" at the Seventeenth Claremont Reading Conference in 1952. The speech was published as a paper in 1952 in the Seventeenth Claremont Reading Conference Yearbook.

Christ, a den of thieves, a house of ill fame, a dwelling of iniquity. Whatever name more horrible to be found, it could never be worse than the synagogue deserves.

I would say the same things about their souls. Debauchery and drunkenness have brought them to the level of lusty goat and pig. They know only one thing: to satisfy their stomachs and get drunk, kill, and beat each other up. Why should we salute them? We should not even have the slightest converse with them. They are lustful, rapacious, greedy, perfidious robbers.

Now who wrote that? Perhaps you say Hitler, or Goebbels, or one of our local anti-Semites? No, it was written by Saint John Chrysostom, in the fourth century A.D. Saint John Chrysostom, as you know, gave us the first liturgy in the Christian church, still used in the Orthodox churches today. From it all services of the Holy Communion derive. Episcopalians will recognize him also as the author of that exalted prayer that closes the offices of both matins and evensong in the *Book of Common Prayer*. I include this incident to show how complex the problem is. Religious people are by no means necessarily free from prejudice. In this regard be patient even with our saints.

What do these four instances have in common? You notice that all of them indicate that somebody is "down" on somebody else — a feeling of rejection, or hostility. But also, in all these four instances, there is indication that the person is not "up" on his subject — not really informed about Americans, Irish, Jews, or bodily odors.

So I would offer, first a slang definition of prejudice: *Prejudice is being down on somebody you're not up on.* If you dislike slang, let me offer the same thought in the style of St. Thomas Aquinas. Thomists have defined prejudice as *thinking ill of others without sufficient warrant.*

You notice that both definitions, as well as the examples I gave, specify two ingredients of prejudice. First there is some sort of faulty generalization in thinking about a group. I'll call this the process of *categorization.* Then there is the negative, rejective, or hostile ingredient, a *feeling* tone. "Being down on something" is the hostile ingredient; "that you're not up on" is the categorization ingredient; "thinking ill of others" is the hostile ingredient; "without sufficient warrant" is the faulty categorization.

Parenthetically I should say that of course there is such a thing 10 as *positive* prejudice. We can be just as prejudiced *in favor of* as we are *against.* We can be biased in favor of our children, our neighborhood, or our college. Spinoza makes the distinction neatly. He says that *love prejudice* is "thinking well of others, through love, more than is right." *Hate prejudice,* he says, is "thinking ill of others, through hate, more than is right."

Reading and Discussion Questions

1. This was a speech, obviously not delivered extemporaneously but read to the audience. What characteristics suggest an oral presentation? If you were to revise this essay into a paper, what changes would you make? Why?
2. Allport has arranged his anecdotes carefully. What principle of organization has he used?
3. This essay was written in 1952. Are there any references or examples that seem dated? Why or why not?

Writing Suggestions

4. Some media critics claim that negative prejudice exists in the treatment of certain groups in movies and television. If you agree, select a group that seems to you to be the object of prejudice in these media, and offer evidence of the prejudice and the probable reasons for it. Or disagree with the media critics and provide evidence that certain groups are *not* the object of prejudice.
5. Can you think of examples of what Allport calls *positive prejudice*? Perhaps you can find instances that are less obvious than the ones Allport mentions. Explain in what way these prejudices represent a love that is "more than is right."

What Sexual Harassment Is — and Is Not

ELLEN BRAVO and ELLEN CASSEDY

Louette Colombano was one of the first female police officers in her San Francisco district. While listening to the watch commander, she and the other officers stood at attention with their hands behind their backs. The officer behind her unzipped his fly and rubbed his penis against her hands.

Diane, a buyer, was preparing to meet an out-of-town client for dinner when she received a message: her boss had informed the client that she would spend the night with him. Diane sent word that she couldn't make it to dinner. The next day she was fired.

Ellen Bravo is the national director of 9to5, an organization for working women. Ellen Cassedy, a founder of 9to5, writes a column for the *Philadelphia Daily News*. This article is excerpted from their book, *The 9 to 5 Guide to Combating Sexual Harassment* (New York: John Wiley & Sons, 1992). Reprinted by permission of John Wiley & Sons, Inc.

Few people would disagree that these are clear-cut examples of sexual harassment. Touching someone in a deliberately sexual way, demanding that an employee engage in sex or lose her job — such behavior is clearly out of bounds. (It's also *illegal.* . . .) But in less obvious cases, many people are confused about where to draw the line.

Is It Harassment?

Is all sexual conversation inappropriate at work? Is every kind of touching off limits? Consider the following examples. In your opinion, which, if any, constitute sexual harassment?

- A male manager asks a female subordinate to lunch to discuss a new project.
- A man puts his arm around a woman at work.
- A woman tells an off-color joke.
- These comments are made at the workplace:

    "Your hair looks terrific."

    "That outfit's a knockout."

    "Did you get any last night?"

The answer in each of these cases is, "It depends." Each one   5
could be an example of sexual harassment — or it could be acceptable behavior.

Take the case of the manager asking a female subordinate to lunch to discuss a new project. Suppose this manager often has such lunchtime meetings with his employees, male and female. Everyone is aware that he likes to get out of the office environment in order to get to know the associates a little better and to learn how they function — for example, whether they prefer frequent meetings or written reports, detailed instructions or more delegation of responsibility. The female subordinate in this case may feel she's being treated just like other colleagues and be glad to receive the individual attention.

On the other hand, suppose this subordinate has been trying for some time, unsuccessfully, to be assigned to an interesting project. The only woman who does get plum assignments spends a lot of time out of the office with the boss; the two of them are rumored to be sleeping together. The lunch may represent an opportunity to move ahead, but it could mean that the manager expects a physical relationship in return. In this case, an invitation to lunch with the boss is laden with unwelcome sexual overtones.

An arm around the shoulder, an off-color joke, comments about someone's appearance, or even sexual remarks may or may not be offensive. What matters is the relationship between the two parties and how each of them feels.

"Your hair looks terrific," for instance, could be an innocuous compliment if it were tossed off by one co-worker to another as they passed in the hall. But imagine this same phrase coming from a male boss bending down next to his secretary's ear and speaking in a suggestive whisper. Suddenly, these innocent-sounding words take on a different meaning. The body language and tone of voice signify something sexual. While the comment itself may not amount to much, the secretary is left to wonder *what else the boss has in mind.*

On the other hand, even words that may seem grossly inappro- 10 priate — "Did you get any last night?" — can be harmless in certain work situations. One group of male and female assembly-line workers talked like this all the time. What made it okay? They were friends and equals — no one in the group had power over any of the others. They were all comfortable with the banter. They hadn't drawn up a list specifying which words were acceptable to the group and which were not. But they had worked together for some time and knew one another well. Their remarks were made with affection and accepted as good-natured. No one intended to offend — and no one was offended. The assembly-line area was relatively isolated, so the workers weren't in danger of bothering anyone outside their group. Had a new person joined the group who wasn't comfortable with this kind of talk, the others would have stopped it. They might have thought the new person uptight, they might not have liked the new atmosphere, but they would have respected and honored any request to eliminate the remarks.

This is the essence of combating sexual harassment — creating a workplace that is built on mutual respect.

Looking at Harassment

Try assessing whether each of the following scenarios constitutes sexual harassment. Then consider the analysis that follows.

Scenario 1: Justine works in a predominantly male department. She has tried to fit in, even laughing on occasion at the frequent sexual jokes. The truth is, though, that she gets more irritated by the jokes each day. It is well known in the department that Justine has an out-of-town boyfriend whom she sees most weekends. Nonetheless, Franklin, one of Justine's co-workers, has said he has the "hots" for her and that — boyfriend or not — he's willing to do almost anything to get a date with her. One day, Sarah, another of Justine's co-workers, over-heard their boss talking to Franklin in the hallway. "If you can get her to go to bed with you," the boss said, "I'll take you out to dinner. Good luck." They chuckled and went their separate ways. (From the consulting firm of Jane C. Edmonds & Associates, Inc., *Boston Globe,* 10/24/91.)

The boss is out of line. True, he probably didn't intend anyone to overhear him. But why was he having this conversation in the hallway? What was he doing having the conversation at all? The boss is responsible for keeping the workplace free of harassment. Instead, he's giving Franklin an incentive to make sexual advances to a co-worker and then to brag about it.

The conversation may constitute harassment not only of Justine 15 but also of Sarah, who overheard the conversation. A reasonable woman might easily wonder, "Who's he going to encourage to go after *me*?" Ideally, Sarah should tell the two men she was offended by their remarks. But given that one of them is her boss, it would be understandable if she were reluctant to criticize his behavior.

Franklin isn't just romantically interested in Justine; he "has the hots" for her and is willing to "do almost anything" to get a date with her. Justine could well be interested in a "fling" with Franklin. But she's irritated by the sexual remarks and innuendoes in the workplace. It's unlikely that she would be flattered by attention from one of the men responsible for this atmosphere.

Justine can just say no to Franklin. But she may well object to having to say no over and over. And most women are not pleased to be the brunt of jokes and boasts. Some may argue that whether Franklin and Justine get together is a personal matter between the two of them. The moment it becomes the subject of public boasting, however, Franklin's interest in Justine ceases to be just a private interaction.

The law doesn't say Justine should be tough enough to speak up on her own — it says the company is responsible for providing an environment free of offensive or hostile behavior. As the person in charge, the boss ought to know what kind of remarks are being made in the workplace and whether employees are offended by them. Instead of making Franklin think the way to win favor with him is to pressure a co-worker into bed, the manager might want to arrange for some training on sexual harassment.

Scenario 2: Freda has been working for Bruce for three years. He believes they have a good working relationship. Freda has never complained to Bruce about anything and appears to be happy in her job. Bruce regularly compliments Freda on her clothing; in his opinion, she has excellent taste and a good figure. Typically, he'll make a remark like "You sure look good today." Last week, Freda was having a bad day and told Bruce that she was "sick and tired of being treated like a sex object." Bruce was stunned. (From the consulting firm of Jane C. Edmonds & Associates, Inc., *Boston Globe,* 10/24/91.)

There's really not enough information to come to any conclu- 20 sion in this case. The scenario explains how Bruce feels, but not Freda. In the past, when he said, "Hey, you look good today," did Freda usually answer, "So do you"? Or did he murmur, "Mmm, you look go-o-o-o-d," and stare at her chest while she crossed her arms and said, "Thank you, sir"? In addition to complimenting Freda's appearance, did Bruce ever praise her work? Did he compliment other women? Men?

It is plausible that Freda might have been upset earlier. She probably wouldn't say she was tired of being treated like a sex object unless she'd felt that way before. Why didn't she speak up sooner? It's not uncommon for someone in Freda's situation to be reluctant to say anything for fear of looking foolish or appearing to be a "bad sport." Remember, Bruce is her boss.

Bruce states that he was stunned when Freda blew up at him. He needs to consider whether Freda might have given him any signals he ignored. He should ask himself how his compliments fit in with the way he treats other employees. Has he really given Freda an opening to object to his remarks?

The most comfortable solution might be for Bruce and Freda to sit down and talk. Perhaps Freda doesn't really mind the compliments themselves but wants more attention paid to her work. If Freda has been upset about the compliments all along, Bruce is probably guilty only of not paying close attention to her feelings. He should let her know that he values her work *and* her feelings, listen carefully to what she has to say, and encourage her to speak up promptly about issues that may arise in the future.

Scenario 3: Barbara is a receptionist for a printing company. Surrounding her desk are five versions of ads printed by the company for a beer distributor. The posters feature women provocatively posed with a can of beer and the slogan, "What'll you have?" On numerous occasions, male customers have walked in, looked at the posters, and commented, "I'll have you, baby." When Barbara tells her boss she wants the posters removed, he responds by saying they represent the company's work and he's proud to display them. He claims no one but Barbara is bothered by the posters.

The legal standard in this case is not how the boss feels, but 25 whether a "reasonable woman" might object to being surrounded by such posters. The company has other products it could display. Barbara has not insisted that the company refuse this account or exclude these posters from the company portfolio. She has merely said she doesn't want the posters displayed around *her* desk. Barbara's view is substantiated by how she's been treated; the posters seem to give customers license to make suggestive remarks to her.

Scenario 4: Therese tells Andrew, her subordinate, that she needs him to escort her to a party. She says she's selecting him because he's the most handsome guy on her staff. Andrew says he's busy. Therese responds that she expects people on her staff to be team players.

Therese may have wanted Andrew merely to accompany her to the party, not to have a sexual relationship with her. And Andrew might have been willing to go along if he hadn't been busy. Nevertheless, a reasonable employee may worry about what the boss means by such a request, particularly when it's coupled with remarks about personal appearance.

Andrew might not mind that Therese finds him handsome. But most people would object to having their job tied to their willingness to make a social appearance with the boss outside of work. The implicit threat also makes Therese's request unacceptable. The company should prohibit managers from requiring subordinates to escort them to social engagements.

Scenario 5: Darlene invites her co-worker Dan for a date. They begin a relationship that lasts several months. Then Darlene decides she is no longer interested and breaks up with Dan. He wants the relationship to continue. During the workday, he frequently calls her on the interoffice phone and stops by her desk to talk. Darlene tries to brush him off, but with no success. She asks her manager to intervene. The manager says he doesn't get involved in personal matters.

Most managers are rightly reluctant to involve themselves in employees' personal relationships. Had Darlene asked for help dealing with Dan outside of work, the manager would have been justified in staying out of it. He could have referred her to the employee assistance program, if the company had one.

Once Dan starts interfering with Darlene's work, however, it's a different story. The company has an obligation to make sure the work environment is free from harassment. If Darlene finds herself less able to do her job or uncomfortable at work because of Dan and if her own efforts have failed, the manager has both the right and the responsibility to step in and tell Dan to back off.

Scenario 6: Susan likes to tell bawdy jokes. Bob objects. Although he doesn't mind when men use such language in the office, he doesn't think it's appropriate for women to do so.

An employee who objects to off-color jokes shouldn't have to listen to them at work, and management should back him up. Bob's problem, however, is restricted to jokes told by women. If he doesn't have the same problem when men tell such jokes, it's his problem — not the company's. Management can't enforce Bob's double standard.

Scenario 7: Janet is wearing a low-cut blouse and short shorts. John, her co-worker, says, "Now that I can see it, you gotta let me have some." Janet tells him to buzz off. All day, despite Janet's objections,

John continues to make similar remarks. When Janet calls her supervisor over to complain, John says, "Hey, can you blame me?"

The company has a right to expect clothing appropriate to the 35
job. If Janet's clothes are inappropriate, management should tell her
so. But Janet's outfit doesn't give John license to say or do whatever
he likes. Once she tells him she doesn't like his comments, he
should stop — or be made to do so.

Scenario 8:   Someone posts a Hustler *magazine centerfold in the
employee men's room. No women use this room.*

Some would say that if the women aren't aware of the pinups in
the men's room, they can't be offensive. But when men walk out of the
restroom with such images in their mind's eye, how do they view their
female co-workers? And when the women find out about the pinups
— as they will — how will they feel? As the judge ruled in a 1991
Florida case involving nude posters at a shipyard, the presence of
such pictures, even if they aren't intended to offend women, "sexualizes the work environment to the detriment of all female employees."

A Common-Sense Definition

Sexual harassment is not complicated to define. To harass someone is to bother him or her. Sexual harassment is bothering someone in a sexual way. The harasser offers sexual attention to someone
who didn't ask for it and doesn't welcome it. The unwelcome behavior might or might not involve touching. It could just as well be spoken words, graphics, gestures, or even looks (not any look — but
the kind of leer or stare that says, "I want to undress you").

Who decides what behavior is offensive at the workplace? The
recipient does. As long as the recipient is "reasonable" and not unduly sensitive, sexual conduct that offends him or her should be
changed.

That doesn't mean there's a blueprint for defining sexual harass- 40
ment. "Reasonable" people don't always agree. Society celebrates
pluralism. Not everyone is expected to have the same standards of
morality or the same sense of humor. Still, reasonable people will
agree *much of the time* about what constitutes offensive behavior or
will recognize that certain behavior or language can be expected to
offend some others. Most people make distinctions between how
they talk to their best friends, to their children, and to their elderly
relatives. Out of respect, they avoid certain behavior in the presence
of certain people. The same distinctions must be applied at work.

Sexual harassment is different from the innocent mistake — that
is, when someone tells an off-color joke, not realizing the listener will
be offended, or gives what is meant as a friendly squeeze of the arm to
a co-worker who doesn't like to be touched. Such behavior may repre-

sent insensitivity, and that may be a serious problem, but it's usually not sexual harassment. In many cases, the person who tells the joke that misfires or who pats an unreceptive arm *knows right away* that he or she has made a mistake. Once aware or made aware, this individual will usually apologize and try not to do it again.

Do They Mean It?

Some offensive behavior stems from what University of Illinois psychologist Louise Fitzgerald calls "cultural lag." "Many men entered the workplace at a time when sexual teasing and innuendo were commonplace," Fitzgerald told the *New York Times*. "They have no idea there's anything wrong with it." Education will help such men change their behavior.

True harassers, on the other hand, *mean* to offend. Even when they know their talk or action is offensive, they continue. Sexual harassment is defined as behavior that is not only unwelcome but *repeated*. (Some kinds of behavior are *always* inappropriate, however, even if they occur only once. Grabbing someone's breast or crotch, for example, or threatening to fire a subordinate who won't engage in sexual activity does not need repetition to be deemed illegal.)

The true harasser acts not out of insensitivity but precisely because of the knowledge that the behavior will make the recipient uncomfortable. The harasser derives pleasure from the momentary or continuing powerlessness of the other individual. In some cases, the harasser presses the victim to have sex, but sexual pleasure itself is not the goal. Instead, the harasser's point is to dominate, to gain power over another. As University of Washington psychologist John Gottman puts it, "Harassment is a way for a man to make a woman vulnerable."

Some harassers target the people they consider the most likely   45
to be embarrassed and the least likely to file a charge. Male harassers are sometimes attempting to put "uppity women" in their place. In certain previously all-male workplaces, a woman who's simply attempting to do her job may be considered uppity. In this instance, the harassment is designed to make the woman feel out of place, if not to pressure her out of the job. Such harassment often takes place in front of an audience or is recounted to others afterwards ("pinch and tell").

Dr. Frances Conley, the renowned neurosurgeon who quit her job at Stanford Medical School after nearly twenty-five years of harassment, told legislators at a sexual harassment hearing in San Diego, California, that the "unsolicited touching, caressing, comments about my physical attributes" she experienced "were always for effect in front of an audience. . . ."

Part of the Job

Some harassers who don't consciously set out to offend are nevertheless unwilling to curb their behavior even after they're told it's offensive. If a woman doesn't like it, they figure that's her problem. And some harassers consider sexual favors from subordinates to be a "perk," as much a part of the job as a big mahogany desk and a private executive bathroom. A young woman on President Lyndon Johnson's staff, according to *A Sexual Profile of Men in Power* (Prentice-Hall, 1977), by Sam Janus and others, "was awakened in her bedroom on his Texas ranch in the middle of the night by a searching flashlight. Before she could scream, she heard a familiar voice: 'Move over. This is your president.'"

Men can be harassed by women, or both harasser and victim can be of the same sex. Overwhelmingly, however, sexual harassment is an injury inflicted on women by men. While the number of hard-core harassers is small, their presence is widely felt. Sexual harassment is ugly. And it's damaging — to the victims, to business, and to society as a whole.

DEFINING SEXUAL HARASSMENT   .

Sexual harassment means bothering someone in a sexual way.

Sexual harassment is behavior that is not only unwelcome but in most cases *repeated*.

The goal of sexual harassment is not sexual pleasure but gaining power over another.

Some male harassers want to put "uppity women" in their place.

The essence of combating sexual harassment is fostering mutual respect in the workplace.

Reading and Discussion Questions

1. What characteristics make this essay easy to read? Why do you think the authors have chosen to make their definition so accessible?
2. Most of the essay is devoted to specific examples. Where do the authors give a general definition of sexual harassment? Does the definition seem too broad or too narrow? Explain.
3. Why is the use of specific examples a particularly effective strategy for defining sexual harassment?
4. The authors say, " 'Reasonable' people will agree *much of the time* about what constitutes offensive behavior. . . ." Are there any examples of sexual harassment in this article with which you disagree? If so, explain your objection.
5. How would you characterize the tone of the article? Does it contribute to the effectiveness of the definition? Tell why or why not.

Writing Suggestions

6. Consider the reasons that sexual harassment has become a national issue. What social, political, and economic factors might account for the rise in complaints and public attention? Are some reasons more important than others?
7. The Clarence Thomas–Anita Hill case in October 1991 was a nationally televised hearing on sexual harassment which continues to reverberate. Look up the facts in several national news magazines. Then summarize them and come to a conclusion of your own about the justice of the accusations, emphasizing those areas of the debate that support your claim.

Heroes on Our Doorstep

MIKE BARNICLE

On the sidewalk outside Children's Hospital yesterday, the nurse stood in the breezy sunlight smoking a cigarette and eating an apple for lunch. As soon as she finished one Marlboro, her hand went right to the pack for another.

"Don't start," she said, "I know all about it. I've quit a hundred times. The problem is I've gone back a hundred and one."

"Maybe it's the job?" she was told.

"Nah," she laughed. "It's me. It's just me. I'm a weak individual."

She has been a nurse for a long time. She tends to children who 5 show up here looking for miracles. The kids come with cancer, a disease that does not discriminate, an often fatal illness that feeds on the human system without regard to any calendar: four or fifty-four, it doesn't matter to cancer.

She is part of a staff — doctors, nurses, even orderlies — who minister to the dying. The patients arrive from all over this country. Some buy time. Some others die on the ward.

"You see how some of these little children fight," the nurse was saying. "You see how brave they are and in its own way it is kind of thrilling to be part of the experience because you feel blessed to be among them, they are so strong."

"They are sick but they are strong. They have this spirit, you know," she said. "Certainly, it's sad but it's also uplifting because they have so much courage they make you feel good. They don't feel sorry for themselves. They deal with their situation and they make you deal with it too."

Mike Barnicle writes a thrice-weekly column in the *Boston Globe*, where this selection appeared on June 21, 1994.

O. J. Simpson made more in a month than this woman earned in the last two years. And for a week, all I have read in the paper, over and over again, is the constant reference to him as a hero, fallen now from a pedestal.

We have a horrendous problem in this country with violence and disorder of every kind. We have become adept at making excuses, creating legal loopholes and avoiding any framework of individual responsibility. All this is common knowledge.

But we may have a larger problem of semantics, with the use and application of language and labels. We constantly confuse heroism with celebrity, figuring that because someone is famous or skilled at a specific task — carrying a football, hitting a baseball, acting out a scene in a movie — that they are mythic figures incapable of disappointing us with any of the evils committed by ordinary human beings. We consistently misinterpret what these people do on a field or a sound stage with who they are. But neither life nor individuals are that simple.

Yet we do it all the time: We confuse wealth with wisdom, figuring anyone worth millions must be smart. We rush to attach ourselves emotionally to people who are pretty, people who score touchdowns, sing songs on MTV, play great parts in action movies. We want to feel good about the famous so we allow them to lead make-believe lives, our very own contrivance, in the desperate hope that we will somehow feel better about ourselves because we heard or read or saw that this false idol or that creation of some political consultant was nice.

And as a result of being star-struck, we rarely notice the courage at our doorstep or heroes on the sidewalk alongside us. Firefighters rush into burning buildings seeking to save total strangers and it is only when one dies that we take the time to pay attention. Nurses labor with kids who cry from chemotherapy, holding them, hugging them, often willing life back into them and we take it for granted. Teachers act as educators, surrogate parents, and drug counselors and we resent their demand for higher pay. Police throw their bodies between the lawless and the innocent and their reward is a never-ending level of dissatisfaction because crime, like cancer, grows everywhere. There are mothers and fathers with several jobs who struggle to keep families together while their kids attend schools where others show up with handguns instead of history books.

This is an increasingly strange country, made more so by the foolish clamor over celebrity. It is a country in danger of losing what little is left of our institutional memory, a mental safeguard that allows us to establish priorities of what and who is truly important, based on performance as well as history. It is a country with the attention span of a cricket, where instant gratification is paramount: I want it now, with no effort and if I don't like it I will toss it out; doesn't matter what it is either — a marriage, a relationship, a pregnancy, a friend.

O. J. Simpson was a wonderful athlete who beat up a woman and   15 may even have killed her. He was famous and gifted but never a hero. To find one of them, you have to stand on a city sidewalk and stare at a nurse who can't quit cigarettes because her nerves are frazzled from caring for all the dying children.

Reading and Discussion Questions

1. How does Barnicle make the transition from the nurse's comments to his definition of heroism? Is it effective? Why or why not?
2. Point out the use of transitional words and phrases that establish connections.
3. Barnicle changes his use of language at some point in the essay. What is the purpose of the change?
4. According to Barnicle, what is the outstanding characteristic of true heroism? Summarize his definition of heroism in one sentence.
5. Do you agree with Barnicle about our confusion of heroism with celebrity? Is he also right in arguing that our regard for celebrities "somehow [makes us] feel better about ourselves"?
6. As you read his list of the kinds of people to whom we attach ourselves emotionally, did the names of real people come to mind? Would his argument have been more persuasive if the author had mentioned real people by name?
7. In the next-to-last paragraph, Barnicle recommends establishing priorities that are truly important, "based on performance as well as history." How is this related to a discussion of a nurse and O. J. Simpson?

Writing Suggestions

8. In one class a student remarked that a man who had risked his life to save a stranger from drowning was not a hero but a fool, since the life of the rescuer, which might have been lost, was just as valuable as that of the stranger. (The sentiment expressed by the student is not new. As cited in Dixon Wecter, *The Hero in America* [Ann Arbor: Ann Arbor Paperbacks, 1963], p. 490, a 1914 antiwar poster proclaimed that anyone "who gave an arm or a leg for his country was 'a sucker'".) Write an essay agreeing or disagreeing with the student. Try to make clear a definition of heroism that would include or exclude the action of the would-be rescuer.
9. Can you think of someone you once regarded as a hero or heroine about whom you feel differently now? Is it because your own values have changed? If so, what caused the change?
10. If you have knowledge of a culture with different values from those of most Americans, describe a hero or heroine who exemplifies the virtues of that culture. Point out both the differences and the similarities.

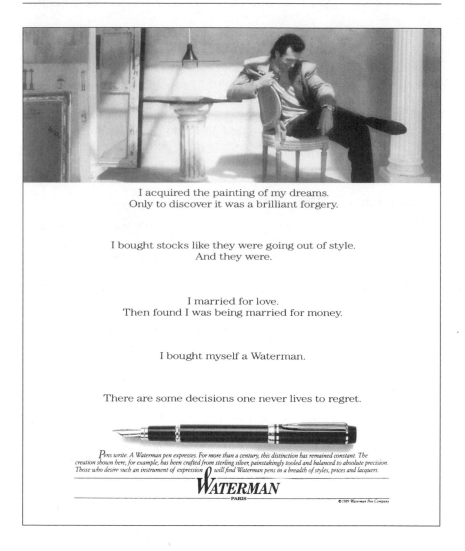

I acquired the painting of my dreams.
Only to discover it was a brilliant forgery.

I bought stocks like they were going out of style.
And they were.

I married for love.
Then found I was being married for money.

I bought myself a Waterman.

There are some decisions one never lives to regret.

Pens write. A Waterman pen expresses. For more than a century, this distinction has remained constant. The creation shown here, for example, has been crafted from sterling silver, painstakingly tooled and balanced to absolute precision. Those who desire such an instrument of expression will find Waterman pens in a breadth of styles, prices and lacquers.

WATERMAN
—— PARIS ——

© 1989 Waterman Pen Company

Discussion Questions

1. This ad is divided into two parts. The part in small print extols the distinctive attributes of the Waterman pen. Why does the advertiser relegate the description of his pen to the small print?
2. How does the advertiser define a superior "instrument of expression"? Does calling a pen an "instrument of expression" add something to the definition?
3. What contrast is the reader invited to examine in the humorous first part of the ad?

Penalize the Unwed Dad?
Fat Chance

LISA SCHIFFREN

America faces no problem more urgent than our skyrocketing illegitimacy rate. Last year, 30 percent of all babies were born out of wedlock, and the rate is expected to rise. Illegitimacy almost always sentences children to a life struggling against overwhelming odds that they will be poor and poorly educated and, for girls, prone to repeating the cycle of unwed motherhood and dependence on welfare.

For teenage mothers, completing school and acquiring marketable skills become major struggles. Marriage becomes less likely. Seventy-five percent of families headed by unmarried women live on $25,000 a year or less. The higher earners in that group are divorced; the income of most never-married mothers hovers between zero and the poverty line. In a society where work and marriage are the I-beams of a middle-class life, nothing that encourages illegitimacy can be considered in the interest of women or children.

It is important to keep these facts in mind when the Senate resumes its work on welfare reform next month. For even though all sides in the debate cite them repeatedly, few proposals actually address them.

The length of benefits and the work requirements for them may have some marginal effect on the people now receiving welfare. But considering the failure of every workfare program ever devised, tinkering is unlikely to help most of those who are in the system to transcend it.

The first goal should be to prevent girls who are not yet trapped 5 from having babies. The way to begin is to cut off the most obvious distorting incentives — cash, housing, and other subsidies — given to unwed teens for self-destructive decisions.

President Clinton recently asserted that there is a consensus not to do any such thing because it would punish innocent children.

How then would he change behavior? Like the feminist-welfare advocacy lobby, he would blame men. And along with Senator Bob

---

This article by Lisa Schiffren, a former speechwriter for Vice President Dan Quayle, appeared in the *New York Times* on August 10, 1995.

Dole, he believes that intensified efforts to get "deadbeat dads" of illegitimate children to pay child support and become involved in their children's lives will solve the problem.

The idea of punishing men for seduction and desertion is of course attractive. Unfortunately, it won't work. The nation already spends nearly $2 billion a year on child support enforcement, with state bureaucracies employing 40,000 people to collect money from divorced and never-married fathers.

Census Bureau data show that nearly 80 percent of the divorced women entitled to child support receive payments, while only 12 percent of women on Aid to Families with Dependent Children receive even negligible sums from their children's fathers.

But increased enforcement won't significantly narrow the gap. A 10 disproportionate number of unmarried fathers are unemployed, unemployable, or too young to work. Liberals were right when they argued that getting these men to pay was like squeezing blood from a stone.

Beyond that, it is bad policy for the state to enforce a contract that does not exist. We make divorced fathers support children they don't live with because marriage carries an obligation to offspring. Casual sex and teenage romance carries no such obligation. When teenagers are impregnated by older men or under coercive circumstances, the policy answers, in effect, are rape and statutory rape charges.

Blurring the distinction between legitimacy and illegitimacy undermines marriage at the very moment it most needs to be strengthened. (Notice how successfully liberals have destroyed the moral and substantive differences between divorced or widowed mothers and never-married mothers — all of whom we now call "single mothers.")

What teenage girls need most is a brutally realistic picture of what their lives will be like if they choose unwed motherhood. Society's unenforceable promise to make casual sexual partners behave like real fathers sends the wrong message. After all, as middle-class women learned during the sexual revolution, a man who indicates that he is interested in sex but not commitment should always be taken at his word.

Even granting that the men involved are scum, the inescapable fact is that women bear children. Since women and girls have sexual autonomy, they can and should be held accountable for how they use it. Before I am accused of blaming the victim, or wishing to deny women sexual freedom, recall that the women in question are not the classic victim caricature that the feminist-welfare lobby likes to cite. These are not wives bound by law or financial dependence to husbands. They are single women who control economic resources, in this case the AFDC check.

Contraception to prevent pregnancy is available — including 15 Norplant, Depo-Provera, and the pill. Abortion is an option.

Girls have the same educational opportunities and most of the economic opportunities boys have. This makes the choice of dependence less acceptable for poor women, just as it has for middle-class women.

The most useful thing we can do for girls on the verge of becoming welfare mothers is to make education, work, and marriage preferable to subsisting on a welfare check.

Sins of the Fathers

JOSEPH P. SHAPIRO and ANDREA R. WRIGHT

The problem with teen sex is not simply that teens are having sex. Adults, in disturbing numbers, are having sex with teens. It is not just Joey Buttafuoco and Amy Fisher, Woody Allen and Soon-Yi Previn or the fact that O. J. Simpson was thirty when he began dating an eighteen-year-old waitress named Nicole Brown. Federal and state surveys suggest that adult males are the fathers of some two-thirds of the babies born to teenage girls. According to the Alan Guttmacher Institute, 39 percent of fifteen-year-old mothers say the fathers of their babies are twenty years old or older. For seventeen-year-old teenage moms, 55 percent of the fathers are adults; for nineteen-year-olds, it is 78 percent.

Little inspires more national hand-wringing these days than the reality of teenage pregnancy. Americans blame impulsive kids and their raging hormones, ignoring the role of adult males. But in fact, teenage girls having sex with men is hardly a new phenomenon. In 1920, for example, 93 percent of babies born to teenagers were fathered by adults. What has changed is that more often than not, pregnant teens no longer marry the father. Today, 65 percent of teenage moms are unmarried, up from 48 percent in 1980. These teens and their children are at high risk of poverty, school failure, and welfare dependency.

Welfare reform, sex education, and teen pregnancy prevention programs are doomed to failure when they ignore the prevalence of adult-teen sex. The welfare reform bill passed by the House of Representatives would deny benefits to unmarried mothers under the age of eighteen, a provision that has become one of the most contentious points of the current debate in the Senate. But most studies suggest that curbing benefits alone will not stem the tide of teen pregnancies.

Joseph P. Shapiro is a senior editor and Andrea R. Wright a reporter-researcher at *U.S. News & World Report*, where this article appeared on August 14, 1995.

What drives teenage girls to become sexually involved with adult males is complex, and often does not follow the logic of Washington policymakers. In the minds of many teens, choosing an older boyfriend makes sense. Francisca Cativo was a sixteen-year-old high school junior when her daughter, Vanessa, was born last September. Her boyfriend, Jose Confesor, is twenty-four. To Cativo, who says she chose to get pregnant, Confesor's age was a plus; it meant he was more mature and more likely to support her child. "The boys around my age just want to be out in the streets playing around," she says. Still, on Confesor's salary as a part-time janitor, the couple is forced to live with his mother in a crowded apartment.

Older men seek out young girls for equally complex reasons — from believing there is less risk of disease to more chance of control. They often hold exaggerated power over their young companions. When teens get pregnant, for example, they are half as likely to have an abortion when their partners are twenty or older.

More disturbing, a sizable amount of teen sex is not consensual. Girls under the age of eighteen are the victims of about half of the nation's rapes each year, according to Justice Department data. When researchers Debra Boyer and David Fine surveyed poor and pregnant teens at Washington State's public health clinics, they were startled to find that two-thirds of these girls reported prior sexual abuse, almost always by parents, guardians, or relatives. Even more shocking: On average, the girls were less than ten years old at the time of the first abuse while the offending male was twenty-seven.

Other adult-teen relationships simply blur the lines between unwanted and consensual sex. Eilene Stanley, who runs a Big Sisters teen-parent program in Tacoma, Washington, says girls — particularly those from broken families or who have been abused — are easy prey for men who show the smallest kindness, even something as simple as giving flowers.

"The justice system does not take care of these girls," complains Hazel Woods-Welborne, who runs a San Diego school program for teenage mothers. Police refused her request to invoke statutory-rape laws and prosecute a fifty-one-year-old man who had a child by a supposedly willing thirteen-year-old. Woods-Welborne is also disturbed by the recent increase in relationships between very young teens and older men. "I'm talking about twelve, thirteen, fourteen-year-old girls. Most times, they cannot even spell intercourse."

The role played by older men raises doubts about pregnancy-prevention programs aimed at teens. "It's hard to teach teens about sex if one of the sexual partners is not sitting in the classroom," notes Kristin Moore of the research group Child Trends. She points to the adult-teen–sex numbers as one reason why high school sex education classes have failed to curb teen pregnancy rates, which after several years of leveling off have been climbing since 1987, fueled primarily by increases among white teens. One answer, Moore says, is to extend sex education to where the boys are — to such places as vocational schools and the military.

Similarly, welfare reform can work only if it targets both teenage 10 moms and their adult partners. Some legislative plans, including ones put forward by Senate Majority Leader Bob Dole and President Clinton, would give cash payments to pregnant girls only if they lived with a parent or another responsible adult. But to Tina in Tacoma, getting pregnant was a conscious decision that had nothing to do with the size of her welfare check. Tina left home at fifteen when her parents objected to her twenty-one-year-old boyfriend, Rocky. She says her parents would have insisted that she give up her son, Kevin, for adoption and end her relationship with Rocky. Three years later, Rocky and Tina plan to marry soon. Her child, she says, gives her the type of bond "I never had with my mom or with my dad."

Welfare reformers have recognized that adult fathers are more likely to hold jobs and be able to pay child support. Most welfare proposals would require hospitals to establish paternity at birth and then create a national database of fathers' names, so that men who refused to support a child would have their wages withheld or lose their driver's licenses. Yet there are limits to how much money can be collected: One Baltimore study found that 32 percent of the adult male partners of teenage girls were neither working nor in school at the time of a child's birth.

Still, teenage girls have become convenient scapegoats for what are really adult problems, argues Mike Males, a graduate student at the University of California at Irvine who has written extensively on adult-teen sex. Indeed, teenage pregnancy patterns are not that different from those of adults: Rates of pregnancy among teens correlate more closely to class and ethnic background than they do to age demographics. Motherhood outside of marriage is on the rise for women of all ages. According to Child Trends, in 1991, for the first time, women over twenty accounted for more of the first births to unmarried women than did teenage girls. While single motherhood is becoming more acceptable for adult women, it remains a stigma for the unmarried teenage mother. As yet, there is little censure for the adult partners of these teenage girls.

Discussion Questions

1. A great deal has been written about the reasons that teenage girls choose to become pregnant. Do some research to discover what the experts say. Do these two debate articles address any of the reasons?
2. Schiffren suggests making "education, work and marriage preferable to subsisting on a welfare check." But she is vague about how to achieve

this. If you have ideas about solutions, write a paper defending one or two ideas.

3. The two articles take opposite sides on the question of primary responsibility for teenage pregnancy. Do you find one view more persuasive than the other? Explain why.

4. Both authors suggest reasons for the failure of attempted solutions to the problem. What explanations do they offer? Can you think of others?

EXERCISES

1. Choose one of the following statements and define the italicized term. Make the context as specific as possible (for example, by referring to the Declaration of Independence or your own experience).
   a. All men are created *equal.*
   b. I believe in *God.*
   c. This school doesn't offer a *liberal education.*
   d. The marine corps needs *good men.*
   e. *Friends* is a *better* television show than *Seinfeld.*

2. Many recent controversial movements and causes are identified by terms that have come to mean different things to different people. Choose one of the following and define it, explaining both the favorable and unfavorable connotations of the term. Use examples to clarify the meaning.
   a. comparative worth
   b. Palestinian homeland
   c. affirmative action
   d. co-dependency
   e. nationalism

3. Choose two words that are sometimes confused and define them to make their differences clear. *Examples:* authoritarianism and totalitarianism; envy and jealousy; sympathy and pity; cult and established church; justice and equality; liberal and radical; agnostic and atheist.

4. Define a good parent, a good teacher, a good husband or wife. Try to uncover the assumptions on which your definition is based. (For example, in defining a good teacher, students sometimes mention the ability of the teacher to maintain order. Does this mean that the teacher alone is responsible for classroom order?)

5. Define any popular form of entertainment, such as the soap opera, western, detective story, or science fiction story or film. Support your definition with references to specific shows or books. *Or* define an idealized type from fiction, film, the stage, advertising, or television, describing the chief attributes of that type and the principal reasons for its popularity.

6. From your own experience write an essay describing a serious misunderstanding that arose because two people had different meanings for a term they were using.

7. Write about an important or widely used term whose meaning has changed since you first learned it. Such terms often come from the

slang of particular groups: drug users, rock music fans, musicians, athletes, computer programmers or software developers.

8. Define the differences between *necessities, comforts,* and *luxuries.* Consider how they have changed over time.

Critical Listening

9. Listen for several nights to the local or national news on television or radio. Keep a record of the *kinds* of news items that are repeated. How do you think news is defined by the broadcasters? Is it relevant that radio, TV, and film have been characterized as the "dramatic media"? Is the definition of broadcast news different from that of the print media? If so, how do you account for it?

10. You and your friends have probably often argued about subjects that required definition — for example, a good teacher, a good parent, a good popular singer or band, a good movie or TV show. Think of a specific discussion. Were you able to reach agreement? How did the acts of listening and talking affect the outcome?

CHAPTER FIVE

Support

TYPES OF SUPPORT: EVIDENCE AND APPEALS TO NEEDS AND VALUES

All the claims you make — whether of fact, of value, or of policy — must be supported. Support for a claim represents the answer to the question, "What have you got to go on?"[1] There are two basic kinds of support in an argument: evidence and appeals to needs and values.

Evidence, as one dictionary defines it, is "something that tends to prove; ground for belief." When you provide evidence, you use facts, including statistics, and opinions, or interpretations of facts, both your own and those of experts. In the following conversation, the first speaker offers facts and the opinion of an expert to convince the second speaker that robots are exceptional machines.

> *"You know, robots do a lot more than work on assembly lines in factories."*
>
> *"Like what?"*
>
> *"They shear sheep, pick citrus fruit, and even assist in neurosurgery. And by the end of the century, every house will have a robot slave."*
>
> *"No kidding. Who says so?"*
>
> *"An engineer who's the head of the world's largest manufacturer of industrial robots."*

---

[1]Stephen Toulmin, *The Uses of Argument* (Cambridge: Cambridge University Press, 1958), p. 98.

A writer often appeals to readers' needs, that is, requirements for physical and psychological survival and well-being, and values, or standards for right and wrong, good and bad. In the following conversation, the first speaker makes an appeal to the universal need for self-esteem and to the principle of helping others, a value the second speaker probably shares.

> *"I think you ought to come help us at the nursing home. We need an extra hand."*
>
> *"I'd like to, but I really don't have the time."*
>
> *"You could give us an hour a week, couldn't you? Think how good you'd feel about helping out, and the old people would be so grateful. Some of them are very lonely."*

Although they use the same kinds of support, conversations are less rigorous than arguments addressed to larger audiences in academic or public situations. In the debates on public policy that appear in the media and in the courts, the quality of support can be crucial in settling urgent matters. The following summary of a well-known court case demonstrates the critical use of both evidence and value appeals in the support of opposing claims.

On March 30, 1981, President Ronald Reagan and three other men were shot by John W. Hinckley, Jr., a young drifter from a wealthy Colorado family. Hinckley was arrested at the scene of the shooting. In his trial the factual evidence was presented first: There were dozens of reliable witnesses who had seen the shooting at close range. Hinckley's diaries, letters, and poems revealed that he had planned the shooting to impress actress Jodie Foster. Opinions, consisting of testimony by experts, were introduced by both the defense and the prosecution. This evidence was contradictory. Defense attorneys produced several psychiatrists who defined Hinckley as insane. If this interpretation of his conduct convinced the jury, then Hinckley would be confined to a mental hospital rather than a prison. The prosecution introduced psychiatrists who interpreted Hinckley's motives and actions as those of a man who knew what he was doing and knew it was wrong. They claimed he was *not* insane by legal definition. The fact that experts can make differing conclusions about the meaning of the same information indicates that interpretations are less reliable than other kinds of support.

Finally, the defense made an appeal to the moral values of the jury. Under the law, criminals judged to be insane are not to be punished as harshly as criminals judged to be sane. The laws assume that criminals who cannot be held responsible for their actions are entitled to more compassionate treatment, confinement to a mental hospital rather than prison. The jury accepted the interpretive evidence supporting the claim of the defense, and Hinckley was pronounced not guilty by reason of insanity. Clearly the moral concern for the rights of the insane proved to be decisive.

In your arguments you will advance your claims, not unlike a lawyer, with these same kinds of support. But before you begin, you should ask two questions: Which kind of support should I use in convincing an audience to accept my claim? and How do I decide that each item of support is valid and worthy of acceptance? This chapter presents the different types of evidence and appeals you can use to support your claim and examines the criteria by which you can evaluate the soundness of that support.

EVIDENCE

Factual Evidence

In Chapter 3, we defined facts as statements possessing a high degree of public acceptance. In theory, facts can be verified by experience alone. Eating too much will make us sick; we can get from Hopkinton to Boston in a half hour by car; in the Northern Hemisphere it is colder in December than in July. The experience of any individual is limited in both time and space, so we must accept as fact thousands of assertions about the world that we ourselves can never verify. Thus we accept the report that human beings landed on the moon in 1969 because we trust those who can verify it. (Country people in Morocco, however, received the news with disbelief because they had no reason to trust the reporters of the event. They insisted on trusting their senses instead. One man said, "I can see the moon very clearly. If a man were walking around up there, wouldn't I be able to see him?")

Factual evidence appears most frequently as examples and statistics, which are a numerical form of examples.

Examples

Examples are the most familiar kind of factual evidence. In addition to providing support for the truth of a generalization, examples can enliven otherwise dense or monotonous prose.

In the following paragraph the writer supports the claim in the topic sentence by offering a series of specific examples. (The article claims that most airport security is useless.)

> Meanwhile, seven hijacking incidents occurred last year (twenty-one in 1980 and eleven the year before), despite the security system. Two involved the use of flammable liquids. . . . In four other cases, hijackers claimed to have flammables or explosives but turned

out to be bluffing. In the only incident involving a gun, a man brushed past the security system and brandished the weapon on the plane before being wrestled to the ground. One other hijacking was aborted on the ground, and the remaining five were concluded after some expense, fright, and delay — but no injuries or deaths.[2]

Hypothetical examples, which create imaginary situations for the audience and encourage them to visualize what might happen under certain circumstances, can also be effective. The following paragraph, taken from the same article as the preceding paragraph, illustrates the use of hypothetical examples.

> But weapons can get through nonetheless. Some are simply over-looked; imagine being one of those 10,000 "screeners" staring at X-rayed baggage, day in and day out. Besides, a gun can be broken down into unrecognizable parts and reassembled past the checkpoint. A hand grenade can be hidden in an aerosol shaving-cream can or a photographer's lens case. The ingredients of a Molotov cocktail can be carried on quite openly; any bottle of, say, duty-free liquor or perfume can be emptied and refilled with gasoline. And the possibilities for bluffing should not be forgotten; once on board, anyone could claim that a bottle of water was really a Molotov cocktail, or that a paper bag contained a bomb.[3]

All claims about vague or abstract terms would be boring or un-intelligible without examples to illuminate them. For example, if you claim that a movie contains "unusual sound effects," you will certainly have to describe some of the effects to convince the reader that your generalization can be trusted.

Statistics

Statistics express information in numbers. In the following example statistics have been used to express raw data in numerical form.

> Surveys have shown that almost half of all male high school seniors — and nearly 20 percent of all ninth grade boys — can be called "problem drinkers." . . . Over 5,000 teenagers are killed yearly in auto accidents due to drunken driving.[4]

These grim numbers probably have meaning for you, partly because you already know that alcoholism exists even among young teenagers and partly because your own experience enables you to evaluate the numbers. But if you are unfamiliar with the subject, such numbers

---

[2]Patrick Brogan, "The $310 Million Paranoia Subsidy," *Harper's*, September 1982, p. 18.

[3]Ibid.

[4]"The Kinds of Drugs Kids Are Getting Into" (Spring House, Pa.: McNeil Pharmaceutical, n.d.).

may be difficult or impossible to understand. Statistics, therefore, are more effective in comparisons that indicate whether a quantity is relatively large or small and sometimes even whether a reader should interpret the result as gratifying or disappointing. For example, if a novice gambler were told that for every dollar wagered in a state lottery, 50 percent goes back to the players as prizes, would the gambler be able to conclude that the percentage is high or low? Would he be able to choose between playing the state lottery and playing a casino game? Unless he had more information, probably not. But if he were informed that in casino games, the return to the players is over 90 percent and in slot machines and racetracks the return is around 80 percent, the comparison would enable him to evaluate the meaning of the 50 percent return in the state lottery and even to make a decision about where to gamble his money.[5]

Comparative statistics are also useful for measurements over time. A national survey by The Institute for Social Research of the University of Michigan, in which 17,000 of the nation's 2.7 million high school seniors were questioned about their use of drugs, revealed a continuing downward trend.

> 50.9 percent of those questioned in 1989 reported that they had at least tried an illicit drug like marijuana or cocaine, as against 53.9 percent in 1988 and 56.6 percent in 1987.[6]

Diagrams, tables, charts, and graphs can make clear the relations among many sets of numbers. Such charts and diagrams allow readers to grasp the information more easily than if it were presented in paragraph form. The bar graph[7] that is shown on page 143 summarizes the information produced by a poll on gambling habits. A pie chart[8] such as the one on page 144 can also clarify lists of data.

Opinions: Interpretations of the Facts

We have seen how opinions of experts influenced the verdict in the trial of John Hinckley. Facts alone were not enough to substantiate the claim that Hinckley was guilty of attempted assassination. Both the defense and the prosecution relied on experts — psychiatrists — to interpret the facts. Opinions or interpretations about the facts are the inferences discussed in Chapter 3. They are an indispensable source of support for your claims.

Suppose a nightclub for teenagers has opened in your town. That is a fact. What is the significance of it? Is the club's existence

---

[5]Curt Suphee, "Lotto Baloney," *Harper's,* July 1983, p. 201.
[6]*New York Times,* February 14, 1990, Sec. A, p. 16.
[7]*New York Times,* May 28, 1989, p. 24.
[8]*Wall Street Journal,* February 2, 1990, Sec. B, p. 1.

Want to Bet?

Please tell me whether or not you have done any of the following in the past 12 months:

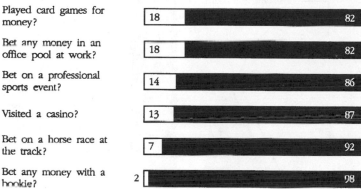

Based on a phone survey of 1,412 people nationwide conducted April 13–16, 1989.

Bar graph

good or bad? What consequences will it have for the community? Some parents oppose the idea of a nightclub, fearing that it may allow teenagers to escape from parental control and engage in dangerous activities. Other parents approve of a club, hoping that it will serve as a substitute for unsupervised congregation in the streets. The importance of these interpretations is that they, not the fact itself, help people decide what actions they should take. If the community accepts the interpretation that the club is a source of delinquency, they may decide to revoke the owner's license and close it. As one writer puts it, "The interpretation of data becomes a struggle over power."

Opinions or interpretations of facts generally take three forms: (1) They may suggest the cause for a condition or a causal connection between two sets of data; (2) they may offer predictions about the future; (3) they may suggest solutions to a problem.

1. Causal Connection

Anorexia is a serious, sometimes fatal, disease, characterized by self-starvation. It is found largely among young women. Physicians, psychologists, and social scientists have speculated about the causes, which remain unclear. A leading researcher in the field, Hilde Bruch, believes that food refusal expresses a desire to postpone sexual development. Another authority, Joan Blumberg, be-

Plastic that Goes to Waste

Components of municipal solid waste, by volume

Types of plastic in municipal solid waste, by weight

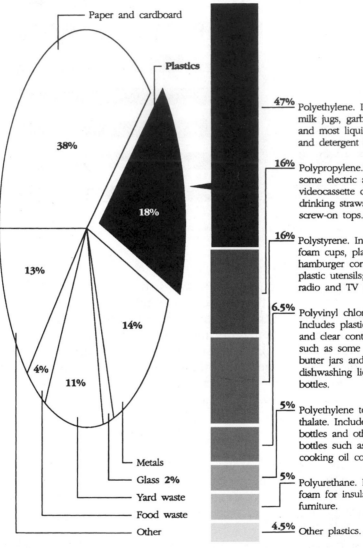

Paper and cardboard

Plastics

38%

18%

13%

14%

4%

11%

Metals

Glass 2%

Yard waste

Food waste

Other

47% Polyethylene. Includes milk jugs, garbage bags, and most liquid soap and detergent bottles.

16% Polypropylene. Includes some electric appliances, videocassette cases, drinking straws, and screw-on tops.

16% Polystyrene. Includes foam cups, plates and hamburger containers; plastic utensils; and radio and TV cabinets.

6.5% Polyvinyl chloride. Includes plastic wrap and clear containers such as some peanut butter jars and dishwashing liquid bottles.

5% Polyethylene tereph-thalate. Includes soda bottles and other clear bottles such as some cooking oil containers.

5% Polyurethane. Includes foam for insulation and furniture.

4.5% Other plastics.

Source: Franklin Associates Ltd.

Pie chart

lieves that one cause may be biological, a nervous dysfunction of the hypothalamus. Still others infer that the causes are cultural, a response to the admiration of the thin female body.[9]

2. Predictions about the Future

In the fall and winter of 1989–1990 extraordinary events shook Eastern Europe, toppling Communist regimes and raising more popular forms of government. Politicians and scholars offered predictions about future changes in the region. One expert, Zbigniew Brzezinski, former national security adviser under President Carter, concluded that the changes for the Soviet Union might be destructive.

> It would be a mistake to see the recent decisions as marking a breakthrough for democracy. Much more likely is a prolonged period of democratizing chaos. One will see the rise in the Soviet Union of increasingly irreconcilable conflicts between varying national political and social aspirations, all united by a shared hatred for the existing Communist nomenklatura. One is also likely to see a flashback of a nationalist type among the Great Russians, fearful of the prospective breakup of the existing Great Russian Empire.[10]

3. Solutions to Problems

How shall we solve the problems caused by young people in our cities "who commit crimes and create the staggering statistics in teenage pregnancies and the high abortion rate"? The minister emeritus of the Abyssinian Baptist Church in New York City proposes establishment of a national youth academy with fifty campuses on inactive military bases. "It is a 'parenting' institution. . . . It is not a penal institution, not a prep school, not a Job Corps Center, not a Civilian Conservation Camp, but it borrows from them." Although such an institution has not been tried before, the author of the proposal thinks that it would represent an effort "to provide for the academic, moral, and social development of young people, to cause them to become responsible and productive citizens."[11]

Expert Opinion

For many of the subjects you discuss and write about, you will find it necessary to accept and use the opinions of experts. Based on their reading of the facts, experts express opinions on a variety of

[9]Phyllis Rose, "Hunger Artists," *Harper's,* July 1988, p. 82.
[10]*New York Times,* February 9, 1990, Sec. A, p. 13.
[11]Samuel D. Proctor, "To the Rescue: A National Youth Academy," *New York Times,* September 16, 1989, Sec. A, p. 27.

controversial subjects: whether capital punishment is a deterrent to crime; whether legalization of marijuana will lead to an increase in its use; whether children, if left untaught, will grow up honest and cooperative; whether sex education courses will result in less sexual activity and fewer illegitimate births. The interpretations of the data are often profoundly important because they influence social policy and affect our lives directly and indirectly.

For the problems mentioned above, the opinions of people recognized as authorities are more reliable than those of people who have neither thought about nor done research on the subject. But opinions may also be offered by student writers in areas in which they are knowledgeable. If you were asked, for example, to defend or refute the statement that work has advantages for teenagers, you could call on your own experience and that of your friends to support your claim. You can also draw on your experience to write convincingly about your special interests.

One opinion, however, is not as good as another. The value of any opinion depends on the quality of the evidence and the trustworthiness of the person offering it.

EVALUATION OF EVIDENCE

Before you begin to write, you must determine whether the facts and opinions you have chosen to support your claim are sound. Can they convince your readers? A distinction between the evaluation of facts and the evaluation of opinions is somewhat artificial because many facts are verified by expert opinion, but for our analysis we discuss them separately.

Evaluation of Factual Evidence

As you evaluate factual evidence, you should keep in mind the following questions:

1. Is the evidence up to date? The importance of up-to-date information depends on the subject. If you are defending the claim that suicide is immoral, you will not need to examine new data. For many of the subjects you write about, recent research and scholarship will be important, even decisive, in proving the soundness of your data. "New" does not always mean "best," but in fields where research is ongoing — education, psychology, technology, medicine, and all the natural and physical sciences — you should be sensitive to the dates of the research.

In writing a paper a few years ago warning about the health hazards of air pollution, you would have used data referring only to outdoor pollution produced by automobile and factory emissions. But writing about air pollution today, you would have to take into account new data about indoor pollution, which has become a serious problem as a result of attempts to conserve energy. Because research studies in indoor pollution are continually being updated, recent evidence will probably be more accurate than past research.

2. Is the evidence sufficient?   The amount of evidence you need depends on the complexity of the subject and the length of your paper. Given the relative brevity of most of your assignments, you will need to be selective. For the claim that indoor pollution is a serious problem, one example would obviously not be enough. For a 750-to-1,000-word paper, three or four examples would probably be sufficient. The choice of examples should reflect different aspects of the problem: in this case, different sources of indoor pollution — gas stoves, fireplaces, kerosene heaters, insulation — and the consequences for health.

Indoor pollution is a fairly limited subject for which the evidence is clear. But more complex problems require more evidence. A common fault in argument is generalization based on insufficient evidence. In a 1,000-word paper you could not adequately treat the causes of conflict in the Middle East; you could not develop workable solutions for the health-care crisis; you could not predict the development of education in the next century. In choosing a subject for a brief paper, determine whether you can produce sufficient evidence to convince a reader who may not agree with you. If not, the subject may be too large for a brief paper.

3. Is the evidence relevant?   All the evidence should, of course, contribute to the development of your argument. Sometimes the arguer loses sight of the subject and introduces examples that are wide of the claim. In defending a national health-care plan, one student offered examples of the success of health maintenance organizations, but such organizations, although subsidized by the federal government, were not the structure favored by sponsors of a national health-care plan. The examples were interesting but irrelevant.

Also keep in mind that not all readers will agree on what is relevant. Is the unsavory private life of a politician relevant to his or her performance in office? If you want to prove that a politician is unfit to serve because of his or her private activities, you may first have to convince some members of the audience that private activities are relevant to public service.

4. Are the examples representative?   This question emphasizes your responsibility to choose examples that are typical of all the examples you do not use. Suppose you offered Vermont's experience to support your claim that passage of a bottle bill would reduce litter. Is the experience of Vermont typical of what is happening or may happen in other states? Or is Vermont, a small, mostly rural New England state, different enough from other states to make the example unrepresentative?

5. Are the examples consistent with the experience of the audience?   The members of your audience use their own experiences to judge the soundness of your evidence. If your examples are unfamiliar or extreme, they will probably reject your conclusion. Consider the following hypothetical description, which is meant to represent the thinking of your generation.

> Imagine coming to a beach at the end of a long summer of wild goings-on. The beach crowd is exhausted, the sand shopworn, hot, and full of debris — no place for walking barefoot. You step on a bottle, and some cop yells at you for littering. The sun is directly overhead and leaves no patch of shade that hasn't already been taken. You feel the glare beating down on a barren landscape devoid of secrets or innocence. You look around at the disapproving faces and can't help but sense, somehow, that the entire universe is gearing up to punish you.
>
> This is how today's young people feel, as members of the 13th generation (born 1961–1981).[12]

If most members of the audience find that such a description doesn't reflect their own expectations or those of their friends, they will probably question the validity of the claim.

Evaluation of Statistics

The questions you must ask about examples also apply to statistics. Are they recent? Are they sufficient? Are they relevant? Are they typical? Are they consistent with the experience of the audience? But there are additional questions directed specifically to evaluation of statistics.

1. Do the statistics come from trustworthy sources?   Perhaps you have read newspaper accounts of very old people, some reported to be as old as 135, living in the Caucasus or the Andes, nourished by yogurt and hard work. But these statistics are hearsay; no birth records or other official documents exist to verify them. Now two anthropologists have concluded that the numbers were part of a rural mythology and that the ages of the people were actually within the normal range for human populations elsewhere.[13]

---

[12]Neil Howe and Bill Strauss, *13th GEN: Abort, Retry, Ignore, Fail?* (New York: Vintage Books, 1993), p. 13.

[13]Richard B. Mazess and Sylvia H. Forman, "Longevity and Age Exaggeration in Vilcabamba, Ecuador," *Journal of Gerontology* (1979), pp. 94–98.

Hearsay statistics should be treated with the same skepticism accorded to gossip or rumor. Sampling a population to gather statistical information is a sophisticated science; you should ask whether the reporter of the statistics is qualified and likely to be free of bias. Among the generally reliable sources are polling organizations such as Gallup, Roper, and Louis Harris and agencies of the U.S. government such as the Census Bureau and the Bureau of Labor Statistics. Other qualified sources are well-known research foundations, university centers, and insurance companies that prepare actuarial tables. Statistics from underdeveloped countries are less reliable for obvious reasons: lack of funds, lack of trained statisticians, lack of communication and transportation facilities to carry out accurate censuses.

2. Are the terms clearly defined? In an example in Chapter 4, the reference to "poverty" (p. 95) made clear that any statistics would be meaningless unless we knew exactly how "poverty" was defined by the user. "Unemployment" is another term for which statistics will be difficult to read if the definition varies from one user to another. For example, are seasonal workers "employed" or "unemployed" during the off-season? Are part-time workers "Employed"? (In Russia they are "unemployed.") Are workers on government projects "employed"? (During the 1930s they were considered "employed" by the Germans and "unemployed" by the Americans.) The more abstract or controversial the term, the greater the necessity for clear definition.

3. Are the comparisons between comparable things? Folk wisdom warns us that we cannot compare apples and oranges. Population statistics for the world's largest city, for example, should indicate the units being compared. Greater London is defined in one way, greater New York in another, and greater Tokyo in still another. The population numbers will mean little unless you can be sure that the same geographical units are being compared.

4. Has any significant information been omitted? *The Plain Truth,* a magazine published by the World-Wide Church of God, advertises itself as follows:

> *The Plain Truth* has now topped 5,000,000 copies per issue. It is now the fastest-growing magazine in the world and one of the widest circulated mass-circulation magazines on earth. Our circulation is now greater than *Newsweek.* New subscribers are coming in at the rate of around 40,000 per week.

What the magazine neglects to mention is that it is *free.* There is no subscription fee, and the magazine is widely distributed in drugstores, supermarkets, and airports. *Newsweek* is sold on newsstands and by subscription. The comparison therefore omits significant information.

Evaluation of Opinions

When you evaluate the reliability of opinions in subjects with which you are not familiar, you will be dealing almost exclusively with opinions of experts. Most of the following questions are directed to an evaluation of authoritative sources. But you can also ask these questions of students or of others with opinions based on their own experience and research.

1. Is the source of the opinion qualified to give an opinion on the subject? The discussion on credibility in Chapter 1 (pp. 14–17) pointed out that certain achievements by the interpreter of the data — publications, acceptance by colleagues — can tell us something about his or her competence. Although these standards are by no means foolproof — people of outstanding reputations have been known to falsify their data — nevertheless they offer assurance that the source is generally trustworthy. The answers to questions you must ask are not hard to find: Is the source qualified by education? Is the source associated with a reputable institution — a university or a research organization? Is the source credited with having made contributions to the field — books, articles, research studies? Suppose that in writing a paper on organ transplants you came across an article by Peter Medawar. He is identified as follows:

> Sir Peter Medawar, British zoologist, winner of the 1960 Nobel Prize in Physiology or Medicine, for proving that the rejection by the body of foreign organs can be overcome; president of the Royal Society; head of the National Institute for Medical Research in London; a world leader in immunology.

These credentials would suggest to almost any reader that Medawar was a reliable source for information about organ transplants.

If the source is not so clearly identified, you should treat the data with caution. Such advice is especially relevant when you are dealing with popular works about such subjects as miracle diets, formulas for instant wealth, and sightings of monsters and UFOs. Do not use such data until you can verify them from other, more authoritative sources.

In addition, you should question the identity of any source listed as "spokesperson" or "reliable source" or "an unidentified authority." The mass media are especially fond of this type of attribution. Sometimes the sources are people in public life who plant stories anonymously or off the record for purposes they prefer to keep hidden.

Even when the identification is clear and genuine, you should ask if the credentials are relevant to the field in which the authority claims expertise. So specialized are areas of scientific study today that scientists in one field may not be competent to make judgments in another. William Shockley is a distinguished engineer, a Nobel Prize winner for his contribution to the invention of the electronic transistor. But when he made the claim, based on his own research, that blacks are genetically inferior to whites, geneticists accused Shockley of venturing into a field where he was unqualified to make judgments. Similarly, advertisers invite stars from the entertainment world to express opinions about products with which they are probably less familiar than members of their audience. All citizens have the right to express their views, but this does not mean that all views are equally credible or worthy of attention.

2. Is the source biased for or against his or her interpretation? Even authorities who satisfy the criteria for expertise may be guilty of bias. Bias arises as a result of economic reward, religious affiliation, political loyalty, and other interests. The expert may not be aware of the bias; even an expert can fall into the trap of ignoring evidence that contradicts his or her own intellectual preferences. A British psychologist has said:

> The search for meaning in data is bound to involve all of us in distortion to greater or lesser degree. . . . Transgression consists not so much in a clear break with professional ethics, as in an unusually high-handed, extreme or self-deceptive attempt to promote one particular view of reality at the expense of all others.[14]

Before accepting the interpretation of an expert, you should ask: Is there some reason why I should suspect the motives of this particular source?

Consider, for example, an advertisement claiming that sweetened breakfast cereals are nutritious. The advertisement, placed by the manufacturer of the cereal, provides impeccable references from scientific sources to support its claims. But since you are aware of the economic interest of the company in promoting sales, you may wonder if they have reproduced only facts that favor their claims. Are there other facts that might prove the opposite? As a careful researcher you would certainly want to look further for data about the advantages and disadvantages of sugar in our diets.

It is harder to determine bias in the research done by scientists and university members even when the research is funded by companies interested in a favorable review of their products. If you dis-

---

[14]Liam Hudson, *The Cult of the Fact* (New York: Harper and Row, 1972), p. 125.

cover that a respected biologist who advocates the use of sugar in baby food receives a consultant's fee from a sugar company, should you conclude that the research is slanted and that the scientist has ignored contrary evidence? Not necessarily. The truth may be that the scientist arrived at conclusions about the use of sugar legitimately through experiments that no other scientist would question. But it would probably occur to you that a critical reader might ask about the connection between the results of the research and the payment by a company that profits from the research. In this case you would be wise to read further to find confirmation or rejection of the claim by other scientists.

The most difficult evaluations concern ideological bias. Early in our lives we learn to discount the special interest that makes a small child brag, "My mother (or father) is the greatest!" Later we become aware that the claims of people who are avowed Democrats or Republicans or supply-side economists or Yankee fans or zealous San Franciscans or joggers must be examined somewhat more carefully than those of people who have no special commitment to a cause or a place or an activity. This is not to say that all partisan claims lack support. They may, in fact, be based on the best available support. But whenever special interest is apparent, there is always the danger that an argument will reflect this bias.

3. Has the source bolstered the claim with sufficient and appropriate evidence? In an article attacking pornography, one author wrote, "Statistics prove that the recent proliferation of porno is directly related to the increasing number of rapes and assaults on women."[15] But the author gave no further information — neither statistics nor proof that a cause-effect relation exists between pornography and violence against women. The critical reader will ask, "What are the numbers? Who compiled them?"

Even those who are reputed to be experts in the subjects they discuss must do more than simply allege that a claim is valid or that the data exist. They must provide facts to support their interpretations.

When Experts Disagree

Authoritative sources can disagree. Such disagreement is probably most common in the social sciences. They are called the "soft" sciences precisely because a consensus about conclusions in these areas is more difficult to arrive at than in the natural and physical sciences. Consider the controversy over what determines the best

[15]Charlotte Allen, "Exploitation for Profit," *Daily Collegian* [University of Massachusetts], October 5, 1976, p. 2.

interests of the child where both biological and foster parents are engaged in trying to secure custody. Experts are deeply divided on this issue. Dr. Daniel J. Cohen, a child psychologist and director of the Yale Child Study Center, argues that the psychological needs of the child should take precedence. If the child has a stable and loving relationship with foster parents, that is where he should stay. But Bruce Bozer and Bernadine Dohrn of the Children and Family Justice Center at Northwestern University Law School, insist that "such a solution may be overly simplistic." The child may suffer in later life when he learns that he has been prevented from returning to biological parents "who fought to get him back."[16]

But even in the natural and physical sciences, where the results of observation and experiment are more conclusive, we encounter heated differences of opinion. A popular argument concerns the extinction of the dinosaurs. Was it the effect of a comet striking the earth? Or widespread volcanic activity? Or a cooling of the planet? All these theories have their champions among the experts.

Environmental concerns also produce lively disagreements. Scientists have lined up on both sides of a debate about the importance of protecting the tropical rain forest as a source of biological, especially mammalian, diversity. Dr. Edward O. Wilson, a Harvard biologist, whose books have made us familiar with the term *biodiversity*, says, "The great majority of organisms appears to reach maximum diversity in the rain forest. There is no question that the rain forests are the world's headquarters of diversity." But in the journal *Science* another biologist, Dr. Michael Mares, a professor of zoology at the University of Oklahoma, argues that "if one could choose only a single South American habitat in which to preserve the greatest mammalian diversity, it would be the dry lands. . . . The dry lands are very likely far more highly threatened than the largely inaccessible rain forests."[17] A debate of more immediate relevance concerns possible dangers in cross-species transplants. One such transplant occurred in December 1995 when a man suffering from AIDS received bone marrow from a baboon in an experiment designed to boost the patient's immune system. Dr. Jonathan S. Allan, of the Southwest Foundation for Biomedical Research in San Antonio, is one of several doctors critical of the guidelines for these procedures, which in his opinion do not protect against possible introduction of new viruses into the general population. In an article for a medical journal, he writes:

> Once the door is opened and a new virus is unleashed, it will be a monumental task to identify a new pathogen, develop adequate screening tests and prevent the spread of that new infection.[18]

---

[16]*New York Times,* September 4, 1994, Sec. E, p. 3.
[17]*New York Times,* April 7, 1992, Sec. C, p. 4.
[18]*New York Times,* January 9, 1996, Sec. C, p. 11.

But other doctors feel that this alarm is unjustified. Dr. Frederick R. Murphy, the dean of the veterinary school at the University of California at Davis, says that "over the years unsterilized biological products derived from animals, products that differ little in risk from xenografts, have often been injected into patients" without major problems.[19]

How can you choose between authorities who disagree? If you have applied the tests discussed so far and discovered that one source is less qualified by training and experience or makes claims with little support or appears to be biased in favor of one interpretation, you will have no difficulty in rejecting that person's opinion. If conflicting sources prove to be equally reliable in all respects, then continue reading other authorities to determine whether a greater number of experts support one opinion rather than another. Although numbers alone, even of experts, don't guarantee the truth, nonexperts have little choice but to accept the authority of the greater number until evidence to the contrary is forthcoming. Finally, if you are unable to decide between competing sources of evidence, you may conclude that the argument must remain unsettled. Such an admission is not a failure; after all, such questions are considered controversial because even the experts cannot agree, and such questions are often the most interesting to consider and argue about.

APPEALS TO NEEDS AND VALUES

Good factual evidence is usually enough to convince an audience that your factual claim is sound. Using examples, statistics, and expert opinion, you can prove, for example, that women do not earn as much as men for the same work. But even good evidence may not be enough to convince your audience that unequal pay is wrong or that something should be done about it. In making value and policy claims, an appeal to the needs and values of your audience is absolutely essential to the success of your argument. If you want to persuade the audience to change their minds or adopt a course of action — in this case, to demand legalization of equal pay for equal work — you will have to show that assent to your claim will bring about what they want and care deeply about.

As a writer, you cannot always know who your audience is; it's impossible, for example, to predict exactly who will read a letter you write to a newspaper. Even in the classroom, you have only partial knowledge of your readers. You may not always know or be able to

---

[19]*New York Times,* January 9, 1996, Sec. C, p. 11.

infer what the goals and principles of your audience are. You may not know how they feel about big government, the draft, private school education, feminism, environmental protection, homosexuality, religion, or any of the other subjects you might write about. If the audience concludes that the things you care about are very different from what they care about, if they cannot identify with your goals and principles, they may treat your argument with indifference, even hostility, and finally reject it. But you can hope that decent and reasonable people will share many of the needs and values that underlie your claims.

Appeals to Needs

Suppose that you are trying to persuade Joan Doakes, a friend who is still undecided, to attend college. In your reading you have come across a report about the benefits of a college education written by Howard Bowen, a former professor of economics at Claremont (California) Graduate School, former president of Grinnell College, and a specialist in the economics of higher education. Armed with his testimony, you write to Joan. As support for your claim that she should attend college, you offer evidence that (1) college graduates earn more throughout their lifetime than high school graduates; (2) college graduates are more active and exert greater influence in their communities than high school graduates; and (3) college graduates achieve greater success as partners in marriage and as thoughtful and caring parents.[20]

Joan writes back that she is impressed with the evidence you've provided — the statistics, the testimony of economists and psychologists — and announced that she will probably enroll in college instead of accepting a job offer.

How did you succeed with Joan Doakes? If you know your friend pretty well, the answer is not difficult. Joan has needs that can be satisfied by material success; more money will enable her to enjoy the comforts and luxuries that are important to her. She also needs the esteem of her peers and the sense of achievement that political activity and service to others will give her. Finally, she needs the rootedness to be found in close and lasting family connections.

Encouraged by your success with Joan Doakes, you write the same letter to another friend, Fred Fox, who has also declined to apply for admission to college. This time, however, your argument fails. Fred, too, is impressed with your research and evidence. But college is not for him, and he repeats that he has decided not to become a student.

---

[20]"The Residue of Academic Learning," *Chronicle of Higher Education,* November 14, 1977, p. 13.

Why such a different response? The reason, it turns out, is that you don't know what Fred really wants. Fred Fox dreams of going to Alaska to live alone in the wilderness. Money means little to him, influence in the community is irrelevant to his goals, and at present he feels no desire to become a member of a loving family.

Perhaps if you had known Fred better, you would have offered different evidence to show that you recognized what he needed and wanted. You could have told him that Bowen's study also points out that "college-educated persons are healthier than are others," that "they also have better ability to adjust to changing times and vocations," that "going to college enhances self-discovery" and enlarges mental resources, which encourage college graduates to go on learning for the rest of their lives. This information might have persuaded Fred that college would also satisfy some of his needs.

As this example demonstrates, you have a better chance of persuading your reader to accept your claim if you know what he or she wants and what importance he or she assigns to the needs that we all share. Your reader must, in other words, see some connection between your evidence and his or her needs.

The needs to which you appealed in your letters to Joan and Fred are the requirements for physiological or psychological well-being. The most familiar classification of needs was developed by the psychologist Abraham H. Maslow in 1954.[21] These needs, said Maslow, motivate human thought and action. In satisfying our needs, we attain both long- and short-term goals. Because Maslow believed that some needs are more important than others, he arranged them in hierarchical order from the most urgent biological needs to the psychological needs that are related to our roles as members of a society.

Physiological Needs. Basic bodily requirements: food and drink; health; sex

Safety Needs. Security; freedom from harm; order and stability

Belongingness and Love Needs. Love within a family and among friends; roots within a group or a community

Esteem Needs. Material success; achievement; power, status, and recognition by others

Self-actualization Needs. Fulfillment in realizing one's potential

For most of your arguments you won't have to address the audience's basic physiological needs for nourishment or shelter. The desire for health, however, now receives extraordinary attention.

[21]*Motivation and Personality* (New York: Harper and Row, 1954), pp. 80–92.

Appeals to buy health foods, vitamin supplements, drugs, exercise and diet courses, and health books are all around us. Many of the claims are supported by little or no evidence, but readers are so eager to satisfy the need for good health that they often overlook the lack of facts or authoritative opinion. The desire for physical well-being, however, is not so simple as it seems; it is strongly related to our need for self-esteem and love.

Appeals to our needs to feel safe from harm, to be assured of order and stability in our lives are also common. Insurance companies, politicians who promise to rid our streets of crime, and companies that offer security services all appeal to this profound and nearly universal need. (We say "nearly" because some people are apparently attracted to risk and danger.) At this writing those who monitor global warming are attempting both to arouse fear for our safety and to suggest ways of reducing the dangers that make us fearful.

The last three needs in Maslow's hierarchy are the ones you will find most challenging to appeal to in your arguments. It is clear that these needs arise out of human relationships and participation in society. Advertisers make much use of appeals to these needs.

Belongingness and Love Needs

"Whether you are young or old, the need for companionship is universal." (ad for dating service)

"Share the Fun of High School with Your Little Girl!" (ad for a Barbie Doll)

Esteem Needs

"Enrich your home with the distinction of an Oxford library."

"Apply your expertise to more challenges and more opportunities. Here are outstanding opportunities for challenge, achievement, and growth." (Perkin-Elmer Co.)

Self-actualization Needs

"Be all that you can be." (U.S. Army)

"Are you demanding enough? Somewhere beyond the cortex is a small voice whose mere whisper can silence an army of arguments. It goes by many names: integrity, excellence, standards. And it stands alone in final judgment as to whether we have demanded enough of ourselves and, by that example, have inspired the best in those around us." (*New York Times*)

Of course, it is not only advertisers who use these appeals. We hear them from family and friends, from teachers, from employers, from editorials and letters to the editor, from people in public life.

Appeals to Values

Needs give rise to values. If we feel the need to belong to a group, we learn to value commitment, sacrifice, and sharing. And we then respond to arguments that promise to protect our values. It is hardly surprising that values, the principles by which we judge what is good or bad, beautiful or ugly, worthwhile or undesirable, should exercise a profound influence on our behavior. Virtually all claims, even those that seem to be purely factual, contain expressed or unexpressed judgments. The two scientists quoted in Chapter 3 (pp. 52–53) who presented evidence that cocaine was "deadlier than we thought," did so not for academic reasons but because they hoped to persuade people that using the drug was bad.

For our study of argument, we will speak of groups or systems of values because any single value is usually related to others. People and institutions are often defined by such systems of values. We can distinguish, for example, between those who think of themselves as traditional and those who think of themselves as modern by listing their differing values. One writer contrasts such values in this way:

> Among the values of traditionalism are: merit, accomplishment, competition, and success; self-restraint, self-discipline, and the postponement of gratification; the stability of the family; and a belief in certain moral universals. The modernist ethos scorns the pursuit of success; is egalitarian and redistributionist in emphasis; tolerates or encourages sensual gratification; values self-expression as against self-restraint; accepts alternative or deviant forms of the family; and emphasizes ethical relativism.[22]

Systems of values are neither so rigid nor so distinct from one another as this list suggests. Some people who are traditional in their advocacy of competition and success may also accept the modernist values of self-expression and alternative family structures. Values, like needs, are arranged in a hierarchy; that is, some are clearly more important than others to the people who hold them. Moreover, the arrangement may shift over time or as a result of new experiences. In 1962, for example, two speech teachers prepared a list of what they called "Relatively Unchanging Values Shared by Most Americans."[23] Included were "puritan and pioneer standards of morality" and "perennial optimism about the future." More than thirty years later, an appeal to these values might fall on a number of deaf ears.

You should also be aware of not only changes over time but also different or competing value systems that reflect a multitude of sub-

[22]Joseph Adelson, "What Happened to the Schools," *Commentary,* March 1981, p. 37.
[23]Edward Steele and W. Charles Redding, "The American Value System: Premises for Persuasion," *Western Speech,* Vol. 26 (Spring 1962), pp. 83–91.

cultures in our country. Differences in age, sex, race, ethnic background, social environment, religion, even in the personalities and characters of its members define the groups we belong to. Such terms as "honor," "loyalty," "justice," "patriotism," "duty," "responsibility," "equality," "freedom," and "courage" will be interpreted very differently by different groups.

All of us belong to more than one group, and the values of the several groups may be in conflict. If one group to which you belong, say, peers of your own age and class, is generally uninterested in and even scornful of religion, you may nevertheless hold to the values of your family and continue to place a high value on religious belief.

How can a knowledge of your readers' values enable you to make a more effective appeal? Suppose you want to argue in favor of a sex education program in the junior high school you attended. The program you support would not only give students information about contraception and venereal disease but also teach them about the pleasures of sex, the importance of small families, and alternatives to heterosexuality. If the readers of your argument are your classmates or your peers, you can be fairly sure that their agreement will be easier to obtain than that of their parents, especially if their parents think of themselves as conservative. Your peers are more likely to value experimentation, tolerance of alternative sexual practices, freedom, and novelty. Their parents are more likely to value restraint, conformity to conventional sexual practices, obedience to family rules, and foresight in planning for the future.

Knowing that your peers share your values and your goals will mean that you need not spell out the values supporting your claim; they are understood by your readers. Convincing their parents, however, who think that freedom, tolerance, and experimentation have been abused by their children, will be a far more challenging task. In one written piece you have little chance of changing their values, a result that might be achieved only over a longer period of time. So you might first attempt to reduce their hostility by suggesting that, even if a community-wide program were adopted, students would need parental permission to enroll. This might convince some parents that you share their values regarding parental authority and primacy of the family. Second, you might look for other values to which the parents subscribe and to which you can make an appeal. Do they prize maturity, self-reliance, responsibility in their children? If so, you could attempt to prove, with authoritative evidence, that the sex education program would promote these qualities in students who took the course.

But familiarity with the value systems of prospective readers may also lead you to conclude that winning assent to your argument will be impossible. It would probably be fruitless to attempt to persuade a group of lifelong pacifists to endorse the use of nuclear weapons. The beliefs, attitudes, and habits that support their value systems are too fundamental to yield to one or two attempts at persuasion.

EVALUATION OF
APPEALS TO NEEDS AND VALUES

If your argument is based on an appeal to the needs and values of your audience, the following questions will help you evaluate the soundness of your appeal.

1. Have the values been clearly defined? If you are appealing to the patriotism of your readers, can you be sure that they agree with your definition? Does patriotism mean "Our country, right or wrong!" or does it mean dissent, even violent dissent, if you think your country is wrong? Because value terms are abstractions, you must make their meaning explicit by placing them in context and providing examples.

2. Are the needs and values to which you appeal prominent in the reader's hierarchy at the time you are writing? An affluent community, fearful of further erosion of quiet and open countryside, might resist an appeal to allow establishment of a high-technology firm, even though the firm would bring increased prosperity to the area.

3. Is the evidence in your argument clearly related to the needs and values to which you appeal? Remember that the reader must see some connection between your evidence and his or her goals. Suppose you were writing an argument to persuade a group of people to vote in an upcoming election. You could provide evidence to prove that only 20 percent of the town voted in the last election. But this evidence would not motivate your audience to vote unless you could provide other evidence to show that their needs were not being served by such a low turnout.

Single-Sex Education Benefits Men Too

CLAUDIUS E. WATTS III

Last week Virginia Military Institute, an all-male state college, got the good news from a federal judge that it can continue its single-sex program if it opens a leadership program at Mary Baldwin College, a nearby private women's school. But it is likely that the government will appeal the decision. Meanwhile, the Citadel, another such institution in Charleston, S.C., remains under attack. Unwittingly, so are some fundamental beliefs prevalent in our society: namely, the value of single-sex education, the need for diversity in education, and the freedom of choice in associating with, and not associating with, whomever one chooses.

When Shannon Faulkner received a preliminary injunction to attend day classes with the Citadel's Corps of Cadets, she was depicted as a nineteen-year-old woman fighting for her constitutional rights, while the Citadel was painted as an outdated and chauvinistic Southern school that had to be dragged into the twentieth century.

But the Citadel is not fighting to keep women out of the Corps of Cadets because there is a grandiose level of nineteenth-century machismo to protect. Rather, we at the Citadel are trying to preserve an educational environment that molds young men into grown men of good character, honor, and integrity. It is part of a single-sex educational system that has proven itself successful throughout history.

The benefits of single-sex education for men are clear: Says Harvard sociologist David Riesman, not only is single-sex education an optimal means of character development, but it also removes the distractions of the "mating-dating" game so prevalent in society and enables institutions to focus students on values and academics.

In short, the value of separate education is, simply, the fact it is separate. 5

In October 1992, a federal appeals court ruled that "single-sex education is pedagogically justifiable." Indeed, a cursory glance at some notable statistics bears that out. For instance, the Citadel has

---

Lieutenant General Claudius E. Watts III, retired from the Air Force, is president of the Citadel in South Carolina. This selection is from the May 3, 1995, edition of the *Wall Street Journal*.

the highest retention rate for minority students of any public college in South Carolina: 67 percent of black students graduate in four years, which is more than $2\frac{1}{2}$ times the national average. Additionally, the Citadel's four-year graduation rate for all students is 70 percent, which compares with 48 percent nationally for all other public institutions and 67 percent nationally for private institutions. Moreover, many of the students come from modest backgrounds. Clearly, the Citadel is not the bastion of male privilege that the U.S. Justice Department, in briefs filed by that agency, would have us all believe.

While the Justice Department continues to reject the court's ruling affirming the values of single-sex education, others continue to argue that because the federal military academies are coeducational, so should the Citadel be. However, it is not the Citadel's primary mission to train officers for the U.S. armed forces. We currently commission approximately 30 percent of our graduates, but only 18 percent actually pursue military careers. At the Citadel, the military model is a means to an end, not the end itself.

Today there are eighty-four women's colleges scattered throughout the United States, including two that are public. These colleges defend their programs as necessary to help women overcome intangible barriers in male-dominated professions. This argument has merit; women's colleges produce only 4.5 percent of all female college graduates, but have produced one-fourth of all women board members of Fortune 500 companies and one-half of the women in Congress. However, the educational benefits of men's colleges are equally clear; and to allow women alone to benefit from single-sex education seems to perpetuate the very stereotypes that women — including Ms. Faulkner — are trying to correct.

If young women want and need to study and learn in single-sex schools, why is it automatically wrong for young men to want and need the same? Where is the fairness in this assumption?

"At what point does the insistence that one individual not be deprived of choice spill over into depriving countless individuals of choice?" asks Emory University's Elizabeth Fox Genovese in an article by Jeffrey Rosen published in the February 14 *New Republic*. 10

Yet, so it is at the Citadel. While one student maintains that she is protecting her freedom to associate, we mustn't forget that the Citadel's cadets also have a freedom — the freedom not to associate. While we have read about one female student's rights, what hasn't been addressed are the rights of the 1,900 cadets who chose the Citadel — and the accompanying discipline and drill — because it offered them the single-sex educational experience they wanted. Why do one student's rights supersede all theirs?

One might be easily tempted to argue on the grounds that Ms. Faulkner is a taxpayer and the Citadel is a tax-supported institution. But if the taxpayer argument holds, the next step is to forbid all public support for institutions that enroll students of only one sex. A draconian measure such as this would surely mean the end of private — as well as public — single-gender colleges.

Most private colleges — Columbia and Converse, the two all-female schools in South Carolina, included — could not survive without federal financial aid, tax exemptions, and state tax support in the form of tuition grants. In fact, nearly 900 of Columbia and Converse's female students receive state-funded tuition grants, a student population that is almost half the size of the Corps of Cadets. In essence, South Carolina's two private women's colleges may stand or fall with the Citadel.

Carried to its logical conclusion, then, the effort to coeducate the Citadel might mean the end of all single-sex education — for women as well as men, in private as well as public schools.

Analysis: Support

In 1993 Shannon Faulkner, a woman, was rejected for admission to the Citadel, an all-male state-supported military academy in South Carolina. In 1995, after a long court battle, she was admitted but resigned after a week of physical and emotional stress. The Court was asked to decide if an education equal to that of the Citadel could be provided for women at a nearby school.

Claudius Watts III tackles a subject that is no longer controversial in regard to women's colleges: the virtues of single-sex education. But in this essay he argues that colleges for men only deserve the same right as women's colleges to exclude the opposite sex.

The author has taken care in the limited space available to cover all the arguments that have emerged in the case of Shannon Faulkner. At the end of the opening paragraph he lays out the three ideas he will develop — the value of single-sex education, the need for diversity in education, and freedom of choice. In paragraphs 3–6 he supports his case for the benefits of separate education by first quoting a prominent sociologist and then offering statistics to prove that the Citadel population is both diverse and successful. In paragraph 7 he refutes a popular analogy — that since the service academies, like West Point and the Naval Academy, admit women, so should the Citadel. The goals of the Citadel, he says, are broader than those of the service academies. But he does more. In paragraph 8 he provides data that women's colleges produce successful graduates. This reinforces his claim that separate education has advantages over coed schooling. Perhaps it also helps to make friends of opponents who might otherwise be hostile to arguments favoring male privileges.

Notice the transition in paragraph 10. This leads the author to the defense of his last point, the far more elusive concept of freedom of choice and the rights of individuals, ideas whose validity cannot be measured in numbers. He introduces this part of his argument by quoting the words of a supporter of single-sex education, a woman professor at Emory University. He makes a strong appeal to the reader's sense of fairness and belief in the rights of the majority, represented here by the male students at the Citadel. There is also an obvious appeal to fear, an implied threat of the danger to women's colleges, in the next-to-last sentence of the essay. Finally, he invokes logic. If single-sex education cannot be defended for males, neither can it be defended for females. He assumes that against logic there can be no real defense.

Some leading advocates for women's rights have, in fact, agreed with General Watts's arguments for that reason. But those who support both Shannon Faulkner's admission to the Citadel and the sanctity of women's colleges will claim that women, as a disadvantaged group, deserve special consideration, while men do not. (One writer even insisted that the Citadel *needed* women as a civilizing influence.) General Watts's argument, however, should go some distance toward reopening the dialogue.

READINGS FOR ANALYSIS

Not Just Read and Write, but Right and Wrong

KATHLEEN KENNEDY TOWNSEND

In a suburban high school's crowded classroom, a group of juniors explained to me why drugs are difficult to control. "You see, Mrs. Townsend, what if you want a new pair of Reeboks? You could sell drugs and make $250 in an afternoon. It's a lot easier and quicker than working at McDonald's. You'd have to work there a whole week."

In my work helping teachers, I've walked into countless high schools where I could have filled a garbage bag with the trash in the halls. Yet I rarely hear teachers asking students to pick up the garbage — or telling them not to litter in the first place.

Of course, many students obey the law, stay away from drugs, and perform selfless acts: They tutor, work with the elderly, or run

Kathleen Kennedy Townsend is the lieutenant-governor of Maryland. This article first appeared in *The Washington Monthly,* January 1990.

antidrug campaigns. But too many lack a sense of duty to a larger community.

A survey conducted for People for the American Way asked just over 1,000 Americans between fifteen and twenty-four what goals they considered important. Three times as many selected career success as chose community service — which finished dead last. Only one-third said they could countenance joining the military or working on a political campaign. During one focus group interview for the study, some young people were asked to name qualities that make this country special. There was a long silence until one young man came up with an answer: "Cable TV."

The study concluded, "Young people have learned only half of 5
America's story. . . . [They] reveal notions of America's unique character that emphasize freedom and license almost to the complete exclusion of service or participation . . . they fail to perceive a need to reciprocate by exercising the duties and responsibilities of good citizenship."

Failure of Schools

While it is easy enough to blame this problem on the "me-ism" of the Reagan years, it's time to recognize that *it's also the result of deliberate educational policy.* One principal I know speaks for too many others. "Schools," she says, "cannot impose duties on the students. Students come from different backgrounds. They have different standards."

Twice since 1982 the Maryland Department of Education has sent out questionnaires to local education departments soliciting opinions about values education. The answers are typical of those found across the United States. Many respondents were indifferent, simply stating that values education is "inherent" in teaching. Other answers were more hostile: "Specific training in values is a new development which we do not consider essential," and "A special effort would cause trouble."

The consensus of the high school teachers and administrators participating in a curriculum workshop I ran last summer said it all: "Values — we can't get into that."

Schools across America have simply refused to take responsibility for the character of their students. They wash their hands of the teaching of virtue, doing little to create an environment that teaches children the importance of self-discipline, obligation, and civic participation. As one teacher training text says, "There is no right or wrong answer to any question of value."

Is it any surprise that students tend to agree? These days it 10
seems they're all relativists. A collection of high school interviews quotes one eleventh-grader as saying, "What one person thinks is

bad or wrong, another person might think that it is good or right. I don't think morals should be taught because it would cause more conflicts and mess up the student's mind." One of her classmates adds, "Moral values cannot be taught and people must learn what works for them. In other words, 'Whatever gets you through the night, it's alright.'"

Sensitivity Needed

Now it's obvious that the public schools are a ticklish arena for instilling values. Our pluralistic society is justly worried about party lines of any kind. That means that teaching values in the schools — whether as an integral part of the traditional classes or as a separate course — requires subtle skills and real sensitivity to student and community needs. Of course, families and churches should play a part, but neither are as strong or effective as they were a generation ago. Only the schools are guaranteed to get a shot at kids. That's why their current fumbling of anything smacking of right and wrong is so disastrous.

The importance of teaching values in the schools was barely mentioned at the education summit presided over by George Bush at the University of Virginia. The meeting was dominated by talk of federal funding and drug education. The underlying valuelessness of American education — an obstacle to the intelligent use of scarce resources and a root cause of drug problems — really didn't come up.

Such a curious oversight at Thomas Jefferson's school! Jefferson fought for public education because he believed that the citizen's virtue is the foundation of democracy. Only virtuous citizens, he knew, would resist private gain for the public good. And to know the public good, you have to study literature, philosophy, history, and religion.

For many years, Jefferson's wisdom about education prevailed. James Q. Wilson attributes America's low level of crime during the nineteenth century to the efforts of educators to instill self-discipline. "In the 1830s," he explains, "crime began to rise rapidly. New York had more murders than London, even though New York was only a tiny fraction of the size of London. However, rather than relying on police forces or other government programs, the citizens concentrated on education.

"Sunday schools were started. It was an all-day effort to provide 15 education in morality, education in punctuality, in decency, in following rules, and accepting responsibility, in being generous, in being kind.

"The process was so successful that in the second half of the nineteenth century, despite urbanization, despite the enormous influx into this country of immigrants from foreign countries all over

Europe, despite the widening class cleavages, despite the beginning of an industrial proletariat, despite all those things which textbooks today teach us cause crime to go up, crime went down. And it went down insofar as I, or any historian, can tell because this effort to substitute the ethic of self-control for what appeared to be the emerging ethic of self-expression succeeded." In 1830 the average American drank ten gallons of distilled liquor a year. By 1850, it was down to two.

Basic Values

The flavor of this nineteenth-century approach to education is preserved today in many state constitutions. North Dakota's is typical in declaring that public schools should "emphasize all branches of knowledge that tend to impress upon the mind the importance of truthfulness, temperance, purity, public spirit, and respect for honest labor of every kind." In current educational jargon, this approach is called "values inculcation." . . .

In 1981 the California State Assembly considered a bill that spelled out values that should be included in public school instructional materials. Among those values were: honesty, acceptance of responsibility, respect for the individuality of others, respect for the responsibility inherent in being a parent or in a position of authority, the role of the work ethic in achieving personal goals, universal values of right and wrong, respect for property, the importance of the family unit, and the importance of respect for the law.

The bill was defeated.

How have we reached the point where a list of basic values like that is considered unsuitable for schools? . . .   20

The major criticism of not teaching values is very simple: There are some values that teachers should affirm. Not all values are the same. My daughter is the only girl on her soccer team, and recently some of the boys on the team spit at her. The coach shouldn't have the boys *justify* their actions. He should have them *stop.* He should make sure they know they were wrong. That's what he should do. What he actually did tells you a lot about the schools today. He did nothing.

Reading and Discussion Questions

1. An editorial writer has supplied three subheadings for parts of the essay. The first part lacks a heading. What do you think it should be? Is "Sensitivity Needed" an appropriate headline for the third part?
2. Mention some of the devices Townsend uses to make her essay easy to read and understand.
3. What different kinds of support does Townsend provide to establish her claim? Is the evidence sufficient to prove that instruction in values is necessary?

4. What values above all others would the author seek to promote? Why do you think she has chosen these particular values?
5. Would the nineteenth-century Sunday school effort described by James Q. Wilson work today to reduce crime? Why or why not?
6. Do you think any of the values listed in the 1981 California bill are controversial? Explain.

Writing Suggestions

7. If you have been a student in a public, private, or Sunday school where specific values were taught, directly or through literature and history, describe and evaluate the experience. Was it successful — that is, did the values taught have a meaningful influence on your life?
8. Are there some actions that are always right or wrong, regardless of the circumstances? If you think there are, choose one or two and defend your choice. (You would probably agree with Ted Koppel, who reminds us that they are the Ten Commandments, not the Ten Suggestions.) If, on the other hand, you believe that all values are relative or situational — dependent, that is, on particular circumstances — argue the proposition that any view on the rightness or wrongness of a specific action is contingent on the situation.

Talking Up Close
DEBORAH TANNEN

Fighting to Be Friends

It is frequently observed that male speakers are more likely to be confrontational by arguing, issuing commands, and taking opposing stands for the sake of argument, whereas females are more likely to avoid confrontation by agreeing, supporting, and making suggestions rather than commands. . . . Cultural linguist Walter Ong argues that "adversativeness" — a tendency to fight — is universal, but "conspicuous or expressed adversativeness is a larger element in the lives of males than of females." In other words, females may well fight, but males are more likely to fight often, openly, and for the fun of it.

But what does it mean to say that males fight more than females? One thing it does not mean is that females therefore are more connected to each other. Because status and connection are

Deborah Tannen, professor of Linguistics at Georgetown University, is the author of *You Just Don't Understand: Women and Men in Conversation* (1989) and *Talking from 9 to 5* (1994), from which this excerpt is taken.

mutually evocative, both fighting with each other and banding together to fight others can create strong connections among males, for example by affiliation within a team. In this regard, a man recalled that when he was young, he and his friends amused themselves after school by organizing fights among themselves. When school let out, the word would go out about who was going to fight whom in whose backyard. Yet these fights were part of the boys' friendship and did not evidence mutual animosity. (Contrast this with a group of girls banding together to pick on a low-status girl, without anyone landing a physical blow.)

I think, as well, of my eighty-five-year-old uncle who still meets yearly with his buddies from World War II, even though the members of his battalion are from vastly different cultural and geographic backgrounds. It is difficult to imagine anything other than war that could have bonded men from such different backgrounds into a group whose members feel such lasting devotion. Indeed, a man who was sent to Vietnam because of an error gave this as the reason he did not try to set the record straight and go home: "I found out I belonged in Vietnam," he said. "The bonding of men at war was the strongest thing I'd felt in my life."

Folklore provides numerous stories in which fighting precipitates friendship among men. Robert Bly recounts one such story which he identifies as Joseph Campbell's account of the Sumerian epic *Gilgamesh*. In Bly's rendition, Gilgamesh, a young king, wants to befriend a wild man named Enkidu. When Enkidu is told of Gilgamesh,

> . . . his heart grew light. He yearned for a friend. "Very well!" he said. "And I shall challenge him."

Bly paraphrases the continuation: "Enkidu then travels to the city and meets Gilgamesh; the two wrestle, Enkidu wins, and the two become inseparable friends."

A modern-day equivalent of the bonding that results from ritual opposition can be found in business, where individuals may compete, argue, or even fight for their view without feeling personal enmity. Opposition as a ritualized format for inquiry is institutionalized most formally in the legal profession, and it is expected that each side will do its best to attack the other and yet retain friendly relations when the case is closed.

These examples show that aggression can be a way of establishing connection to others. Many cultures see arguing as a pleasurable sign of intimacy. Linguist Deborah Schiffrin examined conversations among lower-middle-class men *and women* of East European Jewish background in Philadelphia and found that friendly banter was one

of the fundamental ways they enjoyed and reinforced their friendship. A similar ethic obtains among Germans, who like to engage in
combative intellectual debate about such controversial topics as
politics and religion, according to linguist Heidi Byrnes, who was
born and raised in Germany. Byrnes points out that this has rather
negative consequences in cross-cultural contact. German students
try to show their friendliness to American students by provoking
heated arguments about American foreign policy. But the Americans, who consider it inappropriate to argue with someone they
have just met, refuse to take part. The German students conclude
that Americans are uninformed and uncommitted, while the Americans go away convinced that Germans are belligerent and rude.

Linguist Christina Kakava shows that modern Greek conversation is also characterized by friendly argument. She found, by taping
dinner-table conversation, that members of a Greek family enjoyed
opposing each other. In a study we conducted together, Kakava and
I showed that modern Greek speakers routinely disagree when they
actually agree, a practice that explains my own experience — and
discomfort — when I lived in Greece.

I was in a suburb of Athens, talking to an older woman whom I
call Ms. Stella, who had just told me about complaining to the police
because a construction crew working on the house beside hers illegally continued drilling and pounding through the siesta hours, disturbing her midafternoon nap. I tried to be nice by telling her she
was right, but she would not accept my agreement. She managed to
maintain her independence by restating her position in different
terms. Our conversation (which I taped), translated into English,
went like this:

> *Deborah:* You're right.
>
> *Stella:*   I *am* right. My dear girl, I don't know if I'm right or I'm not
>   right. But I am watching out for my interests and my rights.

Clearly, Ms. Stella thought she was right, but she did not want the
lively conversation to dissipate in so dull a way as her accepting my
statement, "You're right," so she managed to disagree: "I don't know
if I'm right or I'm not right." Disagreeing allowed her to amplify her
position as well.

This was typical of conversations I found myself in when I lived
in Greece. I vividly recall my frustration when I uttered what to me
were fairly automatic expressions of agreement and support and
found myself on the receiving end of what seemed like hostile refusal to accept my agreement. I frequently felt distanced and put
down when my attempts to agree were met with contentious responses. In an effort to make things right, I would try harder to be
agreeable, so that my conversations became veritable litanies of

agreement: Exactly!, Absolutely!, Without a doubt! But my Greek interlocutors probably were puzzled, irritated, and bored by my relentless agreement, and stepped up their contentiousness in their efforts to liven up the interactions.

As evidence that contentious argument helps create connection   10
among Greek friends, I offer an example taken from the study by Kakava, who was also a participant. The other two speakers were her friends, two brothers she calls George and Alkis. George was showing off a belt he had received as a gift, and the three friends argued animatedly about its color:

George: I've got burgundy shoes, but the belt's got black in it too.

Kakava: Does it have black in it? Let me see.

George: It has a stripe in it that's kind of black.

Alkis: Dark brown.

George: It's kind of dark.

Alkis: It's tobacco-colored, dummy! It goes with everything.

George: Tobacco-colored? What are you talking about?! Are you color-blind?!

Conversations in this spirit often give Americans the impression that Greeks are fighting when they are just having an animated conversation.

The discussion of fighting, silence, and interrupting is intended to show that it is impossible to determine what a way of speaking "really means" because the same way of speaking can create either status differences or connection, or both at the same time.

"Is It You or Me?"

Again and again, when I have explained two different ways of saying or doing the same thing, I am asked, "Which way is best?" or "Which way is right?" We are all in pursuit of the right way of speaking, like the holy grail. But there is no one right way, any more than there is a holy grail — at least not one we can hope to find. Most important, and most frustrating, the "true" intention or motive of any utterance cannot be determined merely by considering the linguistic strategy used.

Intentions and effects are not identical. When people have differing conversational styles, the effect of what they say may be very different from their intention. And anything that happens between two people is the result of both their actions. Sociolinguists talk about this by saying that all interaction is "a joint production." The double meaning of status and connection makes every utterance potentially ambiguous and even polysemous (meaning many things at once).

When we think we have made ourselves clear, or think we understand what someone else has said, we feel safe in the conviction that we know what words mean. When someone insists those words meant something else, we can feel like Alice trying to talk to Humpty-Dumpty, who isn't fazed by her protest that "glory doesn't mean a nice knock-down argument" but claims with aplomb, "When I use a word it means what I want it to mean, neither more nor less." If others get to make up their own rules for what words mean, the earth starts slipping beneath our feet. One of the sources of that slippage is the ambiguity and polysemy of status and connection — the fact that the same linguistic means can reflect and create one or the other or both. Understanding this makes it easier to understand the logic behind others' apparently willful misinterpretations and makes the earth feel a little more firm beneath our feet.

Reading and Discussion Questions

1. Tannen's expository strategy is to move back and forth between generalized explanations and specific examples. Does this make reading and comprehension easier or more difficult? Explain your reaction.
2. How does Tannen make a connection between the fighting of young males and the main point of the essay, which is about speech?
3. What different kinds of support does Tannen offer?
4. Point out the sentence or sentences where she summarizes her claim about language.

Writing Suggestions

5. Tannen refers to opposition as a linguistic convention among Jews, Germans, and Greeks. If you have had experiences with these or other ethnic groups in which differences in language rituals played a significant role, tell the story of the encounter and explain what it meant.
6. What have been the principal means of bonding with your friends? Did language play a role? Explain the significance of the examples you choose.

Gas comes from the big utility.
They don't know my name.
They don't know my family.

If you need prompt service from them,
you have to say, "I smell gas."

That's what scares me most. I think gas heat
is dangerous . . . too dangerous
for my home, my kids.

I heat with oil.

Oil heat...The Intelligent Choice
Metropolitan Energy Council, Inc.

66 Morris Ave., P.O. Box 359, Springfield, NJ 07081 • (201) 379-1100

Discussion Questions

1. What strong emotional appeal does the ad make? Is it justified?
2. How would you verify the validity of the appeal?

Animal Research
Saves Human Lives

HELOISA SABIN

That scene in "Forrest Gump" in which young Forrest runs from his schoolmate tormentors so fast that his leg braces fly apart and his strong legs carry him to safety may be the only image of the polio epidemic of the 1950s etched in the minds of those too young to remember the actual devastation the disease caused. Hollywood created a scene of triumph far removed from the reality of the disease.

Some who have benefited directly from polio research, including that of my late husband, Albert, think winning the real war against polio was just as simple. They have embraced a movement that denounces the very process that enables them to look forward to continued good health and promising futures. This "animal rights" ideology — espoused by groups such as People for the Ethical Treatment of Animals, the Humane Society of the United States and the Fund for Animals — rejects the use of laboratory animals in medical research and denies the role such research played in the victory over polio.

The leaders of this movement seem to have forgotten that year after year in the early fifties, the very words "infantile paralysis" and "poliomyelitis" struck great fear in young parents that the disease would snatch their children as they slept. Each summer public beaches, playgrounds, and movie theaters were places to be avoided. Polio epidemics condemned millions of children and young adults to lives in which debilitated lungs could no longer breathe on their own and young limbs were left forever wilted and frail. The disease drafted tiny armies of children on crutches and in wheelchairs who were unable to walk, run, or jump. In the United States, polio struck down nearly 58,000 children in 1952 alone.

Unlike the braces on Forrest Gump's legs, real ones would be replaced only as the children's misshapen legs grew. Other children and young adults were entombed in iron lungs. The only view of the world these patients had was through mirrors over their heads.

Heloisa Sabin is honorary director of Americans for Medical Progress in Alexandria, Virginia. This essay appeared in the *Wall Street Journal* on October 18, 1995.

These memories, however, are no longer part of our collective cultural memory.

Albert was on the front line of polio research. In 1961, thirty years after he began studying polio, his oral vaccine was introduced in the United States and distributed widely. In the nearly forty years since, polio has been eradicated in the Western Hemisphere, the World Health Organization reports, adding that, with a full-scale effort, polio could be eliminated from the rest of the world by the year 2000.

Without animal research, polio would still be claiming thousands of lives each year. "There could have been no oral polio vaccine without the use of innumerable animals, a very large number of animals," Albert told a reporter shortly before his death in 1993. Animals are still needed to test every new batch of vaccine that is produced for today's children.

Animal activists claim that vaccines really didn't end the epidemic — that, with improvements in social hygiene, polio was dying out anyway, before the vaccines were developed. This is untrue. In fact, advanced sanitation was responsible in part for the dramatic *rise* in the number of paralytic polio cases in the fifties. Improvements in sanitation practices reduced the rate of infection, and the average age of those infected by the polio virus went up. Older children and young adults were more likely than infants to develop paralysis from their exposure to the polio virus.

Every child who has tasted the sweet sugar cube or received the drops containing the Sabin vaccine over the past four decades knows polio only as a word, or an obscure reference in a popular film. Thank heavens it's not part of their reality.

These polio-free generations have grown up to be doctors, teachers, business leaders, government officials, and parents. They have their own concerns and struggles. Cancer, heart disease, strokes, and AIDS are far more lethal realities to them now than polio. Yet, those who support an "animal rights" agenda that would cripple research and halt medical science in its tracks are slamming the door on the possibilities of new treatments and cures.

My husband was a kind man, but he was impatient with those who refused to acknowledge reality or to seek reasoned answers to the questions of life.

The pioneers of polio research included not only the scientists but also the laboratory animals that played a critical role in bringing about the end of polio and a host of other diseases for which we now have vaccines and cures. Animals will continue to be as vital as the scientists who study them in the battle to eliminate pain, suffering, and disease from our lives.

That is the reality of medical progress.

Why We Don't Need Animal Experimentation

PEGGY CARLSON — points out flaw, but no benefits → clearly more benefits > flaws in research, hence the definition of research

The issue of animal experimentation has become so polarized that rational thinking seems to have taken a back seat. Heloisa Sabin's October 18 editorial-page article "Animal Research Saves Lives" serves only to further misinform and polarize. She does a great disservice to science to incorrectly portray the debate about animal experimentation as occurring between "animal rights activists" and scientists. The truth is, the value of animal experimentation is being questioned by many scientists.

Mrs. Sabin uses the example of the polio vaccine developed by her husband to justify animal experimentation. However, in the case of the polio vaccine, misleading animal experiments detoured scientists away from reliable clinical studies thereby, according to Dr. Sabin himself, delaying the initial work on polio prevention. It was also unfortunate that the original polio vaccine was produced using monkey cells instead of available human cells as can be done today. The use of monkey cells resulted in viruses with the potential to cause serious disease being transferred to humans when the polio vaccine was administered.

The polio vaccine example cannot logically be used to justify the current level of animal experimentation — several billion dollars and about 30 million animals yearly. Although most people would prefer to believe that the death and suffering of all these animals is justified, the facts do not support that conclusion.

Money

Nearly everything that medicine has learned about what substances cause human cancer and birth defects has come from human clinical and epidemiological studies because animal experiments do not accurately predict what occurs in humans. Dr. Bross, the former Director of Biostatistics at the Roswell Institute for Cancer Research states, "While conflicting animal results have often delayed and hampered advances in the war on cancer, they have never produced a single substantial advance either in the prevention or treatment of cancer." A 1990 editorial in *Stroke* notes that none of the twenty-five compounds "proven" efficacious for treating stroke in animal experiments over the preceding ten years had been effective for use in humans. From human studies alone we have learned how to lessen the risk of heart attacks. Warnings to the public that

riddles v store

Peggy Carlson, M.D., is research director of the Physicians Committee for Responsible Medicine in Washington, D.C. Her letter appeared in the *Wall Street Journal* on November 7, 1995.

smoking cigarettes leads to an increased risk of cancer were delayed as researchers sought, unsuccessfully, to confirm the risk by using animals.

Animal tests for drug safety, cancer-causing potential, and toxic- 5
ity are unreliable, and science is leading us to more accurate meth- *not there*
ods that will offer greater protection. But if we refuse to *yet!*
acknowledge the inadequacies of animal tests we put a stranglehold *examples?*
on the very progress that will help us. Billions of precious health-
care dollars have been spent to fund animal experiments that are *examples!*
repetitious or that have no human relevance.

An uncritical acceptance of the value of animal experiments leads to its overfunding, which, in turn, leads to the underfunding of other more beneficial areas. *→ such as:*
human research funding?
alternatives?

Discussion Questions

1. Sabin uses the vaccine against polio as the principal example in her support of animal research. Does this limit her argument? Should she have been more specific in her references to other diseases?
2. What is the significance of Sabin's repeated references to "reality"?
3. Mention all the kinds of support that Carlson provides. Which of the supporting materials is most persuasive?
4. Does Carlson refute all the arguments in Sabin's article? Be specific.
5. Sabin makes strong emotional appeals. Describe them, and decide how large a part such appeals play in her argument. Does Carlson appeal to the emotions of her readers?

EXERCISES

1. What kind of evidence would you offer to prove to a skeptic that the moon landings — or any other space ventures — have actually occurred? What objections would you anticipate?
2. A group of heterosexual people in a middle-class community who define themselves as devout Christians have organized to keep a group of homosexuals from joining their church. What kind of support would you offer for your claim that the homosexuals should be welcomed into the church? Address your argument to the heterosexuals unwilling to admit the group of homosexuals.
3. In the summer of 1983, after an alarming rise in the juvenile crime rate, the mayor of Detroit instituted a curfew for young people under the age of eighteen. What kind of support can you provide for or against such a curfew?
4. "Racism [or sexism] is [not] a major problem on this campus [or home town or neighborhood]." Produce evidence to support your claim.
5. Write a full-page advertisement to solicit support for a project or cause that you believe in.

6. How do you account for the large and growing interest in science fiction films and literature? In addition to their entertainment value, are there other less obvious reasons for their popularity?

7. According to some researchers soap operas are influential in transmitting values, life-styles, and sexual information to youthful viewers. Do you agree? If so, what values and information are being transmitted? Be specific.

8. Choose one of the following stereotypical ideas and argue that it is true or false or partly both. Discuss the reasons for the existence of the stereotype.
   a. Jocks are stupid.
   b. The country is better than the city for bringing up children.
   c. TV is justly called "the boob tube."
   d. A dog is man's best friend.
   e. Beauty contests are degrading to women.

9. Defend or refute the view that organized sports build character.

10. The philosopher Bertrand Russell said, "Most of the work that most people have to do is not in itself interesting, but even such work has certain advantages." Defend or refute this assertion. Use your own experience as support.

Critical Listening

11. Choose a product advertised on TV by many different makers. (Cars, pain relievers, fast food, cereals, and soft drinks are some of the most popular products.) What kinds of support do the advertisers offer? Why do they choose these particular appeals? Would the support be significantly different in print?

12. From time to time advocates of causes speak on campus. The causes may be broadly based — minority rights, welfare cuts, abortion, foreign aid — or they may be local issues, having to do with harassment policy, course requirements, or tuition increases. Attend a meeting or a rally at which a speaker argues his or her cause. Write an evaluation of the speech, paying particular attention to the kinds of support. Did the speaker provide sufficient and relevant evidence? Did he or she make emotional appeals? What signs, if any, reflected the speaker's awareness of the kinds of audience he or she was addressing?

CHAPTER SIX

Warrants

We now come to the third element in the structure of the argument — the warrant. In the first chapter we defined the warrant as an *assumption,* a belief we take for granted, or a general principle. Claim and support, the other major elements we have discussed, are more familiar in ordinary discourse, but there is nothing mysterious or unusual about the warrant. All our claims, both formal and informal, are grounded in warrants or assumptions that the audience must share with us if our claims are to prove acceptable.

These warrants reflect our observations, our personal experience, and our participation in a culture. But because these observations, experiences, and cultural associations will vary, the audience may not always agree with the warrants or assumptions of the writer. The British philosopher Stephen Toulmin, who developed the concept of warrants, dismissed more traditional forms of logical reasoning in favor of a more audience-based, courtroom-derived approach to argumentation. He refers to warrants as "general, hypothetical statements, which can act as bridges" and "entitle one to draw conclusions or make claims."[1] The word *bridges* to denote the action of the warrant is crucial. One dictionary defines warrant as a "guarantee or justification." We use the word *warrant* to emphasize that in an argument it guarantees a connecting link — a bridge — between the claim and the support. This means that even if a reader agrees that the support is sound, the support cannot prove the validity of the claim unless the reader also agrees with the underlying warrant. Recall the sample argument outlined in Chapter 1 (p. 12):

---

[1]Stephen Toulmin, *The Uses of Argument* (Cambridge: Cambridge University Press, 1958), p. 98.

CLAIM: Adoption of a vegetarian diet leads to healthier and longer life.

SUPPORT: The authors of *Becoming a Vegetarian Family* say so.

WARRANT: The authors of *Becoming a Vegetarian Family* are reliable sources of information on diet.

Notice that the reader must agree with the assumption that the testimony of experts is trustworthy before he or she arrives at the conclusion that a vegetarian diet is healthy. Simply providing evidence that the authors say so is not enough to prove the claim.

The following dialogue offers another example of the relationship between the warrant and the other elements of the argument.

"I don't think that Larry can do the job. He's pretty dumb."

"Really? I thought he was smart. What makes you say he's dumb?"

"Did you know that he's illiterate — can't read above third-grade level? In my book that makes him dumb."

If we put this into outline form, the warrant or assumption in the argument becomes clear.

CLAIM: Larry is pretty dumb.

EVIDENCE: He can't read above third-grade level.

WARRANT: Anybody who can't read above third-grade level must be dumb.

We can also represent the argument in diagram form, which shows the warrant as a bridge between the claim and the support.

Support ——————————————➤ *Claim*

Warrant
(Expressed or Unexpressed)

The argument above can then be written like this:

Support ————————————➤ *Claim*
Larry can't read above   He's pretty dumb.
  third-grade level.
Warrant
Anybody who can't read above third-grade
level must be pretty dumb.

Is this warrant valid? We cannot answer this question until we consider the *backing*. Every warrant or assumption rests on something else that gives it authority; this is what we call backing. Backing or authority for the warrant in this example would consist of research data that prove a relationship between stupidity and illiteracy. This particular warrant, we would discover, lacks backing because we know that the failure to learn to read may be due to a number of things unrelated to intelligence. So, if the warrant is unprovable, the claim — that Larry is dumb — is also unprovable, even if the evidence is true. In this case, then, the evidence does not guarantee the soundness of the claim.

Now consider this example of a somewhat more complicated warrant: The beautiful and unspoiled Eastern Shore of Maryland is being discovered by thousands of tourists, vacationers, and developers who will, according to the residents, change the landscape and the way of life, which is now based largely on fishing and farming. In a few years the Eastern Shore may become a noisy, crowded string of resorts. Mrs. Walkup, the Kent County commissioner, says,

> Catering to the wealthy puts property back on the tax rolls, but it's going to make the Eastern Shore look like the rest of the country. Everything that made our way of life so special is being eroded. We are a fragile area. The Eastern Shore is still special, but it is feeling pressure from all directions. Lots of people don't seem to appreciate the fact that God made us to need a little peace and quiet now and then.[2]

In simplified form the argument of those opposed to development would be outlined this way:

CLAIM: Development will bring undesirable changes to the present way of life on the Eastern Shore, a life of farming and fishing, peace and quiet

SUPPORT: Developers will build express highways, condominiums, casinos, and nightclubs.

WARRANT: A pastoral life of fishing and farming is superior to the way of life brought by expensive, fast-paced modern development.

Notice that the warrant is a broad generalization that can apply to a number of different situations, while the claim is about a specific place and time. It should be added that in other arguments the warrant may not be stated in such general terms. However, even in arguments in which the warrant makes a more specific reference to the claim, the reader can infer an extension of the warrant to other similar arguments. In the vegetarian diet example (p. 3, outlined on p. 12) the warrant mentions a specific book. But it is clear that such

---

[2]Michael Wright, "The Changing Chesapeake," *New York Times Magazine,* July 10, 1983, p. 27.

warrants can be generalized to apply to other arguments in which we accept a claim based on the credibility of the sources.

To be convinced of the validity of Mrs. Walkup's claim, you must first find that the support is true, that the developers plan to introduce drastic changes that will destroy the pastoral life of the Eastern Shore. You may, however, believe that the support is not entirely sound, that the development will be much more modest than residents fear, and that the Eastern Shore will not be seriously altered. Next, you may want to see more justification for the warrant. Is pastoral life superior to the life that will result from large-scale development? Perhaps you have always thought that a life of fishing and farming means poverty and limited opportunities for the majority of the residents. Although the superiority of a way of life is largely a matter of taste and therefore difficult to prove, Mrs. Walkup may need to produce backing for her belief that the present way of life is more desirable than one based on developing the area for new residents and summer visitors. If you find either the support or the warrant unconvincing, you cannot accept the claim.

Remember that a claim is often modified by one or more qualifiers, which limit the claim. Mrs. Walkup might have said, "Development will *probably* destroy *some aspects of* the present way of life on the Eastern Shore." Warrants can also be modified or limited by *reservations,* which remind the reader that there are conditions under which the warrants will not be relevant. Mrs. Walkup might have added, ". . . unless increased prosperity and exposure to the outside world brought by development improve some aspects of our lives."

A diagram of Mrs. Walkup's argument shows the additional elements:

Support ⟶	*Claim*
The developers will build highways, condos, casinos, nightclubs.	Development will bring undesirable changes to life on the Eastern Shore.
Warrant	*Qualifier*
A way of life devoted to farming and fishing is superior to a way of life brought by development.	Development will *most likely* bring undesirable changes.

Backing
We have experienced crowds, traffic, noise, rich strangers, high-rises, and they destroy peace and quiet.

Reservation
But increased development might improve some aspects of our lives.

Claim and support (or lack of support) are relatively easy to uncover in most arguments. One thing that makes the warrant different is that it is often unexpressed and therefore unexamined by both writer and reader because they take it for granted. In the argument about Larry's intelligence, the warrant was stated. But in the argument about development on the Eastern Shore, Mrs. Walkup did not state her warrant directly, although her meaning is perfectly clear. She probably felt that it was not necessary to be more explicit because her readers would understand and supply the warrant.

We can make the discovery of warrants even clearer by examining another argument, in this case a policy claim. We've looked at a factual claim — that Larry is dumb — and a value claim — that Eastern Shore development is undesirable. Now we examine a policy claim that rests on one expressed and one unexpressed warrant. Policy claims are usually more complicated than other claims because the statement of policy is preceded by an array of facts and values. In addition, such claims may represent chains of reasoning in which one argument is dependent on another. These complicated arguments may be difficult or impossible to summarize in a simple diagram, but careful reading, asking the same kinds of questions that the author may have asked about his claim, can help you to find the warrant or chain of warrants that must be accepted before evidence and claim can be linked.

In the article we examine,[3] the author argues for a radical reform in college sports — the elimination of subprofessional intermural team sports, as practiced above all in football and basketball. The claim is clear, and evidence for the professional character of college sports not hard to find: the large salaries paid to coaches, the generous perquisites offered to players, the recruitment policies which ignore academic standing, the virtually full-time commitment of the players, the lucrative contracts with TV. But can this evidence support the author's claim that such sports do not belong on college campuses? Advocates of these sports may ask, Why not? In the conclusion of the article the author states one warrant or assumption underlying his claim.

> Even if the money to pay college athletes could be found, though, a larger question must be answered — namely, why should a system of professional athletics be affiliated with universities at all? For the truth is that the requirements of athletics and academics operate at cross purposes, and the attempt to play both games at once serves only to reduce the level of performance of each.

In other words, the author assumes that the goals of an academic education on the one hand and the goals of big-time college sports

[3]D. G. Myers, "Why College Sports?" *Commentary*, December 1990, pp. 49–51.

on the other hand are incompatible. In the article he develops the ways in which each enterprise harms the other.

But the argument clearly rests on another warrant that is not expressed because the author takes for granted that his readers will supply it: The academic goals of the university are primary and should take precedence over all other collegiate activities. This is an argument based on an authority warrant, the authority of those who define the goals of the university — scholars, public officials, university administrators, and others. (Types of warrants are discussed in the following section.)

This warrant makes clear that the evidence of the professional nature of college sports cited above supports the claim that they should be eliminated. If quasiprofessional college sports are harmful to the primary educational function of the college or university, then they must go. In the author's words, "The two are separate enterprises, to be judged by separate criteria. . . . For college sports, the university is not an educational institution at all; it is merely a locus, a means of coordinating the different aspects of the sporting enterprise."

Arguers will often neglect to state their warrants for one of two reasons: First, like Mrs. Walkup, they may believe that the warrant is obvious and need not be expressed; second, they may want to conceal the warrant in the hope that the reader will overlook its weakness.

What kinds of warrants are so obvious that they need not be expressed? Here are a few that will probably sound familiar.

Mothers love their children.

The more expensive the product, the more satisfactory it will be.

A good harvest will result in lower prices for produce.

First come, first served.

These statements seem to embody beliefs that most of us would share and that might be unnecessary to make explicit in an argument. The last statement, for example, is taken as axiomatic, an article of faith that we seldom question in ordinary circumstances. Suppose you hear someone make the claim, "I deserve to get the last ticket to the concert." If you ask why he is entitled to a ticket that you also would like to have, he may answer in support of his claim, "Because I was here first." No doubt you accept his claim without further argument because you understand and agree with the warrant that is not expressed: "If you arrive first, you deserve to be served before those who come later." Your acceptance of the warrant probably also takes into account the unexpressed backing that is based on a belief in justice: "It is only fair that those who sacrifice time and comfort to be first in line should be rewarded for their trouble."

In this case it may not be necessary to expose the warrant and examine it. Indeed, as Stephen Toulmin tells us, "If we demanded the credentials of all warrants at sight and never let one pass unchallenged, argument could scarcely begin."[4]

But even those warrants that seem to express universal truths invite analysis if we can think of claims for which these warrants might not, after all, be relevant. "First in line," for example, may justify the claim of a person who wants a concert ticket, but it cannot in itself justify the claim of someone who wants a vital medication that is in short supply. Moreover, offering a rebuttal to a long-held but unexamined warrant can often produce an interesting and original argument. If someone exclaims, "All this buying of gifts! I think people have forgotten that Christmas celebrates the birth of Christ," she need not express the assumption — that the buying of gifts violates what ought to be a religious celebration. It goes unstated by the speaker because it has been uttered so often that she knows the hearer will supply it. But one writer, in an essay titled "God's Gift: A Commercial Christmas," argued that, contrary to popular belief, the purchase of gifts, which means the expenditure of time, money, and thought on others rather than oneself, is not a violation but an affirmation of the Christmas spirit.[5]

The second reason for refusal to state the warrant lies in the arguer's intention to disarm or deceive the reader, although the arguer may not be aware of this. For instance, failure to state the warrant is common in advertising and politics, where the desire to sell a product or an idea may outweigh the responsibility to argue explicitly. The following advertisement is famous not only for what it says but for what it does not say:

> In 1918 Leona Currie scandalized a New Jersey beach with a bathing suit cut above her knees. And to irk the establishment even more, she smoked a cigarette. Leona Currie was promptly arrested.
>
> Oh, how Leona would smile if she could see you today.
>
> You've come a long way, baby. *Virginia Slims*. The taste for today's woman.

What is the unstated warrant? The manufacturer of Virginia Slims hopes we will agree that being permitted to smoke cigarettes is a significant sign of female liberation. But many readers would insist that proving "You've come a long way, baby" requires more evidence than women's freedom to smoke (or wear short bathing suits). The shaky warrant weakens the claim.

Politicians, too, conceal warrants that may not survive close scrutiny. In the 1983 mayoral election in Chicago, one candidate re-

---

[4]*The Uses of Argument* (Cambridge: Cambridge University Press, 1958), p. 106.
[5]Robert A. Sirico, *Wall Street Journal,* December 21, 1993, Sec. A, p. 12.

vealed that his opponent had undergone psychiatric treatment. He did not have to state the warrant supporting his claim. He knew that many in his audience would assume that anyone who had undergone psychiatric treatment was unfit to hold public office. This same assumption contributed to the withdrawal of a vice-presidential candidate from the 1972 campaign.

TYPES OF WARRANTS

Arguments may be classified according to the types of warrants offered as proof. Because warrants represent the reasoning process by which we establish the relationship between support and claim, analysis of the major types of warrants enables us to see the whole argument as a sum of its parts.

Warrants may be organized into three categories: "*authoritative, substantive,* and *motivational.*"[6] We have already given examples of these types of warrants in this chapter and in Chapter 1. The *authoritative warrant* (see p. 12) is based on the credibility or trustworthiness of the source. If we assume that the source of the data is authoritative, then we find that the support justifies the claim. A *substantive warrant* is based on beliefs about reliability of factual evidence. In the example on page 180 the speaker assumes, although mistakenly, that the relationship between illiteracy and stupidity is a verifiable datum, one that can be proved by objective research. A *motivational warrant,* on the other hand, is based on the needs and values of the audience. For example, the warrant on page 12 reflects a preference for individual freedom, a value that would cause a reader who held it to agree that laws against marijuana should be repealed.

Each type of warrant requires a different set of questions for testing its soundness. The following list of questions will help you to decide whether a particular warrant is valid and can justify a particular claim.

1. *Authoritative* (based on the credibility of the sources)
   Is the authority sufficiently respected to make a credible claim?
   Do other equally reputable authorities agree with the authority cited?
   Are there equally reputable authorities who disagree?
2. *Substantive* (based on beliefs about the reliability of factual evidence)
   Are sufficient examples given to convince us that a general statement is justified? That is, are the examples given representative of the whole community?

---

[6]D. Ehninger and W. Brockriede, *Decision by Debate* (New York: Dodd, Mead, 1953).

If you have argued that one event or condition can bring about another (a cause-effect argument), does the cause given seem to account entirely for the effect? Are other possible causes equally important as explanations for the effect?

If you have used comparisons, are the similarities between the two situations greater than the differences?

If you have used analogies, does the analogy explain or merely describe? Are there sufficient similarities between the two elements to make the analogy appropriate?

3. *Motivational* (based on the values of the arguer and the audience)

Are the values ones that the audience will regard as important? Are the values relevant to the claim?

SAMPLE ANALYSIS

The Case for Torture

MICHAEL LEVIN

It is generally assumed that torture is impermissible, a throwback to a more brutal age. Enlightened societies reject it outright, and regimes suspected of using it risk the wrath of the United States.

I believe this attitude is unwise. There are situations in which torture is not merely permissible but morally mandatory. Moreover, these situations are moving from the realm of imagination to fact.

Suppose a terrorist has hidden an atomic bomb on Manhattan Island which will detonate at noon on July 4 unless . . . (here follow the usual demands for money and release of his friends from jail). Suppose, further, that he is caught at 10 A.M. of the fateful day, but — preferring death to failure — won't disclose where the bomb is. What do we do? If we follow due process — wait for his lawyer, arraign him — millions of people will die. If the only way to save those lives is to subject the terrorist to the most excruciating possible pain, what grounds can there be for not doing so? I suggest there are none. In any case, I ask you to face the question with an open mind.

Torturing the terrorist is unconstitutional? Probably. But millions of lives surely outweigh constitutionality. Torture is barbaric? Mass murder is far more barbaric. Indeed, letting millions of inno-

Michael Levin is a professor of philosophy at the City College of New York. This essay is reprinted from the June 7, 1982, issue of *Newsweek*.

cents die in deference to one who flaunts his guilt is moral cowardice, an unwillingness to dirty one's hands. If *you* caught the terrorist, could you sleep nights knowing that millions died because you couldn't bring yourself to apply the electrodes?

Once you concede that torture is justified in extreme cases, you   5
have admitted that the decision to use torture is a matter of balancing innocent lives against the means needed to save them. You must now face more realistic cases involving more modest numbers. Someone plants a bomb on a jumbo jet. He alone can disarm it, and his demands cannot be met (or if they can, we refuse to set a precedent by yielding to his threats). Surely we can, we must, do anything to the extortionist to save the passengers. How can we tell 300, or 100, or 10 people who never asked to be put in danger, "I'm sorry, you'll have to die in agony, we just couldn't bring ourselves to . . ."

Here are the results of an informal poll about a third, hypothetical, case. Suppose a terrorist group kidnapped a newborn baby from a hospital. I asked four mothers if they would approve of torturing kidnappers if that were necessary to get their own newborns back. All said yes, the most "liberal" adding that she would administer it herself.

I am not advocating torture as punishment. Punishment is addressed to deeds irrevocably past. Rather, I am advocating torture as an acceptable measure for preventing future evils. So understood, it is far less objectionable than many extant punishments. Opponents of the death penalty, for example, are forever insisting that executing a murderer will not bring back his victim (as if the purpose of capital punishment were supposed to be resurrection, not deterrence or retribution). But torture, in the cases described, is intended not to bring anyone back but to keep innocents from being dispatched. The most powerful argument against using torture as a punishment or to secure confessions is that such practices disregard the rights of the individual. Well, if the individual is all that important — and he is — it is correspondingly important to protect the rights of individuals threatened by terrorists. If life is so valuable that it must never be taken, the lives of the innocents must be saved even at the price of hurting the one who endangers them.

Better precedents for torture are assassination and preemptive attack. No Allied leader would have flinched at assassinating Hitler, had that been possible. (The Allies did assassinate Heydrich.) Americans would be angered to learn that Roosevelt could have had Hitler killed in 1943 — thereby shortening the war and saving millions of lives — but refused on moral grounds. Similarly, if nation A learns that nation B is about to launch an unprovoked attack, A has a right to save itself by destroying B's military capability first. In the same way, if the police can by torture save those who would otherwise die at the hands of kidnappers or terrorists, they must.

There is an important difference between terrorists and their victims that should mute talk of the terrorists' "rights." The terrorist's victims are at risk unintentionally, not having asked to be endangered. But the terrorist knowingly initiated his actions. Unlike his victims, he volunteered for the risks of his deed. By threatening to kill for profit or idealism, he renounces civilized standards, and he can have no complaint if civilization tries to thwart him by whatever means necessary.

Just as torture is justified only to save lives (not extort confessions or recantations), it is justifiably administered only to those *known* to hold innocent lives in their hands. Ah, but how can the authorities ever be sure they have the right malefactor? Isn't there a danger of error and abuse? Won't We turn into Them? 10

Questions like these are disingenuous in a world in which terrorists proclaim themselves and perform for television. The name of their game is public recognition. After all, you can't very well intimidate a government into releasing your freedom fighters unless you announce that it is your group that has seized its embassy. "Clear guilt" is difficult to define, but when 40 million people see a group of masked gunmen seize an airplane on the evening news, there is not much question about who the perpetrators are. There will be hard cases where the situation is murkier. Nonetheless, a line demarcating the legitimate use of torture can be drawn. Torture only the obviously guilty, and only for the sake of saving innocents, and the line between Us and Them will remain clear.

There is little danger that the Western democracies will lose their way if they choose to inflict pain as one way of preserving order. Paralysis in the face of evil is the greater danger. Some day soon a terrorist will threaten tens of thousands of lives, and torture will be the only way to save them. We had better start thinking about this.

Analysis

Levin's controversial essay attacks a popular assumption which most people have never thought to question — that torture is impermissible under any circumstances. Levin argues that in extreme cases torture is morally justified in order to bring about a greater good than the rights of the individual who is tortured.

Against the initial resistance that most readers may feel, Levin makes a strong case. Its strength lies in the backing he provides for the warrant that torture is sometimes necessary. This backing consists in the use of two effective argumentative strategies. One is the anticipation of objections. Unprecedented? No. Unconstitutional? No. Barbaric? No. Second, and more important, are the hypothetical examples that compel readers to rethink their positions and possibly arrive at agreement with the author. Levin chooses extreme examples — kidnapping of a newborn child, planting a bomb on a jumbo jet, detonating an atomic bomb in Manhattan — that draw a line between clear and murky cases and make agreement easier. And he bolsters his moral position by insisting that torture is not to be used as punishment or revenge but only in order to save innocent lives.

To support such an unpopular assumption the writer must convey the impression that he is a reasonable man, and this Levin attempts to do by a searching definition of terms, the careful organization and development of his argument, including references to the opinions of other people, and the expression of compassion for innocent lives.

Another strength of the article is its readability — the use of contractions, informal questions, conversational locutions. This easy, familiar style is disarming; the reader doesn't feel threatened by heavy admonitions from a writer who affects a superior, moral attitude.

READINGS FOR ANALYSIS

A Proposal to Abolish Grading
PAUL GOODMAN

Let half a dozen of the prestigious Universities — Chicago, Stanford, the Ivy League — abolish grading, and use testing only and entirely for pedagogic purposes as teachers see fit.

Anyone who knows the frantic temper of the present schools will understand the transvaluation of values that would be effected by this modest innovation. For most of the students, the competitive grade has come to be the essence. The naive teacher points to the beauty of the subject and the ingenuity of the research; the shrewd student asks if he is responsible for that on the final exam.

Let me at once dispose of an objection whose unanimity is quite fascinating. I think that the great majority of professors agree that grading hinders teaching and creates a bad spirit, going as far as cheating and plagiarizing. I have before me the collection of essays, *Examining in Harvard College,* and this is the consensus. It is uni-

Paul Goodman (1911–1972) was a college professor and writer whose outspoken views were popular with students during the 1960s. This essay is from *Compulsory Miseducation* (1964).

formly asserted, however, that the grading is inevitable; for how else will the graduate schools, the foundations, the corporations *know* whom to accept, reward, hire? How will the talent scouts know whom to tap?

By testing the applicants, of course, according to the specific task-requirements of the inducting institution, just as applicants for the Civil Service or for licenses in medicine, law, and architecture are tested. Why should Harvard professors do the testing *for* corporations and graduate schools?

The objection is ludicrous. Dean Whitla, of the Harvard Office of 5 Tests, points out that the scholastic-aptitude and achievement tests used for *admission* to Harvard are a superexcellent index for all-around Harvard performance, better than high-school grades or particular Harvard course-grades. Presumably, these college-entrance tests are tailored for what Harvard and similar institutions want. By the same logic, would not an employer do far better to apply his own job-aptitude test rather than to rely on the vagaries of Harvard section-men? Indeed, I doubt that many employers bother to look at such grades; they are more likely to be interested merely in the fact of a Harvard diploma, whatever that connotes to them. The grades have most of their weight with the graduate schools — here, as elsewhere, the system runs mainly for its own sake.

It is really necessary to remind our academics of the ancient history of Examination. In the medieval university, the whole point of the grueling trial of the candidate was whether or not to accept him as a peer. His disputation and lecture for the Master's was just that, a masterpiece to enter the guild. It was not to make comparative evaluations. It was not to weed out and select for an extramural licensor or employer. It was certainly not to pit one young fellow against another in an ugly competition. My philosophic impression is that the medievals thought they knew what a good job of work was and that we are competitive because we do not know. But the more status is achieved by largely irrelevant competitive evaluation, the less will we ever know.

(Of course, our American examinations never did have this purely guild orientation, just as our faculties have rarely had absolute autonomy; the examining was to satisfy Overseers, Elders, distant Regents — and they as paternal superiors have always doted on giving grades, rather than accepting peers. But I submit that this set-up itself makes it impossible for the student to *become* a master, to *have* grown up, and to commence on his own. He will always be making A or B for some overseer. And in the present atmosphere, he will always be climbing on his friend's neck.)

Perhaps the chief objectors to abolishing grading would be the students and their parents. The parents should be simply disregarded; their anxiety has done enough damage already. For the stu-

dents, it seems to me that a primary duty of the university is to de-
prive them of their props, their dependence on extrinsic valuation
and motivation, and to force them to confront the difficult enterprise
itself and finally lose themselves in it.

A miserable effect of grading is to nullify the various uses of testing. Testing, for both student and teacher, is a means of structuring,
and also of finding out what is blank or wrong and what has been as-
similated and can be taken for granted. Review — including
high-pressure review — is a means of bringing together the fragments, so that there are flashes of synoptic insight.

There are several good reasons for testing, and kinds of test. But 10
if the aim is to discover weakness, what is the point of down-grading
and punishing it, and thereby inviting the student to conceal his
weakness, by faking and bulling, if not cheating? The natural conclusion of synthesis is the insight itself, not a grade for having had it.
For the important purpose of placement, if one can establish in the
student the belief that one is testing *not* to grade and make invidious
comparisons but for his own advantage, the student should normally seek his own level, where he is challenged and yet capable,
rather than trying to get by. If the student dares to accept himself as
he is, a teacher's grade is a crude instrument compared with a student's self-awareness. But it is rare in our universities that students
are encouraged to notice objectively their vast confusion. Unlike
Socrates, our teachers rely on power-drives rather than shame and
ingenuous idealism.

Many students are lazy, so teachers try to goad or threaten
them by grading. In the long run this must do more harm than good.
Laziness is a character-defense. It may be a way of avoiding learning,
in order to protect the conceit that one is already perfect (deeper,
the despair that one *never* can be). It may be a way of avoiding just
the risk of failing and being down-graded. Sometimes it is a way of
politely saying, "I won't." But since it is the authoritarian grown-up
demands that have created such attitudes in the first place, why repeat the trauma? There comes a time when we must treat people as
adult, laziness and all. It is one thing courageously to fire a do-
nothing out of your class; it is quite another thing to evaluate him
with a lordly F.

Most important of all, it is often obvious that balking in doing
the work, especially among bright young people who get to great
universities, means exactly what it says: The work does not suit me,
not this subject, or not at this time, or not in this school, or not in
school altogether. The student might not be bookish; he might be
school-tired; perhaps his development ought now to take another direction. Yet unfortunately, if such a student is intelligent and is not
sure of himself, he *can* be bullied into passing, and this obscures
everything. My hunch is that I am describing a common situation.

What a grim waste of young life and teacherly effort! Such a student will retain nothing of what he has "passed" in. Sometimes he must get mononucleosis to tell his story and be believed.

And ironically, the converse is also probably commonly true. A student flunks and is mechanically weeded out, who is really ready and eager to learn in a scholastic setting, but he has not quite caught on. A good teacher can recognize the situation, but the computer wreaks its will.

Reading and Discussion Questions

1. Goodman divides his argument into several parts, each of which develops a different idea. How would you subtitle these parts?
2. Are some parts of the argument stronger than others? Does Goodman indicate what points he wants to emphasize?
3. Why do you think Goodman calls on "half a dozen of the prestigious Universities" instead of all universities to abolish grading?
4. Where does the author reveal the purposes of his proposal?
5. Most professors, Goodman argues, think that grading hinders teaching. Why, then, do they continue to give grades? How does Goodman reply to their objections?
6. What does Goodman think the real purpose of testing should be? How does grading "nullify the various uses of testing"?

Writing Suggestions

7. Do you agree that grading prevents you from learning? If so, write an essay in which you support Goodman's thesis by reporting what your own experience has been.
8. If you disagree with Goodman, write an essay that outlines the benefits of grading.
9. Is there a better way than grading to evaluate the work of students — a way that would achieve the goals of education Goodman values? Suggest a method and explain why it would be superior to grading.

A Nation of Enemies

PHILIP K. HOWARD

Finding a public bathroom in New York City is not easy. Most subway toilets were closed down years ago because of vandalism and crime. Museums require people to pay admission. Restaurant bathrooms are restricted to patrons' use. As public toilets became scarce, the nooks and crannies around the city began to exude the malodorous costs of this shortage. "No one needed to be told that this was a serious problem," observed Joan Davidson, a director of a private foundation, the J. M. Kaplan Fund.

Ms. Davidson was nonetheless surprised at the outpouring of enthusiasm when, in 1991, the Kaplan Fund put forward a modest proposal to finance a test of six sidewalk toilet kiosks in different sections of the city. The coin-operated toilets would be imported from Paris, where the municipal government provides them for the convenience of residents and tourists. Perfected over years of experience in Paris, these facilities were almost too good to be true. They clean themselves with a shower of water and disinfectant after each use. The doors open automatically after fifteen minutes so they cannot be used as a place to spend the night. They are small, only five feet in diameter, which means that New York's crowded sidewalks would not be blocked. And while the City of Paris rents them, they would cost budget-strapped New York nothing: Advertising panels would be added on the outside to pay the freight. City Hall was ready to move. The six-month test, in sites from Harlem down to City Hall, would show whether they would work in New York.

Then came the glitch. Wheelchairs couldn't fit inside them. New York's antidiscrimination law provides that it is illegal to "withhold or deny" from the disabled any access to "public accommodation." Ann Emermen, the head of the Mayor's Office of the Disabled, characterized the sidewalk toilet proposal as "discrimination in its purest form." When the city's chief lawyer, Victor Kovner, whose credentials as a champion of liberal causes stretch back thirty years, sought a legislative amendment to permit the six-month test, another lobbyist for the disabled accused him of "conspiring to violate the law." Never mind that he was seeking to amend the law through the democratic process.

Suggestions that disabled-accessible bathrooms might be provided in nearby buildings or restaurants were dismissed out-of-

---

Philip K. Howard is a founding partner of the New York law firm Howard, Darby, and Levin. This selection is from his book *The Death of Common Sense: How Law Is Suffocating America* (1994).

hand: "The law requires that everyone go to the bathroom in exactly the same place." When someone had the nerve, at a public forum, to ask how many wheelchair users there might be compared with other citizens who might benefit (including blind and deaf citizens), the questioner was hooted down for asking a politically incorrect question. At stake, at least for the disabled, were their "rights." When you have a right to something, it doesn't matter what anyone thinks or whether you are, in fact, reasonable.

A kiosk accommodating wheelchairs had in fact been tried in 5 both London and Paris, but it had to be much larger and, because of its size, it could be placed only in locations where there was ample pedestrian room. Also, it was not self-cleaning. Because of the different needs of wheelchair users, it would not self-open until after thirty minutes, and experience showed that it became a refuge for prostitution and drug use. The lobby for the disabled demanded this larger kiosk or nothing.

Good-government groups and editorial boards were livid at the selfishness and intractability of the lobby. The leaders of the disabled lobby, who refer to the general public as the "temporarily abled," cast us as shortsighted bigots. Compromise was unthinkable. Politicians, ever eager to please, ducked for cover.

The ultimate resolution, while arguably legal, was undeniably silly: Two toilet kiosks would be at each of three locations, one for the general public and another, with a full-time attendant, available only for wheelchair users. Mrs. Emerman and other advocates for the disabled were still upset. Their credo is "mainstreaming": the legal right to do everything in the same way as everyone else. They still wanted the disabled to use the same toilet — not one made specifically for them — or wanted no toilet for anyone.

The test proved how great the demand was in New York. The regular units averaged over three thousand flushes per month, or 50 percent more than the average in Paris. The larger units reserved for the disabled were basically unused, the cost of the full-time attendant wasted. The test also made enemies of everyone; even liberals who had championed the cause of the disabled began to see their advocates as unreasonable zealots.

Making trade-offs in situations like this is much of what government does: Almost every government act, whether allocating use of public property, creating new programs, or granting subsidies, benefits one group more than another, and usually at the expense of everyone else. Most people expect their elected and appointed leaders to balance the pros and cons and make decisions in the public interest. The government of New York, however, lacked this power, because it had passed an innocuous-sounding law that created "rights" elevating the interests of any disabled person over other public purpose.

Rights, almost no one needs to be told, are all around us. The lan- 10
guage of rights is used everywhere in modern America — not only in
public life, but in the workplace, in school, in welfare offices, in health
care. There are rights for children and the elderly; the disabled; the
mentally disabled; workers under twenty-five and over forty; alcoholics and the addicted; the homeless; spotted owls and snail darters.

Rights are considered as American as apple pie. This is a country where citizens have *rights*. The Bill of Rights is the best-known
part of the Constitution: Government can't tell us what to say, and
can't take away our "life, liberty or property" except by due process.
Rights are basic. Until the last few decades, however, rights were
not something to shout about. They were the bedrock of our society, something we would give our lives to defend, but not something
people thought much about as they made it through each day.
Rights were synonymous with freedom, protection against being ordered around by government or others.

Rights have taken on a new role in America. Whenever there is a
perceived injustice, new rights are created to help the victims.
These rights are different: While the rights-bearers may see them as
"protection," they don't protect so much as provide. These rights
are intended as a new, and often invisible, form of subsidy. They are
provided at everyone else's expense, but the amount of the check is
left blank. For example, in New York, the unintended consequence of
giving the disabled the "right" to do everything in the same way was
the imposition of a de facto prohibition of sidewalk toilets.

Handing out rights like land grants has become the preferred
method of staking out a place for those who feel disadvantaged.
Lawmakers and courts, confronted with evidence of past abuses,
scramble over each other to define and take credit for handing out
new rights. When refused entry to a movie because his two-year-old
son might disturb the other patrons, Rolando Acosta, then deputy
commissioner of New York City's Human Rights Commission, had an
easy fix; the commission ruled that banning children was age discrimination. In 1993, a judge in Rhode Island found rights for obese
employees. Mari Matsuda, a feminist legal scholar, has advocated
rights for those who are discriminated against on account of unusual accents — people who talk differently would be able to sue if
they feel their accent is being held against them. In 1990, the federal
government enacted a comprehensive disabled law, the Americans
with Disabilities Act (known as the ADA), to serve similar purposes
as New York's. "Let the shameful wall of exclusion finally come tum-
bling down," said President Bush on the South Lawn of the White
House upon signing the bill. The law had passed with virtually no
opposition. After all, rights cost little or nothing out of the budget.
It's only a matter of being fair. Or so we think.

Rights, however, leave no room for balance, or for looking at it
~verybody's point of view as well. Rights, as the legal philoso-

pher Ronald Dworkin has noted, are a trump card. Rights give open-ended power to one group, and it comes out of everybody else's hide. What about the three hundred other moviegoers when the two-year-old starts crying or demanding candy in a loud voice? Too bad; we gave children a right. Rights cede control to those least likely to use them wisely, usually partisans like disabled activists who have devoted their lives to remedying their own injustices. Government, for all its flaws, at least has interest in a balanced result.

This abdication has led to an inverted feudalism in which the rights-bearer, by assertion of legal and moral superiority, lords it over everyone else. Rights-bearers do warfare independent of the constraints of democracy: *Give Us Our Rights.* We cringe, lacking even a vocabulary to respond.   15

It was only three decades ago that John F. Kennedy stirred the nation when, in his inaugural address, he said, "Ask not what your country can do for you, but what you can do for your country." Thirty years later, we have disintegrated into factions preoccupied only with our due, not what we can do.

What went wrong?

Reading and Discussion Questions

1. The organization of this essay for almost half its length is that of a narrative related as the events unfold. Is this an effective strategy? Would it have been better to state the claim at the very beginning?
2. If you were annotating this essay, are there some places where you would ask questions? How would you find the answers?
3. What is Howard's claim? Who are the enemies in the title?
4. What kinds of evidence does Howard provide to support his claim? Which evidence do you think is most convincing?
5. In one sentence summarize the warrant or assumption that underlies the claim. Is the warrant stated or merely understood? Does it seem valid?
6. What distinction does Howard make between rights as guaranteed in the Bill of Rights and rights as demanded by those with disabilities? Do you think Howard is fair to those with disabilities? Explain your answer.

Writing Suggestions

7. Do you feel that, as a student or a young person, you have been deprived of a right or rights that you can justly claim? For example, mandatory school dress codes in high school are becoming increasingly common. Are they a violation of student rights? Write a defense of your position on some relevant issue. Make clear the warrant on which you base your claim.
8. At the end of this selection, Howard asks, "What went wrong?" Do you have an answer that would explain why many of us have become preoccupied with our own rights to the exclusion of the rights of others? Perhaps some things you have learned in history or sociology classes can provide a clue.

Discussion Questions

1. What advantages of natural gas does this ad stress? Are butterflies superior to plants or other animals as persuasive elements?
2. What warrants or assumptions about the user underlie the advertiser's approach?
3. Contrast this ad with the ad on page 173. Which argument is stronger? Notice that one is negative, the other positive. Does that fact influence your choice?

Against the Death Penalty

JOHN P. CONRAD

Whatever the outcome of this debate in the minds of our readers, it is clear to me — and, of course, to my stern opponent as well — that at this stage of our history, capital punishment is a winning cause in America, if nowhere else in the civilized world. Abolitionists may win some of their cases in the courts, in spite of the retentionists' furious denial that the courts should have jurisdiction over the nature and quality of the punishment that the state may impose on criminals. It is still possible for abolitionists to attain high office from the electorate and subsequently to "sabotage" the executioner's craft by commuting the sentences of condemned murderers. Nevertheless, I must gloomily concede that the public opinion polls, in which the hangman now receives a handsome plurality of the respondents' votes, are corroborated in statewide referendums. If the general public has its way, Dr. van den Haag's cause is won, and without the benefit of his robust arguments.

I construe this predilection for the executioner as the outcome of the common man's yearning for a tough stand, a hard line, a crushing response to the nation's surfeit of criminals. The common man may never have met a criminal, but he knows what will deter him and what he deserves — the gallows, no less, or its local equivalent. In this certainty, the electorate is encouraged by demagogues who tell the world that the return of the executioner will signal to criminals everywhere that they can no longer expect leniency from the courts, and that the state will resume an implacable severity that prevented crimes in the old days and will soon prevent it again.

What humbug! Political candidates and their advisors know that, regardless of the deterrent value of the gallows, the death penalty has nothing to do with the nonhomicidal criminal. The arduous and costly tasks that society must undertake if crime is to be prevented still have to be defined and faced — even if we settle on an unswerving program of killing all murderers and stick to it. The signal that is really conveyed by the noose and the electric chair will be understood by thoughtful criminals and ignored by the reckless. That sig-

John P. Conrad has served as chief of research at the California Department of Corrections and the U.S. Bureau of Prisons. This essay is from *The Death Penalty Pro and Con: A Debate* (1983). [All notes are Conrad's.]

nal will tell those who receive it that Americans do not understand the crime problem in spite of all the exposure they have had. Whether thoughtful or reckless, criminals know that neither the gallows nor the prison awaits them, whatever their offense may be, if they are not caught, prosecuted, and convicted. They know that the police do not catch them often enough (although there is reason to suppose that most are eventually arrested), that busy prosecutors are only too willing to settle for a guilty plea to crimes less serious than those with which they are charged, and that, if they are convicted in court, the chance of probation is pretty good unless the crime is so heinous as to have become a matter of public notoriety.

Under the circumstances, how can the criminal justice system deter any man or woman desperate enough to gamble on engaging in a criminal career? The police solve a higher percentage of homicides than any other crime reported to them, but, as my well-informed opponent never tires of pointing out, the number of murders increases every year at an unacceptable rate. There are plenty of potential killers who will accept the 70-30 odds against them, perhaps because they calculate that well-planned murders by disinterested and anonymous murderers constitute most of the 30% that are uncleared. Spouse-killers and rapist-murderers are usually brought to justice, homicidal robbers and contract hit men almost never.

We distract public attention from the expensive requirements 5 of more police, more courts, and more prisons in the stentorian advocacy of capital punishment as a panacea for violent crime. The public officials responsible for this clamor know better. They also know that the execution of a contemptible killer comes cheap, compared to all the measures that must be taken to combat crime effectively.

I do not include my profoundly reflective opponent among the disingenuous office-seekers, office-holders, and editorialists who have somehow convinced the majority of the public that killing killers is the solution to the crime problem. Dr. van den Haag has for many years been a sincere believer in the efficacy of the death penalty as a deterrent of homicide, just as he has advocated more severe punishment for those who commit lesser crimes. He has not convinced me, nor has he persuaded many other abolitionists. Nevertheless, he makes what he can of a mixture of commonsense propositions about deterrence, he invokes the *lex talionis,* and he thrusts the indisputable and deplorable facts about the rising murder rate into the attention of anyone who will listen. His case for the resumption of the death penalty is rational and well argued. He is undisturbed by the overwhelming rejection of his argument by psychologists, sociologists, economists, and statisticians — with the lonely and generally discredited exception of Dr. Isaac Ehrlich.

What a stark and dismal world my bleak opponent contemplates! It is not a far cry from the world that Thomas Hobbes defined as a "time of war," when there is "continual fear and danger of violent death; and the life of man, solitary, poor, nasty, brutish, and short."[1] In this van den Haagian world, everyone must be on his guard against every neighbor, for everyone is a potential murderer, prevented from committing the most horrible of crimes only by the tenuous threat of the death penalty. Especially likely to commit such crimes are the poor, who enviously observe the comfortable classes and determine to take by force what they could not gain by merit and industry. The vertiginously rising crime rate must be attributed in very large part to the desperation of the underclasses. It follows that these people must be stringently controlled. The death penalty must be imposed on those of them who carry their crimes to the point of killing.

When pressed for evidence of the superior deterrent effect of capital punishment, as compared with life imprisonment, Dr. van den Haag will first assert that the lack of evidence does not prove that the death penalty does not deter potential killers; it merely means that statisticians and social scientists have yet to discover a methodology to prove what is self-evident to the ordinary citizen with rudimentary common sense. For those who are unimpressed with this reasoning, he invokes the ancient *lex talionis;* it is right that unlawful killers should themselves be killed.

That is a symmetry that cannot be achieved with respect to any other crime. Rapists cannot be raped; robbers cannot be robbed; burglars cannot be burglarized. The state cannot retaliate against these criminals by treating them as they treated their victims. It is nevertheless possible for the state to kill, as it must — in my righteous opponent's opinion — when a man or a woman stands convicted of murder. Only because murder, the crime of crimes, is punishable by death is it regarded with proper horror. Any lesser response would trivialize the death of an innocent victim.

I say that nothing can trivialize murder. Good men and women   10
abhor violence and particularly abhor it when it is homicidal. To suppose that ordinary citizens will accept murder as a matter of course unless the executioner impresses the horror of it upon them is to state a case for which there is not the slightest supporting evidence. It is a misanthropic fallacy that emerges from the most pessimistic misinterpretation of Freudian doctrine — that all human beings are potential killers, restrained from acting on their primitive

---

[1]Thomas Hobbes, *Leviathan; or the Matter, Forme, and Power of a Commonwealth* (London: Andrew Crooke, 1651; Penguin Books, 1975), p. 186.

and destructive urges only by the threat of extreme punishment. The truth is that in this violent country, where the punishment of criminals is more severe than in any other nation except the Soviet Union and South Africa, fewer than 20,000 murderers are found each year — less than 0.01 percent of our total population. Even if we adjust the population at risk by discounting the infants and the aged, even if we allow for the murders that take place and are not recognized as such, and even if we allow for the murderous assaults in which the victim survived, our annual crop of killers could not exceed 0.05 percent of the population. Perhaps there is another 0.05 percent of potential killers who have abstained from murder for one reason or another, and we have 0.1 percent of the population to worry about. Call for a ten-year cohort of these killers and potential killers and we can elevate the danger level to 1 percent. But what reason is there to believe that the remaining 99 percent are restrained only by the threat of the hangman? Is a society imbued with this belief about its members better than a nation of paranoids?

I insist that the murderer is an exceptional person and so is the citizen who can be persuaded only by threats to abstain from acts of violence. Let the reader consider his own experience and his observation of his friends and enemies. How many truly murderous men, women, and children does he know?

The anachronism that is capital punishment originated in an era when physical punishments were all that could be imposed on criminals. In this debate we have both alluded often to the old days when sentences of truly horrifying cruelty were imposed on men and women guilty of crimes far less grave than capital murder. It is a stain on Western civilization that children could be hanged for theft, men could be broken on the rack for robbery, and women burned to death for witchcraft and adultery as recently as the eighteenth and nineteenth centuries, when many of the brightest achievements of European and American culture flowered. It should not have taken so long for a man like Beccaria to emerge with a protest against the evils of punishment as administered in the eighteenth century, or for men like Bentham and Romilly to make their case against the idiocies of nineteenth-century criminal justice in England. Not only did it take centuries too long for such men to appear, but their opposition was intransigent to the last ditch. The only way to understand the diehards of the times is to remember the dread in the upper classes that upheavals like the French Revolution might take place in their own countries if social controls were eased. Even if a major political convulsion were to be avoided, the security of the comfortable classes required the support of the death penalty. The impassioned arguments in favor of the hangman in both the English Houses of Parliament exposed the transparent apprehensions of the privileged and their trust in the gallows as the best possible prevention of crime. Those were the days when there were over 200 offenses in the statutes that called for execution.

Romilly and his friends prevailed, as did their counterparts elsewhere in Europe. Their success may be partly laid to Yankee ingenuity, which had contributed the penitentiary to the administration of criminal justice. It was adopted with alacrity throughout Europe. The penitentiary is not the brightest gem of American social technology, but it is a feasible alternative to capital punishment. The whip was eliminated for ordinary offenders, and the gallows was reserved for murderers.

The question that I have raised so often in this debate must be confronted again. *Why should we retain capital punishment when a life sentence in prison will serve the deterrent purpose at least as well?* Implicit in that question is my complete disbelief that there exists a population of potential murderers who would be deterred by the gallows — or the lethal needle — but would proceed with their killings if the worst they could expect was a life sentence in prison. If such extraordinary people exist, a supposition for which there is absolutely no evidence, they would be balanced by an equally extraordinary, and equally hypothetical, few who are tempted to commit murder to achieve the notoriety of public execution. There may be a few in each of these classes, but in the absence of any positive evidence of their existence in significant numbers, no debating points can be claimed for them by either side.

The adequacy of a life sentence in prison as a deterrent to murder — if deterrence is truly our aim — is obvious to those who know what that experience does to the prisoner. The term begins in ignominy. It is lived out in squalor. It ends when youth is long since gone, or, more often than most people know, in the death of the senile in a prison ward for the aged and infirm. Those who fancy that life in prison bears any resemblance to the gaiety of a resort hotel or the luxury of a country club have been beguiled by dishonest demagogues. Commitment to an American prison is a disaster for all but the most vicious human predators, men who discover a false manhood in the abuse of the weak. The unique combination of ennui and chronic dread of one's fellows, of idleness and wasted years, and of lives spent with wicked, vicious, or inane men and women should be — and for most people certainly is — a terrifyingly deterrent prospect. Those who find it tolerable are manifesting the meaninglessness of their lives before commitment.

In his now classic disquisition on punishment, the great Norwegian criminologist, Johannes Andenaes, acknowledged that "it can hardly be denied that any conclusion as to the real nature of general prevention involves a great deal of guess work. Claims based on the 'demands of general prevention,' therefore, can often be used to cloak strictly conservative demands for punishment or mere conservative resistance to change."[2]

Jack Gibbs carries this point a good deal further in his comprehensive survey of thought and rhetoric generated by the deterrence controversy:

> Hypocrisy is not likely to be a question in debates over penal policy when a protagonist either (1) opposes punishment regardless of the deterrence presumably realized or (2) advocates punishment for the sake of retribution alone. However, a party to the debate may endorse punishment, but only *insofar as it deters crime,* meaning that a value judgement at least appears to be contingent on scientific evidence. When that argument is made, hypocrisy does become an issue, and the very notion of scientific evidence becomes disputable. No scientific finding necessarily (i.e., logically) gives rise to a moral conclusion or value judgement, and the compunction to bridge the gap readily leads to personalized evidential criteria. Thus, one may believe that crimes should be punished for the sake of vengeance alone but conceal that belief by arguing that punishment deters crime and dismiss all manner of research findings as irrelevant or insufficient. At the other extreme, if one views punishment as intrinsically wrong, that value judgement can be covertly defended by invoking rigorous criteria for positive evidence of deterrence.[3]

I do not accuse my upright opponent of hypocrisy, but I think the weakness of any case to be made for the superior deterrent effect of the death penalty — as compared to long incarceration — should be apparent to the reader. It is natural in our goal-oriented culture to adopt the deterrent theory. It promises to accomplish steps toward the prevention of the worst of crimes with each cadaver hauled away from the place of execution. Some day, the retentionist hopes, science will justify the killing by showing the effectiveness of capital punishment as measured by the numbers of innocent lives saved. This is the hope that Dr. van den Haag and his friends express so ardently.

It is a hope that will not be realized. The power of the criminal 20
justice system to prevent any category of crimes is very limited. An organized society must administer criminal justice because it cannot ignore crime. Crimes must be punished in the interests of the society's cohesion and solidarity. The methods we have devised to punish criminals will intimidate some of them, will prevent the

---

[2] Johannes Andenaes, *Punishment and Deterrence* (Ann Arbor: University of Michigan Press, 1974), pp. 9–10.
    [3] Jack Gibbs, *Crime, Punishment and Deterrence* (New York, Oxford, and Amsterdam: Elsevier, 1975), pp. 9–10.

crimes that imprisoned criminals might commit, and may deter some potential criminals from engaging in violations of the law. To suppose that the criminal justice system can or should prevent crime is to expect too much of it and too little of the larger social system of which criminal justice is only a part.

I contend that the criminal justice system must be process-oriented, not engaged in achieving goals that are beyond its reach. The police should be efficient in apprehending criminals, the courts should be fair in trying them, and the penal system should be humane but secure. The process-oriented hanging of criminals as their just desert for the crime of murder is an archaism surviving from a bygone and primitive age. The assertion that some day it will be shown that it is a necessary deterrent to murder is, at best, a naive indulgence in wishful thinking.

Throughout this debate I have insisted on the primacy of retributivism in the administration of justice. My utilitarian opponent scorns retributivism as a theory, and in the strict sense in which that word is used by scientists, he may be right.[4] He supposes that deterrence qualifies as a theory because it may be subjected to verification tests. The reader may judge whether Professor van den Haag has cited any tests whatsoever that offer a satisfactory verification of the hypothesis on which his special case of the deterrent "theory" must rest.[5]

I take up my position somewhere between the two extremes defined by Gibbs. I do indeed hold that it is necessary to punish crimes in the interest of retribution.[6] There are enough empirical supports for the notion that punishment will deter in many situations. There are none at all for the notion that the death penalty will deter criminals more effectively than a protracted prison sentence. I do not accept the argument that punishment is intrinsically wrong, but I do

---

[4] On the usage, "theories of punishment," to which Dr. van den Haag has objected, see H. L. A. Hart, *Punishment and Responsibility* (Oxford: Clarendon Press, 1968), p. 70: "theories of punishment are not theories in any normal sense. They are not, as scientific theories are, assertions or contentions as to what is or is not the case. . . . On the contrary, those major positions concerning punishment which are called deterrent or retributive or reformative 'theories' of punishment are *moral* claims as to what justifies the practice of punishment — claims as to why, morally, it should or may be used." Hart goes on to write that if we claim that capital punishment protects society from harm, then we should call "this implicit moral claim 'the utilitarian position.'" I agree with Hart's fastidious use of terms, but the word *theory* is by now too deeply embedded in criminological discourse to be summarily uprooted.

[5] By "special case," of course, I mean the deterrence that is ascribed to capital punishment that is beyond the reach of life imprisonment.

[6] I readily concede that I am too squeamish to justify punishment for the sake of vengeance. I insist that there is a significant difference between primitive vengeance — the *lex talionis* of Hammurabi, Leviticus, and the Twelve Tables of republican Rome — and the denunciatory, reprobative functions of retribution.

hold that punishment must not be inflicted beyond simple necessity. It is not necessary to punish anyone with a sanction more severe than the gravity of the crimes committed and the criminal's record of recidivism for serious crimes. I see no great problem in achieving a consensus on the scale of sanctions, with a life term in prison for the first degree murderer at the apex of the scale.

The rule is that we should punish no more than we must. The death penalty is needless in an age when the maximum-security prison is available. Adherence to the principle of necessity as the limiting factor in determining the nature and quality of punishment will go far toward preventing our nation from ever descending to the horrible depths of degraded justice that are to be seen in Eastern Europe, in South Africa, and in Argentina.

The executioner does what he has to do in behalf of the citizens 25 of the state that employs him. His hand is on the lever that releases the cyanide, switches on the current, or springs the trap. We, as citizens, cannot escape a full share of his responsibility. We voted into office the legislators who make killers of us all. If the deliberate killing of another human being is the most abhorrent of crimes, we are all guilty, even though we shall be scot-free from legal punishment. The pity and terror that an execution inspires in even the most callous is punishment enough for the perceptive citizen. Pity and terror, mixed with the knowledge that what has been done is futile.

As my stoical opponent has repeatedly reminded us, we must all die. Many of us will die in conditions far more painful than sudden oblivion from a whiff of gas or a lethal charge of electricity. None of us has to inflict death on another. The statutes that make such deaths occasionally possible must be repealed in the interest of decency and good conscience. The sooner the better.

For the Death Penalty

ERNEST VAN DEN HAAG

There are two basic arguments for the death penalty; they are independent of, yet consistent with, one another.

The first argument is moral: The death penalty is just; it is deserved for certain crimes. One can explain why one feels that certain crimes deserve the death penalty. But as usual with moral arguments, one cannot show this conviction to be *factually* correct (or, for that matter, incorrect) since moral arguments rest not on facts but on our evaluation of them. My evaluation leads me to believe that, e.g., premeditated murder or treason (a fact) is so grave and horrible a crime (an evaluation) as to deserve nothing less than the death penalty, that only the death penalty (a fact) is proportionate to the gravity of the crime (an evaluation).

My widely shared view is opposed by abolitionists, who claim that the death penalty is unjust for any crime, and inconsistent with human dignity. Professor Conrad's arguments in favor of this position seem unconvincing to me. Since most abolitionists believe, as I do, that punishments should be proportionate to the perceived gravity of crimes, the abolitionist claim seems to me logically precarious. It implies either that murder is not so horrible after all — not horrible enough, at any rate to deserve death — or that the death penalty is too harsh a punishment for it, and indeed for any conceivable crime. I find it hard to believe that one can hold either view seriously, let alone both. But I am wrong: Professor Conrad does, and he is by no means alone in the academic world.

I must confess that I have never understood the assorted arguments claiming that the death penalty is inconsistent with human dignity or that, somehow, society has no right to impose it. One might as well claim that death generally, or at least death from illness, is inconsistent with human dignity, or that birth is, or any suffering or any undesirable social condition. Most of these are unavoidable. At least death by execution can be avoided by not killing someone else, by not committing murder. One can preserve one's dignity in this respect if one values it. Incidentally, execution may be physically less humiliating and painful than death in a hospital. It is, however, morally more humiliating and meant to be: It indicates the extreme blame we attach to the crime of murder by deliberately expelling the murderer from among the living.

Ernest van den Haag is the retired John M. Olin Professor of Jurisprudence and Public Policy at Fordham University and a Distinguished Scholar at the Heritage Foundation. This essay is from *The Death Penalty Pro and Con: A Debate* (1983).

As for the dignity of society, it seems to me that by executing 5 murderers it tries to keep its promise to secure the lives of innocents, to vindicate the law, and to impose retribution on those who so horribly violate it. To do anything less would be inconsistent with the dignity of society.

I see no evidence for society somehow not having "the right" to execute murderers. It has always done so. Traditional laws and Scriptures have always supported the death penalty. I know of no reasoning, even in a religious (theocratic) state, that denies the right of secular courts to impose it. We in America have a secular republic, of course, and therefore, the suggestion that the right to punish belongs only to God, or that the right to impose capital punishment does, is clearly out of place. It is not a religious but a secular task to put murderers to death. Our Constitution does provide for it (Amendments V and XIV). However much we believe in divine justice, it is to occur after, not in, this life. As for justice here and now, it is done by the courts, which are authorized in certain cases to impose the death penalty. A secular state cannot leave it to God. And incidentally, no theocratic state ever has. If they make mistakes, one can hope that God will correct the courts hereafter — but this is no ground for depriving courts of their duty to impose the penalties provided by law where required, nor is it a ground for depriving the law of the ability to prescribe the punishments felt to be just, including the death penalty.

The second argument in favor of capital punishment is material, grounded on empirical facts. They are contested, as readers of this book know, but no one would deny that what is contested are facts. The factual question is: Does the death penalty deter murder more than life imprisonment, or does it make no difference?

I do not agree with Professor Conrad's wishful idea that the work of Professor Isaac Ehrlich has been discredited. I believe that Ehrlich's findings — that the death penalty does indeed deter more than any other penalty currently inflicted, so that each execution saves between seven and nine innocent lives, the lives of victims who will not be murdered in the year of execution because of the deterrent effects of executions — have been confirmed by subsequent studies and have stood up sturdily under criticism competent and incompetent, which Ehrlich has convincingly refuted. However, Ehrlich's work is controversial. Anything is, if a sufficient number of people attack it. It is fair, therefore, to say that although the preponderance of evidence is now supporting the hypothesis that capital punishment deters more than any other punishment, the statistical demonstration has not been conclusive enough to convince everybody. Certainly not Professor Conrad and his friends. They have not changed their pre-Ehrlich convictions, and indeed tend to dismiss his work.

But Conrad's fellow abolitionists have admitted that they would want to abolish the death penalty even if it were shown statistically that each execution does reduce the homicide rate by 500 murders per year. Why then worry about statistical proof? And why take seriously people so irrational that they would sacrifice the lives of 500 innocents to preserve the life of one convicted murderer?

Statistics have their place. But here I think they scarcely are 10 needed. Harsher penalties are more deterrent than milder ones. Not only does our whole criminal justice system accept this view; we all do to the extent to which deterrence is aimed at in our everyday life. All other things equal, we penalize our children, our friends, or our business partners the more harshly the more we feel we must deter them and others in the future from a wrong they have done. Social life would not be possible if we did not believe that we can attract people to actions we desire by giving them incentives, and deter them from actions we do not desire by disincentives. The incentives and disincentives are usually proportionate to the felt desirability or undesirability of what we want to attract to or deter from. Why should murder be an exception? Why should we not believe that the greatest disincentive — the threat of death — is most likely to be the greatest deterrent?

Where there is life there is hope. This certainly is one major argument in favor of the death penalty. The murderer who premeditates his crime — and crimes of passion are not subject to capital punishment — if he contemplates the risk of life imprisonment is not likely to believe that, if convicted, he will remain in prison for life. He knows, however inchoately, about parole, pardons, commutations — he believes above all that he, a smart and superior fellow, will find a way to escape. Few prisoners actually do escape. But practically all "lifers" believe that they will, at least when they start their sentence. So believing, they do not greatly fear a sentence of life imprisonment and are not deterred by it. This is why the rate of stranger-murders — murders in which victim and murderer do not know one another and to which the threat of the death penalty should apply — as a proportion of all murders has steadily climbed in the last twenty years. The murderers knew that in practice they would get away with life imprisonment, from which they would be paroled after a few years. Or they hoped they would escape. After all, we executed all of five prisoners in 1981, only one of whom was executed against his wishes. (All of them were white, to the great disappointment of the civil liberties lobby.) At this rate no murderer can foresee execution or be deterred by it.

I find it hard to believe, as Professor Conrad does, that most men are incapable of murder. I admire his optimism. But I find it hard to share. I do not see how he can cling to his faith after Stalin and Hitler, in the presence of assorted tyrants and murderers in power from Albania to Iran to China. But faith obviously is not subject to empirical verification. I am optimistic, however, in my own way, which seems more realistic to me: I believe that most men can be deterred from murder by the threat of the death penalty.

Even if Conrad were right, even if his claim that only a few men would ever become murderers in the absence of the threat of punishment were correct, I should continue to advocate the death penalty to deter these few men. And even if only some of these men need the threat of capital punishment to be deterred, while others would be deterred by the threat of life imprisonment, I should advocate the death penalty to deter the very few who, according to Conrad, do, or even just may, require it to be deterred. The lives of the innocents that will or may be spared because of the death penalty are more valuable to me, and to any civilized society, than the lives of murderers. I do not want to risk their lives for the sake of the lives of murderers.

The reader will have to decide for himself on which side he wants to be.

Discussion Questions

1. These arguments are the conclusions of a book-long debate. Do you think the debaters have omitted any significant issues?
2. Both Conrad and van den Haag accuse each other of holding views of human nature based on faulty warrants. Explain their respective views. Do they offer sufficient support for them?
3. Why does Conrad think the death penalty is unnecessary as a deterrent? Is there a contradiction in his argument that life imprisonment is just as bad as, if not worse than, capital punishment?
4. What are van den Haag's two main arguments in favor of the death penalty? How can you tell which he considers to be more important?
5. To what extent do statistics and other facts play a role in these arguments?

EXERCISES

1. What are some of the assumptions underlying the preference for *natural* foods and medicines? Can *natural* be clearly defined? Is this preference part of a broader philosophy? Try to evaluate the validity of the assumption.
2. Is plagiarism wrong? What assumptions about education are relevant to the issue of plagiarism? (Some students defend it. What kinds of arguments do they provide?)
3. Choose an advertisement and examine the warrants on which the advertiser's claim is based.
4. "Religious beliefs are (or are not) necessary to a satisfactory life." Explain the warrants underlying your claim. Define any ambiguous terms.

5. Should students be given a direct voice in the hiring of faculty members? On what warrants about education do you base your answer?
6. Discuss the validity of the warrant in this statement from *The Watch Tower* (a publication of the Jehovah's Witnesses) about genital herpes: "The sexually loose are indeed 'receiving in themselves the full recompense, which was due for their error' (Romans 1:27)."
7. Read the following passage about suicide by the Greek philosopher Aristotle (adapted from his *Ethics*). Then defend or attack his argument, being careful to make clear both Aristotle's and your own warrants.

> Just as a murderer does not have the right to take a mother from her family or a child from her parents and simultaneously to deny society the use of a productive citizen, so the suicide, even though he or she freely chooses to be his or her own victim, does not possess the right to thus diminish the welfare of so many others.

8. In view of the increasing attention to health in general, and nutrition and exercise in particular, do you think that universities and colleges should impose physical education requirements? If so, what form should they take? If not, why not? Defend your reasons.
9. In recent years both state and federal governments have been embroiled in controversies concerning the rights of citizens to engage in harmful practices. In Massachusetts, for example, a mandatory seat belt law was repealed by rebellious voters who considered the law an infringement of their freedom. What principles do you think ought to guide government regulation of dangerous practices?
10. The author of the following passage, Katherine Butler Hathaway, became a hunchback as a result of a childhood illness. Here she writes about the relationship between love and beauty from the point of view of someone who is deformed. Discuss the warrants on which the author bases her conclusion.

> I could secretly pretend that I had a lover . . . but I could never risk showing that I thought such a thing was possible for me . . . with any man. Because of my repeated encounters with the mirror and my irrepressible tendency to forget what I had seen, I had begun to force myself to believe and to remember, and especially to remember, that I would never be chosen for what I imagined to be the supreme and most intimate of all experience. I thought of sexual love as an honor that was too great and too beautiful for the body in which I was doomed to live.

Critical Listening

11. People often complain that they aren't listened to. Children complain about parents, patients about doctors, wives about husbands, citizens about government. Are the complaints to be taken literally? Or are they based on unexpressed warrants or assumptions about communication? Choose a specific situation with which you're familiar and explain the meaning of the complaint.

12. Barbara Ehrenreich, in a *Time* essay, defends "talk shows of the *Sally Jessy Raphael* variety" as highly moralistic. Listen to a few of these shows — *Ricki Lake, Geraldo, Hard Copy* — and determine what moral assumptions about personal relationships and behavior underlie the advice given to the participants by the host and the audience. Do you think Ehrenreich is correct?

CHAPTER SEVEN

Language
and Thought

THE POWER OF WORDS

Words play such a critical role in argument that they deserve special treatment. Elsewhere we have referred directly and indirectly to language: Chapter 4 discusses definitions and Part Two discusses style — the choice and arrangement of words and sentences — and shows how successful writers express arguments in language that is clear, vivid, and thoughtful. An important part of these writers' equipment is a large and active vocabulary, but no single chapter in a book can give this to you; only reading and study can widen your range of word choices. Even in a brief chapter, however, we can point out how words influence the feelings and attitudes of an audience, both favorably and unfavorably.

One kind of language responsible for shaping attitudes and feelings is *emotive language,* language that expresses and arouses emotions. Understanding it and using it effectively is indispensable to the arguer who wants to move an audience to accept a point of view or undertake an action.

Long before you thought about writing your first argument, you learned that words had the power to affect you. Endearments and affectionate and flattering nicknames evoked good feelings about the speaker and yourself. Insulting nicknames and slurs produced dislike for the speaker and bad feelings about yourself. Perhaps you were told, "Sticks and stones may break your bones, but words will never hurt you." But even to a small child it is clear that ugly words are as painful as sticks and stones and that the injuries are sometimes more lasting.

Nowhere is the power of words more obvious and more familiar than in advertising, where the success of a product may depend on the feelings that certain words produce in the prospective buyer. Even the names of products may have emotive significance. In recent years a new industry, composed of consultants who supply names for products, has emerged. Although most manufacturers agree that a good name won't save a poor product, they also recognize that the right name can catch the attention of the public and persuade people to buy a product at least once. According to an article in the *Wall Street Journal,* a product name not only should be memorable but also should "remind people of emotional or physical experiences." One consultant created the name Magnum for a malt liquor from Miller Brewing Company: "The product is aimed at students, minorities, and lower-income customers." The president of the consulting firm says that Magnum "implies strength, masculinity, and more bang for your buck."[1] This naming of products has been called the "Rumpelstiltskin effect," a phrase coined by a linguist. "The whole point," he said, "is that when you have the right name for a thing, you have control over it."[2]

Even scientists recognize the power of words to attract the attention of other scientists and the public to discoveries and theories that might otherwise remain obscure. A good name can even enable the scientist to visualize a new concept. One scientist says that "a good name," such as "quark," "black hole," "big bang," "chaos," or "great attractor," "helps in communicating a theory and can have substantial impact on financing."

It is not hard to see the connection between the use of words in conversation and advertising and the use of emotive language in the more formal arguments you will be writing. Emotive language reveals your approval or disapproval, assigns praise or blame — in other words, makes a judgment about the subject. Keep in mind that unless you are writing purely factual statements, such as scientists write, you will find it hard to avoid expressing judgments. Neutrality does not come easily, even where it may be desirable, as in news stories or reports of historical events. For this reason you need to attend carefully to the statements in your argument, making sure that you have not disguised judgments as statements of fact. Of course, in attempting to prove a claim, you will not be neutral. You will be revealing your judgment about the subject, first in the selection of facts and opinions and the emphasis you give to them and second in the selection of words.

Like the choice of facts and opinions, the choice of words can be effective or ineffective in advancing your argument, moral or im-

---

[1] *Wall Street Journal,* August 5, 1982, p. 19.
[2] *Harvard Magazine,* July–August 1995, p. 18.

moral in the honesty with which you exercise it. The following discussions offer some insights into recognizing and evaluating the use of emotive language in the arguments you read, as well as into using such language in your own arguments where it is appropriate and avoiding it where it is not.

CONNOTATION

The connotations of a word are the meanings we attach to it apart from its explicit definition. Because these added meanings derive from our feelings, connotations are one form of emotive language. For example, the word *rat* denotes or points to a kind of rodent, but the attached meanings of "selfish person," "evil-doer," "betrayer," and "traitor" reflect the feelings that have accumulated around the word.

In Chapter 4 we observed that definitions of controversial terms, such as *poverty* and *unemployment*, may vary so widely that writer and reader cannot always be sure that they are thinking of the same thing. A similar problem arises when a writer assumes that the reader shares his or her emotional response to a word. Emotive meanings originate partly in personal experience. The word *home*, defined merely as "a family's place of residence," may suggest love, warmth, and security to one person; it may suggest friction, violence, and alienation to another. The values of the groups to which we belong also influence meaning. Writers and speakers count on cultural associations when they refer to our country, our flag, and heroes and enemies we have never seen. The arguer must also be aware that some apparently neutral words trigger different responses from different groups — words such as *cult, revolution, police, beauty contest,* and *corporation.*

Various reform movements have recognized that words with unfavorable connotations have the power not only to reflect but also to shape our perceptions of things. The words *Negro* and *colored* were rejected by the civil rights movement in the 1960s because they bore painful associations with slavery and discrimination. Instead, the word *black,* which was free from such associations, became the accepted designation; more recently, the Reverend Jesse Jackson suggested another change, African American, to reflect ethnic origins. People of "Spanish-Hispanic" origin (as they are designated on the 1990 census) are now engaged in a debate about the appropriate term for a diverse population of more than 22 million American residents from Mexico, Puerto Rico, Cuba, and more than a dozen Central and South American countries. To some, the word *Hispanic* is unacceptable because it is an Anglicization and recalls the colonization of America by Spain and Portugal.

The women's liberation movement also insisted on changes that would bring about improved attitudes toward women. The movement condemned the use of *girl* for a female over the age of eighteen and the use in news stories of descriptive adjectives that emphasized the physical appearance of women. And the homosexual community succeeded in reintroducing the word *gay,* a word current centuries ago, as a substitute for words they considered offensive. Now *queer,* a word long regarded as offensive, has been adopted as a substitute for *gay* by a new generation of gays and lesbians, although it is still considered unacceptable by many members of the homosexual community.

Members of certain occupations have invented terms to confer greater respectability on their work. The work does not change, but the workers hope that public perceptions will change if janitors are called custodians, if garbage collectors are called sanitation engineers, if undertakers are called morticians, if people who sell makeup are called cosmetologists. Events considered unpleasant or unmentionable are sometimes disguised by polite terms, called *euphemisms.* During the 1992–1993 recession new terms emerged which disguised, or tried to, the grim fact that thousands of people were being dismissed from their jobs: "skill mix adjustment," "work force imbalance correction," "redundancy elimination," "downsizing," "indefinite idling," even a daring "career-change opportunity." Many people refuse to use the word *died* and choose *passed away* instead. Some psychologists and physicians use the phrase "negative patient care outcome" for what most of us would call "death." Even when referring to their pets, some people cannot bring themselves to say "put to death" but substitute "put to sleep" or "put down." In place of a term to describe an act of sexual intercourse, some people use "slept together" or "went to bed together" or "had an affair."

Polite words are not always so harmless. If a euphemism disguises a shameful event or condition, it is morally irresponsible to use it to mislead the reader into believing that the shameful condition does not exist. In his powerful essay "Politics and the English Language" George Orwell pointed out that politicians and reporters have sometimes used terms like "pacification" or "rectification of frontiers" to conceal acts that result in torture and death for millions of people. An example of such usage was cited by a member of Amnesty International, a group monitoring human rights violations throughout the world. He objected to a news report describing camps in which the Chinese were promoting "reeducation through labor." This term, he wrote, "makes these institutions seem like a cross between Police Athletic League and Civilian Conservation Corps camps." On the contrary, he went on, the reality of "reeducation through labor" was that the victims were confined to "rather unpleasant prison camps." The details he offered about the conditions under which people lived and worked gave substance to his claim.[3] More recently, when news organizations referred to the expulsion of Romanian gypsies from Germany as part of a "deportation treaty," an official of Germany's press agency objected to the use of the word "deportation." "You must know that by using words such as 'deportation' you are causing great sadness. . . . We prefer that you use the term readmission or retransfer."[4]

Some of the most interesting changes in language usage occur in modern Bible translations. The vocabulary and syntax of earlier versions have been greatly simplified in order to make the Bible more accessible to that half of the American public who cannot read above eighth-grade level. Another change responds to arguments by feminists, environmentalists, and multiculturalists for more "inclusive language." God is no longer the "Father," human beings no longer have "dominion" over creation, and even the word "blindness" as a metaphor for sin or evil has been replaced by other metaphors.

Perhaps the most striking examples of the way that connotations influence our perceptions of reality occur when people are asked to respond to questions of poll-takers. Sociologists and students of poll-taking know that the phrasing of a question, or the choice of words, can affect the answers and even undermine the validity of the poll. In one case poll-takers first asked a selected group of people if they favored continuing the welfare system. The majority answered no. But when the poll-takers asked if they favored government aid to the poor, the majority answered yes. Although the terms "welfare" and "government aid to the poor" refer to essentially the same forms of government assistance, "welfare" has acquired for many people negative connotations of corruption and shiftless recipients.

A *New York Times*/CBS News poll conducted in January 1989 asked, "If a woman wants to have an abortion and her doctor agrees to it, should she be allowed to have an abortion or not?" Sixty-one percent said yes, 25 percent said no, and 25 percent said it depended on the circumstances. But when the pollsters asked, "Should abortion be legal as it is now, or legal only in such cases as rape, incest, or to save the life of the mother, or should it not be permitted at all?" a much higher percentage said that abortion depended on the circumstances. Only 46 percent said it should be legal as it is now, and 41 percent said it should be legal only in such cases as rape, incest, or to save the life of the mother. According to polling experts, people are far more likely to say that they support abortion

---

[3]Letter to the *New York Times,* August 30, 1982, p. 25.
[4]*International Herald Tribune,* November 5, 1992.

when the question is asked in terms of the "woman's right to choose" than when the question asks about "protecting the unborn child." "How the question is framed," say the experts, "can affect the answers."[5]

This is also true in polls concerning rape, another highly charged subject. Dr. Neil Malamuth, a psychologist at the University of California at Los Angeles, says, "When men are asked if there is any likelihood they would force a woman to have sex against her will if they could get away with it, about half say they would. But if you ask them if they would rape a woman if they knew they could get away with it, only about 15 percent say they would." The men who change their answers aren't aware that "the only difference is in the words used to describe the same act."[6]

The wording of an argument is crucial. Because readers may interpret the words you use on the basis of feelings different from your own, you must support your word choices with definitions and with evidence that allows readers to determine how and why you made them.

SLANTING

Slanting, says one dictionary, is "interpreting or presenting in line with a special interest." The term is almost always used in a negative sense. It means that the arguer has selected facts and words with favorable or unfavorable connotations to create the impression that no alternative view exists or can be defended. For some questions it is true that no alternative view is worthy of presentation, and emotionally charged language to defend or attack a position that is clearly right or wrong would be entirely appropriate. We aren't neutral, nor should we be, about the tragic abuse of human rights anywhere in the world or even about less serious infractions of the law, such as drunk driving or vandalism, and we should use strong language to express our disapproval of these practices.

Most of your arguments, however, will concern controversial questions about which people of goodwill can argue on both sides. In such cases, your own judgments should be restrained. Slanting will suggest a prejudice — that is, a judgment made without regard to all the facts. Unfortunately, you may not always be aware of your bias or special interest; you may believe that your position is the only correct one. You may also feel the need to communicate a passionate belief about a serious problem. But if you are interested in persuading a reader to accept your belief and to act on it, you must

---

[5]*New York Times,* January 1, 1989, p. 21.
[6]*New York Times,* August 29, 1989, Sec. C, p. 1.

also ask: If the reader is not sympathetic, how will he or she respond? Will he or she perceive my words as "loaded" — one-sided and prejudicial — and my view as slanted?

R. D. Laing, a Scottish psychiatrist, defined prayer in this way: "Someone is gibbering away on his knees, talking to someone who is not there."[7] This description probably reflects a sincerely held belief. Laing also clearly intended it for an audience that already agreed with him. But the phrases "gibbering away" and "someone who is not there" would be offensive to people for whom prayer is sacred.

The following remark by an editor of *Penthouse* appeared in a debate on women's liberation.

> I haven't noticed that there is such a thing as a rise in the women's liberation movement. It seems to me that it's a lot of minor sound and a tiny fury. There are some bitty bitty groups of some disappointed ladies who have some objective or other.[8]

An unfriendly audience would resent the use of language intended to diminish the importance of the movement: "minor sound," "tiny fury," "bitty bitty groups of some disappointed ladies," "some objective or other." But even audiences sympathetic to the claim may be repelled or embarrassed by intense, colorful, obviously loaded words. In the mid-1980s an English environmental group, *London Greenpeace,* began to distribute leaflets accusing the McDonald's restaurants of a wide assortment of crimes. The leaflets said in part:

> McDollars, McGreedy, McCancer, McMurder, McDisease, McProfits, McDeadly, McHunger, McRipoff, McTorture, McWasteful, McGarbage.
>
> This leaflet is asking you to think for a moment about what lies behind McDonald's clean, bright image. It's got a lot to hide. . . .
>
> McDonald's and Burger King are two of the many U.S. corporations using lethal poisons to destroy vast areas of Central American rain forest to create grazing pastures for cattle to be sent back to the States as burgers and pet food. . . .
>
> What they don't make clear is that a diet high in fat, sugar, animal products and salt . . . and low in fiber, vitamins and minerals — which describes an average McDonald's meal — is linked with cancers of the breast and bowel, and heart disease. . . .[9]

Even readers who share the belief that McDonald's is not a reliable source of good nutrition might feel that *London Greenpeace* has gone

---

[7]"The Obvious," in *The Dialectics of Liberation,* edited by David Cooper (Penguin Books, 1968), p. 17.

[8]"Women's Liberation: A Debate" (Penthouse International Ltd., 1970).

[9]*New York Times,* August 6, 1995, Sec. E, p. 7. (In 1990 McDonald's sued the group for libel; the trial began in 1994 and will probably last until 1996, the longest libel trial in British history.)

too far, that the name-calling, loaded words, and exaggeration have damaged the credibility of the attackers more than the reputation of McDonald's.

We find slanting everywhere, not only in advertising and propaganda, where we expect to find it, but in news stories, which should be strictly neutral in their recounting of events, and in textbooks. In the field of history, for example, it is often difficult for scholars to remain impartial about significant events. Like the rest of us, they may approve or disapprove, and their choice of words will reflect their judgments.

The following passage by a distinguished Catholic historian describes the events surrounding the momentous decision by Henry VIII, king of England, to break with the Roman Catholic Church in 1534, in part because of the Pope's refusal to grant him a divorce from the Catholic princess Catherine of Aragon so that he could marry Anne Boleyn.

> The *protracted* delay in receiving an annulment was very *irritating* to the *impulsive* English king. . . . Gradually Henry's former *effusive* loyalty to Rome gave way to a settled conviction of the tyranny of the papal power, and there *rushed* to his mind the recollections of efforts of earlier English rulers to restrict that power. A few *salutary* enactments against the Church might *compel* a favorable decision from the Pope.
>
> Henry seriously opened his campaign against the Roman Church in 1531, when he *frightened* the clergy into paying a fine of over half a million dollars for violating an *obsolete* statute . . . and in the same year he *forced* the clergy to recognize himself as supreme head of the Church. . . .
>
> His *subservient* Parliament then empowered him to stop the payments of annates to the Pope and to appoint bishops in England without recourse to the papacy. *Without waiting longer* for the decision from Rome, he had Cranmer, *one of his own creatures,* whom he had just named Archbishop of Canterbury, declare his marriage null and void. . . .
>
> Yet Henry VIII encountered considerable *opposition* from the *higher clergy,* from the monks, and from many *intellectual leaders.* . . . A *popular uprising* — the Pilgrimage of Grace — was *sternly* suppressed, and such men as the *brilliant* Sir Thomas More and John Fisher, the *aged* and *saintly* bishop of Rochester, were beheaded because they retained their former belief in papal supremacy.[10] [Italics added]

In the first paragraph the italicized words help make the following points: that Henry was rash, impulsive, and insincere and that he was intent on punishing the church (the word *salutary* means healthful or beneficial and is used sarcastically). In the second paragraph the choice of words stresses Henry's use of force and the cowardly submission of his followers. In the third paragraph the adjectives de-

---

[10]Carlton J. H. Hayes, *A Political and Cultural History of Modern Europe,* Vol. 1 (New York: Macmillan Company, 1933), pp. 172–173.

scribing the opposition to Henry's campaign and those who were executed emphasize Henry's cruelty and despotism. Within the limits of this brief passage the author has offered support for his strong indictment of Henry VIII's actions, both in defining the statute as obsolete and in describing the popular opposition. In a longer exposition you would expect to find a more elaborate justification with facts and authoritative opinion from other sources.

The advocate of a position in an argument, unlike the reporter or the historian, must express a judgment, but the preceding examples demonstrate how the arguer should use language to avoid or minimize slanting and to persuade readers that he or she has come to a conclusion after careful analysis. The careful arguer must not conceal his or her judgments by presenting them as if they were statements of fact, but must offer convincing support for his or her choice of words and respect the audience's feelings and attitudes by using temperate language.

Depending on the circumstances, *exaggeration* can be defined, in the words of one writer, as "a form of lying." An essay in *Time* magazine, "Watching Out for Loaded Words," points to the danger for the arguer in relying on exaggerated language as an essential part of the argument.

> The trouble with loaded words is they tend to short-circuit thought. While they may describe something, they simultaneously try to seduce the mind into accepting a prefabricated opinion about the something described.[11]

PICTURESQUE LANGUAGE

Picturesque language consists of words that produce images in the mind of the reader. Students sometimes assume that vivid picture-making language is the exclusive instrument of novelists and poets, but writers of arguments can also avail themselves of such devices to heighten the impact of their messages.

Picturesque language can do more than render a scene. It shares with other kinds of emotive language the power to express and arouse deep feelings. Like a fine painting or photograph, it can draw readers into the picture where they partake of the writer's experience as if they were also present. Such power may be used to delight, to instruct, or to horrify. In 1741 the Puritan preacher Jonathan Edwards delivered his sermon "Sinners in the Hands of an Angry God," in which people were likened to repulsive spiders hanging over the flames of Hell to be dropped into the fire whenever a wrath-

---

[11]*Time,* May 24, 1982, p. 86.

ful God was pleased to release them. The congregation's reaction to Edwards's picture of the everlasting horrors to be suffered in the netherworld included panic, fainting, hysteria, and convulsions. Subsequently Edwards lost his pulpit in Massachusetts, in part as a consequence of his success at provoking such uncontrollable terror among his congregation.

Language as intense and vivid as Edwards's emerges from very strong emotion about a deeply felt cause. In an argument against abortion, a surgeon recounts a horrifying experience as if it were a scene in a movie.

> You walk toward the bus stop. . . . It is all so familiar. All at once you step on something soft. You feel it with your foot. Even through your shoe you may have the sense of something unusual, something marked by a special "give." It is a foreignness upon the pavement. Instinct pulls your foot away in an awkward little movement. You look down, and you see . . . a tiny naked body, its arms and legs flung apart, its head thrown back, its mouth agape, its face serious. A bird, you think, fallen from the nest. But there is no nest here on 73rd Street, no bird so big. It is rubber, then. A model, a . . . a joke. And you bend to see. Because you must. And it is no joke. Such a gray softness can be but one thing. It is a baby, and dead. You cover your mouth, your eyes. You are fixed. Horror has found its chink and crawled in, and you will never be the same as you were. Years later you will step from a sidewalk to a lawn, and you will start at its softness and think of that upon which you have just trod.[12]

Here the use of the pronoun *you* serves to draw readers into the scene and intensify their experience.

The rules governing the use of picturesque language are the same as those governing other kinds of emotive language. Is the language appropriate? Is it too strong, too colorful for the purpose of the message? Does it result in slanting or distortion? What will its impact be on a hostile or indifferent audience? Will they be angered, repelled? Will they cease to read or listen if the imagery is too disturbing?

We expect strong language in arguments about life and death. For subjects about which your feelings are not so passionate, your choice of words will be more moderate. The excerpt below, from an article arguing against repeal of Sunday closing laws, creates a sympathetic picture of a market-free Sunday. Most readers, even those who oppose Sunday closing laws, would enjoy the picture and perhaps react more favorably to the argument.

> Think of waking in the city on Sunday. Although most people no longer worship in the morning, the city itself has a reverential air. It comes to life slowly, even reluctantly, as traffic lights blink their orders

---

[12]Richard Selzer, *Mortal Lessons: Notes on the Art of Surgery* (New York: Simon and Schuster, 1974), pp. 153–154.

to empty streets. Next, joggers venture forth, people out to get the paper, families going to church or grandma's. Soon the city is its Sunday self: People cavort with their children, discuss, make repairs, go to museums, gambol. Few people go to work, and any shopping is incidental. The city on Sunday is a place outside the market. Play dominates, not the economy.[13]

CONCRETE AND ABSTRACT LANGUAGE

Writers of argument need to be aware of another use of language — the distinction between concrete and abstract. Concrete words point to real objects and real experiences. Abstract words express qualities apart from particular things and events. *Beautiful roses* is concrete; we can see, touch, and smell them. *Beauty* in the eye of the beholder is abstract; we can speak of the quality of beauty without reference to a particular object or event. *Returning money found in the street to the owner, although no one has seen the discovery* is concrete. *Honesty* is abstract. In abstracting we separate a quality shared by a number of objects or events, however different from each other the individual objects or events may be.

Writing that describes or tells a story leans heavily on concrete language. Although arguments also rely on the vividness of concrete language, they use abstract terms far more extensively than other kinds of writing. Using abstractions effectively, especially in arguments of value and policy, is important for two reasons: (1) Abstractions represent the qualities, characteristics, and values that the writer is explaining, defending, or attacking; and (2) they enable the writer to make generalizations about his or her data. Equally important is knowing when to avoid abstractions that obscure the message.

In some textbook discussions of language, abstractions are treated as inferior to concrete and specific words, but such a distinction is misleading. Abstractions allow us to make sense of our experience, to come to conclusions about the meaning of the bewildering variety of emotions and events we confront throughout a lifetime. One writer summarized his early history as follows: "My elementary school had the effect of *destroying any intellectual motivation,* of *stifling* all *creativity,* of *inhibiting personal relationships* with either my teachers or my peers" (emphasis added). Writing in the humanities and in some social and physical sciences would be impossible without recourse to abstractions that express qualities, values, and conditions.

---

[13]Robert K. Manoff, "New York City, It Is Argued, Faces 'Sunday Imperialism,'" *New York Times,* January 2, 1977, Sec. IV, p. 13.

You should not, however, expect abstract terms alone to carry the emotional content of your message. The effect of even the most suggestive words can be enhanced by details, examples, and anecdotes. One mode of expression is not superior to the other; both abstractions and concrete detail work together to produce clear, persuasive argument. This is especially true when the meanings assigned to abstract terms vary from reader to reader.

In establishing claims based on the support of values, for example, you may use such abstract terms as *religion, duty, freedom, peace, progress, justice, equality, democracy,* and *pursuit of happiness.* You can assume that some of these words are associated with the same ideas and emotions for almost all readers; others require further explanation. Suppose you write, "We have made great progress in the last fifty years." One dictionary defines *progress* as "a gradual betterment," another abstraction. How will you define "gradual betterment" for your readers? Can you be sure that they have in mind the same references for progress that you do? If not, misunderstandings are inevitable. You may offer examples: supersonic planes, computers, shopping malls, nuclear energy. Many of your readers will react favorably to the mention of these innovations, which to them represent progress; others, for whom these inventions represent change but not progress, will react unfavorably. You may not be able to convince all of your readers that "we have made great progress," but all of them will now understand what you mean by "progress." And intelligent disagreement is preferable to misunderstanding.

Abstractions tell us what conclusions we have arrived at; details tell us how we got there. But there are dangers in either too many details or too many abstractions. For example, a writer may present only concrete data without telling readers what conclusions are to be drawn from them. Suppose you read the following:

> To Chinese road-users, traffic police are part of the grass . . . and neither they nor the rules they're supposed to enforce are paid the least attention. . . . Ignoring traffic-lights is only one peculiarity of Chinese traffic. It's normal for a pedestrian to walk straight out into a stream of cars without so much as lifting his head; and goodness knows how many Chinese cyclists I've almost killed as they have shot blindly in front of me across busy main roads.[14]

These details would constitute no more than interesting gossip until we read, "It's not so much a sign of ignorance or recklessness . . . but of fatalism." The details of specific behavior have now acquired a significance expressed in the abstraction *fatalism.*

---

[14]Philip Short, "The Chinese and the Russians," *The Listener,* April 8, 1982, p. 6.

A more common problem, however, in using abstractions is omission of details. Either the writer is not a skilled observer and cannot provide the details, or he or she feels that such details are too small and quiet compared to the grand sounds made by abstract terms. These grand sounds, unfortunately, cannot compensate for the lack of clarity and liveliness. Lacking detailed support, abstract words may be misinterpreted. They may also represent ideas that are so vague as to be meaningless. Sometimes they function illegitimately as short cuts (discussed on pp. 227–34), arousing emotions but unaccompanied by good reasons for their use. The following paragraph exhibits some of these common faults. How would you translate it into clear English?

> We respectively petition, request, and entreat that due and adequate provision be made, this day and the date hereinafter subscribed, for the satisfying of these petitioners' nutritional requirements and for the organizing of such methods of allocation and distribution as may be deemed necessary and proper to assure the reception by and for said petitioners of such quantities of baked cereal products as shall, in the judgment of the aforesaid petitioners, constitute a sufficient supply thereof.[15]

If you had trouble decoding this, it was because there were almost no concrete references — the homely words *baked* and *cereal* leap out of the paragraph like English signposts in a foreign country — and too many long words or words of Latin origin when simple words would do: *requirements* instead of *needs*, *petition* instead of *ask*. An absence of concrete references and an excess of long Latinate words can have a depressing effect on both writer and reader. The writer may be in danger of losing the thread of the argument, the reader at a loss to discover the message.

The paragraph above, according to James B. Minor, a lawyer who teaches courses in legal drafting, is "how a federal regulation writer would probably write, 'Give us this day our daily bread.'" This brief sentence with its short, familiar words and its origin in the Lord's Prayer has a deep emotional effect. The paragraph composed by Minor deadens any emotional impact because of its preponderance of abstract terms and its lack of connection with the world of our senses.

That passage was invented to educate writers in the government bureaucracy to avoid inflated prose. But writing of this kind is not uncommon among professional writers, including academics. If the subject matter is unfamiliar and the writer an acknowledged expert, you may have to expend a special effort in penetrating the language. But you may also rightly wonder if the writer is making unreasonable demands on you.

---

[15]*New York Times,* May 10, 1977, p. 35.

The human race is now entering upon a new phase of evolutionary consciousness and progress, a phase in which, impelled by the forces of evolution itself, it must converge upon itself and convert itself into one single human organism infused by a reconciliation of knowing and being in their inner unity and destined to make a qualitative leap into a higher form of consciousness as we know it, or otherwise destroy itself. For the entire universe is one vast field, potential for incarnation, and achieving incandescence here and there of reason and spirit. And in the whole world of *quality* with which by the nature of our minds we necessarily make contact, we here and there apprehend preeminent value. This can be achieved only if we recognize that we are unable to focus our attention on the particulars of the whole, without diminishing our comprehension of the whole, and of course, conversely, we can focus on the whole only by diminishing our comprehension of the particulars which constitute the whole.[16]

You probably found this paragraph even more baffling than the previous example. Although there is some glimmer of meaning here — that mankind must attain a higher level of consciousness, or perish — you should ask whether the extraordinary overload of abstract terms is justified. In fact, most readers would be disinclined to sit still for an argument with so little reference to the real world. One critic of social science prose maintains that if preeminent thinkers like Bertrand Russell can make themselves clear but social scientists continue to be obscure, "then you can justifiably suspect that it might all be nonsense."[17]

Finally, there are the moral implications of using abstractions that conceal a disagreeable reality. George Orwell pointed them out more than forty years ago in "Politics and the English Language." Another essayist, Joseph Wood Krutch, in criticizing the attitude that cheating "doesn't really hurt anybody," observed, " 'It really doesn't hurt anybody' means it doesn't do that abstraction called society any harm." The following news story reports a proposal with which Orwell and Krutch might have agreed. His intention, says the author, is to "slow the hand of any President who might be tempted to unleash a nuclear attack."

> It has long been feared that a President could be making his fateful decision while at a "psychological distance" from the victims of a nuclear barrage; that he would be in a clean, air-conditioned room, surrounded by well-scrubbed aides, all talking in abstract terms about appropriate military responses in an international crisis, and that he might well push to the back of his mind the realization that hundreds of millions of people would be exterminated.

---

[16]Ruth Nanda Anshen, "Credo Perspectives," introduction to *Two Modes of Thought* by James Bryant Conant (New York: Simon and Schuster, 1964), p. x.

[17]Stanislav Andreski, *Social Sciences as Sorcery* (New York: St. Martin's Press, 1972), p. 86.

So Roger Fisher, professor of law at Harvard University, offers a simple suggestion to make the stakes more real. He would put the codes needed to fire nuclear weapons in a little capsule, and implant the capsule next to the heart of a volunteer, who would carry a big butcher knife as he accompanied the President everywhere. If the President ever wanted to fire nuclear weapons, he would first have to kill, with his own hands, that human being.

He has to look at someone and realize what death is — what an innocent death is. "It's reality brought home," says Professor Fisher.[18]

The moral lesson is clear: It is much easier to do harm if we convince ourselves that the object of the injury is only an abstraction.

SHORT CUTS

Short cuts are arguments that depend on readers' responses to words. Short cuts, like other devices we have discussed so far, are a common use of emotive language but are often mistaken for valid argument.

Although they have power to move us, these abbreviated substitutes for argument avoid the hard work necessary to provide facts, expert opinion, and analysis of warrants. Even experts, however, can be guilty of using short cuts, and the writer who consults an authority should be alert to that authority's use of language. Two of the most common uses of short cuts are clichés and slogans.

Clichés

"I'm against sloppy, emotional thinking. I'm against fashionable thinking. I'm against the whole cliché of the moment."[19] This statement by the late Herman Kahn, the founder of the Hudson Institute, a famous think tank, serves as the text for this section. A cliché is an expression or idea grown stale through overuse. Clichés in language are tired expressions that have faded like old photographs; readers no longer see anything when clichés are placed before them. Clichés include phrases like "cradle of civilization," "few and far between," "rude awakening," "follow in the footsteps of," "fly in the ointment."

But more important to recognize and avoid are clichés of thought. A cliché of thought may be likened to a formula, which one dictionary defines as "any conventional rule or method for doing something, especially when used, applied, or repeated without thought." Clichés of thought represent ready-made answers to questions, stereotyped solutions to problems, "knee-jerk" reactions. Two writers who call these

---

[18]*New York Times,* September 7, 1982, Sec. C, p. 1.
[19]*New York Times,* July 8, 1983, Sec. B, p. 1.

forms of expression "mass language" describe it this way: "Mass language is language which presents the reader with a response he is expected to make without giving him adequate reason for having this response."[20] These "clichés of the moment" are often expressed in single words or phrases. For example, the phrase "Gen X" has been repeated so often that it has come to represent an indisputable truth for many people, one they no longer question. The acceptance of this cliché, however, conceals the fact that millions of very different kinds of people from ages eighteen to thirty-five are being thoughtlessly lumped together as apathetic and lazy.

Certain cultural attitudes encourage the use of clichés. The liberal American tradition has been governed by hopeful assumptions about our ability to solve problems. A professor of communications says that "we tell our students that for every problem there must be a solution."[21] But real solutions are hard to come by. In our haste to provide them, to prove that we can be decisive, we may be tempted to produce familiar responses that resemble solutions.

History teaches us that a solution to an old and serious problem is almost always accompanied by unexpected drawbacks. As the writer quoted in the previous paragraph warns us, "Life is not that simple. There is no one answer to a given problem. There are multiple solutions, all with advantages and disadvantages." By solving one problem, we often create another. Automobiles, advanced medical techniques, industrialization, and liberal divorce laws have all contributed to the solution of age-old problems: lack of mobility, disease, poverty, domestic unhappiness. We now see that these solutions bring with them new problems that we nevertheless elect to live with because the advantages seem greater than the disadvantages. A well-known economist puts it this way: "I don't look for solutions; I look for trade-offs. I think the person who asks, 'What is the solution to this problem?' has a fundamental misconception of the way the world works. We have trade-offs, and that's all we have."[22]

This means that we should be skeptical of solutions promising everything and ignoring limitations and criticism. Such solutions have probably gone around many times. Having heard them so often, we are inclined to believe that they have been tried and proven. Thus they escape serious analysis.

Some of these problems and their solutions represent the fashionable thinking to which Kahn objected. They confront us every-

---

[20]Richard E. Hughes and P. Albert Duhamel, *Rhetoric: Principles and Usage* (Englewood Cliffs, N.J.: Prentice-Hall, 1962), p. 161.

[21]Malcolm O. Sillars, "The New Conservatism and the Teacher of Speech," *Southern Speech Journal* 21 (1956), p. 240.

[22]Thomas Sowell, "Manhattan Report" (edited transcript of *Meet the Press*) (New York: International Center for Economic Policy Studies, 1981), p. 10.

where, like the public personalities who gaze at us week after week from the covers of magazines and tabloid newspapers at the checkout counter in the supermarket. Alarms about the failures of public education, about drug addiction or danger to the environment or teenage pregnancy are sounded throughout the media continuously. The same solutions are advocated again and again: "Back to basics"; "Impose harsher sentences"; "Offer sex education." Their popularity, however, should not prevent us from asking: Are the problems as urgent as their prominence in the media suggests? Are the solutions workable? Does sufficient evidence exist to justify their adoption?

Your arguments will not always propose solutions. They will sometimes provide interpretations of or reasons for social phenomena, especially for recurrent problems. Some explanations have acquired the status of folk wisdom, like proverbs, and careless arguers will offer them as if they needed no further support. One object of stereotyped responses is the problem of juvenile delinquency, which liberals attribute to poverty, lack of community services, meaningless education, and violence on TV. Conservatives blame parental permissiveness, decline in religious influence, lack of individual responsibility, lenient courts. Notice that the interpretations of the causes of juvenile delinquency are related to an ideology, to a particular view of the world that may prevent the arguer from recognizing any other way of examining the problem. Other stereotyped explanations for a range of social problems include inequality, competition, self-indulgence, alienation, discrimination, technology, lack of patriotism, excessive governmental regulation, and lack of sufficient governmental regulation. All of these explanations are worthy of consideration, but they must be defined and supported if they are to be used in a thoughtful, well-constructed argument.

Although formulas change with the times, some are unexpectedly hardy and survive long after critics have revealed their weaknesses. Overpopulation is an often-cited cause of poverty, disease, and war. It can be found in the writing of the ancient Greeks 2,500 years ago. "That perspective," says the editor of *Food Monitor,* a journal published by World Hunger Year, Inc., "is so pervasive that most Americans have simply stopped thinking about population and resort to inane clucking of tongues."[23] If the writer offering overpopulation as an explanation for poverty were to look further, he or she would discover that the explanation rested on shaky data. Singapore, the most densely populated country in the world (11,574 persons per square mile) is also one of the richest ($16,500 per capita income per year). Chad, one of the most sparsely populated (11 persons per square mile) is also one of the poorest ($190 per capita in-

---

[23]Letter to the *New York Times,* October 4, 1982, Sec. A, p. 18.

come per year).[24] Strictly defined, overpopulation may serve to explain some instances of poverty; obviously it cannot serve as a blanket to cover all or even most instances. "By repeating stock phrases," one columnist reminds us, "we lose the ability, finally, to hear what we are saying."

Slogans

> I have always been rather impressed by those people who wear badges stating where they stand on certain issues. The badges have to be small, and therefore the message has to be small, concise, and without elaboration. So it comes out as "I hate something" or "I love something," or ban this or ban that. There isn't space for argument, and I therefore envy the badge-wearer who is so clear-cut about his or her opinions.[25]

The word *slogan* has a picturesque origin. A slogan was the war cry or rallying cry of a Scottish or Irish clan. From that early use it has come to mean a "catchword or rallying motto distinctly associated with a political party or other group" as well as a "catch phrase used to advertise a product."

Slogans, like clichés, are short, undeveloped arguments. They represent abbreviated responses to often complex questions. As a reader you need to be aware that slogans merely call attention to a problem; they cannot offer persuasive proof for a claim in a dozen words or less. As a writer you should avoid the use of slogans that evoke an emotional response "without giving [the reader] adequate reason for having this response."

Advertising slogans are the most familiar. Some of them are probably better known than nursery rhymes: "Reach out and touch someone," "It costs more, but I'm worth it," "Don't leave home without it." Advertisements may, of course, rely for their effectiveness on more than slogans. They may also give us interesting and valuable information about products, but most advertisements give us slogans that ignore proof — short cuts substituting for argument.

The persuasive appeal of advertising slogans is heavily dependent on the connotations associated with products. In Chapter 5 (see p. 157, under "Appeals to Needs and Values"), we discussed the way in which advertisements promise to satisfy our needs and protect our values. Wherever evidence is scarce or nonexistent, the advertiser must persuade us through skillful choice of words and phrases (as well as pictures), especially those that produce pleasur-

[24]*World Almanac and Book of Facts,* 1995 (New York: World Almanac, 1995), pp. 754 and 818.

[25]Anthony Smith, "Nuclear Power — Why Not?" *The Listener,* October 22, 1981, p. 463.

able feelings. "Let it inspire you" is the slogan of a popular liqueur. It suggests a desirable state of being but remains suitably vague about the nature of the inspiration. Another familiar slogan — "Noxzema, clean makeup" — also emphasizes a quality that we approve of, but what is "clean" makeup? Since the advertisers are silent, we are left with warm feelings about the word and not much more.

Advertising slogans are persuasive because their witty phrasing and punchy rhythms produce an automatic "yes" response. We react to them as we might react to the lyrics of popular songs, and we treat them far less critically than we treat more straightforward and elaborate arguments. Still, the consequences of failing to analyze the slogans of advertisers are usually not serious. You may be tempted to buy a product because you were fascinated by a brilliant slogan, but if the product doesn't satisfy, you can abandon it without much loss. However, ignoring ideological slogans, coined by political parties or special interest groups, may carry an enormous price, and the results are not so easily undone.

Ideological slogans, like advertising slogans, depend on the power of connotation, the emotional associations aroused by a word or phrase. In the 1960s and 1970s, a period of well-advertised social change, slogans flourished; they appeared by the hundreds of thousands on buttons, T-shirts, and bumper stickers. One of them read, "Student Power!" To some readers of the slogan, distrustful of young people and worried about student unrest on campuses and in the streets, the suggestion was frightening. To others, mostly students, the idea of power, however undefined, was intoxicating. Notice that "Student Power!" is not an argument; it is only a claim. (It might also represent a warrant.) As a claim, for example, it might take this form: Students at this school should have the power to select the faculty. Of course, the arguer would need to provide the kinds of proof that support his or her claim, something the slogan by itself cannot do. Many people, whether they accepted or rejected the claim, supplied the rest of the argument without knowing exactly what the issues were and how a developed argument would proceed. They were accepting or rejecting the slogan largely on the basis of emotional reaction to words.

American political history is, in fact, a repository of slogans. Leaf through a history of the United States and you will come across "Tippecanoe and Tyler, too," "manifest destiny," "fifty-four forty or fight," "make the world safe for democracy," "the silent majority," "the domino theory," "the missile gap," "the window of vulnerability." Each administration tries to capture the attention and allegiance of the public by coining catchy phrases. Roosevelt's New Deal in 1932 was followed by the Square Deal and the New Frontier. Today, slogans must be carefully selected to avoid offending groups that are sensitive to the ways in which words affect their interests.

In 1983 Senator John Glenn, announcing his candidacy for president, talked about bringing "old values and new horizons" to the White House. "New horizons" apparently carried positive connotations. His staff, however, worried that "old values" might suggest racism and sexism to minorities and women.

A professor of politics and international affairs at Princeton University explains why public officials use slogans, despite their obvious shortcomings:

> Officials long have tried to capture complicated events and to dominate public discussion of foreign policy by using simple phrases and slogans. They engage in phrase-making in order to reach wide audiences. . . .
>
> Slogans and metaphors often express the tendencies of officials and academics who have a common wish to be at once sweeping, unequivocal, easily understood, and persuasive. The desire to capture complicated phenomena through slogans stems also from impatience with the particular and unwillingness or inability to master interrelationships.[26]

Over a period of time slogans, like clichés, can acquire a life of their own and, if they are repeated often enough, come to represent an unchanging truth we no longer need to examine. "Dangerously," says the writer quoted above, "policy makers become prisoners of the slogans they popularize."

The arguments you write will not, of course, be one-sentence slogans. Unfortunately, many longer arguments amount to little more than sloganeering or series of suggestive phrases strung together to imitate the process of argumentation. Following are two examples. The first is taken from a full-page magazine advertisement in 1983, urging the formation of a new political party. The second is part of the second inaugural address of George C. Wallace, governor of Alabama, in 1971. These extracts are typical of the full advertisement and the full speech.

> We can't dislodge big money from its domination over the two old parties, but we can offer the country something better: a new party that represents the people and responds to their needs. . . . How can we solve any problem without correcting the cause — the structure of the Dem/Rep machine and the power of the military-industrial establishment? . . . The power of the people could be a commanding force if only we could get together — Labor, public-interest organizations, blacks, women, antinuclear groups, and all the others.[27]

> The people of the South and those who think like the South, represent the majority viewpoint within our constitutional democracy, but they are not organized and do not speak with a loud voice. Until the day

---

[26]Henry Bienen, "Slogans Aren't the World," *New York Times,* January 16, 1983, Sec. IV, p. 19.

[27]*The Progressive,* September 1983, p. 38.

arrives when the voice of the people of the South and those who think like us is, within the law, thrust into the face of the bureaucrats, only then can the "people's power" express itself legally and ethically and get results. . . . Too long, oh, too long, has the voice of the people been silenced by their own disruptive government — by governmental bribery in quasi-governmental handouts such as H.E.W. and others that exist in America today! An aroused people can save this nation from those evil forces who seek our destruction. The choice is yours. The hour is growing late![28]

Whatever power these recommendations might have if their proposals were more clearly formulated, as they stand they are collections of slogans and loaded words. (Even the language falters: Can the voice of the people be thrust into the face of the bureaucrats?) We can visualize some of the slogans as brightly colored banners: "Dislodge Big Money!" "Power to the People!" "Save This Nation from Evil Forces!" "The Choice Is Yours!" Do all the groups mentioned share identical interests? If so, what are they? Given the vagueness of the terms, it is not surprising that arguers on opposite sides of the political spectrum — loosely characterized as liberal and conservative — sometimes resort to the same clichés and slogans: the language of populism, or a belief in the virtues of the "common people" in these examples.

Slogans have numerous shortcomings as substitutes for the development of an argument. First, their brevity presents serious disadvantages. Slogans necessarily ignore exceptions or negative instances that might qualify a claim. They usually speak in absolute terms without describing the circumstances in which a principle or idea might not work. Their claims therefore seem shrill and exaggerated. In addition, brevity prevents the sloganeer from revealing how he or she arrived at conclusions.

Second, slogans may conceal unexamined warrants. When Japanese cars were beginning to compete with American cars, the slogan "Made in America by Americans" appeared on the bumpers of thousands of American-made cars. A thoughtful reader would have discovered in this slogan several implied warrants: American cars are better than Japanese cars; the American economy will improve if we buy American; patriotism can be expressed by buying American goods. If the reader were to ask a few probing questions, he or she might find these warrants unconvincing.

Silent warrants that express values hide in other popular and influential slogans. "Pro-life," the slogan of those who oppose abortion, assumes that the fetus is a living being entitled to the same rights as individuals already born. "Pro-choice," the slogan of those

---

[28]Second Inaugural Address as governor of Alabama, January 18, 1971.

who favor abortion, suggests that the freedom of the pregnant woman to choose is the foremost or only consideration. The words *life* and *choice* have been carefully selected to reflect desirable qualities, but the words are only the beginning of the argument.

Third, although slogans may express admirable sentiments, they often fail to tell us how to achieve their objectives. They address us in the imperative mode, ordering us to take an action or refrain from it. But the means of achieving the objectives may be nonexistent or very costly. If the sloganeer cannot offer workable means for implementing his or her goals, he or she risks alienating the audience.

Sloganeering is one of the recognizable attributes of propaganda. Propaganda for both good and bad purposes is a form of slanting, of selecting language and facts to persuade an audience to take a certain action. Even a good cause may be weakened by an unsatisfactory slogan. The slogans of some organizations devoted to fundraising for the physically handicapped have come under attack for depicting the handicapped as helpless. According to one critic, the popular slogan "Jerry's kids" promotes the idea that Jerry Lewis is the sole support of children with muscular dystrophy. Perhaps increased sensitivity to the needs of the disabled will produce new words and new slogans. If you assume that your audience is sophisticated and alert, you will probably write your strongest arguments, devoid of clichés and slogans.

Sample Analysis

A Gen-X Rip Van Winkle

JOSHUA B. JANOFF

Ever read the story of Rip Van Winkle? These days I'd recommend it to anyone. The story is one of those uniquely American folk tales, about a work-shy gentleman farmer who falls asleep under a tree — for twenty years. When he awakes, he finds that the world is a very different place. I read the story as a young boy, and it wasn't until recently that I began to have some inkling of what poor Rip must have been feeling the day he finally opened his eyes and rejoined the world.

I'm a twenty-two-year-old freshman at a small New England liberal-arts college. I take classes in subjects like writing and sociol-

When this "My Turn" column appeared in the April 24, 1995, issue of *Newsweek,* Joshua B. Janoff was a freshman at Emerson College in Boston.

ogy. The school newspaper I write for is filled with aspiring muck-rakers, and most people here followed Teddy Kennedy's reelection bid with enthusiasm. A casual outside observer might say I fit the mold of the left-wing, out-of-touch, spotted-owl-saving, liberal-loving college student. A stereotypical Generation Xer suffering from a short bout of college-induced idealism, right?

Not so fast. I don't and never have fit such a label. When I was seventeen, I enlisted for a four-year hitch in the U.S. Navy. I entered the service as a young kid — bored, complacent, and cloistered. At the end of my completed time in the navy, I was a noncommissioned officer and Desert Storm veteran. My military service was a series of stark contrasts. I often worked for cruel idiots, scrubbed countless toilets and decks, and chipped away acres of paint. I also gazed at the hypnotic grin on the Mona Lisa, visited the birthplace of Mozart, stood inside the Roman Colosseum, climbed the Great Pyramid of Cheops and put my hand on the reputed tomb of Jesus Christ.

I'm not bragging. The day I was discharged was one of the happi-est of my life. It was also my first Rip Van Winkle experience. I turned on my car radio to begin the long drive home. I realized I was listen-ing to bands I'd never heard of. (Who the hell is Pearl Jam? Who or what is Alice in Chains?) I'd grown apart from my age group.

When I got home I told people about serving overseas, about   5
how the pride we felt came of very hard work. My old friends just stared at me and said I sounded like their father. Or their grandfa-ther. Suddenly I felt very, very old. It seemed I now possessed values that contemporaries saw as chauvinistic, archaic, or hopelessly tra-ditional. Their reaction was odd, since people in the navy consid-ered me very liberal.

My first mass exposure to Generation X, which was when I hit college, accentuated my confusion. I'd never even heard the term until I got to school. I was surprised to learn that, because of my age, I was considered a member of this lazy, apathetic group of flannel-wearing misfits. At first I laughed. Then the suggestion started to bother me. I denied any complicity. Hey, I'd been away when this inane nomenclature was hatched. "No good," my fellow students said. "By virtue of your age, you are a part of it. Think about it."

So I did. But their claims just weren't true. The more I searched for common ground with my peers, the more I began to notice the habits that set me apart. When I'd tell friends I was in Desert Storm, I kept getting the same reaction. "Wow, what was it like? Were you scared? Wow, I could never have done that."

Now I'd be curious. Exactly what did that last statement mean? "Well, you know. I mean, it's not like I'd ever put on some uniform and go to war like in the movies. There's just no way."

That response disturbed me. When Desert Storm was going on, everyone I knew expressed total support and sympathy for the American servicepersons risking their safety to free Kuwait. Just a few years later, the idea of serving in such a way seems unthinkable to my generation. I don't believe it's because of an abundance of conscientious objectors among them. A true conscientious objector has strong, carefully thought out convictions and acts out of a sense of moral compulsion. I think those who told me they wouldn't go were just plain lazy.

The average age of an American combat soldier in the Korean 10 War was twenty, and in the Vietnam War, it was nineteen. I know there was a draft in effect, but besides the relative few who went to Canada, these young Americans proved that they were doers rather than talkers. Even the ones who went north *acted* on their beliefs. Today's youth, by contrast, seem willing to talk about their convictions, but not act on them.

I've seen other, more commonplace examples of my peers' laziness. Physical fitness was expected growing up in my family, and that attitude was reinforced in the navy. Now most of my friends look at me like I'm nuts when I say that I go to the gym regularly. Hell, forget the gym. To a lot of my fellow students, just walking a mile to the dining hall is unthinkable. Thank God for that shuttle bus, eh?

Sometimes, just getting out of bed is a problem. Most of the people in my college regard 8 A.M. classes as a fate between death and a world without Quentin Tarantino movies. I'm tempted to tell these people that 6 A.M. was considered "sleeping in" in the navy, but I doubt it would change anything.

Finally, there's the whole apathy thing. At first I felt certain that the idea of a generationwide sense of total indifference was crazy. It had to be an invention of the mass media. Unfortunately, the media assertions appear to be true. We as a generation have yet to produce any defining traits, except perhaps to show a defeatist belief that we will do worse than our parents.

Not that the situation is completely untenable. No living generation can honestly claim to have a general consensus on any one issue, whether the topic is politics, abortion, or health-care reform. If my age group can agree to resolve its indifference before it's too late, then maybe we can go ahead to make a more constructive future. It's time to stop channel surfing and looking for new ways to procrastinate, and to desist from blaming problems on those in authority. Perhaps what's needed is a good swift kick in the rear. Playtime is over, and there is a big bad world out there. It's waiting to see what we've got, but it's also ours for the taking. Let's lose the remote and do it.

Analysis

Most of the arguments in this book might be described as formal and objective — that is, the personality of the author is not present, and our full attention falls on the argument itself without regard to the

characteristics of the individual behind it. Editorials are good examples of the formal essay, whose authors almost always remain anonymous. This is as it should be for many subjects of general interest.

But there is another way of arriving at a claim, even about these
subjects, and that is through a narrative of personal experience. The
essay by Janoff, a twenty-two-year-old student, is an example of such
a strategy. Because the "I" is not suppressed, as in an editorial, but
becomes, in fact, the central focus of the argument, the writer can
exercise greater freedom in his choice of language. He can treat his
idea as if it were a subject for conversation, and he can express his
own feelings, which may not be appropriate or relevant in a more
formal essay. (Organization is simpler because it follows the
chronology of the events.)

Since he is telling a story about himself, the author uses "I"
freely throughout. He adopts language that is close to colloquial
speech, using contractions and sentence fragments, as well as slang
and mild profanity, all of which are usually frowned on in more formal contexts. He also repeats the direct speech of fellow students, a
device that emphasizes the narrative element.

There is, however, a danger in the use of "I" and the introduction
of the self as part of the argument. In paragraph 7 the "I" that had
previously been engaged in telling us an interesting story about
events with which we might sympathize begins to change, to distance itself from the students in the story — and the readers of it —
and to claim a certain superiority to them. I am a doer, not a talker;
active, not lazy; involved, not apathetic; grown-up, not childish. Listening to this new and different voice, we are probably not surprised
to be lectured rather severely in the last two paragraphs. And notice
that here the language deteriorates, especially in the last paragraph,
descending from vivid details and clear colloquial speech into cliché
and vague formulas without much force. Perhaps this means that
even the author felt uncomfortable speaking in this voice.

Whether or not the author is right about his moral superiority,
to compare his readers unfavorably to himself is not an effective
persuasive strategy. Authors often scold their readers, but by removing the subjective element — by declining to refer to themselves — they can take refuge in the defense that "It's nothing
personal." Here, of course, the attack comes from someone we
know, who has made himself the hero of his story. Needless to say,
readers prefer modesty in their heroes. A careful writer of a personal experience essay can take advantage of the greater flexibility
of language without allowing the "I" to overwhelm the argument.

The Speech the Graduates Didn't Hear

JACOB NEUSNER

We the faculty take no pride in our educational achievements with you. We have prepared you for a world that does not exist, indeed, that cannot exist. You have spent four years supposing that failure leaves no record. You have learned at Brown that when your work goes poorly, the painless solution is to drop out. But starting now, in the world to which you go, failure marks you. Confronting difficulty by quitting leaves you changed. Outside Brown, quitters are no heroes.

With us you could argue about why your errors were not errors, why mediocre work really was excellent, why you could take pride in routine and slipshod presentation. Most of you, after all, can look back on honor grades for most of what you have done. So, here grades can have meant little in distinguishing the excellent from the ordinary. But tomorrow, in the world to which you go, you had best not defend errors but learn from them. You will be ill-advised to demand praise for what does not deserve it, and abuse those who do not give it.

For four years we created an altogether forgiving world, in which whatever slight effort you gave was all that was demanded. When you did not keep appointments, we made new ones. When your work came in beyond the deadline, we pretended not to care.

Worse still, when you were boring, we acted as if you were saying something important. When you were garrulous and talked to hear yourself talk, we listened as if it mattered. When you tossed on our desks writing upon which you had not labored, we read it and even responded, as though you earned a response. When you were dull, we pretended you were smart. When you were predictable, unimaginative, and routine, we listened as if to new and wonderful things. When you demanded free lunch, we served it. And all this why?

Despite your fantasies, it was not even that we wanted to be 5
liked by you. It was that we did not want to be bothered, and the easy way out was pretense: smiles and easy Bs.

Jacob Neusner, formerly university professor at Brown University, is Distinguished Professor of Religious Studies at the University of South Florida in Tampa. His speech appeared in Brown's *The Daily Herald* on June 12, 1983.

It is conventional to quote in addresses such as these. Let me quote someone you've never heard of: Professor Carter A. Daniel, Rutgers University (*Chronicle of Higher Education,* May 7, 1979):

> College has spoiled you by reading papers that don't deserve to be read, listening to comments that don't deserve a hearing, paying attention even to the lazy, ill-informed, and rude. We had to do it, for the sake of education. But nobody will ever do it again. College has deprived you of adequate preparation for the last fifty years. It has failed you by being easy, free, forgiving, attentive, comfortable, interesting, unchallenging fun. Good luck tomorrow.

That is why, on this commencement day, we have nothing in which to take much pride.

Oh, yes, there is one more thing. Try not to act toward your co-workers and bosses as you have acted toward us. I mean, when they give you what you want but have not earned, don't abuse them, insult them, act out with them your parlous relationships with your parents. This too we have tolerated. It was, as I said, not to be liked. Few professors actually care whether or not they are liked by peer-paralyzed adolescents, fools so shallow as to imagine professors care not about education but about popularity. It was, again, to be rid of you. So go, unlearn the lies we taught you. To Life!

Reading and Discussion Questions

1. Neusner condemns students for various shortcomings. But what is he saying, both directly and indirectly, about teachers? Find places where he reveals his attitude toward them, perhaps inadvertently.
2. Pick out some of the language devices — connectives, parallel structures, sentence variety — that Neusner uses effectively.
3. Pick out some of the words and phrases — especially adjectives and verbs — used by Neusner to characterize both students and teachers. Do you think these terms are loaded? Explain.
4. Has Neusner chosen "facts" to slant his article? If so, point out where slanting occurs. If not, point out where the article seems to be truthful.
5. As a student you will probably object to Neusner's accusations. How would you defend your behavior as a student in answer to his specific charges?

Writing Suggestions

6. Rewrite Neusner's article with the same "facts" — or others from your experience — using temperate language and a tone of sadness rather than anger.
7. Write a letter to Neusner responding to his attack. Support or attack his argument by providing evidence from your own experience.
8. Write your own short commencement address. Do some things need to be said that commencement speakers seldom or never express?

9. Write an essay using the same kind of strong language as Neusner uses about some aspect of your education of which you disapprove. Or write a letter to a teacher using the same form as "The Speech the Graduates Didn't Hear."

Jack and the Beanstalk
JAMES FINN GARNER

Once upon a time, on a little farm, there lived a boy named Jack. He lived on the farm with his mother, and they were very excluded from the normal circles of economic activity. This cruel reality kept them in straits of direness, until one day Jack's mother told him to take the family cow into town and sell it for as much as he could.

Never mind the thousands of gallons of milk they had stolen from her! Never mind the hours of pleasure their bovine animal companion had provided! And forget about the manure they had appropriated for their garden! She was now just another piece of property to them. Jack, who didn't realize that nonhuman animals have as many rights as human animals — perhaps even more — did as his mother asked.

On his way to town, Jack met an old magic vegetarian, who warned Jack of the dangers of eating beef and dairy products.

"Oh, I'm not going to eat this cow," said Jack. "I'm going to take her into town and sell her."

"But by doing that, you'll just perpetuate the cultural mythos of 5 beef, ignoring the negative impact of the cattle industry on our ecology and the health and social problems that arise from meat consumption. But you look too simple to be able to make these connections, my boy. I'll tell you what I'll do: I'll offer a trade of your cow for these three magic beans, which have as much protein as that entire cow but none of the fat or sodium."

Jack made the trade gladly and took the beans home to his mother. When he told her about the deal he had made, she grew very upset. She used to think her son was merely a conceptual rather than a linear thinker, but now she was sure that he was downright differently abled. She grabbed the three magic beans and threw them out the window in disgust. Later that day, she attended her first support-group meeting with Mothers of Storybook Children.

The next morning, Jack stuck his head out the window to see if the sun had risen in the east again (he was beginning to see a pattern in

James Finn Garner is a writer and performer in Chicago who has written for the *Chicago Tribune* and appeared on Chicago Public Radio. This chapter is from *Politically Correct Bedtime Stories* (1994).

this). But outside the window, the beans had grown into a huge stalk that reached through the clouds. Because he no longer had a cow to milk in the morning, Jack climbed the beanstalk into the sky.

At the top, above the clouds, he found a huge castle. It was not only big, but it was built to larger-than-average scale, as if it were the home of someone who just happened to be a giant. Jack entered the castle and heard beautiful music wafting through the air. He followed this sound until he found its source: a golden harp that played music without being touched. Next to this self-actualized harp was a hen sitting on a pile of golden eggs.

Now, the prospect of easy wealth and mindless entertainment appealed to Jack's bourgeois sensibilities, so he picked up both the harp and the hen and started to run for the front door. Then he heard thundering footsteps and a booming voice that said:

> FEE, FIE, FOE, FUM,
> I smell the blood of an English person!
> I'd like to learn about his culture and views on life!
> And share my own perspectives in an open and generous way!

Unfortunately, Jack was too crazed with greed to accept the 10 giant's offer of a cultural interchange. "It's only a trick," thought Jack. "Besides, what's a giant doing with such fine, delicate things? He must have stolen them from somewhere else, so I have every right to take them." His frantic justifications — remarkable for someone with his overtaxed mental resources — revealed a terrible callousness to the giant's personal rights. Jack apparently was a complete sizeist, who thought that all giants were clumsy, knowledge-impaired, and exploitable.

When the giant saw Jack with the magic harp and the hen, he asked, "Why are you taking what belongs to me?"

Jack knew he couldn't outrun the giant, so he had to think fast. He blurted out, "I'm not taking them, my friend. I am merely placing them in my stewardship so that they can be properly managed and brought to their fullest potential. Pardon my bluntness, but you giants are too simple in the head and don't know how to manage your resources properly. I'm just looking out for your interests. You'll thank me for this later."

Jack held his breath to see if the bluff would save his skin. The giant sighed heavily and said, "Yes, you are right. We giants do use our resources foolishly. Why, we can't even discover a new beanstalk before we get so excited and pick away at it so much that we pull the poor thing right out of the ground!"

Jack's heart sank. He turned and looked out the front door of the castle. Sure enough, the giant had destroyed his beanstalk. Jack grew frightened and cried, "Now I'm trapped here in the clouds with you forever!"

The giant said, "Don't worry, my little friend. We are strict vege- 15
tarians up here, and there are always plenty of beans to eat. And besides, you won't be alone. Thirteen other men of your size have
already climbed up beanstalks to visit us and stayed."

So Jack resigned himself to his fate as a member of the giant's
cloud commune. He didn't miss his mother or their farm much, because up in the sky there was less work to do and more than enough
to eat. And he gradually learned not to judge people based on their
size ever again, except for those shorter than he.

Reading and Discussion Questions

1. A comic writer often assumes a *persona*. This persona is not the author
   but a character that the author has created and whose voice he or she
   adopts. How would you describe the person that Garner pretends to be
   in this story?
2. Explain the title of the book from which this story is taken.
3. Point out the targets of Garner's satire. How did you recognize them?
   Would some readers find certain references offensive?
4. What language elements — vocabulary, sentence structure, metaphors —
   does Garner use to comic advantage? How do they reflect the character
   of the persona?

Writing Suggestions

5. Perhaps you feel that some of the things that Garner makes fun of
   should not be subjected to ridicule. Write a serious piece defending the
   politically correct attitude toward one of these targets.
6. If you are brave, write a funny piece about some subject whose absurdi-
   ties have either amused or angered you. The subjects are everywhere.
   Some may even be found in the serious arguments you have been reading in this book: malls, mandatory school attendance, sexual harassment, gun control, single-sex schools. (Not surprisingly, all of these
   subjects have, in fact, been treated satirically by columnists like Russell
   Baker, Dave Barry, Mike Royko, and Maureen Dowd.) And, of course, advertisements can also be used as objects of humorous attack.

Amtrak® is a registered service mark of the National Railroad Passenger Corporation.

Discussion Questions

1. What feelings does the advertiser want to evoke? Find words that make your answer clear.
2. The words *real* and *good* are italicized. Why are they so important? Is the advertiser making a contrast with something else?
3. How does the graphic design underscore the spirit and language of the ad?

Kessler's a Drag

ALEXANDER VOLOKH

During World War II, you could unmask a Nazi soldier masquerading as an American GI by asking him, "Who won the World Series?" Today, in the nicotine debate, one question is a similar giveaway. Ask someone, "Is smoking addictive, and do people know this?"

"No" to the first part means you're talking to a tobacco company president. "No" to the second part means you're talking to Food and Drug Administration Commissioner David Kessler.

Whoever doesn't know that cigarettes are addictive and deadly has been living in a cave. People have known that cigarettes, tar and nicotine are bad at least since the 1950s. When the cancer connection was first proposed, low-tar and low-nicotine cigarettes quickly appeared on the market with no prodding from the government. Cigarette companies aggressively tried to gain market share by scaring smokers about their competitors' tar and nicotine levels — even though the Federal Trade Commission banned such advertising in 1954. From 1957 to 1959, tar and nicotine contents dropped 40 percent because of consumer demand. The FTC eventually cracked down on violators in 1959, but then it reversed course, allowing nicotine advertising in 1966 and mandating it in 1970. Today, all cigarette ads indicate tar and nicotine contents.

According to Kip Viscusi, professor of economics at Duke University, people today actually overestimate the risks of smoking. The average American estimates the risk of dying from lung cancer because of smoking at 38 percent. The true risk is between 6 percent and 13 percent. The average American estimates the total risk of dying because of smoking at 54 percent. The true risk is between 18 percent and 36 percent. Professor Viscusi calculates that if people had accurate perceptions of smoking risks, smoking actually would increase by about 7 percent.

Dr. Kessler tells us: "The public thinks of cigarettes as simply 5 blended tobacco rolled in paper. But they are much more than that. Some of today's cigarettes may, in fact, qualify as high-technology

---

This column by Alexander Volokh, a policy analyst at the Redson Foundation in Los Angeles, appeared in the *Wall Street Journal* on August 8, 1995.

nicotine delivery systems that deliver nicotine in precisely calcu-
lated quantities." But smokers don't need tobacco companies to manipulate their nicotine intake — they do it themselves all the time.
They do it by choosing which brand to smoke (nicotine contents
range from 0.05 mg to 2 mg), how often to light up, and how deeply
and often to puff. Smokers may not know exactly what secret herbs
and spices cigarette companies add to tobacco, but they're well
aware of the risk.

The surprising thing about the modern antismoking movement
isn't that it wants to regulate a personal choice. That's nothing new.
What is new is how disingenuous the movement has become. In the
early 1900s, during the first wave of anticigarette sentiment, people
at least said that they opposed smoking on moral grounds. Today,
the Kesslers of the world pretend to be scientists, acting as if their
recommendations hinged on some new evidence. They don't, and
it's dishonest to say otherwise. But while everyone sees through tobacco companies' dubious claims, Dr. Kessler's are working.

Underage smoking is a real concern, and there are probably
steps that the government should take to reduce children's access
to cigarettes. But what sort of society are the antismokers creating
for our children? Says Sam Kazman, general counsel of the Competitive Enterprise Institute, "Personally, I don't want my children to
smoke when they grow up. I also don't want them to ride motor-
cycles or fly hang-gliders. But most of all, I don't want them to grow
up thinking these aren't their decisions to make."

A Former Smoker Cheers

DAVID RAKOFF

When I quit my two-pack-a-day smoking habit three years ago, I
told myself that I would take it up again when I turned sixty-five.
Thirty-five smoke-free years and then I could resuscitate a romance
with my old habit and, as S. J. Perelman might say, go to hell my own
way.

But unless I plan to spend my retirement years in Paris or Bei-
jing, that might not be an option: New York is slowly becoming a
smoke-free zone. And you know, that's fine by me. In fact, I cheered
from my bed when I woke up Monday morning, switched on the
radio, and heard that the ban on smoking had gone into effect.

David Rakoff works for a publisher in New York. His essay appeared in the *New York Times* on April 14, 1995.

Lest you think I'm one of those zealous exsmokers, I assure you I am not. I still understand that feeling when one's next cigarette seems more important than food or shelter. I smoked through nine months of chemotherapy, after all, so why can't I just live and let live?

Well, for one thing, smoking can kill you. End of story. It's incredibly bad for you. But far more importantly, it can kill *me*. And, frankly, I'm already cranky enough without being endangered by people who are neither relatives nor friends. If we've never met and you increase the level of poison in my already toxic New York life, watch out.

Besides, we should finally have the decency to try to take care of   5
one another. There used to be a billboard at Houston and Broadway that read: "Welcome to America. The only developed country other than South Africa without universal health care!" Nelson Mandela was still in prison when that billboard was up, and here we are still grappling with people's right to universal coverage. How can we, as a society, say that we care about our citizens' health and not agree to remove this most visible and dangerous threat? Otherwise, we all put our lives at risk of being nasty, brutish and short.

I've been told that, as a nonnational (I moved to the United States thirteen years ago), I can't fully appreciate the ferocity with which Americans regard their personal freedoms, that it is a slippery slope from stopping people smoking in restaurants to installing Orwellian telescreens in their homes. But surely my right to avoid the increased risk of another bout of cancer outweighs my neighbor's right to blow smoke on my $20 entree (except, bizarrely, in a space intimate enough to contain fewer than thirty-five seats).

Finally, smoking is just not as glamorous as it used to be. It's been a long time since Jean-Paul Belmondo and Jean Seberg langorously puffed their way through Paris in the aptly titled "Breathless." And don't even mention that much touted cigar renaissance that has young and old blithely lighting up as if they had never heard the name Sigmund Freud. Smoking is somewhat passé, and surely in New York that has to count for something.

It does seem ridiculous to make Central Park smoke-free, and I feel doubly sorry for the waiters working in tiny restaurants; somehow their health has been deemed less worthy of protection under the new law, and now they're likely to see even more business from serious smokers turned away from everywhere else. But when I think of the acute nausea, pain, burned skin, side effects of medication and hair loss of cancer treatment, I can only think: "Been there. Done that." And so I cheer from my bed.

Discussion Questions

1. These two essays use different stylistic approaches to the subject. Point out examples of differences in language and appeals to an audience.

2. Both Volokh and Rakoff introduce their essay in mind-catching ways. Describe the introductions and tell how they work to lead the reader into their arguments.
3. How does Rakoff indicate the different parts of his essay? What idea does each part develop?
4. How does Rakoff try to persuade the reader that he is a reasonable fellow? Why does he think it necessary to include this declaimer in his argument? Do you find it persuasive?
5. Does Volokh offer any data that surprised you? Would they encourage you to take up or continue smoking?
6. What are Volokh's main objections to Dr. Kessler's crusade? What is the main point of the essay? Or is there more than one point?

EXERCISES

1. Select one or two related bumper stickers visible in your neighborhood. Examine the hidden warrants on which they are based and assess their validity.
2. For a slogan found on a bumper sticker or elsewhere, supply the evidence to support the claim in the slogan. Or find evidence that disproves the claim.
3. Examine a few periodicals from fifty or more years ago. Select either an advertising or a political slogan in one of them and relate it to beliefs or events of the period. Or tell why the slogan is no longer relevant.
4. Discuss the origin of a cliché or slogan. Describe, as far as possible, the backgrounds and motives of its users.
5. Make up your own slogan for a cause that you support. Explain and defend your slogan.
6. Discuss the appeal to needs and values of some popular advertising or political slogan.
7. Choose a cliché and find evidence to support or refute it. *Examples:* People were much happier in the past. Mother knows best. Life was much simpler in the past. Money can't buy happiness.
8. Choose one of the statements in exercise 7 or another statement and write a paper telling why you think such a statement has persisted as an explanation.
9. Select a passage, perhaps from a textbook, written largely in abstractions, and rewrite it using simpler and more concrete language.

Critical Listening

10. In watching TV dramas about law and medicine (*Law and Order, The Client, ER, Chicago Hope*) do you find that the professional language, some of which you may not fully understand, plays a positive or negative role in your enjoyment of the show? Explain your answer.
11. Listen to a radio or television report of a sports event. Do the announcers use a kind of language, especially jargon, that would not be used in print reports? One critic thinks that sports broadcasting has had a "destructive effect . . . on ordinary American English." Is he right or wrong?

CHAPTER EIGHT

Induction, Deduction, and Logical Fallacies

Throughout the book we have pointed out the weaknesses that cause arguments to break down. In the vast majority of cases these weaknesses represent breakdowns in logic or the reasoning process. We call such weaknesses *fallacies,* a term derived from the Latin. Sometimes these false or erroneous arguments are deliberate; in fact, the Latin word *fallere* means to deceive. But more often these arguments are either carelessly or unintentionally constructed. Thoughtful readers learn to recognize them; thoughtful writers learn to avoid them.

The reasoning process was first given formal expression by Aristotle, the Greek philosopher, almost 2,500 years ago. In his famous treatises, he described the way we try to discover the truth — observing the world, selecting impressions, making inferences, generalizing. In this process Aristotle identified two forms of reasoning: *induction* and *deduction.* Both forms, he realized, are subject to error. Our observations may be incorrect or insufficient, and our conclusions may be faulty because they have violated the rules governing the relationship between statements. The terms we've introduced may be unfamiliar, but the processes of reasoning, as well as the fallacies that violate these processes, are not. Induction and deduction are not reserved only for formal arguments about important problems; they also represent our everyday thinking about the most ordinary matters. As for the fallacies, they, too, unfortunately, may crop up anywhere, whenever we are careless in our use of the reasoning process.

In this chapter we will examine some of the most common fallacies. First, however, a closer look at induction and deduction will make clear what happens when fallacies occur.

INDUCTION

Induction is the form of reasoning in which we come to conclusions about the whole on the basis of observations of particular instances. If you notice that prices on the four items you bought in the campus bookstore are higher than similar items in the bookstore in town, you may come to the conclusion that the campus store is a more expensive place to shop. If you also noticed that all three of the instructors you saw on the first day of school were wearing faded jeans and running shoes, you might say that your teachers are generally informal in their dress. In both cases you have made an *inductive leap,* reasoning from what you have learned about a few examples to what you think is true of a whole class of things.

How safe are you in coming to these conclusions? As we've noticed in discussing data and generalization warrants, the reliability of your conclusion depends on the quantity and quality of your observations. Were four items out of the thousands available in the campus store a sufficiently large sample? Would you come to the same conclusion if you chose fifty items? Might another selection have produced a different conclusion? As for the casually dressed instructors, perhaps further investigation would disclose that the teachers wearing jeans were all teaching assistants and that associate and full professors usually wore business clothes. Or the difference might lie in the academic discipline; anthropology teachers might turn out to dress less formally than business school teachers.

In these two situations, you could come closer to verifying your conclusions by further observation and experience, that is, by buying more items at both stores over a longer period of time and by coming into contact with a greater number of professors during a whole semester. Even without pricing every item in both stores or encountering every instructor on campus, you would be more confident of your generalization as the quality and quantity of your samples increased.

In some cases you can observe all the instances in a particular situation. For example, by acquiring information about the religious beliefs of all the residents of the dormitory, you can arrive at an accurate assessment of the number of Buddhists. But since our ability to make definitive observations about everything is limited, we must also make an inductive leap about categories of things that we ourselves can never encounter in their entirety. For some generalizations, as we have learned about evidence, we rely on the testimony of reliable witnesses who report that they have experienced or observed many more instances of the phenomenon. A television documentary may give us information about unwed teenage mothers in a city neighborhood; four girls are interviewed and followed for several days by the reporter. Are these girls typical of thousands of others? A sociologist on the program assures us that, in fact, they are. She herself has consulted with hundreds of other young mothers and can vouch for the fact that a conclusion about them, based on our observation of the four, will be sound. Obviously, though, our conclusion can only be probable, not certain. The sociologist's sample is large, but she can account only for hundreds, not thousands, and there may be unexamined cases that will seriously weaken our conclusions.

In other cases, we may rely on a principle known in science as "the uniformity of nature." We assume that certain conclusions about oak trees in the temperate zone of North America, for example, will also be true for oak trees growing elsewhere under similar climatic conditions. We also use this principle in attempting to explain the causes of behavior in human beings. If we discover that institutionalization of some children from infancy results in severe emotional retardation, we think it safe to conclude that under the same circumstances all children would suffer the same consequences. As in the previous example, we are aware that certainty about every case of institutionalization is impossible. With rare exceptions, the process of induction can offer only probability, not certain truth.

SAMPLE ANALYSIS:
AN INDUCTIVE ARGUMENT

Not All Men Are Sly Foxes

ARMIN A. BROTT

If you thought your child's bookshelves were finally free of openly (and not so openly) discriminatory materials, you'd better check again. In recent years groups of concerned parents have persuaded textbook publishers to portray more accurately the roles that women and minorities play in shaping our country's history and culture. *Little Black Sambo* has all but disappeared from library and bookstore shelves; feminist fairy tales by such authors as Jack Zipes have, in many homes, replaced the more traditional (and obviously sexist) fairy tales. Richard Scarry, one of the most popular children's writers, has reissued new versions of some of his classics; now fe-

Armin A. Brott is a freelance writer. This article appeared in *Newsweek* on June 1, 1992.

male animals are pictured doing the same jobs as male animals. Even the terminology has changed: males and females are referred to as mail "carriers" or "firefighters."

There is, however, one very large group whose portrayal continues to follow the same stereotypical lines as always: fathers. The evolution of children's literature didn't end with *Goodnight Moon* and *Charlotte's Web.* My local public library, for example, previews 203 new children's picture books (for the under-five set) each *month.* Many of these books make a very conscious effort to take women characters out of the kitchen and the nursery and give them professional jobs and responsibilities.

Despite this shift, mothers are by and large still shown as the primary caregivers and, more important, as the primary nurturers of their children. Men in these books — if they're shown at all — still come home late after work and participate in the child rearing by bouncing baby around for five minutes before putting the child to bed.

In one of my two-year-old daughter's favorite books, *Mother Goose and the Sly Fox,* "retold" by Chris Conover, a single mother (Mother Goose) of seven tiny goslings is pitted against (and naturally outwits) the sly Fox. Fox, a neglectful and presumably unemployed single father, lives with his filthy, hungry pups in a grimy hovel littered with the bones of their previous meals. Mother Goose, a successful entrepreneur with a thriving lace business, still finds time to serve her goslings homemade soup in pretty porcelain cups. The story is funny and the illustrations marvelous, but the unwritten message is that women take better care of their kids and men have nothing else to do but hunt down and kill innocent, law-abiding geese.

The majority of other children's classics perpetuate the same 5 negative stereotypes of fathers. Once in a great while, people complain about *Babar*'s colonialist slant (little jungle-dweller finds happiness in the big city and brings civilization — and fine clothes — to his backward village). But I've never heard anyone ask why, after his mother is killed by the evil hunter, Babar is automatically an "orphan." Why can he find comfort only in the arms of another female? Why do Arthur's and Celeste's mothers come alone to the city to fetch their children? Don't the fathers care? Do they even have fathers? I need my answers ready for when my daughter asks.

I recently spent an entire day on the children's floor of the local library trying to find out whether these same negative stereotypes are found in the more recent classics-to-be. The librarian gave me a list of the twenty most popular contemporary picture books and I read every one of them. Of the twenty, seven don't mention a parent at all. Of the remaining thirteen, four portray fathers as much less loving and caring than mothers. In *Little Gorilla,* we are told that the little gorilla's "mother loves him" and we see Mama gorilla giving her little one a warm hug. On the next page we're also told that his "father loves him," but in the illustration, father and son aren't even touching. Six of the remaining nine books mention or portray mothers as the only parent, and only three of the twenty have what could be considered "equal" treatment of mothers and fathers.

The same negative stereotypes also show up in literature aimed at the *parents* of small children. In "What to Expect the First Year," the authors answer almost every question the parents of a newborn or toddler could have in the first year of their child's life. They are meticulous in alternating between references to boys and girls. At the same time, they refer almost exclusively to "mother" or "mommy." Men, and their feelings about parenting, are relegated to a nine-page chapter just before the recipe section.

Unfortunately, it's still true that, in our society, women do the bulk of the child care, and that thanks to men abandoning their families, there are too many single mothers out there. Nevertheless, to say that portraying fathers as unnurturing or completely absent is simply "a reflection of reality" is unacceptable. If children's literature only reflected reality, it would be like prime-time TV and we'd have books filled with child abusers, wife beaters, and criminals.

Young children believe what they hear — especially from a parent figure. And since, for the first few years of a child's life, adults select the reading material, children's literature should be held to a high standard. Ignoring men who share equally in raising their children, and continuing to show nothing but part-time or no-time fathers is only going to create yet another generation of men who have been told since boyhood — albeit subtly — that mothers are the truer parents and that fathers play, at best, a secondary role in the home. We've taken major steps to root out discrimination in what our children read. Let's finish the job.

Analysis

An inductive argument proceeds by examining particulars and arriving at a generalization that represents a probable truth. After reading a number of children's books in which the fathers, if they appear at all, are mostly portrayed as irresponsible and uncaring, Brott concludes that fathers are discriminated against in children's literature. Brott reports that he has examined twenty books. Only three of them give equal treatment to fathers and mothers. Even a book of advice for parents treats fathers with comparative indifference.

Because the subject is likely to be familiar to most readers, they will be able to participate in finding their own examples in children's literature to support — or refute — his claim. The success of Brott's argument will depend on finding that the examples in the article are sufficient, representative, and up-to-date. We know that the books he refers to are up-to-date (Brott mentions this in paragraph 6), but they may not be representative (the librarian gave him a list of the twenty "most popular contemporary picture books"), and whether twenty of 203 new books received by the library *each month* is sufficient is somewhat doubtful. Like all inductive arguments, this one too must be judged for probability, not certainty, but high probability would require a much bigger sample.

The examples in the article are not simply a list, however. Brott presents his conclusion within a broad context. In the first and second paragraphs he points out that while many negative racial and sexual stereotypes are disappearing from children's literature, one damaging stereotype remains, that of fathers. In the final paragraph he summarizes the dangers to society of allowing children — and the potential fathers among them — to believe that fathers are unimportant or indifferent to their children. One may find the latter conclusion valid, of course, even if one finds Brott's sample insufficient.

DEDUCTION

While induction attempts to arrive at the truth, deduction guarantees sound relationships between statements. If each of a series of statements, called *premises*, is true, deductive logic tells us that the conclusion must also be true. Unlike the conclusions from induction, which are only probable, the conclusions from deduction are certain. The simplest deductive argument consists of two premises and a conclusion. In outline such an argument looks like this:

MAJOR PREMISE:	All students with 3.5 averages and above for three years are invited to become members of Kappa Gamma Pi, the honor society.
MINOR PREMISE:	George has had a 3.8 average for over three years.
CONCLUSION:	Therefore, he will be invited to join Kappa Gamma Pi.

This deductive conclusion is *valid* or logically consistent because it follows necessarily from the premises. No other conclusion is possible. Validity, however, refers only to the form of the argument. The argument itself may not be satisfactory if the premises are not true — if Kappa Gamma Pi has imposed other conditions or if George has only a 3.4 average. The difference between truth and validity is important because it alerts us to the necessity for examining the truth of the premises before we decide that the conclusion is sound.

One way of discovering how the deductive process works is to look at the methods used by Sherlock Holmes, that most famous of literary detectives, in solving his mysteries. His reasoning process follows a familiar pattern. Through the inductive process — that is, observing the particulars of the world — he came to certain conclusions about those particulars. Then he applied deductive reasoning to come to a conclusion about a particular person or event.

On one occasion Holmes observed that a man sitting opposite him on a train had chalk dust on his fingers. From this observation Holmes deduced that the man was a schoolteacher. If his thinking were outlined, it would take the form of the syllogism, the classic form of deductive reasoning:

MAJOR PREMISE:	All men with chalk dust on their fingers are schoolteachers.
MINOR PREMISE:	This man has chalk dust on his fingers.
CONCLUSION:	Therefore, this man is a schoolteacher.

One dictionary defines the syllogism as "a formula of argument consisting of three propositions." The first proposition is called the major premise and offers a generalization about a large group or class. This generalization has been arrived at through inductive reasoning or observation of particulars. The second proposition is called the minor premise, and it makes a statement about a member of that group or class. The third proposition is the conclusion, which links the other two propositions, in much the same way that the warrant links the support and the claim.

If we look back at the syllogism that summarizes Holmes's thinking, we see how it represents the deductive process. The major premise, the first statement, is an inductive generalization, a statement arrived at after observation of a number of men with chalk on their fingers. The minor premise, the second statement, assigns a particular member, the man on the train, to the general class of those who have dust on their fingers.

But although the argument may be logical, it is faulty. The deductive argument is only as strong as its premises. As Lionel Ruby pointed out, Sherlock Holmes was often wrong.[1] Holmes once deduced from the size of a large hat found in the street that the owner was intelligent. He obviously believed that a large head meant a large brain and that a large brain indicated intelligence. Had he lived one hundred years later, new information about the relationship of

---

[1] *The Art of Making Sense* (Philadelphia: Lippincott, 1954), ch. 17.

brain size to intelligence would have enabled him to come to a different and better conclusion.

In this case, we might first object to the major premise, the generalization that all men with chalk dust on their fingers are schoolteachers. Is it true? Perhaps all the men with dusty fingers whom Holmes had so far observed had turned out to be schoolteachers, but was his sample sufficiently large to allow him to conclude that all dust-fingered men, even those with whom he might never have contact, were teachers? Were there no other vocations or situations that might require the use of chalk? Draftsmen or carpenters or tailors or artists might have fingers just as white as those of schoolteachers. In other words, Holmes may have ascertained that all schoolteachers have chalk dust on their fingers, but he had not determined that *only* schoolteachers can be thus identified. Sometimes it is helpful to draw circles representing the various groups in their relation to the whole.

If a large circle (see the figure below) represents all those who have chalk dust on their fingers, we see that several different groups may be contained in this universe. To be safe, Holmes should have deduced that the man on the train *might* have been a schoolteacher; he was not safe in deducing more than that. Obviously, if the inductive generalization or major premise is false, the conclusion of the particular argument is also false or invalid.

The deductive argument may also go wrong elsewhere. What if the minor premise is untrue? Could Holmes have mistaken the source of the white powder on the man's fingers? Suppose it was not chalk dust but flour or confectioner's sugar or talcum or heroin? Any of these possibilities would weaken or invalidate his conclusion.

Another example, closer to the kinds of arguments you will examine, reveals the flaw in the deductive process.

MAJOR
PREMISE: All Communists oppose organized religion.

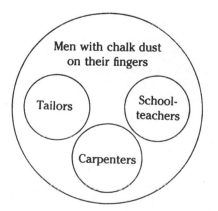

MINOR PREMISE:	Robert Roe opposes organized religion.
CONCLUSION:	Therefore, Robert Roe is a Communist.

The common name for this fallacy is "guilt by association." The fact that two things share an attribute does not mean that they are the same thing. As in the first example, the diagram above makes clear that Robert Roe and Communists do not necessarily share all attributes. Remembering that Holmes may have misinterpreted the signs of chalk on the traveler's fingers, we may also want to question whether Robert Roe's opposition to organized religion has been misinterpreted.

An example from history shows us how such an argument may be used. In a campaign speech during the summer of 1952, Senator Joseph McCarthy, who had made a reputation as a tireless enemy of communism, said, "I do not tell you that Schlesinger, Stevenson's number one man, number one braintrust, I don't tell you he's a Communist. I have no information on that point. But I do know that if he were a Communist he would also ridicule religion as Schlesinger has done."[2] This is an argument based on a sign warrant. Clearly the sign referred to by Senator McCarthy, ridicule of religion, would not be sufficient to characterize someone as a Communist.

Some deductive arguments give trouble because one of the premises, usually the major premise, is omitted. As in the warrants we examined in Chapter 6, a failure to evaluate the truth of the unexpressed premise may lead to an invalid conclusion. When only two parts of the syllogism appear, we call the resulting form an *enthymeme*. Suppose we overhear the following snatch of conversation:

> *"Did you hear about Jean's father? He had a heart attack last week."*

---

[2]Joseph R. McCarthy, "The Red-Tinted Washington Crowd," speech delivered to a Republican campaign meeting at Appleton, Wisconsin, November 3, 1952.

"That's too bad. But I'm not surprised. I know he always re-fused to go for his annual physical checkups."

The second speaker has used an unexpressed major premise, the cause-effect warrant "If you have annual physical checkups, you can avoid heart attacks." He does not express it because he assumes that it is unnecessary to do so. The first speaker recognizes the un-spoken warrant and may agree with it. Or the first speaker may pro-duce evidence from reputable sources that such a generalization is by no means universally true, in which case the conclusion of the second speaker is suspect.

A knowledge of the deductive process can help guide you to-ward an evaluation of the soundness of your reasoning in an argu-ment you are constructing. The syllogism is often clearer than an outline in establishing the relations between the different parts of an argument.

Suppose you wanted to argue that your former high school should introduce a dress code. You might begin by asking these questions: What would be the purpose of such a regulation? How would a dress code fulfill that purpose? What reasons could you pro-vide to support your claim?

Then you might set down part of your argument like this:

Dressing in different styles makes students more aware of social differences among themselves.

The students in this school dress in many different styles.

Therefore, they are more aware of differences in social status among the student body.

As you diagram this first part of the argument, you should ask two sets of questions:

1. Is the major premise true? Do differences in dress cause aware-ness of differences in social status? Has my experience con-firmed this?
2. Is the minor premise true? Has my observation confirmed this?

The conclusion, of course, represents something that you don't have to observe. You can deduce with certainty that it is true if both the major and minor premises are true.

So far the testing of your argument has been relatively easy be-cause you have been concerned with the testing of observation and experience. Now you must examine something that does not appear in the syllogism. You have determined certain facts about percep-tions of social status, but you have not arrived at the policy you want to recommend: that a dress code should be mandated. Notice that the dress code argument is based on acceptance of a moral value.

Reducing awareness of social differences is a desirable goal for the school.

A uniform dress code would help to achieve that goal.

Therefore, students should be required to dress uniformly.

The major premise in this syllogism is clearly different from the previous one. While the premise in the previous syllogism can be tested by examining sufficient examples to determine probability, this statement, about the desirability of the goal, is a value judgment and cannot be proved by counting examples. Whether equality of social status is a desirable goal depends on an appeal to other, more basic values.

Setting down your own or someone else's argument in this form will not necessarily give you the answers to questions about how to support your claim, but it should clearly indicate what your claims are and, above all, what logical connections exist between your statements.

SAMPLE ANALYSIS: A DEDUCTIVE ARGUMENT

Advice for the Anti-Smokers: Take a Message from Garcia

ABIGAIL TRAFFORD

Long ago, I used to smoke. I was a student in Paris and I never went out without a red package of Royales and my black cigarette holder. I smoked over an espresso in the afternoon after class. I smoked over a glass of anis late at night.

I smoked because it was a prop along with long hair and poetry, a symbol of coming of age, of living on the edge. It was a year when students at the Sorbonne gathered and marched in protest. It was a year on my own, a time of hope, a celebration of freedom, symbolized by plumes of cigarette smoke.

I smoked for the same reasons my daughters and I and millions of Americans reveled in the music of the Grateful Dead and now mourn the sad end of Jerry Garcia. The Grateful Dead is about attitude, image, and lifestyle, and Jerry Garcia was the rock existentialist whose sound communicated across generations.

Abigail Trafford is health editor of the *Washington Post*. This article appeared in the *Post* on August 15, 1995.

His music was about independence and staking out your own turf and finding a comfortable personality. And so were my cigarettes. I smoked, in the words of the Grateful Dead, because *"All the years combine. . . . In the end there's just a song comes cryin' up the night."* An ashtray of half-smoked Royales. The black cigarette holder on the table. The empty glass. Paris in the sixties. *"It seems like all this life was just a dream. Stella blue. Stella blue."*

By contrast with such images of adventure and poetry, President Clinton's new crackdown on teenage smoking is going to be a tough sell. It focuses on health, but in fact is a direct intervention in the rites of passage for many teenagers.   5

The medical reasons against smoking are indisputable, and Garcia's death last week at age fifty-three gave the president a dramatic example of the consequences of unhealthy living. Captain Trips smoked three packs of cigarettes a day, lived off junk food, took all kinds of drugs and became a heroin addict, dying ignominiously in a rehab center where he was being treated for a relapse. President Clinton warned: "Young people should say: 'I'm not going to die that way.'"

But if the anti-smoking forces are to be successful, they must take a page from the Grateful Dead on how to reach the hearts and minds of young people. So far, do-not-smoke campaigns aimed at teenagers have largely missed the mark. It doesn't work to tell them to just say no.

Yet public health messages are generally written like commandments of medical virtue: Don't smoke, don't drink (too much), don't eat (too much), don't drive (too fast, without a seat belt), don't take illegal drugs, don't accept rides from strangers, don't have sex (before you're ready, before you know how to use a condom, before you're in a monogamous relationship, before you're married).

But as every parent knows, the forbidden fruit is the tastiest to young people. "Teenagers tend to rebel as a routine. The best way to get teenagers to do something is to tell them not to do it," says George D. Lundberg, editor of the *Journal of the American Medical Association.*

Compare the negative public health messages with the songs of 10 the Grateful Dead. The group did not gloss over the fatal realities of growing up, but it talked about them in a way that struck a chord and made young people listen: *"What in the world ever became of sweet Jane. She lost her sparkle, you know she isn't the same. Livin' on reds, vitamin C and cocaine. All a friend can say is 'Ain't it a shame.'"*

For the most part, the Grateful Dead was about optimism. It gave fans a good feeling now, not a promise of better hearts or lungs in middle age. As the song goes: *"Dear Mr. Fantasy play us a tune. Something to make us all feel happy. Do anything to take us out of this gloom. Sing a song, play guitar, make us happy."*

To succeed, a cultural revolution that takes away smoking has to replace it with *"something to make us all feel happy . . . [and] take us out of this gloom."*

Unfortunately, cigarette advertisers have been more successful than anti-smoking forces when it comes to taking the basics of the Grateful Dead message. Billboards advertising cigarettes promise virility, power, sexuality, a message that smoking is an escape from the unbearable feelings of growing up.

The challenge of the president's attack on tobacco is to take the message away from the advertisers and turn it around so that young people will understand that their transition from teenager to adult — their demand to be recognized as an individual — does not depend on smoking. In fact, their lives depend on making this cultural shift.

After Paris, I gave up smoking. Luckily, I never learned to inhale   15 properly, which is the key to not getting addicted. Unlike most smokers, I was able to quit without a second thought.

Yet I never forgot my Paris days or the symbolism of a package of Royales. As the song goes, smoking had been for me *"A box of rain [that] will ease the pain, and Love will see you through."*

Analysis

The title is a play on words. "A Message to Garcia," written by Elbert Hubbard in 1899, is an essay extolling the heroic American army lieutenant who delivered a crucial message to a General Garcia during the Spanish-American War. It enjoyed extraordinary popularity in the early 1900s both in America and abroad.

A deductive argument proceeds from a general statement that the writer assumes to be true to a conclusion that is more specific. Deductive reasoning is commonplace, but it is seldom so pure as the definition suggests. In Trafford's article the generalization, or major premise, on which the conclusion is based, is expressed in paragraph 2: Smoking is an act that symbolizes youthful defiance and an embrace of adult freedom. The minor premise represents her belief that both the kind of life she led in Paris and the music of the Grateful Dead — especially that of the band's leader, Jerry Garcia — could give young people something that, like cigarettes, would "ease the pain." She concludes that anti-smoking advertising must concentrate not on warnings about dangers to health but on messages of optimism, like that offered by Garcia, "something to make us all feel happy."

As in any deductive argument, the validity of the claim or conclusion depends, first of all, on the soundness of the major premise. Trafford uses her own experience as a young woman in rebellion against a conventional life-style to prove that smoking is a way of establishing one's independence and individuality. Young readers will know about the bohemian life that she and others enjoyed in Paris a generation ago only from reading or movies. But Trafford's use of specific details — "the empty glass," "The black cigarette holder on the table," "an espresso in the afternoon after class" — is clear enough, and today's students can supply their own symbols. Even more appealing and original is her use of the lyrics of songs by the Grateful Dead. For her both smoking and the Grateful Dead represented "an attitude, an image, and a life-style" signifying freedom and power.

Is Trafford right, then, in concluding that warnings about health dangers alone are not enough to prevent young people from smoking? We know that cigarette smoking among the young has declined, so perhaps the warnings have taken hold, after all. But Trafford thinks that only "a cultural shift" can work. Cigarette advertisers promise virility, power, sexuality. The anti-smoking forces must somehow convince young people that adulthood can offer the satisfactions symbolized by smoking.

In logic, the conclusion of a deductive argument must be true. In real-life arguments, however, the conclusions do not fall into place quite so easily. Theoretically, Trafford's conclusion — that because of the special appeal of smoking, anti-smoking forces must find a different approach — is sound. But when we try to envision the kinds of persuasion that would produce a cultural shift, we are hard pressed to know exactly what Trafford means. Trafford herself gave up smoking as a rite of passage from teenager to adult, when youthful rebellion apparently was no longer necessary or attractive. She quit smoking easily. But we aren't told how that metamorphosis was accomplished.

A Note on the Syllogism and the Toulmin Model

In examining the classical deductive syllogism, you may have noticed the resemblance of its three-part outline to the three-part structure of claim, support, and warrant that we have used throughout the text to illustrate the elements of argument. We mentioned that the syllogism was articulated over two thousand years ago by the Greek philosopher Aristotle. By contrast, the claim-support-warrant structure is based on the model of argument proposed by the modern British philosopher Stephen Toulmin.

Now, there is every reason to think that all models of argument will share some similarities. Nevertheless, the differences between the formal syllogism and the informal Toulmin model suggest that the latter is a more effective instrument for writers who want to know which questions to ask, both before they begin and during the process of developing their arguments.

The syllogism is useful for laying out the basic elements of an argument, as we have seen in several examples. It lends itself more readily to simple arguments. The following syllogism summarizes a familiar argument.

MAJOR
PREMISE: Advertising of things harmful to our health should be legally banned.

MINOR
PREMISE: Cigarettes are harmful to our health.

CONCLUSION: Therefore, advertising of cigarettes should be legally banned.

Cast in the form of a Toulmin outline, the argument looks like this:

CLAIM: Advertising of cigarettes should be legally banned.

SUPPORT
(EVIDENCE):   Cigarettes are harmful to our health.

WARRANT: Advertising of things harmful to our health should be legally banned.

or in diagram form:

Support ——————————————————▶ *Claim*
Cigarettes are harmful   Advertising of cigarettes
to our health.   should be legally banned.

Warrant
Advertising of things harmful to our
health should be legally banned.

In both the syllogism and the Toulmin model the principal elements of the argument are expressed in three statements. You can see that the claim in the Toulmin model is the conclusion in the syllogism — that is, the proposition that you are trying to prove. The evidence (support) in the Toulmin model corresponds to the minor premise in the syllogism. And the warrant in the Toulmin model resembles the major premise of the syllogism.

But the differences are significant. One difference is the use of language. The syllogism represents an argument "in which the validity of the assumption underlying the inference 'leap' is uncontested."[3] That is, the words "major premise" seem to suggest that the assumption has been proved. They do not emphasize that an

[3]Wayne E. Brockenreide and Douglas Ehninger, "Toulmin on Argument: An Interpretation and Application," *Contemporary Theories of Rhetoric: Selected Readings,* ed. Richard L. Johannesen (New York: Harper and Row, 1971), p. 245. This comparative analysis is indebted to Brockenreide and Ehninger's influential article.

analysis of the premise — "Advertising of things harmful to our health should be legally banned" — is necessary before we can decide that the conclusion is acceptable. Of course, a careful arguer will try to establish the truth and validity of all parts of the syllogism, but the terms in which the syllogism is framed do not encourage him or her to examine the real relationship among the three elements. Sometimes the enthymeme (see p. 256), which uses only two elements in the argument and suppresses the third, makes analyzing the relationship even more difficult.

In the Toulmin model, the use of the term *warrant* indicates that the validity of the proposition must be established in order to *guarantee* the claim, or make the crossing from support to claim. It makes clear that the arguer must ask *why* such advertising must be banned.

Nor is the term *minor premise* as useful to the arguer as "support." The word *support* instructs the arguer that he or she must take steps to provide the claim with factual evidence or an appeal to values.

A second difference is that while the syllogism is essentially static, with all three parts logically locked into place, the Toulmin model suggests that an argument is a *movement* from support to claim by way of the warrant, which acts as a bridge. Remember that Toulmin introduced the concept of warrant by asking "How do you get there?" (His first two questions, introducing the claim and support, were, "What are you trying to prove?" and "What have you got to go on?")

Lastly, recall that in addition to the three basic elements, the Toulmin model offers supplementary elements of argument. The *qualifier,* in the form of words like "probably" or "more likely," shows that the claim is not absolute. The *backing* offers support for the validity of the warrant. The *reservation* suggests that the validity of the warrant may be limited. These additional elements, which refine and expand the argument itself, reflect the real flexibility and complexity of the argumentative process.

COMMON FALLACIES

In this necessarily brief review it would be impossible to discuss all the fallacies listed by logicians, but we can examine the ones most likely to be found in the arguments you will read and write. Fallacies are difficult to classify, first, because there are literally dozens of systems for classifying, and second, because under any system there is always a good deal of overlap. Our discussion of the reasoning process, however, tells us where faulty reasoning occurs.

Inductive fallacies, as we know, result from the wrong use of evidence: That is, the arguer leaps to a conclusion on the basis of an insufficient sample, ignoring evidence that might have altered his or her conclusion. Deductive fallacies, on the other hand, result from a failure to follow the logic of a series of statements. Here the arguer neglects to make a clear connection between the parts of his or her argument. One of the commonest strategies is the introduction of an irrelevant issue, one that has little or no direct bearing on the development of the claim and serves only to distract the reader.

It's helpful to remember that, even if you cannot name the particular fallacy, you can learn to recognize it and not only refute it in the arguments of others but avoid it in your own as well.

1. Hasty Generalization

In Chapter 5 (see pp. 146–48) we discussed the dangers in drawing conclusions on the basis of insufficient evidence. Many of our prejudices are a result of hasty generalization. A prejudice is literally a judgment made before the facts are in. On the basis of experience with two or three members of an ethnic group, for example, we may form the prejudice that all members of the group share the characteristics that we have attributed to the two or three in our experience. (See Gordon Allport, "The Nature of Prejudice," on p. 116.)

Superstitions are also based in part on hasty generalization. As a result of a very small number of experiences with black cats, broken mirrors, Friday the thirteenth, or spilled salt, some people will assume a cause-effect relation between these signs and misfortunes. Superstition has been defined as "a notion maintained despite evidence to the contrary." The evidence would certainly show that, contrary to the superstitious belief, in a lifetime hundreds of such "unlucky" signs are not followed by unfortunate events. To generalize about a connection is therefore unjustified.

2. Faulty Use of Authority

The attempt to bolster claims by citing the opinions of experts was discussed in Chapter 5. Both writers and readers need to be especially aware of the testimony of authorities who may disagree with those cited. In circumstances where experts disagree, you are encouraged to undertake a careful evaluation and comparison of credentials.

3. *Post Hoc* or Doubtful Cause

The entire Latin term for this fallacy is *post hoc, ergo propter hoc,* meaning, "After this, therefore because of this." The arguer infers that because one event follows another event, the first event must be the cause of the second. But proximity of events or conditions does not guarantee a causal relation. The rooster crows every morning at 5:00 and, seeing the sun rise immediately after, decides that his crowing has caused the sun to rise. A month after A-bomb tests are concluded, tornadoes damage the area where the tests were held, and residents decide that the tests caused the tornadoes. After the school principal suspends daily prayers in the classroom, acts of vandalism increase, and some parents are convinced that failure to conduct prayer is responsible for the rise in vandalism. In each of these cases, the fact that one event follows another does not prove a causal connection. The two events may be coincidental, or the first event may be only one, and an insignificant one, of many causes that have produced the second event. The reader or writer of causal arguments must determine whether another more plausible explanation exists and whether several causes have combined to produce the effect. Perhaps the suspension of prayer was only one of a number of related causes: a decline in disciplinary action, a relaxation of academic standards, a change in school administration, and changes in family structure in the school community.

In the previous section we saw that superstitions are the result not only of hasty generalization but also of the willingness to find a cause-effect connection in the juxtaposition of two events. A belief in astrological signs also derives from erroneous inferences about cause and effect. Only a very few of the millions of people who consult the astrology charts every day in newspapers and magazines have submitted the predictions to statistical analysis. A curious reader might try this strategy: Save the columns, usually at the beginning or end of the year, in which astrologers and clairvoyants make predictions for events in the coming year, allegedly based on their reading of the stars and other signs. At the end of the year evaluate the percentage of predictions that were fulfilled. The number will be very small. But even if some of the predictions prove true, there may be other less fanciful explanations for their accuracy.

In defending simple explanations against complex ones, philosophers and scientists often refer to a maxim called *Occam's razor,* a principle of the medieval philosopher and theologian William of Occam. A modern science writer says this principle "urges a preference for the simplest hypothesis that does all we want it to do."[4] Bertrand Russell, the twentieth-century British philosopher, explained it this way:

> It is vain to do with more what can be done with fewer. That is to say, if everything in some science can be interpreted without assuming this or that hypothetical entity, there is no ground for assuming it. I have myself found this a most fruitful principle in logical analysis.[5]

---

[4]Martin Gardner, *The Whys of a Philosophical Scrivener* (New York: Quill, 1983), p. 174.
[5]*Dictionary of Mind, Matter and Morals* (New York: Philosophical Library, 1952), p. 166.

In other words, choose the simpler, more credible explanation wherever possible.

We all share the belief that scientific experimentation and research can answer questions about a wide range of natural and social phenomena: evolutionary development, hurricanes, disease, crime, poverty. It is true that repeated experiments in controlled situations can establish what seem to be solid relations suggesting cause and effect. But even scientists prefer to talk not about cause but about an extremely high probability that under controlled conditions one event will follow another.

In the social sciences cause-effect relations are especially susceptible to challenge. Human experiences can seldom be subjected to laboratory conditions. In addition, the complexity of the social environment makes it difficult, even impossible, to extract one cause from among the many that influence human behavior.

4. False Analogy

Many analogies are merely descriptive and offer no proof of the connection between the two things being compared. In recent years a debate has emerged between weight-loss professionals about the wisdom of urging overweight people to lose weight for health reasons. Susan Wooley, director of the eating disorders clinic at the University of Cincinnati and a professor of psychiatry, offered the following analogy in defense of her view that dieting is dangerous.

> We know that overweight people have a higher mortality rate than thin people. We also know that black people have a higher mortality rate than white people. Do we subject black people to torturous treatments to bleach their skin? Of course not. We have enough sense to know skin-bleaching will not eliminate sickle-cell anemia. So why do we have blind faith that weight loss will cure the diseases associated with obesity?"[6]

But it is clear that the analogy between black skin and excessive weight does not work. The color of one's skin does not cause sickle-cell anemia, but there is an abundance of proof that excess weight influences mortality.

Historians are fond of using analogical arguments to demonstrate that particular circumstances prevailing in the past are being reproduced in the present. They therefore feel safe in predicting that the present course of history will follow that of the past. British historian Arnold Toynbee argues by analogy that humans' tenure on earth may be limited.

---

[6]*New York Times,* April 12, 1992, Sec. C, p. 43.

On the evidence of the past history of life on this planet, even the extinction of the human race is not entirely unlikely. After all, the reign of man on the Earth, if we are right in thinking that man established his present ascendancy in the middle paleolithic age, is so far only about 100,000 years old, and what is that compared to the 500 million or 900 million years during which life has been in existence on the surface of this planet? In the past, other forms of life have enjoyed reigns which have lasted for almost inconceivably longer periods — and which yet at last have come to an end.[7]

Toynbee finds similarities between the limited reigns of other animal species and the possible disappearance of the human race. For this analogy, however, we need to ask whether the conditions of the past, so far as we know them, at all resemble the conditions under which human existence on earth might be terminated. Is the fact that human beings are also members of the animal kingdom sufficient support for this comparison?

5. *Ad Hominem*

The Latin term *ad hominem* means "against the man" and refers to an attack on the person rather than on the argument or the issue. The assumption in such a fallacy is that if the speaker proves to be unacceptable in some way, his or her statements must also be judged unacceptable. Attacking the author of the statement is a strategy of diversion that prevents the reader from giving attention where it is due — to the issue under discussion.

You might hear someone complain, "What can the priest tell us about marriage? He's never been married himself." This accusation ignores the validity of the advice the priest might offer. In the same way an overweight patient might reject the advice on diet by an overweight physician. In politics it is not uncommon for antagonists to attack each other for personal characteristics that may not be relevant to the tasks they will be elected to perform. They may be accused of infidelity to their partners, homosexuality, atheism, or a flamboyant social life. Even if certain accusations should be proved true, voters should not ignore the substance of what politicians do and say in their public offices.

This confusion of private life with professional record also exists in literature and the other arts. According to their biographers, the American writers Thomas Wolfe, Robert Frost, and William Saroyan — to name only a few — and numbers of film stars, including Charlie Chaplin, Joan Crawford, and Bing Crosby, made life miserable for those closest to them. Having read about their unpleasant personal characteristics, some people find it hard to separate the artist from

---

[7]*Civilization on Trial* (New York: Oxford University Press, 1948), pp. 162–163.

his or her creation, although the personality and character of the artist are often irrelevant to the content of the work.

Accusations against the person do *not* constitute a fallacy if the characteristics under attack are relevant to the argument. If the politician is irresponsible and dishonest in the conduct of his or her personal life, we may be justified in thinking that the person will also behave irresponsibly and dishonestly in public office.

6. False Dilemma

As the name tells us, the false dilemma, sometimes called the black-white fallacy, poses an either/or situation. The arguer suggests that only two alternatives exist, although there may be other explanations of or solutions to the problem under discussion. The false dilemma reflects the simplification of a complex problem. Sometimes it is offered out of ignorance or laziness, sometimes to divert attention from the real explanation or solution that the arguer rejects for doubtful reasons.

You may encounter the either/or situation in dilemmas about personal choices. "At the University of Georgia," says one writer, "the measure of a man was football. You either played it or worshiped those who did, and there was no middle ground."[8] Clearly this dilemma — "Love football or you're not a man" — ignores other measures of manhood.

Politics and government offer a wealth of examples. In an interview with the *New York Times* in 1975, the Shah of Iran was asked why he could not introduce into his authoritarian regime greater freedom for his subjects. His reply was, "What's wrong with authority? Is anarchy better?" Apparently he considered that only two paths were open to him — authoritarianism or anarchy. Of course, democracy was also an option, which, perhaps fatally, he declined to consider.

7. Slippery Slope

If an arguer predicts that taking a first step will lead inevitably to a second, usually undesirable step, he or she must provide evidence that this will happen. Otherwise, the arguer is guilty of a slippery slope fallacy.

Asked by an inquiring photographer on the street how he felt about censorship of a pornographic magazine, a man replied, "I don't think any publication should be banned. It's a slippery slope when you start making decisions on what people should be permit-

---

[8]Phil Gailey, "A Nonsports Fan," *New York Times Magazine,* December 18, 1983, Sec. VI, p. 96.

ted to read. . . . It's a dangerous precedent." Perhaps. But if questioned further, the man should have offered evidence that a ban on some things leads inevitably to a ban on everything.

Predictions based on the danger inherent in taking the first step are commonplace:

> Legalization of abortion will lead to murder of the old and the physically and mentally handicapped.
>
> The Connecticut law allowing sixteen-year-olds and their parents to divorce each other will mean the death of the family.
>
> If we ban handguns, we will end up banning rifles and other hunting weapons.

Distinguishing between probable and improbable predictions — that is, recognizing the slippery slope fallacy — poses special problems because only future developments can verify or refute predictions. For example, in 1941 the imposition of military conscription aroused some opponents to predict that the draft was a precursor of fascism in this country. Only after the war, when 10 million draftees were demobilized, did it become clear that the draft had been an insufficient sign for a prediction of fascism. In this case the slippery slope prediction of fascism might have been avoided if closer attention had been paid to other influences pointing to the strength of democracy.

Slippery slope predictions are simplistic. They ignore not only the dissimilarities between first and last steps but also the complexity of the developments in any long chain of events.

8. Begging the Question

If the writer makes a statement that assumes that the very question being argued has already been proved, the writer is guilty of begging the question. In a letter to the editor of a college newspaper protesting the failure of the majority of students to meet the writing requirement because they had failed an exemption test, the writer said, "Not exempting all students who honestly qualify for exemption is an insult." But whether the students are honestly qualified is precisely the question that the exemption test was supposed to resolve. The writer has not proved that the students who failed the writing test were qualified for exemption. She has only made an assertion *as if* she had already proved it.

In an effort to raise standards of teaching, some politicians and educators have urged that "master teachers" be awarded higher salaries. Opponents have argued that such a proposal begs the question because it assumes that the term "master teachers" can be or has already been defined.

Circular reasoning is an extreme example of begging the question: "Women should not be permitted to join men's clubs because the clubs are for men only." The question to be resolved first, of course, is whether clubs for men only should continue to exist.

9. Straw Man

This fallacy consists of an attack on a view similar to but not the same as the one your opponent holds. It is a familiar diversionary tactic. The name probably derives from an old game in which a straw man was set up to divert attention from the real target that a contestant was supposed to knock down.

One of the outstanding examples of the straw man fallacy occurred in the famous Checkers speech of Senator Richard Nixon. In 1952 during his vice-presidential campaign, Nixon was accused of having appropriated $18,000 in campaign funds for his personal use. At one point in the radio and television speech in which he defended his reputation, he said:

> One other thing I probably should tell you, because if I don't they will probably be saying this about me, too. We did get something, a gift, after the election.
>
> A man down in Texas heard Pat on the radio mention the fact that our two youngsters would like to have a dog, and, believe it or not, the day before we left on this campaign trip we got a message from Union Station in Baltimore saying they had a package for us. We went down to get it. You know what it was?
>
> It was a little cocker spaniel dog, in a crate that he had sent all the way from Texas, black and white, spotted, and our little girl, Tricia, the six-year-old, named it Checkers.
>
> And, you know, the kids, like all kids, loved the dog, and I just want to say this, right now, that regardless of what they say about it, we are going to keep it.[9]

Of course, Nixon knew that the issue was the alleged misappropriation of funds, not the ownership of the dog, which no one had asked him to return.

10. Two Wrongs Make a Right

This is another example of the way in which attention may be diverted from the question at issue.

After a speech by President Jimmy Carter in March 1977 attacking the human rights record of the Soviet Union, Russian officials responded:

---

[9]Radio and television address of Senator Nixon from Los Angeles on September 23, 1952.

As for the present state of human rights in the United States, it is characterized by the following facts: millions of unemployed, racial discrimination, social inequality of women, infringement of citizens' personal freedom, the growth of crime, and so on.[10]

The Russians made no attempt to deny the failure of *their* human rights record; instead they attacked by pointing out that the Americans are not blameless either.

11. *Non Sequitur*

The Latin term *non sequitur,* which means "it does not follow," is another fallacy of irrelevance. An advertisement for a book, *Worlds in Collision,* whose theories about the origin of the earth and evolutionary development have been challenged by almost all reputable scientists, states:

Once rejected as "preposterous!" Critics called it an outrage! It aroused incredible antagonism in scientific and literary circles. Yet half a million copies were sold and for twenty-seven years it remained an outstanding bestseller.

We know, of course, that the popularity of a book does not bestow scientific respectability. The number of sales, therefore, is irrelevant to proof of the book's theoretical soundness.

12. *Ad Populum*

Arguers guilty of this fallacy make an appeal to the prejudices of the people (*populum* in Latin). They assume that their claim can be adequately defended without further support if they emphasize a belief or attitude that the audience shares with them. One common form of *ad populum* is an appeal to patriotism, which may allow arguers to omit evidence that the audience needs for proper evaluation of the claim. In the following advertisement the makers of Zippo lighters made such an appeal in urging readers to buy their product.

It's a grand old lighter. Zippo — the grand old lighter that's made right here in the good old U. S. A.
We truly make an all-American product. The raw materials used in making a Zippo lighter are all right from this great land of ours.
Zippo windproof lighters are proud to be Americans.

13. Appeal to Tradition

In making an appeal to tradition, the arguer assumes that what has existed for a long time and has therefore become a tradition should continue to exist *because* it is a tradition. If the arguer avoids

---

[10]*New York Times,* March 3, 1977, p. 1.

telling his or her reader *why* the tradition should be preserved, he or she may be accused of failing to meet the real issue.

The following statement appeared in a letter defending the membership policy of the Century Club, an all-male club established in New York City in 1847 that was under pressure to admit women. The writer was a Presbyterian minister who opposed the admission of women.

> I am totally opposed to a proposal which would radically change the nature of the Century. . . . A club creates an ethos of its own over the years, and I would deeply deplore a step that would inevitably create an entirely different kind of place.
>
> A club like the Century should surely be unaffected by fashionable whims. . . .[11]

14. Faulty Emotional Appeals

In some discussions of fallacies, appeals to the emotions of the audience are treated as illegitimate or "counterfeit proofs." All such appeals, however, are *not* illegitimate. As we saw in Chapter 5 on support, appeals to the values and emotions of an audience are an appropriate form of persuasion. You can recognize fallacious appeals if (1) they are irrelevant to the argument or draw attention from the issues being argued or (2) they appear to conceal another purpose. Here we treat two of the most popular appeals — to pity and to fear.

Appeals to pity, compassion, and natural willingness to help the unfortunate are particularly hard to resist. The requests for aid by most charitable organizations — for hungry children, victims of disaster, stray animals — offer examples of legitimate appeals. But these appeals to our sympathetic feelings should not divert us from considering other issues in a particular case. It would be wrong, for example, to allow a multiple murderer to escape punishment because he or she had experienced a wretched childhood. Likewise, if you are asked to contribute to a charitable cause, you should try to learn how many unfortunate people or animals are being helped and what percentage of the contribution will be allocated to maintaining the organization and its officers. In some cases the financial records are closed to public review, and only a small share of the contribution will reach the alleged beneficiaries.

Appeals to fear are likely to be even more effective. But they must be based on evidence that fear is an appropriate response to the issues and that it can move an audience toward a solution to the problem. (Fear can also have the adverse effect of preventing people from taking a necessary action.) Insurance companies, for example,

---

[11]David H. C. Read, letter to the *New York Times,* January 13, 1983, p. 14.

make appeals to our fears of destitution for ourselves and our families as a result of injury, unemployment, sickness, and death. These appeals are justified if the possibilities of such destitution are real and if the insurance will provide relief. It would also be legitimate to arouse fear of the consequences of drunk driving, provided, again, that the descriptions were accurate. On the other hand, it would be wrong to induce fear that fluoridation of public water supplies causes cancer without presenting sound evidence of the probability. It would also be wrong to instill a fear of school integration unless convincing proof were offered of undesirable social consequences.

An emotional response by itself is not always the soundest basis for making decisions. Your own experience has probably taught you that in the grip of a strong emotion like love or hate or anger you often overlook good reasons for making different and better choices. Like you, your readers want to be given the opportunity to consider all the available kinds of support for an argument.

READINGS FOR ANALYSIS

On Nation and Race
ADOLF HITLER

There are some truths which are so obvious that for this very reason they are not seen or at least not recognized by ordinary people. They sometimes pass by such truisms as though blind and are most astonished when someone suddenly discovers what everyone really ought to know. Columbus's eggs lie around by the hundreds of thousands, but Columbuses are met with less frequency.

Thus men without exception wander about in the garden of Nature; they imagine that they know practically everything and yet with few exceptions pass blindly by one of the most patent principles of Nature's rule: the inner segregation of the species of all living beings on this earth.

Even the most superficial observation shows that Nature's restricted form of propagation and increase is an almost rigid basic law of all the innumerable forms of expression of her vital urge.

Adolf Hitler (1889–1945) became the Nazi dictator of Germany in the mid-1930s. "On Nation and Race" (editor's title) begins the eleventh chapter of *Mein Kampf* (*My Struggle*), vol. 1, published in 1925.

Every animal mates only with a member of the same species. The titmouse seeks the titmouse, the finch the finch, the stork the stork, the field mouse the field mouse, the dormouse the dormouse, the wolf the she-wolf, etc.

Only unusual circumstances can change this, primarily the compulsion of captivity or any other cause that makes it impossible to mate within the same species. But then Nature begins to resist this with all possible means, and her most visible protest consists either in refusing further capacity for propagation to bastards or in limiting the fertility of later offspring; in most cases, however, she takes away the power of resistance to disease or hostile attacks.

This is only too natural.   5

Any crossing of two beings not at exactly the same level produces a medium between the level of the two parents. This means: The offspring will probably stand higher than the racially lower parent, but not as high as the higher one. Consequently, it will later succumb in the struggle against the higher level. Such mating is contrary to the will of Nature for a higher breeding of all life. The precondition for this does not lie in associating superior and inferior, but in the total victory of the former. The stronger must dominate and not blend with the weaker, thus sacrificing his own greatness. Only the born weakling can view this as cruel, but he after all is only a weak and limited man; for if this law did not prevail, any conceivable higher development of organic living beings would be unthinkable.

The consequence of this racial purity, universally valid in Nature, is not only the sharp outward delimitation of the various races, but their uniform character in themselves. The fox is always a fox, the goose a goose, the tiger a tiger, etc., and the difference can lie at most in the varying measure of force, strength, intelligence, dexterity, endurance, etc., of the individual specimens. But you will never find a fox who in his inner attitude might, for example, show humanitarian tendencies toward geese, as similarly there is no cat with a friendly inclination toward mice.

Therefore, here, too, the struggle among themselves arises less from inner aversion than from hunger and love. In both cases, Nature looks on calmly, with satisfaction, in fact. In the struggle for daily bread all those who are weak and sickly or less determined succumb, while the struggle of the males for the female grants the right or opportunity to propagate only to the healthiest. And struggle is always a means for improving a species' health and power of resistance and, therefore, a cause of its higher development.

If the process were different, all further and higher development would cease and the opposite would occur. For, since the inferior always predominates numerically over the best, if both had the same possibility of preserving life and propagating, the inferior would multiply so much more rapidly that in the end the best would inevitably be driven into the background, unless a correction of this state of affairs were undertaken. Nature does just this by subjecting the weaker part to such severe living conditions that by them alone the number is limited, and by not permitting the remainder to increase promiscuously, but making a new and ruthless choice according to strength and health.

No more than Nature desires the mating of weaker with stronger 10 individuals, even less does she desire the blending of a higher with a lower race, since, if she did, her whole work of higher breeding, over perhaps hundreds of thousands of years, might be ruined with one blow.

Historical experience offers countless proofs of this. It shows with terrifying clarity that in every mingling of Aryan blood with that of lower peoples the result was the end of the cultured people. North America, whose population consists in by far the largest part of Germanic elements who mixed but little with the lower colored peoples, shows a different humanity and culture from Central and South America, where the predominantly Latin immigrants often mixed with the aborigines on a large scale. By this one example, we can clearly and distinctly recognize the effect of racial mixture. The Germanic inhabitant of the American continent, who has remained racially pure and unmixed, rose to be master of the continent; he will remain the master as long as he does not fall a victim to defilement of the blood.

The result of all racial crossing is therefore in brief always the following:

(a) Lowering of the level of the higher race;

(b) Physical and intellectual regression and hence the beginning of a slowly but surely progressing sickness.

To bring about such a development is, then, nothing else but to 15 sin against the will of the eternal creator.

And as a sin this act is rewarded.

When man attempts to rebel against the iron logic of Nature, he comes into struggle with the principles to which he himself owes his existence as a man. And this attack must lead to his own doom.

Here, of course, we encounter the objection of the modern pacifist, as truly Jewish in its effrontery as it is stupid! "Man's role is to overcome Nature!"

Millions thoughtlessly parrot this Jewish nonsense and end up by really imagining that they themselves represent a kind of conqueror of Nature; though in this they dispose of no other weapon than an idea, and at that such a miserable one, that if it were true no world at all would be conceivable.

But quite aside from the fact that man has never yet conquered 20 Nature in anything, but at most has caught hold of and tried to lift one or another corner of her immense gigantic veil of eternal riddles and secrets, that in reality he invents nothing but only discovers everything, that he does not dominate Nature, but has only risen on the basis of his knowledge of various laws and secrets of Nature to be lord over those other living creatures who lack this knowledge — quite aside from all this, an idea cannot overcome the preconditions for the development and being of humanity, since the idea itself depends only on man. Without human beings there is no human idea in this world; therefore, the idea as such is always conditioned by the presence of human beings and hence of all the laws which created the precondition for their existence.

And not only that! Certain ideas are even tied up with certain men. This applies most of all to those ideas whose content originates, not in an exact scientific truth, but in the world of emotion, or, as it is so beautifully and clearly expressed today, reflects an "inner experience." All these ideas, which have nothing to do with cold logic as such, but represent only pure expressions of feeling, ethical conceptions, etc., are chained to the existence of men, to whose intellectual imagination and creative power they owe their existence. Precisely in this case the preservation of these definite races and men is the precondition for the existence of these ideas. Anyone, for example, who really desired the victory of the pacifistic idea in this world with all his heart would have to fight with all the means at his disposal for the conquest of the world by the Germans; for, if the opposite should occur, the last pacifist would die out with the last German, since the rest of the world has never fallen so deeply as our own people, unfortunately, has for this nonsense so contrary to Nature and reason. Then, if we were serious, whether we liked it or not, we would have to wage wars in order to arrive at pacifism. This and nothing else was what Wilson, the American world savior, intended, or so at least our German visionaries believed — and thereby his purpose was fulfilled.

In actual fact the pacifistic-humane idea is perfectly all right perhaps when the highest type of man has previously conquered and subjected the world to an extent that makes him the sole ruler of this earth. Then this idea lacks the power of producing evil effects in exact proportion as its practical application becomes rare and finally impossible. Therefore, first struggle and then we shall see what can be done. Otherwise mankind has passed the high point of its development and the end is not the domination of any ethical idea but barbarism and consequently chaos. At this point someone or other may laugh, but this planet once moved through the ether for millions of years without human beings and it can do so again some day if men forget that they owe their higher existence, not to the ideas of a few crazy ideologists, but to the knowledge and ruthless application of Nature's stern and rigid laws.

Everything we admire on this earth today — science and art, technology and inventions — is only the creative product of a few peoples and originally perhaps of *one* race. On them depends the existence of this whole culture. If they perish, the beauty of this earth will sink into the grave with them.

However much the soil, for example, can influence men, the result of the influence will always be different depending on the races in question. The low fertility of a living space may spur the one race to the highest achievements; in others it will only be the cause of bitterest poverty and final undernourishment with all its consequences. The inner nature of peoples is always determining for the manner in which outward influences will be effective. What leads the one to starvation trains the other to hard work.

All great cultures of the past perished only because the origi- 25 nally creative race died out from blood poisoning.

The ultimate cause of such a decline was their forgetting that all culture depends on men and conversely; hence that to preserve a certain culture the man who creates it must be preserved. This preservation is bound up with the rigid law of necessity and the right to victory of the best and stronger in this world.

Those who want to live, let them fight, and those who do not want to fight in this world of eternal struggle do not deserve to live.

Even if this were hard — that is how it is! Assuredly, however, by far the harder fate is that which strikes the man who thinks he can overcome Nature, but in the last analysis only mocks her. Distress, misfortune, and diseases are her answer.

The man who misjudges and disregards the racial laws actually forfeits the happiness that seems destined to be his. He thwarts the triumphal march of the best race and hence also the precondition for all human progress, and remains, in consequence, burdened with all the sensibility of man, in the animal realm of helpless misery.

It is idle to argue which race or races were the original represen- 30 tative of human culture and hence the real founders of all that we sum up under the word "humanity." It is simpler to raise the question with regard to the present, and here an easy, clear answer results. All the human culture, all the results of art, science, and technology that we see before us today, are almost exclusively the creative product of the Aryan. This very fact admits of the not unfounded inference that he alone was the founder of all higher humanity, therefore representing the prototype of all that we understand by the word "man." He is the Prometheus of mankind from whose bright forehead the divine spark of genius has sprung at all times, forever kindling anew that fire of knowledge which illumined the night of silent mysteries and thus caused man to climb the path to mastery over the other beings of this earth. Exclude him

— and perhaps after a few thousand years darkness will again descend on the earth, human culture will pass, and the world turn to a desert.

Reading and Discussion Questions

1. Find places in the essay where Hitler attempts to emphasize the scientific objectivity of his theories.
2. Are there some passages which are difficult to understand? (See, for example, paragraph 13.) How do you explain the difficulty?
3. In explaining his ideology, how does Hitler misinterpret the statement that "Every animal mates only with a member of the same species"? How would you characterize this fallacy?
4. Hitler uses the theory of evolution and his interpretation of the "survival of the fittest" to justify his racial philosophy. Find the places in the text where Hitler reveals that he misunderstands the theory in its application to human beings.
5. What false evidence about race does Hitler use in his assessment of the racial experience in North America? Examine carefully the last sentence of paragraph 11: "The Germanic inhabitant of the American continent, who has remained racially pure and unmixed, rose to be master of the continent; he will remain the master as long as he does not fall a victim to defilement of the blood."
6. What criticism of Jews does Hitler offer? How does this criticism help to explain Hitler's pathological hatred of Jews?
7. Hitler believes that pacifism is a violation of "Nature and reason." Would modern scientists agree that the laws of Nature require unremitting struggle and conflict between human beings — until the master race conquers?

Writing Suggestion

8. Do some research in early human history to discover the degree of truth in this statement: "All human culture, all the results of art, science, and technology that we see before us today, are almost exclusively the creative product of the Aryan." You may want to limit your discussion to one area of human culture.

People Like Me

TONY PARKER and HANK SULLIVAN

Yeah sure I'll talk with you, like I wrote and said I would. I just hope it's interesting enough for you to feel you want to hear. My story's very simple you see, it's not at all complex, or least not the way I look at it it's not. I'm your ordinary professional criminal and there's plenty around. Some of us [are] successful, some of us aren't, you know how it goes. What's a professional criminal, what does it mean? Well all it is is someone who makes his living out of crime. Like you do with writing, it's more or less like that. You do your writing, I do my crime. Successful or unsuccessful, which one am I? Well successful of course. I must be, I'm here and still alive. I've never thought of giving up, I'm the same way as you: I just can't imagine doing anything else.

My basic facts are few, shall we start with those? You're talking to a man called Hank and his age is fifty-two. He's doing eight terms of imprisonment for life, plus six sentences consecutive totaling three hundred years. The life terms are for shootings in which people got killed, and the fixed sentences are for different offenses like attempted murder, wounding, armed robbery, possession of explosives, robbery with violence, escape, resisting arrest, and that kind of stuff. All of it straight though, nothing kinky or weird. Parole is something I'll never ever be given, no matter what, which I guess some guys'd take to mean they'd never get out. Not me though, not me my friend, myself I don't look at it that way. Because for sure if I did, well then I'd be dead.

How do I mean? Well let out and get out, they're two different things. They won't let me out ever, not from the front door, sure I know that. So what I have is the only alternative, you know what I mean? If it can't be the front then that only leaves the back. So escape's my ambition and the planning of it is all that keeps me alive. In twenty years I've made it twice so it's not an impossible dream. I'm not that sort of a man. I mean if I was I'd be frustrated wouldn't I, all disappointed and sour and eaten up inside. But I'm not. I'll get out again one day, there's no doubt about that. Believe me, do, okay?

Go back to the beginning for you, my background and childhood, you want to hear about those? Sure I'll tell you then, it won't take too much time. You see there's nothing to tell. I'm from a white middle-class Catholic family, perfectly ordinary, straight down the

---

Tony Parker is a British sociologist who has written several books on criminals and prisons, including *The Violence of Our Lives: Interviews with American Murderers* (1995) from which this interview with career criminal Hank Sullivan is excerpted.

line. As a kid I was happy and we weren't rich, but neither were we poor. We lived in a nice home, we were well raised and wanted for nothing or nothing I recall. My father was a production manager at a factory and my mother was a teacher; both of them are dead now, but they were nice people and good. They were very happy with each other, you know how some people are? They believed in family ties and values, and all that kind of thing. I've a brother and two sisters, all older than me. I've not been in contact with any of them since I was young, but as far as I know they've led conventional lives. Both my sisters are married and I couldn't tell you what their names are. That's about all I can think of that there's to say where my family's concerned. They don't really exist for me for practical purposes in any meaningful kind of way now, because that's how it goes.

Schooling, I guess that'd be interesting if I could remember any-   5
thing of it that left any mark but I'm sorry no, I can't. I went to a Catholic high school for boys and the teachers were priests. I wasn't ever beaten or sexually interfered with. There were none of those things went on you sometimes read about, so there's no interest there, just nothing at all. I think I usually got good grades. My life was not unusual and nothing occurred in it for the first ten years I'd say. No one specially influenced me either for good or for bad, you know what I mean?

The fact I was secretive and had an inner life was all that made me any different, I suppose. If you'd met me then you'd never have imagined more than anyone else what was happening inside. Exteriors conceal, right? In my case I was amusing myself from the age of ten on with stick-ups and fires. They were like kind of my hobbies, but they were much more than that: For me they were my all-consuming interests would be more correct to say. I guess to some folk that'd be unusual in a way, but if it is it didn't seem so to me. It wasn't my life was dull you know and I wanted to escape from it and fizz it up a bit; I just found it interesting to do those things and watch how people would react. Guns were easy to get like they always are, and the first one I had was like a train set for me, I'd clean it and polish it and look after it like it was a treasure or my very best friend. My very first gun, a Colt .45 automatic, gee I'll never forget that one, I loved it I did. Like the way you remember your first woman, you know how I mean?

The other part intrigued me was the psychology thing: People are always more frightened of a kid with a gun than they are of an adult armed robber, have you ever noticed that? Because they think he's not going to be so reasonable and responsible in the way he handles it like a grown-up would I suppose. Might fire a shot at them for just a trivial thing like moving too quick or something of that sort. There was a cabdriver once I stuck up when I was twelve; he'd pulled in an alley where I'd told him to go, and when I let him see the gun and told him to give me all he'd got, he got almost hysterical with fear. "Don't shoot me, don't shoot me" he went on and on. I had to really make a big effort to try and talk him down. I said "Look buddy I'm not going to shoot you" I said, "just so long as you give me all there is." . . . [H]e was so terrified. I mean can you imagine that?

As for those fires, the arson bit I mean, when I first started coming into juvenile institutions and places of that kind, it used to cause so much . . . interest among psychologists and shrinks you wouldn't believe. Very unusual and significant, least that's what they always said. Going to bed with your sister . . . that was ordinary stuff, but a fourteen-year-old who was a serial arsonist, well he really was, he was some special kind of guy. All I did actually was set fire to warehouses and stores and offices and schools and that sort of place. Just for fun you know. But they'd never accept it was that, it always had to be symbolic of something: I found that kind of weird, I really did. One center I was in a psychologist had me write down every single place I'd done. Sixteen as I recall and they divided them in groups: "masculine" and "feminine," "aggressive" and "passive" and some other categories I forget. It was a young woman who done this stuff, and I remember her better than I remember all the shit. She had a real short white overall and a pretty tight little ass, and she'd all the time lean over the table I was sitting at to mark up the blocks So what I did naturally was I stretched it all out, then while she was arranging all the papers and covering them with marks I'd stand round in back of her and peek up her skirt or look down her front. . . . A strange kind of occupation for a young girl to have, studying someone like me. But I let her have her fun though, I didn't mind: one of us was normal and the other one was not. . . .

You know I guess the best part of all though was hearing people talk. They sure caused some chattering, those fires of mine did. "They've caught the arsonist," that I often heard, or words to the effect the owner of the premises was responsible himself, he'd done it for insurance because business was bad. You know what people say. How many I did in total I can't properly recall because I never did something stupid like keeping a list. Sixteen I told the psychologist about, but that sure was not them all; twenty-five or thirty say would be nearer the mark in around about a year. And then it all finished and came to an end. How I was caught was real stupid, no doubt at all. How it is when you're young, right, it's always the same? You want to impress some girl, and that's just what I did. I was boasting one night to her it was me who'd set the fires, and she said she didn't believe it, I was trying to pull her leg. So what did I do? I gave her a forecast: I told her wait and see, on the Saturday night I'd set alight a certain store. So when it went up like I said it would, what happened, well anyone could guess: She told her parents what I'd said. The cops were round my place in five minutes flat, and in my room they found things I'd not had time to hide. My parents were pretty shaken by it, especially my dad. He sat me down I remember and he said he knew I hadn't done such things and I must be protecting someone else, like parents always do. Finally he said he'd help me and in every way he could, but only if I'd swear on the Bible to him to tell the honest truth. I said okay I'd do that, and that's what I did: I swore on the word of God that I'd acted entirely on my own, and I guess that made him feel pretty bad. He was a good man by his lights and he just couldn't understand. It taught me a lesson though, the experience I mean and I've tried to remember it since all through my life but with varying success. What it is you'll know it, like every other man: Never trust a dame.

What happened in the end was I was sent to reform school for an   10 indefinite period, which was precisely four years. I'd say they were some of the best of my life. I mixed with guys like myself whose only aim was crime. There was a thousand juvenile offenders there of every kind you could imagine, and a lot I'm sure you couldn't, you know what I mean? That's an experience you know I'd not otherwise have had. It was good, it taught me possibilities and it opened up my eyes. Also it made me tough. You know I've often thought this since, the guys who do their time better are the ones who started early. That I honestly believe, now I've thought it out, which I've just this minute done.

I don't know what was with my parents after that, somehow we seemed to grow apart. They visited a time or two, but I never went back home; it didn't seem to have no point, we sort of lived in different worlds. I'd say from eighteen up I only associated with all my own kind. Funny, things like that, it's the way it often works. I mean some folks you fit with but others you can only say if they hadn't been your relatives you'd never have known them even for a start. Then someone else you meet and it's like you've known them all your life. That was how it was with me and my first serious girl: She was the sister of a guy I was buddy-buddy with in there. We never talked it over or arranged it any way, but as soon as I got out I went to the apartment she had, and I think all we said was "Hi there" before we then went straight to bed. That's the way it should be, so I've always found. Then you know where you are and you won't get surprised by discovering you're with a vegetarian or someone of that kind.

She was a good kid that girl was, I owe a lot to her: She was the person gave me my first proper chance. Sheila her name was or Sheena, something of the kind. She had some Irish in her you know like I do as well, and we were both brought up Catholic, which was another thing — we were ideally suited to each other in most every way there was. She wasn't much of a looker but I don't think you should let that count: What mattered was she had brains, was good with figures and intelligent. She had a job in the central cashier's office of a chain of carpet and furnishing stores, and she knew the days of the month where their different cash drops were made. That was very useful for me because she could point me to all the places where I needed to be, tell me what time the armored truck with the wages in it would arrive and all stuff like that.

Honestly I did, I learned a lot from that girl: not just where and when to make the strikes but how to plan them out so's they looked like they were at random and no one could trace a pattern in them, point a finger, you know? That stuff was very useful for a young guy like me beginning on a criminal career. I think she was hoping one day I'd make a big enough pile for us to retire and settle down. It was sad for her it didn't happen like that. My trouble was you see I had a wandering eye, something I've never come to terms with in my life. I don't attach myself to people, there's too many risks — lays you open to their moods instead of keeping them to yours. Me and her, Sheena or whatever her name was, things were going along very nice and smoothly for a couple of years till she started talking about wanting to settle down. There was nothing else for it: One night I upped and I didn't come back because you don't want discussions, you just make the break like that. Besides women can peach on you, threaten to tell, and that can lead to awkwardness. I've had it happen and it's not very nice. As soon as they say they might, the best thing to do is make for the door.

I'd say on the whole though I've been lucky with my women, they've mostly given me good times. There was one I remember, now she was one of the best, a feisty little girl; only sixteen, fast-legged and sprinty like a quarter horse. Got me to train her how to use a thirty-eight, and she was the sort to go out and pull jobs I myself'd think twice about first. She was some kid she was, red hair and not all that tall, only came up to here. You know what she'd do? What she was good at especially, it was usually hotels. She'd sit in the bar of one and when some guy propositioned her they'd go up to his room. Ten minutes flat and she'd get him stripped naked, down to his drawers. Then she'd take off all her own clothes and get him so dazzled he'd fall on the bed, and when he did that then she'd reach for her purse, pull out her gun and make him give her his last cent. Takes courage to do that you know, for a girl on her own. I used to tell her if she was my daughter I would, I'd feel real proud. . . .

Women eh, there was other ones too, plenty in my time. I met a 15 broad once, believe me she was sixty-five, she was a little old granny and she drove a big truck and suggested we go into partnership. Only let me tell you, that's something I've never ever done—take on one other guy and the risk grows three ways. One is he could let you down and not play his part; two he could get injured and captured to follow; three if he is he could try to save his neck by telling what he knows. I'd say to any young guy to always bear that in mind: wherever it's practicable, stay on your own.

Let me tell you an example: The first time I ever came to prison, it wasn't my fault. Me and another guy, we'd held up a security truck that was taking wages to a factory. I'd done all the planning about where exactly we'd stop it which was on a bridge over a canal. Then at the last minute I heard it had four armored guards, not two like I'd been told. I always reckoned I could deal with two when I worked on my own, but four was rather different; you'd need eyes in the back of your head. So what did I do but I took on an assistant, and when the shooting started he took a bullet in his hip. He wasn't wearing body armor like I'd told him he should so of course he was caught. They beat it out of him where I was making for and they had twenty police vehicles and dogs and a helicopter too. They got me in the woods and threw a cordon round it, and all because this guy gave them knowledge so they could work out my route. I had no way out except fire power: In the confrontation I shot more accurately than they did but one against twenty's not fair odds and I surrendered in the end. I gave a good account of myself first, I think I took out a total of four, but I finished up with two life sentences plus two hundred years.

Considering for ten years I'd been working nice and steady and never once being caught, as you can imagine I felt very bitter about that result. I still think if I hadn't had that amateur along, I'd most likely have shaken off pursuit. I've learned my lesson about that, or mostly I have. I don't want to be boastful, but if someone wants to hire my services for something big when I'm out I always lay down strict conditions that they leave me alone to work the way I want to, which means on my own. I won't do nothing for anyone if I have to follow their instructions; they must follow mine.

Another thing is this: I won't do just anything, I always make it plain that there's lines. An obvious one from which I'll never deviate is I'll never hurt a woman, not for any sum at all. I don't know if it means I'm softhearted or what. I've been offered contracts and some of them were big ones, but if it's a woman, then the answer's no. I don't touch females, get somebody else. On the whole though taking individuals out, that's really not my line. I've only done two contract hits in the whole of my life, or three at the most. They're sneaky, know what I mean? I wouldn't ever touch them unless business was real bad; I'd sooner stand up and fight. I don't like killing people when they're not armed.

The excitement, you know, that's the part I like: I'm not the sort goes round shooting at random anyone I see. All of my killings they've all had a purpose, I'm a professional criminal, not a . . . psychopath. Those first two I told you about, I was trying to get away, then the next three again, they were all of men with guns who were moving me to a different state or other to face some more charges. The chances of breaching a maximum security establishment are low because you're outnumbered by the guards, so the best times are when they're moving you. Then the same thing again two years ago, there were just two prison guards. That's only seven? One two thr.... Oh yeah you're right, so who the hell was ... yeah wait a minute, I've got it now, the second escape it wasn't three it was four, a state trooper turned up and thought he'd join in. Though I'll be honest with you, there's been a couple of others too that haven't come out and I think they never will. How many in total? Jeez I've no idea, more than ten it must be I guess.

Let me try and tell you how it is. Firstly I don't have to justify   20
myself, there's no need. I guess the way I'd put it would be to say it's like we are at war, me and society I mean. I see myself as a law enforcement officer — only my laws, not yours. Or another way to say it would be there's one set of guys whose uniforms are blue: They try and hang on to things like money and possessions and power. And then there'd be other ones whose uniforms are green: They want to get a slice of things themselves too. The one way they'll not do it is work from nine through five so they have to think of other ways. I've chosen one which I thoroughly enjoy: It's plotting and scheming and working out a strategy, then putting it into action and seeing if it works. And again I'm not boasting in saying this to you because it's true: I've been successful a hundred times more often than I've ever been caught for, that's certainly a fact. We're cleverer than we're given credit for, people like me, we certainly are.

I'm a professional criminal, and I take pride in my trade. An amateur, you see, he's not like that at all. How I'd define him would be a guy who makes a quick hit and relies on his luck for the amount of cash he gets: could be a few hundred bucks, might be nothing at all. But for me I need to know first what the amount is's involved, and the amount of risk I'll take's got to be commensurate with the financial reward. If it looks like it's going to be a combat situation I wouldn't go in underarmed; always at least I've got to have an automatic rifle, two pistols and at least some hand grenades. "Armed to the teeth" would be the phrase.

Obviously if it's something big other guys are going to try and stop me, right? They'll go as far as they think's necessary to do that, including killing me of course. Then I'm saying in return that to stop me that's what they'll have to do, and if they try, then I'm going to try and kill them first. That's common sense, okay? But don't get me wrong like I said before: I wouldn't kill anyone unless it was strictly necessary to get what I wanted or it was my life or theirs.

Would I ever kill you, you want an honest answer to that? Well the answer is no, probably not. I can't envisage the situation arising can you, where it would be necessary? I mean if you were a guard here and I had a gun, if I wanted your key I'd ask you for it. I'd say "Give me your key." And if you were sensible about it as I think you would be and did what I asked and stood to one side, then of course I wouldn't kill you, because there wouldn't be a need. On the other hand though if you crazily decided you wouldn't give me the key and went for your gun, then of course I'd blow your . . . head in. I'd have to wouldn't I, otherwise you might do me harm? That answer your question, do you understand? Good: no hard feelings I hope.

Oh boy Tony I've enjoyed this you know, I truly have. It's been like the kind of conversation you usually have with yourself, know what I mean? Good luck with the book.

Reading and Discussion Questions

1. Do you detect fallacious reasoning in the following statements? Examine the statements that precede or follow them in the interview in order to understand the context.
   a. "What's a professional criminal, what does it mean? Well all it is is someone who makes his living out of crime. Like you do with writing, it's more or less like that." (paragraph 1)
   b. "They got me in the woods and threw a cordon round it, and all because this guy [his accomplice, who was captured] gave them knowledge so they could work out my route. . . . In the confrontation I shot more accurately than they did but one against twenty's not fair odds and I surrendered in the end." (paragraph 16)
   c. " . . . taking individuals out, that's really not my line. I've only done two contract hits in the whole of my life, or three at the most. They're sneaky, know what I mean?" (paragraph 18)
   d. "I'm not the sort goes round shooting at random anyone I see. All my killings they've all had a purpose. I'm a professional criminal, not a . . . psychopath." (paragraph 19)
   e. "I see myself as a law enforcement officer — only my laws, not yours." (paragraph 20)
2. How does Sullivan see himself as a person? Find some of the passages where he describes himself and his personal relations. Does his self-perception strike you as strange? Why or why not?
3. When he talks about "fault," what does he mean? ("The first time I ever went to prison, it wasn't my fault. Me and another guy, we'd held up a security truck that was taking wages to a factory.")

Writing Suggestions

4. Sullivan's definitions seem perverse. Choose some of his ideas and write an analysis of the meanings he gives to them, explaining how they are different from those of most people.
5. *All God's Children: The Bosket Family and the American Tradition of Violence* by Fox Butterfield (1995) is an extraordinary documentation of one family's criminal careers over at least one hundred years. You will

probably want to read the whole book once you begin, but the story of Willie Bosket, a highly intelligent criminal who told police that he had committed 2,000 crimes by age fifteen, will give you some insight into the psychology of the criminal and his defense of his actions. He is far more articulate than Sullivan. Write an analysis of the reasons he gives for his crimes.

CHERYL SILAS had a highway collision, was hit twice from behind, and then sold three cars for us.

When Cheryl unbuckled her shoulder harness and lap belt, it took her a moment to realize her Saturn coupe was really a mess. And that, remarkably, she wasn't. That's when she decided to get another SC.

Several other people arrived at similar conclusions. A policeman at the accident scene came in soon after and ordered himself a sedan. As did a buddy of his, also on the force. Then Cheryl's brother, glad he still had a sister, bought yet another Saturn in Illinois.

Now, good referrals are important to any product. And we're always glad to have them. But we'd be more than happy if our customers found less dramatic ways to help spread the word.

A DIFFERENT KIND *of* COMPANY. A DIFFERENT KIND *of* CAR.

© 1991 Saturn Corporation. M.S.R.P. of 1992 Saturn SC shown is $12,415, including retailer prep and optional sunroof. Tax, license, transportation and other options additional. If you'd like to know more about Saturn, and our new sedans and coupe, please call us at 1-800-522-5000.

Discussion Questions

1. What example of inductive reasoning does the advertiser use? How would you evaluate the probability of the conclusion?
2. To what extent does the use of an alleged real person in a narrative contribute to the effectiveness of the advertiser's pitch? Should the ad have contained more factual information?

UFO Abductions:
An Introduction

JOHN E. MACK

In the fall of 1989, when a colleague asked me if I wished to meet Budd Hopkins, I replied, "Who's he?" She told me that he was an artist in New York who worked with people who reported being taken by alien beings into spaceships. I then said something to the effect that he must be crazy and so must they. No, no, she insisted, it was a very serious and real matter. A day came soon when I would be in New York for another purpose — it was January 10, 1990, one of those dates you remember that mark a time when everything in your life changes — and she took me to see Budd.

Nothing in my then nearly forty years of familiarity with the field of psychiatry prepared me for what Hopkins had to say. I was impressed with his warmth, sincerity, intelligence, and caring for the people with whom he had been working. But more important than that were the stories he told me from people all over the United States who had come forth to tell him about their experiences after reading one of his books or articles or hearing him on television. These corresponded, sometimes in minute detail, to those of other "abductees" or "experiencers," as they are called.

Most of the specific information that the abductees provided about the means of transport to and from the spaceships, the descriptions of the insides of the ships themselves, and the procedures carried out by the aliens during the abductions had never been written about or shown in the media. Furthermore, these individuals were from many parts of the country and had not communicated with each other. They seemed in other respects quite sane, had come forth reluctantly, fearing the discrediting of their stories or outright ridicule they had encountered in the past. They had come to see Hopkins at considerable expense, and, with rare exceptions, had nothing to gain materially from telling their stories. In one example a woman was startled when Hopkins showed her a drawing

---

John E. Mack, M.D., is a Professor of Psychiatry at the Harvard University Medical School. This selection is from *Abduction: Human Experiences with Aliens* (1994). [Bibliographic citations have been cut.]

of an alien being. She asked how he had been able to depict what she had seen when they had only just begun talking. When he explained that the drawing had been made by another person from a different part of the country she became intensely upset, for an experience that she had wanted to believe was a dream, now, she felt, must be in some way real.

My reaction was in some respects like this woman's. What Hopkins had encountered in the more than two hundred abduction cases he had seen over a fourteen-year period were reports of experiences that had the characteristics of real events: highly detailed narratives that seemed to have no obvious symbolic pattern; intense emotional and physical traumatic impact, sometimes leaving small lesions on the experiencers' bodies; and consistency of stories down to the most minute details. But if these experiences were in some sense "real," then all sorts of new questions opened up. How often was this occurring? If there were large numbers of these cases, who was helping these individuals deal with their experiences and what sort of support or treatment was called for? What was the response of the mental health profession? And, most basic of all, what was the source of these encounters? These and many other questions will be addressed in this book.

In response to my obvious but somewhat confused interest, 5 Hopkins asked if I wished to see some of these experiencers myself. I agreed, with curiosity tinged by slight anxiety. At his home a month later Hopkins arranged for me to see four abductees, one man and three women. Each told similar stories of their encounters with alien beings and abduction experiences. None of them seemed psychiatrically disturbed except in a secondary sense; that is, they were troubled as a *consequence* of something that had apparently happened to them. There was nothing to suggest that their stories were delusional, a misinterpretation of dreams, or the product of fantasy. None of them seemed like people who would concoct a strange story for some personal purpose. Sensing my now obvious interest, Hopkins asked if I wanted him to refer cases to me in the Boston area, of which he already knew quite a few. Again I agreed, and in the spring of 1990 I began to see abductees in my home and hospital offices.

In the more than three and a half years I have been working with abductees I have seen more than a hundred individuals referred for evaluation of abductions or other "anomalous" experiences. Of these, seventy-six (ranging in age from two to fifty-seven; forty-seven females and twenty-nine males, including three boys eight and under) fulfill my quite strict criteria for an abduction case: conscious recall or recall with the help of hypnosis, of being taken by alien beings into a strange craft, reported with emotion appropriate to the experience being described and no apparent mental condition that could account for the story. I have done between one and eight several-hour modified hypnosis sessions with forty-nine of these individuals, and have evolved a therapeutic approach I will describe shortly.

Although I have a great debt and profound respect for the pioneers in this field, like Budd Hopkins, who have had the courage to investigate and report information that runs in the face of our culture's consensus reality, this book is based largely on my own clinical experience. For this is a subject that is so controversial that virtually no accepted scientific authority has evolved that I might use to bolster my arguments or conclusions. I will report, therefore, what I have learned primarily from my own cases and will make interpretations and draw conclusions on the basis of this information.

The experience of working with abductees has affected me profoundly. The intensity of the energies and emotions involved as abductees relive their experiences is unlike anything I have encountered in other clinical work. The immediacy of presence, support, and understanding that is required has influenced the way I regard the psychotherapeutic task in general. Furthermore, I have come to see that the abduction phenomenon has important philosophical, spiritual, and social implications. Above all, more than any other research I have undertaken, this work has led me to challenge the prevailing worldview or consensus reality which I had grown up believing and had always applied in my clinical/scientific endeavors. According to this view — called variously the Western, Newtonian/Cartesian, or materialist/dualist scientific paradigm — reality is fundamentally grounded in the material world or in what can be perceived by the physical senses. In this view intelligence is largely a phenomenon of the brain of human beings or other advanced species. If, on the contrary, intelligence *is* experienced as residing in the larger cosmos, this perception is an example of "subjectivity" or a projection of our mental processes.

What the abduction phenomenon had led me (I would now say inevitably) to see is that we participate in a universe or universes that are filled with intelligences from which we have cut ourselves off, having lost the senses by which we might know them. It has become clear to me also that our restricted worldview or paradigm lies behind most of the major destructive patterns that threaten the human future — mindless corporate acquisitiveness that perpetuates vast differences between rich and poor and contributes to hunger and disease; ethno-national violence resulting in mass killing which could grow into a nuclear holocaust; and ecological destruction on a scale that threatens the survival of the earth's living systems.

There are, of course, other phenomena that have led to the chal- 10
lenging of the prevailing materialist/dualistic worldview. These include near death experiences, meditation practices, the use of

psychedelic substances, shamanic journeys, ecstatic dancing, religious rituals, and other practices that open our being to what we call in the West nonordinary states of consciousness. But none of these, I believe, speaks to us so powerfully in the language that we know best, the language of the physical world. For the abduction phenomenon reaches us, so to speak, where we live. It enters harshly into the physical world, whether or not it is *of* this world. Its power, therefore, to reach and alter our consciousness is potentially immense. All of these matters will be discussed more fully in the clinical case examples that constitute the bulk of this book, and, especially, in the concluding chapter.

One of the important questions in abduction research has been whether the phenomenon is fundamentally new — related to the sightings of "flying saucers" and other unidentified flying objects (UFOs) in the 1940s and the discovery in the 1960s that these craft had "occupants" — or is but a modern chapter in a long story of humankind's relationship to vehicles and creatures appearing from the heavens that goes back to antiquity. . . .

The most commonly debated issue, whether abductions are really taking place, leads us to the center of questions about perception and levels of consciousness. The most glaring question is whether there is any reality independent of consciousness. At the level of personal consciousness, can we apprehend reality directly, or are we by necessity bound by the restrictions of our five senses and the mind that organizes our worldview? Is there a shared, collective consciousness that operates beyond our individual consciousness? If there is a collective consciousness, how is it influenced, and what determines its content? Is UFO abduction a product of this shared consciousness? If, as in some cultures, consciousness pervades all elements of the universe, then what function do events like UFO abductions and various mystical experiences play in our psyches and in the rest of the cosmos?

These are questions that are not easily answered. Perhaps all we can do at this point in time is to acknowledge the questions as we listen to the experiences of those who have moved beyond our culturally shared ideas of "reality." The UFO abduction experience, while unique in many respects, bears resemblance to other dramatic, transformative experiences undergone by shamans, mystics, and ordinary citizens who have had encounters with the paranormal. In all of these experiential realms, the individual's ordinary consciousness is radically transformed. He or she is initiated into a non-ordinary state of being which results, ultimately, in a reintegration of the self, an immersion or entrenchment into states and/or knowledge not previously accessible. Sometimes the process is brought on by illness or a traumatic event of some kind, and sometimes the individual is simply pulled into a sequence of states of being from which he or she emerges with new powers and sensitivities. "During his initiation, the Shaman learns how to penetrate into other dimensions of reality and maintain himself there; his trials, whatever the nature of them, endow him with a sensitivity that can perceive and integrate these new experiences ... through the strangely sharpened senses of the Shaman the sacred manifests itself." . . . Like many abductees, the initiate hones his new sensibilities in the service of wisdom that can be used by his people. . . .

The UFO Abduction Phenomenon Worldwide

Another question concerns the worldwide distribution of abductions, or reports of the phenomenon, which may be quite a different matter. UFO abductions have been reported and collected most frequently in Western countries or countries dominated by Western culture and values. Insofar as the abduction phenomenon may be seen as occurring in the context of the global ecological crisis, which is an outcome of the Western materialist/dualistic worldview, it may be that its "medicine" is being administered primarily where it is most needed — in the United States and the other Western industrial countries. Related to this would be the fact that in many cultures the entry into the physical world of vehicles, and even contact with creatures, seemingly from space or another dimension, would not be as noteworthy as in societies where traffic from the spirit world or the "world beyond" into our physical existence would be considered remarkable. . . .

In some countries, where people hold all sorts of beliefs in su- 15 pernatural beings, abduction experiences are confused or simply connected with other visitations. Cynthia Hind, a researcher from South Africa, reports, "Their reactions are as perhaps Westerners would react to ghosts; not necessarily terrified (or not always so) but certainly wary of what they see." . . .

Abductees overseas seem to have contact with a greater variety of entities than Americans. These range from tiny men to tall, hooded beings, and include naked individuals of both sexes and humanoid beings with every manner or shape of head, feet, and hands. A Dutch couple recently described their UFO visitors as being tiny and appearing in rainbow hues — green, orange, and purple. . . .

But universal properties of the abduction experience remain. Most often, abductees everywhere are compellingly drawn toward a powerful light, often while they are driving or asleep in their beds. Invariably, they are later unable to account for a "lost" period of time, and they frequently bear physical and psychological scars of their experience. These range from nightmares and anxiety to chronic nervous agitation, depression, and even psychosis, to actual physical scars — puncture and incision marks, scrapes, burns, and sores.

Some encounters are more sinister, traumatizing, and mysterious. Others seem to bear a healing and educational intent. Most often, say abductees, they are told or warned by the beings or people not to tell about their experiences. In Puerto Rico, Miguel Figueroa, for example, reported receiving threatening phone calls the day after he saw five little, gray men in the middle of the road. . . .

Even less well documented than the actual abductions are the consequences of the experience. In working with abductees, Gilda Moura, a Brazilian psychologist, reports on the paranormal abilities many Brazilian abductees experience after an encounter. These include increased telepathic abilities, clairvoyance, visions, and the receiving of spiritual messages which are often concerned with world ecology, the future of humankind, and social justice. Many abductees decide to change their profession after their experience. . . .

It is likely that with the publicizing of therapeutic and hypnosis techniques currently being pioneered in the United States, much more information about abduction experiences overseas will be available in coming years; for the rest of the world certainly does not lack awareness of the UFO phenomenon, as is evidenced by the proliferation of UFO bureaus, offices, and research organizations abroad.   20

Modern-Day Abductions

The modern history of abductions begins with the experience of Barney and Betty Hill in September 1961. . . . The Hills, a stable, respectable interracial couple living in New Hampshire, had suffered from disturbing symptoms for more than two years when they reluctantly consulted Boston psychiatrist Benjamin Simon. Barney was an insomniac and Betty had frequent nightmares. Both were so persistently anxious that it became intolerable for them to continue their lives without looking into disturbing repercussions of the September night in which they could not account for two hours during the return journey from a holiday in Montreal. Except for the distresses related to the incident they described, Dr. Simon reported no psychiatric illness.

On the night of September 19, 1961, the Hills reported that their car was "flagged down" by small, gray humanoid beings with unusual eyes. Before this they had noticed an erratically moving light and then a strange craft. With binoculars Barney had been able to see the creatures inside the craft. The Hills were amnesic about what happened to them during the missing hours until undergoing repeated hypnosis sessions with Dr. Simon. In their meetings with him, Dr. Simon instructed the Hills not to tell each other details of the memories that were emerging. After being taken from their car the Hills said they were led by the beings against their wills onto a craft. Each reported that on the craft they were placed on a table and subjected to detailed medical-like examinations with taking of skin and hair "samples." A needle was inserted into Betty's abdomen and a "pregnancy test" performed. Researchers have discovered recently that a sperm sample was taken from Barney, a fact that was withheld by him and John Fuller, who later wrote about their case, because it was too humiliating at the time for Barney to admit. . . . The beings communicated with the Hills telepathically, nonverbally, "as if it were in English." The Hills were "told to" forget what had happened.

Despite Dr. Simon's belief that the Hills had experienced some sort of shared dream or fantasy, a kind of folie à deux, they persisted in their conviction that these events really happened, and that they had not communicated the corroborating details to each other during the investigation of their symptoms. Barney, who died in 1969 at the age of forty-six, had been particularly reluctant to believe in the reality of the experience lest he appear irrational. "I wish I could think it was an hallucination," he told Dr. Simon when the doctor pressed him. But in the end Barney concluded, "we had seen and been a part of something different than anything I had seen before," and "these things did happen to me." Betty, who continues to speak publicly about her experience, also believes in the reality of these events. In 1975 a film about the Hill case, *The UFO Incident,* starring James Earl Jones as Barney, was shown on television in the United States.

A number of books and articles documented abduction experiences by other individuals in the years following the Hill's testimony. . . . It has been the pioneering research of New York artist and sculptor Budd Hopkins, however, over almost two decades with hundreds of abductees, that has established the essential consistency of the abduction phenomenon. Hopkins's first book, *Missing Time,* published in 1981, documented the unaccounted-for time periods and associated symptoms that indicate that abduction experiences have taken place, as well as the characteristic details of such experiences. . . . Hopkins also found that abduction experiences were possibly associated with previously unexplainable small cuts, body scars, and scoop marks; the narratives even suggested that small objects or "implants" may have been inserted in victims' noses, legs, and other body parts. In his second book, *Intruders,* published in 1987, Hopkins defined the sexual and reproductive episodes that have come to be associated with the abduction phenomenon. . . . Temple University historian David Jacobs has further refined the basic reported pattern of an abduction experience. . . . Jacobs identifies primary phenomena such as manual or instrument examination, staring, and urological-gynecological procedures; secondary events, including machine examination, visualization, and child presentation; and ancillary events, among them miscellaneous additional physical, mental, and sexual activities and procedures.

None of this work, in my view, has come to terms with the pro- 25
found implications of the abduction phenomenon for the expansion of human consciousness, the opening of perception to realities beyond the manifest physical world and the necessity of changing our place in the cosmic order if the earth's living systems are to survive the human onslaught. . . .

Abductions and Abductionists

CURTIS PEEBLES

This book is a chronicle of the flying saucer myth — the system of beliefs that have developed around the idea that alien spacecraft are being seen in Earth's skies. These beliefs did not suddenly spring into existence fully formed. Rather, a set of conflicting ideas originated, the myth was defined, then the beliefs evolved over nearly half a century. Moreover, the flying saucer myth is not a single, monolithic set of doctrines. As soon as the flying saucer myth was defined, schisms began to develop among "believers" — those people who accepted the idea that flying saucers were extraordinary objects. Not all believers held the same beliefs, and these schisms soon led to open warfare. This interaction between believers has been a major influence on the myth's history.

The flying saucer myth not only concerns disk-shaped spaceships and the aliens who supposedly pilot them. Because it also involves how the believers view the role and nature of government, and how the government relates to the people, the U.S. government has had to deal with the flying saucer myth. Presidents have denied their existence; they were a twenty-two-year headache for the Air Force, and were investigated by Congress and the CIA. This interaction both fed the flying saucer myth and brought about the very things the government sought to avoid.

A similar interaction has taken place between the flying saucer myth and the larger society. The flying saucer myth is a mirror to the events of postwar America — the paranoia of the 1950s, the social turmoil of the 1960s, the "me generation" of the 1970s, and the

---

Curtis Peebles is an aerospace historian whose books include *Watch the Skies! A Chronicle of the Flying Saucer Myth* (1994), from which this selection is taken. [Bibliographic citations have been cut.]

nihilism of the 1980s and the early 1990s. As the flying saucer myth entered popular culture, images and ideas were created which, in turn, shaped the flying saucer myth itself. . . .

Close Encounters of the Third Kind

Although many films had used flying saucer themes, *Close Encounters of the Third Kind* was the only one to fully understand the flying saucer myth. The story is one of ordinary people trying to cope with mythic experiences. Roy Neary (Richard Dreyfuss) is a power company lineman who sees a UFO. He finds himself the victim of subliminal messages which cause him to undertake obsessive, bizarre actions which cause his family to leave. Neary finally realizes he is to go to Devil's Tower, Wyoming. He embarks on an arduous cross-country journey. Overcoming obstacles, he is rewarded with a meeting with the aliens. As the multicolored mothership lifts off with Neary aboard, he rises above his own mundane, earthly existence.

In earlier films, the flying saucers were sources of danger. In   5
Close Encounters of the Third Kind, the meeting with the aliens was not to be feared, but to be anticipated. It was this "sense of wonder" that was so lacking in such films as *The Thing* or *Earth vs. the Flying Saucer.*

Close Encounters of the Third Kind defined the shape of the aliens. In the film, "they" were short, with large heads, slanted dark eyes, and light gray skins. Their noses were small and their ears were only small holes. The aliens' bodies were elongated and very thin. The fingers were also long. Their overall appearance was that of a fetus. By the early 1980s, this "shape" would come to dominate abduction descriptions.

The Growth of Abduction Reports

Certain UFOlogists began to specialize in abduction cases. The first such "abductionist" was Dr. R. Leo Sprinkle, a psychologist at the University of Wyoming. Sprinkle was frequently quoted by the tabloids and was on the *National Enquirer*'s Blue Ribbon Panel. Sprinkle's role was critical in shaping both the development of the abduction myth and its acceptance. His "hypnotic sessions with UFO abductees" began in 1967 and 1968 with three cases. It was not until 1974 that Sprinkle had another abduction case (reflecting the post-Condon Report decline in interest). In 1975 there were two cases. There were three cases each in 1976 and 1977 (after *The UFO Incident*). In 1978 (after *Close Encounters of the Third Kind*), Sprinkle worked with ten subjects, while in 1979 there were eighteen abductees. In 1980 he held the first of his annual conferences for UFO abductees and investigators.

This increase in abduction reports was not limited to Sprinkle. UFOlogist David Webb noted that a 1976 search of UFO literature (covering nearly thirty years) showed only 50 abduction-type cases. Yet, over the next two years, about 100 *more* cases were reported, bringing the total to some 150. By the end of the 1970s, the total number of cases exceeded 200. . . .

Budd Hopkins

With the 1980s, a new abductionist appeared — an artist named Budd Hopkins. Long interested in UFOs, the rise in abduction reports attracted Hopkins's attention in 1976. He met "Steven Kilburn." Kilburn had a vague memory of being afraid of a stretch of road, but no UFO sighting. To this point, people claiming to have been abducted said they had seen a UFO and/or occupant. This was followed by a period of "missing time." The "abduction" itself was "remembered" under hypnosis. Kilburn had no such memory. When he was hypnotized, however, Kilburn said he was grabbed by a "big wrench" and was taken aboard a UFO.

To Hopkins, this implied a person could be an "abductee" *with-* 10 *out* any overt memory. Hopkins began asking people if they had "uneasiness," recurring dreams, or "any event" which might indicate an abduction. It was no longer necessary for a person to have "missing time." *Anyone* could now be an abductee and not realize it. Hopkins believed there might be tens of thousands of abductees — what he called "an invisible multitude."

Hopkins published his conclusions in his 1981 book *Missing Time.* He believed "a very long-term, in-depth study is being made of a relatively large sample of humans." The "human specimens" were first abducted as young children. "Monitoring devices" would be implanted in the abductee's nose. This was described as a tiny ball on a long rod. The ball was left in the nasal cavity. The young abductees were then released with no memories of the (alleged) events. Years later, Hopkins believed, once the abductees reached puberty, they would be abducted a second time.

The aliens in Hopkins's abduction cases all followed the shape of those in *The UFO Incident* and *Close Encounters of the Third Kind* — large heads, thin bodies, slanted eyes, and gray skin. The book had several drawings of what became known as "the Grays." *Missing Time* completed the process of defining the shape of the aliens.

Hopkins also speculated on the alien's motivation. He noted several abductees had scars from childhood. He believed tissue samples were being taken. Hopkins suggested the aliens needed a specific genetic structure. Hopkins also suggested the aliens were taking sperm and ova samples. These, he continued, might be for experiments in producing human/alien hybrids.

This expanded the abduction myth; it was now much more "intrusive." In the Pascagoula case, Hickson claimed he was passively "scanned." Now, tissue samples were being taken which left scars. The alleged abductees also showed emotional scars from their supposed experiences — long-lasting anxiety and fear. The "monitoring devices" were a further intrusion. The taking of sperm and ova was, symbolically, the most intrusive of all. Humans were depicted as helpless before the aliens' overwhelming power, reduced to a lab rat.

Hopkins further developed these themes in his 1987 book *Intruders*. In September 1983, he received a letter from "Kathie Davis." She had read *Missing Time* and wrote him to describe a dream she had had in early 1978 of two small beings in her bedroom. From Davis's accounts and twelve other abductees, Hopkins came to believe the aliens had an unmistakable interest "in the process of human reproduction" going back to the Villas-Boas case. [15]

Hopkins described the process as follows — female abductees were identified as donors during their childhood abductions. The implants allowed the aliens to "track" them. When they reached puberty, they would be reabducted. Ova would be removed, its genetic structure altered with alien characteristics, then replanted back in the human. The female abductees would carry the "baby" several months, then again be abducted. The human/alien child would be removed and brought to term.

Males were not immune to such breeding abductions, according to Hopkins. "Ed Duvall" recalled under hypnosis a sexual encounter with a hybrid alien. In this and other cases, a "suction device" was placed over the penis to remove the sperm. None of these breeding abductions could, according to Hopkins, be described as an erotic experience. "It was very perfunctory," Duvall said, "a detached, clinical procedure."

Once the hybrid children were born, the humans who had "donated" sperm or ova were (yet again) abducted and "shown" their "offspring." The aliens even encouraged the humans to hold the "babies" in a kind of bonding exercise, according to Hopkins. Four women either dreamed or remembered under hypnosis being shown a tiny baby — gray in color and oddly shaped. Kathie Davis claimed to have seen two of her *nine* hybrid children and been allowed to name them. Nor did this cycle of abductions end here. Hopkins claimed the children of abductees were themselves targets for abductions.

Some of Hopkins's abductees gave their impressions of why the aliens were doing these things. "Lucille Forman" had the impression of an alien society "millions of years old, of outstanding technology and intellect but not much individuality or warmth . . . the society was dying . . . children were being born and living to a certain age, perhaps preadolescence, and then dying." The aliens were desperately trying to survive, through both taking new genetic material and exploiting human emotions.

Hopkins painted a progressively darker picture of the "relation- 20 ship" between humans and aliens. "The UFO phenomenon," Hopkins wrote, "seems able to exert nearly complete control over the behavior of the abductees." He continued that the "implants" had "a controlling function as receivers" and that the abductees can "be made to act as surrogates for their abductors." It is a basic tenet of the abduction myth that these alleged events were truly *alien* experiences — that they are not based on science fiction nor psychological aberrations. Hopkins said, "None of these recollections in any way suggests traditional sci-fi gods and devils . . . the aliens are described neither as all-powerful, lordly presences, nor as satanic monsters, but instead as complex, controlling, physically frail beings."

Dr. David Jacobs (a pro-UFO historian) said in a 1986 MUFON[1] paper, "Contactee stories were deeply rooted in a science fiction model of alien behavior [while] abductee stories have a profoundly alien quality to them that are strikingly devoid of cultural programmatic content."

Thomas E. Bullard said that Betty and Barney Hill had no cultural sources from which they could have derived their story, that they were "entirely unpredisposed."

Entirely Unpredisposed?

Consider the following story — a group of men are in a rural area, at night, when they are abducted. They are rendered unconscious, loaded aboard strange flying machines, and taken to a distant place. They are then programmed with false memories to hide the time they were missing. One of them is converted into a puppet of his abductors. They are then released with no overt memories of what happened. But, years later, two of the group begin having strange, surreal dreams about what was done to them.

This story has many elements of abduction stories — loss of control, loss of memory (i.e., one's soul), and loss of humanity. It is not an abduction story. It has nothing to do with UFOs. It is the plot of the 1962 film *The Manchurian Candidate*.

Despite Hopkins's and Jacobs's claims, the abductee myth has 25 numerous similarities with science fiction. Martin Kottmeyer has noted a number of these. In the film *Killers from Space* an abductee has a strange scar and missing memory. In *Invaders from Mars,* the Martians use implants to control humans. This includes not only adults, but their children as well. In the "Cold Hands, Warm Heart"

---

[1]MUFON (Mutual UFO Network) is an international organization dedicated to a scientific study of the UFO phenomenon. — ED.

episode of *The Outer Limits,* an astronaut (William Shatner) orbiting Venus loses contact with Earth for eight minutes. After returning to Earth, he has dreams that he landed on Venus and saw a Venusian approaching the ship. His body also starts changing into a Venusian.

"Dying planets" such as "Lucille Forman" described are a standard feature of science fiction — in H. G. Wells's masterpiece *War of the Worlds,* the Martians attacked because Mars was dying and Earth seemed their only hope for survival. Similar "dying planet" themes appeared in the films *This Island Earth, The 27th Day, Killers from Space,* and *Earth vs. the Flying Saucers. The Invaders* were "alien beings from a dying planet."

Crossbreeding between humans and aliens was a common science fiction film plot. They include *Devil Girl from Mars, I Married a Monster from Outer Space, The Mysterians, Village of the Damned, Mars Needs Women,* and the *Alien* film series.

The shape of aliens in abduction stories is well within the traditions of science fiction. The "bug-eyed monsters" of 1930s and 1940s pulp magazines often had large, bald heads. This was the shape of the projected image of the Wizard in the *Wizard of Oz.* The aliens in the film *Invasion of the Saucer Men* were "bald, bulgy-brained, googly-eyed, no-nosed," fitting the stereotyped image of UFO aliens. Kottmeyer noted that this "prompts worries that abductees are not only plagiarists, but have bad taste as well." In the 1960s, television series such as *The Twilight Zone* and *The Outer Limits* often featured dome-headed aliens. The original pilot for *Star Trek,* "The Cage" (telecast as the two-part episode "The Menagerie"), had short, large-headed, gray-skinned, bald, physically weak aliens with the power to control human minds.

The reasoning behind this particular shape was best expressed by an *Outer Limits* episode called "The Sixth Finger." The story involves the forced forward evolution of a human (David McCallum). As he evolves, his brain grows, his hair recedes, he becomes telepathic, and can control humans. The idea is that apes have small brains, are hairy, and strong. Modern man, in contrast, has a larger brain, has limited body hair, and is weaker. It therefore seems "right" that a future man would have a huge brain, no hair, and be physically frail.

All these similarities between science fiction concepts and the abduction myth caused Kottmeyer to write, "It seems more sensible to flip Hopkins' allegation around. He says nothing about the aliens of UFO abductions resembling 'sci-fi'. I ask, is there anything about UFO aliens that does not resemble science fiction?"

A final note — Hopkins describes a half human/half alien being lacking the ability to feel emotions. It is just such a being which is the most famous character in all of science fiction — Mr. Spock of *Star Trek.* How "logical."

Questions about Hypnosis

Hopkins's abductees had no overt memories until they were hypnotized. The question becomes whether the abduction story is only a product of being hypnotized. A controlled test of hypnotic abduction accounts was conducted in 1977 by Dr. Alvin H. Lawson, a UFOlogist and English professor at California State University, Long Beach. He and others were dissatisfied with the hypnotic regression of abductees. They decided to ask a group of people with no significant UFO knowledge to imagine an abduction under hypnosis. The hypnotic sessions were conducted by Dr. William C. McCall, an M.D. with decades of clinical hypnosis experience. Lawson and the others had expected the imaginary abductees would need prompting. The result was quite different — Lawson wrote later:

> What startled us at first was the [subject's] ease and eagerness of narrative invention. Quite often, after introducing the situation — such as, "describe the interior" — Dr. McCall would sit back and the [subject] would talk freely with no more prompting than an occasional, "what's happening, now?"

Lawson compared four imaginary abduction accounts with features of four "real" abduction stories. The chart was an exact match. He concluded:

> It is clear from the imaginary narratives that a great many apparent patterns may originate in the mind and so be available to a witness — whether imaginary or "real." If a person who is totally uninformed about UFOs suddenly finds himself in the abduction sequence, it seems safe to assume that the individual's own sensibility will be able to provide under hypnotic regression, pattern details of his encounter which he may or may not have actually experienced in a "real" sense.

The implication of the Lawson study was not that there was a massive number of covert abductions. Rather, it shows that nearly anyone can, under hypnosis, provide an abduction story. Not surprisingly, abductionists and UFO groups have criticized and ignored the Lawson test.

The typical questioning during an abduction hypnotic session 35 goes far beyond "what's happening, now." While researching the book *Mute Evidence,* Daniel Kagan was hypnotized by Dr. Sprinkle. During the session, Dr. Sprinkle said, "Imagine yourself in a spacecraft." There were no UFO images in the recurring dream Kagan was describing. Kagan was so shocked by the attempt to insert a UFO that he came out of the trance. Kagan concluded:

> Sprinkle had just demonstrated how much he had probably been responsible for the UFO imagery reported by so many of his hypnotic subjects. It meant that none of Sprinkle's case histories could be taken seriously, because his role as hypnotist could have been the single most powerful factor in introducing UFO images into the subjects' memories.

Another factor is that many of the stories originate with dreams. The dreams are real, but are they dreams of real events? One indication that they are, in fact, only dreams is the wildly irrational and contradictory nature of the stories. This includes one case in which an "abductee" reported hearing a voice from inside a UFO cry out, "I am Jimmy Hoffa!" Other psychological factors include the abductee's own mental state (even "normal" people can have hallucinations) and such organic brain disorders as temporal lobe epilepsy. Finally, there are the effects of personal experiences: under hypnosis, one abductee gave an extremely outlandish description of the aliens; when the hypnotist asked, "Are you sure?" the abductee responded, "No . . . that was something I saw in the Sunday comic section." Clearly, hypnosis is not the foolproof truth-finding technique the abductionists make it out to be.

In retrospect, it seems clear that the flying saucer myth was always an attempt to find a relationship with the aliens. Earlier myths were about contacts/interactions/struggles between humans and humanlike supernatural beings. Even the conservative Keyhoe had "Operation Lure." The contactees had their own "relationship," rooted in the worldview of the 1950s. When this faded, it was replaced, in the 1960s and 1970s, by the abduction myth, yet another attempt to find a relationship with mythological beings.

This human/alien relationship exactly mirrors society's changing attitudes toward authority, science, and sex. During the contactee era of the 1950s, the grandfatherly "Ike" was president. By the mid-1980s, authority was seen as absolutely evil. Science in the 1950s was seen as utopian. By the 1980s, this had changed into the belief science was antihuman. In 1978, Jose Inacio Alvaro described his alien sexual encounter as being pleasurable. By the 1980s, with the specter of AIDS haunting the bedroom, Hopkins was depicting it as a joyless, technological rape.

The function of mythology is to allow a society to relate to the larger world. This has not changed.

Discussion Questions

1. Does the knowledge that John Mack is a professor of psychiatry at Harvard University Medical School influence your judgment of his conclusions?

2. How would you describe the differences between the prose styles of Mack and Peebles? Dr. Mack writes very well — with grace and authority. Do you think the fact that he *sounds* like an expert is also influential? Find instances of language that conveys the idea of authority — through vocabulary, sentence structure, references to unfamiliar phenomena, etc.

3. What kind of evidence does Mack provide? (Go over his "strict criteria for an abduction case.") How much of that evidence might be considered objective or provable by scientific method?

4. Both Mack and Peebles discuss Budd Hopkins. How do you account for their very different views of him?
5. What is Peebles's principal explanation for the abduction phenomenon? Is it persuasive?
6. Mack and Peebles both mention political events and attitudes. What are they and how have they affected belief in visits by aliens?

EXERCISES

Decide whether the reasoning in the following examples is faulty. Explain your answers.

1. The presiding judge of a revolutionary tribunal, on being asked why people were being executed without trial: "Why should we put them on trial when we know that they're guilty?"
2. Since good nutrition is essential to the health of its citizens, the government should punish people who eat junk food.
3. A research study demonstrated that children who watched *Seinfeld* rather than *Friends* received higher grades in school. So it must be true that *Seinfeld* is more educational than *Friends*.
4. The meteorologist was wrong in predicting the amount of rain for May. Obviously the meteorologist is unreliable.
5. Women ought to be permitted to serve in combat. Why should men be the only ones to face death and danger?
6. If Cher uses Equal, it must taste better than Sweet 'n Low.
7. People will gamble anyway, so why not legalize gambling in this state?
8. Because so much money was spent on public education in the last decade while educational achievement declined, more money to improve education can't be the answer to reversing the decline.
9. He's a columnist for the campus newspaper, so he must be a pretty good writer.
10. We tend to exaggerate the need for standard English. You don't need much standard English for most jobs in this country.
11. It's discriminatory to mandate that police officers must conform to a certain height and weight.
12. A doctor can consult books to make a diagnosis, so a medical student should be able to consult books when being tested.
13. Because this soft drink contains so many chemicals, it must be unsafe.
14. Core requirements should be eliminated. After all, students are paying for their education, so they should be able to earn a diploma by choosing the courses they want.
15. We should encourage a return to arranged marriages in this country since marriages based on romantic love haven't been very successful.
16. I know three redheads who have terrible tempers, and since Annabel has red hair, I'll bet she has a terrible temper, too.
17. Supreme Court Justice Byron White was an All-American football player while at college, so how can you say that athletes are dumb?

18. Benjamin H. Sasway, a student at Humboldt State University in California, was indicted for failure to register for possible conscription. Barry Lynn, president of Draft Action, an antidraft group, said, "It is disgraceful that this Administration is embarking on an effort to fill the prisons with men of conscience and moral commitment."

19. You know Jane Fonda's exercise videos must be worth the money. Look at the great shape she's in.

20. James A. Harris, former president of the National Education Association: "Twenty-three percent of schoolchildren are failing to graduate, and another large segment graduate as functional illiterates. If 23 percent of anything else failed — 23 percent of automobiles didn't run, 23 percent of the buildings fell down, 23 percent of stuffed ham spoiled — we'd look at the producer."

21. A professor at Rutgers University: "The arrest rate for women is rising three times as fast as that of men. Women, inflamed by the doctrines of feminism, are pursuing criminal careers with the same zeal as business and the professions."

22. Physical education should be required because physical activity is healthful.

23. George Meany, former president of the AFL-CIO, in 1968: "To these people who constantly say you have got to listen to these younger people, they have got something to say, I just don't buy that at all. They smoke more pot than we do and if the younger generation are the hundred thousand kids that lay around a field up in Woodstock, New York, I am not going to trust the destiny of the country to that group."

24. That candidate was poor as a child, so he will certainly be sympathetic to the poor if he's elected.

25. When the federal government sent troops into Little Rock, Arkansas, to enforce integration of the public school system, the governor of Arkansas attacked the action, saying that it was as brutal an act of intervention as Russia's sending troops into Hungary to squelch the Hungarians' rebellion. In both cases, the governor said, the rights of a freedom-loving, independent people were being violated.

26. Governor Jones was elected two years ago. Since that time constant examples of corruption and subversion have been unearthed. It is time to get rid of the man responsible for this kind of corrupt government.

27. Are we going to vote a pay increase for our teachers or are we going to allow our schools to deteriorate into substandard custodial institutions?

28. You see, the priests were right. After we threw those virgins into the volcano, it quit erupting.

29. The people of Rome lost their vitality and desire for freedom when their emperors decided that the way to keep them happy was to provide them with bread and circuses. What can we expect of our own country now that the government gives people free food and there is a constant round of entertainment provided by television?

30. From Mark Clifton, "The Dread Tomato Affliction" (proving that eating tomatoes is dangerous and even deadly): "Ninety-two point four percent of juvenile delinquents have eaten tomatoes. Fifty-seven point one percent of the adult criminals in penitentiaries throughout the United

States have eaten tomatoes. Eighty-four percent of all people killed in automobile accidents during the year have eaten tomatoes."

31. "But can you doubt that air has weight when you have the clear testimony of Aristotle affirming that all elements have weight, including air, and excepting only fire?" (From Galileo, *Dialogues Concerning Two New Sciences*)

32. Robert Brustein, artistic director of the American Repertory Theatre, commenting on a threat by Congress in 1989 to withhold funding from an offensive art show: "Once we allow lawmakers to become art critics, we take the first step into the world of Ayatollah Khomeini, whose murderous review of *The Satanic Verses* still chills the heart of everyone committed to free expression." (The Ayatollah Khomeini called for the death of the author, Salman Rushdie, because he had allegedly committed blasphemy against Islam in his novel.)

Critical Listening

33. Listen carefully to a speech by a candidate for public office. Note any fallacies or lapses in logical thinking. Do some kinds of fallacies seem more common than others?

PART TWO

Writing and Researching Arguments

CHAPTER NINE

Writing an Argumentative Paper

The person who understands how arguments are constructed has an important advantage in today's world. Television commercials, political speeches, newspaper editorials, and magazine advertisements, as well as many communications between individuals, all draw on the principles we have examined in the preceding chapters. By now you should be fairly adept at picking out claims, support, and warrants (explicit or unstated) in these presentations. The next step is to apply your skills to writing an argument of your own. The process of using what you have learned will enhance your ability to analyze critically the marketing efforts with which we are all bombarded every day. Mastering the writing of arguments also gives you a valuable tool for communicating with other people in school, on the job, and even at home.

In this chapter we will move through the various stages involved in creating an argumentative paper: choosing a topic, defining the issues, organizing the material, writing the essay, and revising. We will also consider the more general question of how to use the principles already discussed in order to convince a real audience. The more carefully you follow the guidelines set out here and the more thought you give to your work at each point, the better you will be able to utilize the art of argument when this course is over.

FINDING AN APPROPRIATE TOPIC

An old British recipe for jugged hare is said to begin, "First, catch your hare." To write an argumentative paper, you first must choose your topic. This is a relatively easy task for someone writing an argument as part of his or her job — a lawyer defending a client, for example, or an advertising executive presenting a campaign. For a student, however, it can be daunting. Which of the many ideas in the world worth debating would make a good subject?

Several guidelines can help you evaluate the possibilities. Perhaps your assignment limits your choices. If you have been asked to write a research paper, you obviously must find a topic on which research is available. If your assignment is more open-ended, you need a topic that is worth the time and effort you expect to invest in it. In either case, your subject should be one that interests you. Don't feel you have to write about what you know — very often finding out what you don't know will turn out to be more satisfying. You should, however, choose a subject that is familiar enough for you to argue about without fearing you're in over your head.

Invention Strategies

As a starting point, think of conversations you've had in the past few days or weeks that have involved defending a position. Is there some current political issue you're concerned about? Some dispute with friends that would make a valid paper topic? One of the best sources is controversies in the media. Keep your project in mind as you watch TV, read, or listen to the radio. You may even run into a potential subject in your course reading assignments or classroom discussions. Fortunately for the would-be writer, nearly every human activity includes its share of disagreement.

As you consider possible topics, write them down. One that looks unlikely at first glance may suggest others or may have more appeal when you come back to it later. Further, simply putting words on paper has a way of stimulating the thought processes involved in writing. Even if your ideas are tentative, the act of converting them into phrases or sentences can often help in developing them.

Evaluating Possible Topics

Besides interesting you, your topic must interest your audience. Who is the audience? For a lawyer it is usually a judge or jury; for a columnist, anyone who reads the newspaper in which his or her column appears. For the student writer, the audience is to some extent hypothetical. You should assume that your paper is directed at readers who are reasonably intelligent and well informed, but who have no specific knowledge of the subject. It may be useful to imagine you are writing for a local or school publication — this may be the case if your paper turns out well.

Be sure, too, that you choose a topic with two sides. The purpose of an argument is to defend or refute a thesis, which means the thesis must be debatable. In evaluating a subject that looks promising, ask yourself: Can a case be made for the opposing view? If not, you have no workable ground for building your own case.

Finally, check the scope of your thesis. Consider how long your paper will be, and whether you can do justice to your topic in that amount of space. For example, suppose you want to argue in favor of worldwide nuclear disarmament. Is this a thesis you can support persuasively in a short paper? One way to find out is by listing the potential issues or points about which arguers might disagree. Consider the thesis: "The future of the world is in danger as long as nuclear weapons exist." Obviously this statement is too general. You would have to specify what you mean by the future of the world (the continuation of human life? of all life? of the earth itself?) and exactly how nuclear weapons endanger it before the claim would hold up. You could narrow it down: "Human beings are error-prone; therefore as long as nuclear weapons exist there is the chance that a large number of people will be killed accidentally." Though this statement is more specific and includes an important warrant, it still depends on other unstated warrants: that one human being (or a small group) is in the position to discharge a nuclear weapon capable of killing a large number of people; that such a weapon could, in fact, be discharged by mistake, given current safety systems. Can you expect to show sufficient evidence for these assumptions in the space available to you?

By now it should be apparent that arguing in favor of nuclear disarmament is too broad an undertaking. A more workable approach might be to defend or refute one of the disarmament proposals under consideration by the U.S. Congress, or to show that nuclear weapons pose some specific danger (such as long-term water pollution) that is sufficient reason to strive for disarmament.

Can a thesis be too narrow? Certainly. If this is true of the one you have chosen, you probably realized it when you asked yourself whether the topic was debatable. If you can prove your point convincingly in a paragraph, or even a page, you need a broader thesis.

At this preliminary stage, don't worry if you don't know exactly how to word your thesis. It's useful to write down a few possible phrasings to be sure your topic is one you can work with, but you need not be precise. The information you unearth as you do research will help you to formulate your ideas. Also, stating a thesis in final terms is premature until you know the organization and tone of your paper.

To This Point

Let's assume you have surveyed a range of possible topics and chosen one that provides you with a suitable thesis for your paper. Before you go on, check your thesis against the following questions:

1. Is this topic one that will interest both me and my audience?
2. Is the topic debatable?
3. Is my thesis appropriate in scope for a paper of this length?
4. Do I know enough about my thesis to have a rough idea of what ideas to use in supporting it and how to go about finding evidence to back up these ideas?

DEFINING THE ISSUES

Preparing an Initial Outline

An outline, like an accounting system or a computer program, is a practical device for organizing information. Nearly every elementary and high school student learns how to make an outline. What will you gain if you outline your argument? Time and an overview of your subject. The minutes you spend organizing your subject at the outset generally save at least double the time later, when you have few minutes to spare. An outline also enables you to see the whole argument at a glance.

Your preliminary outline establishes an order of priority for your argument. Which supporting points are issues to be defended, which are warrants, and which are evidence? Which supporting points are most persuasive? By constructing a map of your territory, you can identify the research routes that are likely to be most productive. You can also pinpoint any gaps in your reasoning.

List each issue as a main heading in your outline. Next, write below it any relevant support (or sources of support) that you are aware of. Then reexamine the list and consider which issues appear likely to offer the strongest support for your argument. You should number these in order of importance.

Case Study: Coed Bathrooms

To see how we raise and evaluate issues in a specific context, let's look at a controversy that surfaced recently at a large university. Students living in coed dorms elected to retain their coed bathrooms. The university administration, however, withdrew its approval, in part because of growing protests from parents and alumni.

The students raised these issues:

1. The rights of students to choose their living arrangements
2. The absence of coercion on those who did not wish to participate
3. The increase in civility between the sexes as a result of sharing accommodations

4. The practicality of coed bathrooms, which preclude the necessity for members of one sex to travel to a one-sex bathroom on another floor
5. The success of the experiment so far

On the other side, the administration introduced the following issues:

1. The role of the university *in loco parentis*
2. The necessity for the administration to retain the goodwill of parents and alumni
3. The dissatisfaction of some students with the arrangement
4. The inability of immature students to respect the right of others and resist the temptation of sexual activity

Now let's analyze these issues, comparing their strengths and weaknesses.

1. It is clear that not all the issues in this dispute were equally important. The arguers decided, therefore, to give greater emphasis to the issues that were most likely to be ultimately persuasive to their audiences and less attention to those that were difficult to prove or narrower in their appeal. The issue of convenience, for example, seemed a minor point. How much cost is imposed in being required to walk up or down a flight of stairs?

2. It was also clear that, as in several of the other cases we have examined, the support consisted of both factual data and appeals to values. In regard to the factual data, each side reported evidence to prove that

a. The experiment was or was not a success.
b. Civility had or had not increased.
c. The majority of students did or did not favor the plan.
d. Coercion had or had not been applied.

The factual data were important. If the administration could prove that the interests of some students had been injured, then the student case for coed bathrooms would be weakened.

But let us assume that the factual claims either were settled or remained in abeyance. We now turn our attention to a second set of issues, a contest over the values to be served.

3. Both sides claimed adherence to the highest principles of university life. Here the issues, while no easier to resolve, offered greater opportunity for serious and fruitful discussion.

The first question to be resolved was that of democratic control. The students asserted, "We should be permitted to have coed bathrooms because we can prove that the majority of us want them." The students hoped that the university community would agree with the implied analogy: that the university community should resemble a political democracy and that students should have full rights as citizens of that community. (This is an argument also made in regard to other areas of university life.)

The university denied that it was a democracy in which students had equal rights and insisted that it should not be. The administration offered its own analogical proof: Students are not permitted to hire their own teachers or to choose their manner of instruction, their courses of study, their grades, or the rules of admission. The university, they insisted, represented a different kind of community, like a home, in which the experienced are required to lead and instruct the inexperienced.

Students responded by pointing out that coed bathrooms or any other aspect of their living arrangements were areas in which *they* were experts and that freedom to choose living arrangements was not to be confused with a demand for equal participation in academic matters. Moreover, it was also true that in recent years the verdict had increasingly been rendered in favor of rights of special groups as against those of institutions. Students' rights have been among those that have benefited from the movement toward freedom of choice.

4. The second issue was related to the first but introduced a practical consideration, namely, the well-being of the university. The administration argued that more important than the wishes of the students in this essentially minor dispute was the necessity for retaining the support and goodwill of parents and alumni, who are ultimately responsible for the very existence of the university.

The students agreed that this support was necessary but felt that parents and alumni could be persuaded to consider the good reasons in the students' argument. Some students were inclined to carry the argument over goals even further. They insisted that if the university could maintain its existence only at the cost of sacrificing principles of democracy and freedom, then perhaps the university had forfeited its right to exist.

In making our way through this debate, we have summarized a procedure for tackling the issues in any controversial problem.

1. Raise the relevant issues and arrange them in order of importance. Plan to devote more time and space to issues you regard as crucial.
2. Produce the strongest evidence you can to support your factual claims, knowing that the opposing side or critical readers may try to produce conflicting evidence.
3. Defend your value claims by finding support in the fundamental principles with which most people in your audience would agree.
4. Argue with yourself. Try to foresee what kinds of refutation are possible. Try to anticipate and meet the opposing arguments.

ORGANIZING THE MATERIAL

Once you are satisfied that you have identified all the issues that will appear in your paper, you should begin to determine what kind of organization will be most effective for your argument. Now is the time to organize the results of your thinking into a logical and persuasive form. If you have read about your topic, answered questions, and acquired some evidence, you may already have decided on ways to approach your subject. If not, you should look closely at your outline now, recalling your purposes when you began your investigation, and develop a strategy for using the information you have gathered to achieve those purposes.

The first point to establish is what type of thesis you plan to present. Is your intention to make readers aware of some problem? To offer a solution to the problem? To defend a position? To refute a position held by others? The way you organize your material will depend to a great extent on your goal. With that goal in mind, look over your outline and reevaluate the relative importance of your issues. Which ones are most convincing? Which are backed up by the strongest support? Which ones relate to facts, and which concern values?

With these points in mind, let us look at various ways of organizing an argumentative paper. It would be foolish to decide in advance how many paragraphs a paper ought to have; however, you can and should choose a general strategy before you begin writing. If your thesis presents an opinion or recommends some course of action, you may choose simply to state your main idea and then defend it. If your thesis argues against an opposing view, you probably will want to mention that view and then refute it. Both these organizations introduce the thesis in the first or second paragraph (called the *thesis paragraph*). A third possibility is to start establishing that a problem exists and then introduce your thesis as the solution; this method is called *presenting the stock issues*. Although these three approaches sometimes overlap in practice, examining each one individually can help you structure your paper. Let's take a look at each arrangement.

Defending the Main Idea

All forms of organization will require you to defend your main idea, but one way of doing this is simple and direct. Early in the paper state the main idea that you will defend throughout your argument. You can also indicate here the two or three points you intend to develop in support of your claim; or you can raise these later as they come up. Suppose your thesis is that widespread vegetarianism would solve a number of problems. You could phrase it this way: "If the majority of people in this country adopted a vegetarian diet, we would see improvements in the economy, in the health of our people, and in moral sensitivity." You would then develop each of the claims in your list with appropriate data and warrants. Notice that the thesis statement in the first (thesis) paragraph has already outlined your organizational pattern.

Defending the main idea is effective for factual claims as well as policy claims, in which you urge the adoption of a certain policy and give the reasons for its adoption. It is most appropriate when your thesis is straightforward and can be readily supported by direct statements.

Refuting the Opposing View

Refuting an opposing view means to attack it in order to weaken, invalidate, or make it less credible to a reader. Since all arguments are dialogues or debates — even when the opponent is only imaginary — refutation of the other point of view is always implicit in your arguments. As you write, keep in mind the issues that an opponent may raise. You will be looking at your own argument as an unsympathetic reader may look at it, asking yourself the same kinds of critical questions and trying to find its weaknesses in order to correct them. In this way every argument you write becomes a form of refutation.

How do you plan a refutation? Here are some general guidelines.

1. If you want to refute the argument in a specific essay or article, read the argument carefully, noting all the points with which you disagree. This advice may seem obvious, but it cannot be too strongly emphasized. If your refutation does not indicate scrupulous familiarity with your opponent's argument, he or she has the right to say, and often does, "You haven't really read what I wrote. You haven't really answered my argument."

2. If you think that your readers are sympathetic to the opposing view or are not familiar with it, summarize it at the beginning of your paper, providing enough information to give readers an understanding of exactly what you plan to refute. When you summarize, it's important to be respectful of the opposition's views. You don't want to alienate readers who might not agree with you at first.

3. If your argument is long and complex, choose only the most important points to refute. Otherwise the reader who does not have the original argument on hand may find a detailed refutation hard to follow. If the argument is short and relatively simple — a claim supported by only two or three points — you may decide to refute all of them, devoting more space to the most important ones.

4. Attack the principal elements in the argument of your opponent.

   a. Question the evidence. (See pp. 146–52 in the text.) Question whether your opponent has proved that a problem exists.

b. Attack the warrants or assumptions that underlie the claim. (See pp. 186–87 in the text.)

c. Attack the logic or reasoning of the opposing view. (Refer to the discussion of fallacious reasoning on pp. 263–73 in the text.)

d. Attack the proposed solution to a problem, pointing out that it will not work.

5. Be prepared to do more than attack the opposing view. Supply evidence and good reasons in support of your own claim.

Finding the Middle Ground

Although an argument, by definition, assumes a difference of opinion, we know that opposing sides frequently find accommodation somewhere in the middle. As you mount your own argument about a controversial issue, you need not confine yourself to support of any of the differing positions. You may want to acknowledge that there is some justice on all sides and that you understand the difficulty of resolving the issue.

Consider these guidelines for an argument that offers a compromise between competing positions:

1. Early in your essay explain the opposing positions. Make clear the major differences separating the two (or more) sides.

2. Point out, whenever possible, that the opposing sides already agree to some exceptions to their stated positions. Such evidence may prove that the opposing sides are not so extreme as their advocates insist. Several commentators, writing about the budget conflict between Democrats and Republicans in late 1995, adopted this strategy, suggesting that compromise was possible because the differences were narrower than the public believed.

3. Make clear your own moderation and sympathy, your own willingness to negotiate. An example of this attitude appears in an essay on abortion in which the author infers how Abraham Lincoln might have treated the question of abortion rights.

> In this debate I have made my own position clear. It is a pro-life position (though it may not please all pro-lifers), and its model is Lincoln's position on slavery from 1854 until well into the Civil War: tolerate, restrict, discourage. Like Lincoln's, its touchstone is the common good of the nation, not the sovereign self. Like Lincoln's position, it accepts the legality but not the moral legitimacy of the institution that it seeks to contain. It invites argument and negotiation; it is a gambit, not a gauntlet.[1]

---

[1]George McKenna, "On Abortion: A Lincolnian Position," *The Atlantic Monthly,* September 1995, p. 68. (A gauntlet or glove is flung down in order to challenge an opponent to combat; a gambit is the opening move in a chess game, or in the words of one dictionary, "a concession that invites discussion." — ED.)

4. If you favor one side of the controversy, acknowledge that opposing views deserve to be considered. For example, in another essay
on abortion, the author, who supports abortion rights, says,

> Those of us who are pro-choice must come to terms with those
> thoughtful pro-lifers who believe that in elevating the right to privacy
> above all other values, the most helpless form of humanity is left unpro-
> tected and is, in fact, defined away. They deserve to have their views
> addressed with sympathy and moral clarity.[2]

5. Provide evidence that accepting a middle ground can offer
marked advantages for the whole society. Wherever possible,
show that continued polarization can result in violence, injustice, and suffering.

6. In offering a solution that finds a common ground, be as specific
as possible, emphasizing the part that you are willing to play in
reaching a settlement. In an essay titled "Pro-Life and Pro-
Choice? Yes!" the author concludes with this:

> Must those of us who abhor abortion, then, reconcile ourselves to
> seeing it spread unchecked? By no means. We can refuse to practice it
> ourselves — or, if we are male, beseech the women who carry our chil-
> dren to let them be born, and promise to support them, and mean it
> and do it. We can counsel and preach to others; those of us who are re-
> ligious can pray. . . . What we must not do is ask the state to impose our
> views on those who disagree.[3]

On a different subject, a debate on pornography, the author, who is
opposed to free distribution of obscene material, nevertheless refuses to endorse censorship.

> I think that, by enlarging the First Amendment to protest, in effect,
> freedom of expression, rather than freedom of speech and of the press,
> the courts made a mistake. The courts have made other mistakes, but I
> do not know a better way of defining the interests of the community
> than through legislation and through the courts. So I am willing to put
> up with things I think are wrong in the hope that they will be corrected.
> I know of no alternative that would always make the right decisions.[4]

Presenting the Stock Issues

Presenting the stock issues, or stating the problem before the
solution, is a type of organization borrowed from traditional debate
format. It works for policy claims when an audience must be con-

[2]Benjamin C. Schwarz, "Judge Ginsburg's Moral Myopia," *New York Times,* July
30, 1993, Sec. A, p. 27.
[3]George Church, *Time,* March 6, 1995, p. 108.
[4]Ernest van den Haag, *Smashing Liberal Icons: A Collection of Debates* (Washington, D.C.: The Heritage Foundation, 1981), p. 101.

vinced that a need exists for changing the status quo (present conditions) and for introducing plans to solve the problem. You begin by establishing that a problem exists (need). You then propose a solution (plan), which is your thesis. Finally, you show reasons for adopting the plan (advantages). These three elements — need, plan, and advantages — are called the stock issues.

For example, suppose you wanted to argue that measures for reducing acid rain should be introduced at once. You would first have to establish a need for such measures by defining the problem and providing evidence of damage. Then you would produce your thesis, a means for improving conditions. Finally you would suggest the benefits that would follow from implementation of your plan. Notice that in this organization your thesis paragraph usually appears toward the middle of your paper, although it may also appear at the beginning.

Ordering Material for Emphasis

Whichever way you choose to work, you should revise your outline to reflect the order in which you intend to present your thesis and supporting ideas. Not only the placement of your thesis paragraph but also the wording and arrangement of your ideas will determine what points in your paper receive the most emphasis.

Suppose your purpose is to convince the reader that cigarette smoking is a bad habit. You might decide to concentrate on three unpleasant attributes of cigarette smoking: (1) it is unhealthy; (2) it is dirty; (3) it is expensive. Obviously, these are not equally important as possible deterrents. You would no doubt consider the first reason the most compelling, accompanied by evidence to prove the relationship between cigarette smoking and cancer, heart disease, emphysema, and other diseases. This issue, therefore, should be given greater emphasis than the others.

There are several ways to achieve emphasis. One is to make the explicit statement that you consider a certain issue the most important.

> Finally, and *most importantly,* human culture is often able to neutralize or reverse what might otherwise be genetically advantageous consequences of selfish behavior.[5]

This quotation also reveals a second way — placing the material to be emphasized in an emphatic position, either first or last in the paper. The end position, however, is generally more emphatic.

A third way to achieve emphasis is to elaborate on the material to be emphasized, treating it at greater length, offering more data and reasons for it than you give for the other issues.

---

[5]Peter Singer, *The Expanding Circle* (New York: New American Library, 1982), p. 171.

Considering Scope and Audience

With a working outline in hand that indicates the order of your thesis and claims, you are almost ready to begin turning your notes into prose. First, however, it is useful to review the limits on your paper to be sure your writing time will be used to the best possible advantage.

The first limit involves scope. As mentioned earlier, your thesis should introduce a claim that can be adequately supported in the space available to you. If your research has opened up more aspects than you anticipated, you may want to narrow your thesis to one major subtopic. Or you could emphasize only the most persuasive arguments for your position (assuming these are sufficient to make your case) and omit the others. In a brief paper (three or four pages), three issues are probably all you have room to develop. On the other hand, if you suspect your thesis can be proved in one or two pages, look for ways to expand it. What additional issues might be brought in to bolster your argument? Alternatively, is there a larger issue for which your thesis could become a supporting idea?

Other limits on your paper are imposed by the need to make your points in a way that will be persuasive to an audience. The style and tone you choose depend not only on the nature of the subject, but also on how you can best convince readers that you are a credible source. *Style* in this context refers to the elements of your prose — simple versus complex sentences, active versus passive verbs, metaphors, analogies, and other literary devices. *Tone* is the approach you take to your topic — solemn or humorous, detached or sympathetic. Style and tone together compose your voice as a writer.

Many students assume that every writer has only one voice. In fact, a writer typically adapts his or her voice to the material and the audience. Perhaps the easiest way to appreciate this is to think of two or three works by the same author that are written in different voices. Or compare the speeches of two different characters in the same story, novel, or film. Every writer has individual talents and inclinations that appear in most or all of his or her work. A good writer, however, is able to amplify some stylistic elements and diminish others, as well as to change tone, by choice.

It is usually appropriate in a short paper to choose an *expository* style, which emphasizes the elements of your argument rather than your personality. You many want to appeal to your readers' emotions as well as their intellects, but keep in mind that sympathy is most effectively gained when it is supported by believable evidence. If you press your point stridently, your audience is likely to be suspicious rather than receptive. If you sprinkle your prose with jokes or metaphors, you may diminish your credibility by detracting from the substance of your case. Both humor and analogy can be useful tools, but they should be used with discretion.

You can discover some helpful pointers on essay style by reading the editorials in newspapers such as the *New York Times,* the *Washington Post,* or the *Wall Street Journal.* The authors are typically addressing a mixed audience comparable to the hypothetical readers of your own paper. Though their approaches vary, each writer is attempting to portray himself or herself as an objective analyst whose argument deserves careful attention.

Again, remember your goals. You are trying to convince your audience of something; an argument is, by its nature, directed at people who may not initially agree with its thesis. Therefore, your voice as well as the claims you make must be convincing.

To This Point

The organizing steps that come between preparation and writing are often neglected. Careful planning at this stage, however, can save much time and effort later. As you prepare to start writing, you should be able to answer the following questions:

1. Is the purpose of my paper to persuade readers to accept a potentially controversial idea, to refute someone else's position, or to propose a solution to a problem?
2. Can or should my solution also incorporate elements of compromise and negotiation?
3. Have I decided on an organization that is likely to accomplish this purpose?
4. Does my outline arrange my thesis and issues in an appropriate order to emphasize the most important issues?
5. Does my outline show an argument whose scope suits the needs of this paper?
6. What questions of style and tone do I need to keep in mind as I write to ensure that my argument will be persuasive?

WRITING

Beginning the Paper

Having found a claim you can defend and the voice you will adopt toward your audience, you must now think about how to begin. An introduction to your subject should consist of more than just the first paragraph of your paper. It should invite the reader to give attention to what you have to say. It should also point you in the direction you will take in developing your argument. You may want to begin the actual writing of your paper with the thesis paragraph. It is useful to consider the whole paragraph rather than simply the thesis statement for two reasons. First, not all theses are effectively expressed in a single sentence. Second, the rest of the paragraph will be closely related to your statement of the main idea. You may show why you have chosen this topic or why your audience will benefit from reading your paper. You may introduce your warrant, qualify your claim, and in other ways prepare for the body of your argument. Because readers will perceive the whole paragraph as a unit, it makes sense to approach it that way.

Consider first the kind of argument you intend to present. Does your paper make a factual claim? Does it address values? Does it recommend a policy or action? Is it a rebuttal of some current policy or belief? The answers to those questions will influence the way you introduce the subject.

If your thesis makes a factual claim, you may be able to summarize it in one or two opening sentences. "Whether we like it or not, money is obsolete. The currency of today is not paper or coin, but plastic." Refutations are easy to introduce in a brief statement: "Contrary to popular views on the subject, the institution of marriage is as sound today as it was a generation ago."

A thesis that defends a value is usually best preceded by an explanatory introduction. "Some wars are morally defensible" is a thesis that can be stated as a simple declarative opening sentence. However, readers who disagree may not read any further than the first line. Someone defending this claim is likely to be more persuasive if he or she first gives an example of a situation in which war is or was preferable to peace or presents the thesis less directly.

One way to keep such a thesis from alienating the audience is to phrase it as a question. "Are all wars morally indefensible?" Still better would be to prepare for the question:

> Few if any of us favor war as a solution to international problems. We are too vividly aware of the human suffering imposed by armed conflict, as well as the political and financial turmoil that inevitably result. Yet can we honestly agree that no war is ever morally defensible?

Notice that this paragraph gains appeal from use of the first person *we*. The author implies that he or she shares the readers' feelings but has good reasons for believing those feelings are not sufficient grounds for condemning all wars. Even if readers are skeptical, the conciliatory phrasing of the thesis should encourage them to continue reading.

For any subject that is highly controversial or emotionally charged, especially one that strongly condemns an existing situation or belief, you may sometimes want to express your indignation directly. Of course, you must be sure that your indignation can be justified. The author of the following introduction, a physician and writer, openly admits that he is about to make a case that may offend readers.

> Is there any polite way to introduce today's subject? I'm afraid not. It must be said plainly that the media have done about as sorry and dishonest a job of covering health news as is humanly possible, and that when the media do not fail from bias and mendacity, they fail from ignorance and laziness.[6]

If your thesis advocates a policy or makes a recommendation, it may be a good idea, as in a value claim, to provide a short background. The following paragraph introduces an argument favoring relaxation of controls in high schools.

> "Free the New York City 275,000" read a button worn by many young New Yorkers some years ago. The number was roughly the total of students enrolled in the City's high schools.
>
> The condition of un-freedom which is described was not, however, unique to the schools of one city. According to the Carnegie Commission's comprehensive study of American public education, *Crisis in the Classroom,* public schools across the country share a common characteristic, namely, "preoccupation with order and control." The result is that students find themselves the victims of "oppressive and petty rules which give their schools a repressive, almost prison-like atmosphere."[7]

There are also other ways to introduce your subject. One is to begin with an appropriate quotation.

> "Reading makes a full man, conversation makes a ready man, and writing makes an exact man." So Francis Bacon told us around 1600. Recently I have been wondering how Bacon's formula might apply to present-day college students.[8]

Or you may begin with an anecdote. In the following introduction to an article about the relation between cancer and mental attitude, the author recounts a personal experience.

> Shortly after I moved to California, a new acquaintance sat in my San Francisco living room drinking rose-hip tea and chainsmoking. Like so many residents of the Golden West, Cecil was "into" all things healthy, from jogging to *shiatsu* massage to kelp. Tobacco didn't seem to fit, but he told me confidently that there was no contradiction. "It all

---

[6]Michael Halberstam, "TVs Unhealthy Approach to Health News," *TV Guide,* September 20–26, 1980, p. 24.

[7]Alan Levine and Eve Carey, *The Rights of Students* (New York: Avon Books, 1977), p. 11.

[8]William Aiken, "The Conversation on Campus Today Is, Uh . . . ," *Wall Street Journal,* May 4, 1982, p. 18.

has to do with energy," he said. "Unless you have a lot of negative energy about smoking cigarettes, there's no way they can hurt you; you won't get cancer."[9]

Finally, you may introduce yourself as the author of the claim.

> I wish to argue an unpopular cause: the cause of the old, free elective system in the academic world, or the untrammeled right of the undergraduate to make his own mistakes.[10]

> My subject is the world of Hamlet. I do not of course mean Denmark, except as Denmark is given a body by the play; and I do not mean Elizabethan England, though this is necessarily close behind the scenes. I mean simply the imaginative environment that the play asks us to enter when we read it or go to see it.[11]

You should, however, use such introductions with care. They suggest an authority about the subject that you shouldn't attempt to assume unless you can demonstrate that you are entitled to it.

Guidelines for Good Writing

In general, the writer of an argument follows the same rules that govern any form of expository writing. Your style should be clear and readable, your organization logical, your ideas connected by transitional phrases and sentences, your paragraphs coherent. The main difference between an argument and other kinds of expository writing, as noted earlier, is the need to persuade an audience to adopt a belief or take an action. You should assume your readers will be critical rather than neutral or sympathetic. Therefore, you must be equally critical of your own work. Any apparent gap in reasoning or ambiguity in presentation is likely to weaken the argument.

As you read the essays in this book and elsewhere, you will discover that good style in argumentative writing shares several characteristics:

- Variety in sentence structure: a mixture of both long and short sentences, different sentence beginnings
- Rich but standard vocabulary: avoidance of specialized terms unless they are fully explained, word choice appropriate to a thoughtful argument
- Use of details and examples to illustrate and clarify abstract terms, principles, and generalizations

---

[9]Joel Guerin, "Cancer and the Mind," *Harvard Magazine,* November–December 1978, p. 11.

[10]Howard Mumford Jones, "Undergraduates on Apron Strings," *Atlantic Monthly,* October 1955, p. 45.

[11]Maynard Mack, "The World of Hamlet," *Yale Review,* June 1952, p. 502.

You should take care to avoid the following:

- Unnecessary repetition: making the same point without new data or interpretation
- Exaggeration or stridency, which can create suspicion of your fairness and powers of observation
- Short paragraphs of one or two sentences, which are common in advertising and newspaper writing to get the reader's attention but are inappropriate in a thoughtful essay

In addition to these stylistic principles, seven general points are worth keeping in mind:

1. Although *you,* like *I,* should be used judiciously, it can be found even in the treatment of weighty subjects. Here is an example from an essay by the distinguished British mathematician and philosopher, Bertrand Russell.

> Suppose you are a scientific pioneer and you make some discovery of great scientific importance and suppose you say to yourself, "I am afraid this discovery will do harm": you know that other people are likely to make the same discovery if they are allowed suitable opportunities for research; you must therefore, if you do not wish the discovery to become public, either discourage your sort of research or control publication by a board of censors.[12]

Don't be afraid to use *you* or *I* when it is useful to emphasize the presence of the person making the argument.

2. Don't pad. This point should be obvious; the word *pad* suggests the addition of unnecessary material. Many writers find it tempting, however, to enlarge a discussion even when they have little more to say. It is never wise to introduce more words into a paper that has already made its point. If the paper turns out to be shorter than you had hoped, it may mean that you have not sufficiently developed the subject or that the subject was less substantial than you thought when you selected it. Padding, which is easy to detect in its repetition and sentences empty of content, weakens the writer's credibility.

3. For any absolute generalization — a statement containing words such as *all* or *every* — consider the possibility that there may be at least one example that will weaken the generalization. Such a precaution means that you won't have to backtrack and admit that your generalization is not, after all, universal. A student who was arguing against capital punishment for the reason that all killing was wrong suddenly paused in her presentation and added, "On the

---

[12]"Science and Human Life," in *What Is Science?* edited by James R. Newman (New York: Simon and Schuster, 1955), p. 12.

other hand, if given the chance, I'd probably have been willing to kill Hitler." This admission meant that she recognized important exceptions to her rule and that she would have to qualify her generalization in some significant way.

4. When offering an explanation, especially one that is complicated or extraordinary, look first for a cause that is easier to accept, one that doesn't strain credibility. (In Chapter 8, we called attention to this principle. See pp. 265–66.) For example, a few years ago a great many people were bemused by reports about the mysterious Bermuda Triangle, which had apparently swallowed up ships and planes since the mid-nineteenth century. The forces at work were variously described as space-time warps, UFOs that transported earthlings to other planets, and sea monsters seeking revenge. But a careful investigation revealed familiar, natural causes. A reasonable person interested in the truth would have searched for more conventional explanations before accepting the bizarre stories of extraterrestrial creatures. He or she would also exercise caution when confronted by conspiracy theories that try to account for controversial political events, such as the assassination of John F. Kennedy.

5. Check carefully for questionable warrants. Your outline should specify your warrants. When necessary, these should be included in your paper to link claims with support. Many an argument has failed because it depended on an unstated warrant with which the reader did not agree. If you were arguing for a physical education requirement at your school, you might make a good case for all the physical and psychological benefits of such a requirement. But you would certainly need to introduce and develop the warrant on which your claim was based — that it is the proper function of a college or university to provide the benefits of a physical education. Many readers would agree that physical education is valuable, but they might question the assumption that an academic institution should introduce a nonintellectual enterprise into the curriculum. At any point where you draw a controversial or tenuous conclusion, be sure your reasoning is clear and logical.

6. Avoid conclusions that are merely summaries. Summaries may be needed in long technical papers, but in brief arguments they create endings that are without force or interest. In the closing paragraph you should find a new idea that emerges naturally from the development of the whole argument.

7. Strive for a paper that is unified, coherent, and emphatic where appropriate. A *unified* paper stays focused on its goal and directs each claim, warrant, and piece of evidence toward that goal. Extraneous information or unsupported claims impair unity. *Coherence* means that all ideas are fully explained and adequately connected by transitions. To ensure coherence, give especially close

attention to the beginnings and ends of your paragraphs: Is each new concept introduced in a way that shows it following naturally from the one that preceded it? *Emphasis,* as we have mentioned, is a function partly of structure and partly of language. Your most important claims should be placed where they are certain of receiving the reader's attention: key sentences at the beginning or end of a paragraph, key paragraphs at the beginning or end of your paper. Sentence structure can also be used for emphasis. If you have used several long, complex sentences, you can emphasize a significant point by stating it briefly and simply. You can also create emphasis with verbal flags, such as "The primary issue to consider . . ." or "Finally, we cannot ignore. . . ."

All clear expository prose will exhibit the qualities of unity, coherence, and emphasis. But the success of an argumentative paper is especially dependent on these qualities because the reader may have to follow a line of reasoning that is both complicated and unfamiliar. Moreover, a paper that is unified, coherent, and properly emphatic will be more readable, the first requisite of an effective argument.

REVISING

The final stage in writing an argumentative paper is revising. The first step is to read through what you have written for mistakes. Next, check your work against the guidelines listed under "Organizing the Material" and "Writing." Have you omitted any of the issues, warrants, or supporting evidence on your outline? Is each paragraph coherent in itself? Do your paragraphs work together to create a coherent paper? All the elements of the argument — the issues raised, the underlying assumptions, and the supporting material — should contribute to the development of the claim in your thesis statement. Any material that is interesting but irrelevant to that claim should be cut. Finally, does your paper reach a clear conclusion that reinforces your thesis?

Be sure, too, that the style and tone of your paper are appropriate for the topic and the audience. Remember that people choose to read an argument because they want the answer to a troubling question or the solution to a recurrent problem. Besides stating your thesis in a way that invites the reader to join you in your investigation, you must retain your audience's interest through a discussion that may be unfamiliar or contrary to their convictions. The outstanding qualities of argumentative prose style, therefore, are clarity and readability.

Style is obviously harder to evaluate in your own writing than organization. Your outline provides a map against which to check the structure of your paper. Clarity and readability, by comparison, are somewhat abstract qualities. Two procedures may be helpful. The first is to read two or three (or more) essays by authors whose style you admire and then turn back to your own writing. Awkward spots in your prose are sometimes easier to see if you get away from it and respond to someone else's perspective than if you simply keep rereading your own writing.

The second method is to read aloud. If you have never tried it, you are likely to be surprised at how valuable this can be. Again, start with someone else's work that you feel is clearly written, and practice until you achieve a smooth rhythmic delivery that satisfies you. And listen to what you are reading. Your objective is to absorb the patterns of English structure that characterize the clearest, most readable prose. Then read your paper aloud and listen to the construction of your sentences. Are they also clear and readable? Do they say what you want them to say? How would they sound to a reader? According to one theory, you can learn the rhythm and phrasing of a language as you learn the rhythm and phrasing of a melody. And you will often *hear* a mistake or a clumsy construction in your writing that has escaped your eye in proofreading.

PREPARING THE MANUSCRIPT

Type on one side of 8½-by-11-inch 20-pound white typing paper, double-spacing throughout. Leave margins of 1 to 1½ inches on all sides and indent each paragraph five spaces, or one-half inch if you are preparing your paper on a computer. Unless a formal outline is part of the paper, a separate title page is unnecessary. Instead, beginning about one inch from the top of the first page and flush with the left margin, type your name, the instructor's name, the course title, and the date, each on a separate line; then double-space and type the title, capitalizing the first letter of the first and last words of the title and all other words except articles, prepositions, and conjunctions. Double-space and type the body of the paper.

Number all pages at the top right corner, typing your last name before each page number in case pages are mislaid. If an outline is included, number its pages with lowercase roman numerals.

Proofread the paper carefully for mistakes in grammar, spelling, and punctuation. Make corrections with liquid correction fluid or, if there are only a few mistakes, cross them out and neatly write the correction above the line. If you have used a word-processing program, correct the errors and reprint the pages in question.

REVIEW CHECKLIST
FOR ARGUMENTATIVE PAPERS

A successful argumentative paper meets the following criteria:

1. It presents a thesis that is of interest to both the writer and the audience, is debatable, and can be defended in the amount of space available.
2. Each statement offered in support of the thesis is backed up with enough evidence to give it credibility. Data cited in the paper come from a variety of sources. All quotations and direct references to primary or secondary sources are fully documented.
3. The warrants linking claims to support are either specified or implicit in the author's data and line of reasoning. No claim should depend on an unstated warrant with which skeptical readers might disagree.
4. The thesis is clearly presented and adequately introduced in a thesis paragraph, which indicates the purpose of the paper.
5. Supporting statements and data are organized in a way that builds the argument, emphasizes the author's main ideas, and justifies the paper's conclusions.
6. All possible opposing arguments are anticipated and refuted.
7. The paper is written in a style and tone appropriate to the topic and the intended audience. The author's prose is clear and readable.
8. The manuscript is clean, carefully proofed, and typed in an acceptable format.

CHAPTER TEN

Researching an Argumentative Paper

The success of any argument, short or long, depends in large part on the quantity and quality of the support behind it. Research, therefore, can be crucial for any argument outside your own experience. Most papers will benefit from research in the library and elsewhere because development of the claim requires facts, examples, statistics, and informed opinions that are available only from primary and secondary research sources. This chapter offers information and advice to help you work through the steps of writing a research paper, from getting started to preparing the finished product.

GETTING STARTED

The following guidelines will help you keep your research on track:

1. Focus your investigation on building your argument, not merely on collecting information about the topic. Do follow any promising leads that turn up from the sources you consult, but don't be diverted into general reading that has no direct bearing on your thesis.

2. Look for at least two pieces of evidence to support each point you make. If you cannot find sufficient evidence, you may need to revise or abandon the point.

3. Use a variety of sources. Check not only different publications (books, magazines, journals, newspapers, and so on) but information drawn from different fields as well.

4. Be sure your sources are authoritative. We have already pointed out elsewhere the necessity for examining the credentials of sources. Although it may be difficult or impossible for those outside the field to conclude that one authority is more trustworthy than another, some guidelines are available. Articles and essays in scholarly journals are probably more authoritative than articles in college newspapers. Authors whose credentials include many publications and years of study at reputable institutions are probably more reliable than newspaper columnists and the so-called man in the street. However, we can judge reliability much more easily if we are dealing with facts and inferences than with values and emotions.

5. Don't let your sources' opinions outweigh your own. Your paper should demonstrate that the thesis and ideas you present are yours, arrived at after careful reflection and supported by research. The thesis need not be original, but your paper should be more than a collection of quotations or a report of the facts and opinions you have been reading. It should be clear to the reader that the quotations and other materials support *your* claim and that *you* have been responsible for finding and emphasizing the important issues, examining the data, and choosing between strong and weak opinions.

6. Prepare for research by learning your way around your local or university library. Locate the computerized catalog access system and practice using the system's search techniques. Identify the reference and information databases that are available electronically or on CD-ROM, noting those which index and abstract articles and those which provide full-text retrieval of the items. Know where the copy machines are and whether you need money or a key-card to use them. Finally, locate the reference center and reference librarians in case you need help.

MAPPING RESEARCH: A SAMPLE OUTLINE

To explore a range of research activities, let's suppose that you are preparing a research paper, six to ten pages long. You have chosen to defend the following thesis: *Conventional zoos should be abolished because they are cruel to animals and cannot provide the benefits to the public that they promise.* To keep your material under control and give direction to your reading, you would sketch a preliminary outline, which might look like this:

Why We Don't Need Zoos

I. Moral Objection: Animals have fundamental right to liberty
  A. Must prove animals are negatively affected by captivity
    1. research?

2. research?

    B. Must refute claims that captivity is not detrimental to animals

        1. Brownlee's description of dolphin: "seeming stupor"; eating "half-heartedly"; not behaving like wild dolphins

        2. Personal experience: watching leopards running in circles in cages for hours

II. Practical Objection: Zoos can't accomplish what they claim to be their goals

    A. "Educational benefits" zoo provides are inaccurate at best: Public is not learning about wild animals at all but about domesticated descendants of same (support with research from [I.A] above)

    B. Conservation programs at zoos are ineffective

        1. It's difficult to breed animals in zoos

        2. Resultant offspring, when there is any, is victim of inbreeding. Leads to inferior stock that will eventually die out (research?)

Now you need to begin the search for the materials that will support your argument. There are two principal ways of gathering the materials — primary research and secondary research. Most writers will not want to limit themselves to one kind of research, but one method may work better than another for a particular project.

USING SOURCES: PRIMARY RESEARCH

The term *primary research* describes the search for firsthand information in the field — that is, outside the library. By firsthand we mean information taken directly from the original source. It can include interviews and conversations, surveys, questionnaires, personal observations, and experiments. If your topic relates to a local issue, one involving your school or your town, or is based on the experience of someone whose story has been unreported, firsthand information may be more useful than library research. The library, however, is also a source of original materials. For example, documents containing raw data that have not yet been interpreted — such as statistics compiled by the Census Bureau of the United States — will be most readily available in the library.

One of the rewards of primary research is that it often generates new information which in turn produces new interpretations of familiar conditions. It is a favored method for anthropologists and sociologists, and most physical and natural scientists use observation and experiment at some point as essential tools in their research. Notice that both of the student research papers at the end of this chapter used firsthand information gained from personal observation and interviews in addition to their secondary library research.

Consider the sample thesis that *zoos should be abolished.* Remember that you need to prove that *zoos are cruel to animals* and that *they cannot provide the benefits to the public that they promise.* It is possible to go directly to primary sources without consulting books or journals. For example:

- Phone the local area chapter of any animal rights group and ask to interview members on their opinions concerning zoos.
- Talk to the veterinarian on call at your local zoo and ask about animal injuries, illnesses, neuroses, and so forth.
- Search the World Wide Web for sites sponsored and developed by the groups associated with the animal rights movement. Many such informational sites will provide the text of current or proposed laws concerning this issue.
- Locate Internet newsgroups or discussion lists devoted to animal rights and identify experts in the field such as animal scientists who would be willing to provide authoritative opinions for your paper.

The information gleaned from primary research can be used directly to support your claim, or can provide a starting point for secondary research at the library.

USING SOURCES: SECONDARY RESEARCH

For freshman research papers the most common resource is still the library. If you were going to write a research paper on why we don't need zoos, you would probably want to rely on materials available in the library for most of your evidence. Although you could collect some firsthand information by visiting a zoo yourself (as did the author of the paper at the end of this chapter) and by interviewing zoo directors and other animal scientists, the published opinions of a wide range of scholars will be far more easily obtained in the library and will probably carry more weight in your argument. Having drawn up a preliminary outline to help map out your reading, how can you most effectively use the library to research the fate of wild animals in captivity?

It's a good idea to consult the librarian before starting your research; he or she will be able to direct you to specific reference works relevant to your subject, which could save you a lot of time.

Your library contains useful systems for retrieving material of all kinds, including the catalog access system; dictionaries and encyclopedias; indexes to magazines, newspapers, journals, and specialized print sources; abstracting services; and on-line and CD-ROM databases that may or may not provide full-text access to selected items.

Catalog Access Systems

Most libraries have replaced their card catalogs with computerized *on-line public access catalogs* (OPACs). These catalog systems use machine-readable cataloging (MARC) records, or bibliographic records, to provide the information traditionally shown on catalog cards. A MARC record includes

- a description of the item, including title, edition, material-specific details, content notes, publication information, and physical description
- main entry and added entry, providing alphabetic catalog access points such as subtitles, authors, series titles, and so on
- subject headings and subject added entries

Sample On-Line Catalog Record
You searched for the TITLE: animal rights movement

```
CALL #       Z7164.C45 M38 1994.
AUTHOR       Manzo, Bettina, 1943-
TITLE        The animal rights movement in the United States, 1975-
                 1990 : an annotated bibliography / by Bettina Manzo.
IMPRINT      Metuchen, N.J. : Scarecrow Press, 1994.
PHYS DESCR   xi, 296 p. ; 23 cm.
NOTE         Includes indexes.
CONTENTS     Animal rights movement -- Activists and organizations --
                 Philosophy, ethics and religion -- Law and legislation
                 -- Factory farming and vegetarianism -- Trapping and
                 fur industry -- Companion animals -- Wildlife --
                 Circuses, zoos, rodeos, dog
SUBJECT      Animal rights movement --United States --Bibliography.
             Animal rights --United States --Bibliography.
             Animal experimentation --United States --Bibliography.
OCLC #       30671149.
ISBN/ISSN    GB95-17241.
```

- call numbers, such as Dewey or Library of Congress
- shelf list information, such as the source of the book and its price

The place provided on the record for each of these pieces of information is called a *field*. The best of the computerized catalog access systems allows users to search many of these fields for selected types of information. For example, you can search for "animal rights" within the Subject or Content Notes fields, or "zoos" within the Title field. Generally, computerized library catalogs can be searched by

- author
- title
- subject, or
- words found in the titles, content notes, and subjects.

Most on-line catalogs also enable users to search efficiently by means of *Boolean logic* that combines search terms using the words AND, OR, and NOT. In Boolean logic searching, combining terms with AND means that the bibliographic record has to contain both terms. For example, when you search for the phrase "animal rights AND zoos," the computer finds MARC records that contain both the terms *animal rights* AND *zoos,* thus sparing you from having to read through many items on zoos which have nothing to say about animal rights. Searching for "dogs OR cats" provides all records that contain either the word *dogs* OR the word *cats.* Using NOT in a search limits the results to records that contain the first search term, but *not* the second one, as in "zoos NOT petting." Additionally, after your initial search, the group of resulting MARC records can also be limited by language, publication date, and so on.

On-line public access catalogs allow much more comprehensive searches for items relevant to your paper topic than were ever possible with the card catalog, because the computer can search the entire library collection at once. When you find a citation for a book or item that interests you, print the MARC record so that you can locate the item on the library shelves by using the Call Number. In addition, if the item is a good fit for your topic, identify its Subject Headings and words in the Content Notes field. By using these terms in another search, you will most likely find similar items. Ideally, a good on-line catalog and focused search will provide you with plenty of material relevant to your topic that can be used to support your claim.

Encyclopedias

General and subject-specific encyclopedias can provide useful overviews and valuable cross references of your topic area. Print versions of these sources will be on your library's shelves, but you should also check to see if the library has any on-line or CD-ROM versions.

In the nonprint versions, it is possible to search every word of the encyclopedia. By combining search terms using Boolean logic, you can quickly obtain a comprehensive collection of information on your topic. In newer on-line and multimedia CD-ROM encyclopedias, entries contain *hyperlinks* to their cross references. Hyperlinks let you click on a photo or a word within the text and instantly access that part of the encyclopedia where the linked topic is located. For example, clicking on the word *zoos* within an entry on the "animal rights movement" will instantly connect you to the "zoo" entry in the encyclopedia. In addition to general encyclopedias, others you might find useful include the following:

- *Encyclopedia of Crime and Justice*
- *Encyclopedia of Psychology*
- *Encyclopedia of Educational Research*
- *Encyclopedia of Environmental Sciences*
- *Encyclopedia of Religion*
- *Encyclopedia of Biological Sciences*
- *International Encyclopedia of Social Sciences*

Indexes and Abstracts

Indexes serve to locate information within other documents, whereas abstracts provide a summary of content. In the print version of indexes and abstracts, entries are usually organized by the author's name, title of the article, or subject of the article. Newer CD-ROM and on-line database versions have powerful search capabilities and allow focused searches on many access points by using Boolean logic to combine terms and limit the information found to the desired topic.

Many of the sources listed below are fast becoming available as full-text databases, in which the full document, paper, or article and all bibliographic citation information are provided. Many newspapers, magazines, and journals are already available in full text on CD-ROM or on-line. In order to simplify your research, ask the reference librarian at your library which databases provide full-text article retrieval, and begin your search with those.

For a controversial or current topic, look at the most recent citations first. If you are researching a specific event, start your search by limiting it to the year in which the event took place. Give yourself enough time to use your library's interlibrary loan system should you need to retrieve articles from journals not available at your university.

General Magazine Sources. In order to locate articles about your subject, you will want to use magazine indexes and abstracts which cover current events, hobbies, education, and popular culture.

- *Readers' Guide to Periodical Literature* indexes more than 200 magazines.
- *Readers' Guide Abstracts* provides summaries of many of the articles.
- *Magazine Index* indexes more than 400 popular magazines.
- *Academic Index* covers more than 400 scholarly and general interest periodicals.
- *Magazine ASAP* provides the full text of over 120 magazines.
- *Periodical Abstracts* includes 450 magazines, with full text available.
- *ArticleFirst* is an index of periodicals.
- *ABI Inform* includes full-text business articles.

Newspaper Sources. Newspaper indexes provide coverage of national, international, regional, and local news topics. Most well-known indexes are now available on CD-ROM and on-line, as well as in print. Many include comprehensive abstracts; more and more are providing the full text of the articles. These indexes are an excellent source for articles on current events and controversial topics.

- *New York Times Index*
- *National Newspaper Index*
- *Newspaper Abstracts*

Many newspapers are available in full text and searchable through on-line databases such as NEXIS, Dow Jones News Retrieval, and Data Times and also through consumer on-line services such as Compuserve, Prodigy, and America Online.

Specialized Sources. Specialized indexes and abstracts focus on more sophisticated articles from scholarly and professional journals and magazines. The articles will be more difficult to read but will be more substantial and authoritative for use as support for your claim. They include

- *Applied Science & Tech Index*
- *Art Index*
- *Biography Index*
- *Book Review Index*
- *Psychological Abstracts*

- *Sociological Abstracts*
- *Education Index*
- *Dissertation Abstracts*
- ERIC (education)
- *Essay and General Literature Index*
- *PsychInfo* (psychological literature)
- *Business Periodicals Index*
- *Biological Abstracts*
- *Chemical Abstracts*
- *Historical Abstracts*

Database Services

Many of the sources listed previously are also available through services that offer access to large collections of databases. Within these databases are millions of documents drawn from a wide array of subject areas. These one-stop-shopping services will allow you to search simultaneously, for example, *Biological Abstracts, ABI Inform,* and *Medline.* Specialized databases exist for almost any discipline you would want to search, but you should find out which services your library subscribes to and what databases are contained there before you decide to consult any one of them.

- DIALOG contains over 450 databases from a broad range of disciplines. Particularly noted for its collection of business, science, and technology databases.
- ERIC, the Educational Research Information Center, provides abstracts of educational research and indexes more than 700 journals.
- DataStar, Europe's leading on-line service, provides over 350 databases.
- LEXIS-NEXIS has 172 "libraries" containing thousands of sources. Noted for its law and business collections.
- Dow Jones News Retrieval contains more than 3,000 publications.
- OCLC, the Online Computer Library Center, provides shared cataloging.
- WorldCat is a database containing more than 26 million records from more than 15,000 libraries worldwide.
- MedLine contains thousands of sources from the medical field.
- OVID Online provides bibliographic access to more than 80 major databases in medicine, education, psychology, sociology, and business.

Internet and World Wide Web

The Internet is a fast-growing web of educational, corporate, and research computer networks around the world. The World Wide Web, a subset of the Internet, consists of millions of "pages," or small collections of text, graphics, pictures, videos, sound, and hyperlinks to other pages containing related material.

The Internet and World Wide Web can be valuable sources of primary and secondary information for your paper. Hundreds of magazines, newspapers, books, and electronic journals have Web and Internet sites that allow searching and provide citations or full-text articles. Web pages exist on practically any topic of current interest, including some of the topics addressed in this book's selections — human and animal rights issues, politics, and immigration.

Many professionals subscribe to E-Mail Discussion Lists devoted to their professional subject areas, and these lists can be used for primary research or as expert support for a claim. Usenet newsgroups are a great source of information on just about any topic. Government sites provide statistical, economic, and census information. Trade and professional associations and many consumer and human interest groups have developed informational, interactive Web pages.

One note of caution: With millions of Internet and World Wide Web sites currently up and running, the reliability of the information found on them is very much a concern. Make sure you know who sponsored or developed the site where the information resides. Most reliable sites will tell you who is updating the information and when the last update was done.

READING WITH A PURPOSE

When you begin studying your sources, read first to acquire general familiarity with your subject. Make sure that you are covering both sides of the question — in this case arguments both for and against the existence of zoos — as well as facts and opinions from a variety of sources. In investigating this subject, you will encounter data from biologists, ecologists, zoo directors, anthropologists, animal-rights activists, and ethical philosophers; their varied points of view will contribute to the strength of your claim.

As you read, look for what seem to be the major issues. They will probably be represented in all or most of your sources. For the claim about zoos the major issues may be summarized as follows: (1) the fundamental right wild animals have to liberty; (2) the harm done to animals who are denied this right and kept in captivity. On the other side, these issues will emerge: (1) the lack of concrete evidence that animals suffer or are harmed by being in zoos; (2) the benefits, in terms of entertainment, education, and conservation efforts that the public derives from zoos. The latter two, of course, are the issues you will have to refute. Your note taking should emphasize these important issues.

Record questions as they occur to you in your reading. Why do zoos exist? What are their major goals, and how well do they meet them? What happens to animals who are removed from the wild and placed in zoos? What happens to animals born and reared in captivity? How do these groups compare with their wild counterparts, who are free to live in their natural habitats? Do animals really have a right to liberty? What are the consequences of denying them this right? Are there consequences to humanity?

Taking Notes

While everyone has his or her own method for taking notes, here are a few suggestions that should be useful to any writer, including those working on a word processor.

*Note
Card
with
Quotation*

Hediger   25

"The wild animal, with its marked tendency to escape, is notorious for the fact that it is never completely released from that all-important activity, avoiding enemies, even during sleep, but is constantly on the alert."

*Note
Card
with
Summary*

Hediger   25

Animals who live in the wild have to be on the watch for predators constantly.

Note
Card
with
Statistics

> Reiger   32
>
> By end of decade, worldwide extinction rate will
> be one species per hour.
>
> Other statistics, too, in Reiger, "The Wages of
> Growth," Field and Stream, July 1981:32.

Bibliography
Note
Card

> Hediger, Heini. The Psychology and Behavior
>   of Animals in Zoos and Circuses. Trans.
>   Geoffrey Sircom. New York: Dover, 1968.

Summarize instead of quoting long passages, unless you feel the quotation is more effective than anything you can write and can provide crucial support for your argument. Summarizing as you read can save you a great deal of time.

When you do quote, make sure to quote exactly. Copy the material word for word, leaving all punctuation exactly as it appears and inserting ellipsis points if you delete material. Make sure to enclose all quotations in quotation marks and to copy complete information about your source, including page numbers and publishing information as well as the author's name and the title of the book or article. If you quote an article that appears in an anthology or collection, make sure you record complete information about the book itself.

Record complete bibliographical information for each source *as you use it*. That way you will have all the information necessary to document your paper when you need it. Some people find it useful to keep two sets of note cards: one set for the bibliographical information and one set for the notes themselves. Each source appears on one card by itself, ready to be arranged in alphabetical order for the Works Cited or References page of the paper.

If you use a word processor, you can record information in any number of ways; the best may be to open a file for each source, enter the bibliographic information, and directly type into the file a series of potentially useful quotations, paraphrases, and summaries. For each entry, make sure to note the correct page reference as you go along, and indicate clearly whether you are quoting, paraphrasing, or summarizing. The material you record can then be readily integrated into your research paper by cutting and pasting from the source files, thus eliminating the need to retype and reducing the chance of error. Resist the temptation to record nothing but direct quotations; this will only postpone the inevitable work of summarizing, paraphrasing, and composing involved in thinking critically about your topic.

As you take notes, refer to your outline frequently to ensure that you are acquiring sufficient data to support all the points you intend to use. You will also be revising your outline during the course of your research, as issues are clarified and new ones emerge. Keeping close track of your outline will prevent you from recording material that is interesting but not relevant. If you aren't sure whether you will want to use a certain piece of information later, don't copy the whole passage. Instead, make a note for future reference so that you can find it again if you need it. Taking too many notes is, however, preferable to taking too few, a problem that will force you to go back to the library for missing information. For the ideas and quotations in your notes, you should always take down enough information to enable you to find the references again as quickly as possible.

When researching your topic, you will find words and ideas put together by other people that you will want to use in your paper. Relying on the knowledge of others is an important part of doing research; expert opinions and eloquent arguments will help support your claims when your own expertise is limited. But remember, this is *your* paper. Your ideas and your insights into other people's ideas are just as important as the information you uncover at the library. Try to achieve a balance between solid information and original interpretation.

Quoting

You may want to quote passages or phrases from your sources if they express an idea in words more effective than your own. In this particular project, you might come across a statement that provides succinct, irrefutable evidence for an issue you wish to support. If the author of this statement is a professional in his or her field, someone with a great deal of authority on the subject, it would be appropriate to quote that author. Suppose, during the course of your research for the zoo paper, you find that many sources agree that zoos don't have the money or space necessary to maintain large enough animal populations to ensure successful captive breeding programs. But so far you only have opinions to that effect. You have been unable to find any concrete documentation of this fact until you come across Ulysses S. Seal's address to the National Zoological Park Symposia for the Public, September 1982. Here is how you could use Seal's words in your paper (using reference citation style of the American Psychological Association):

> Bear in mind that "none of these [zoo] budgets is allocated specifically for species preservation. Zoos have been established primarily as recreational institutions and are only secondarily develop ing programs in conservation, education and research" (Seal, 1982, p. 74).

Notice the use of brackets (not parentheses) in the first sentence, which enclose material that did not appear in the original source but is necessary for clarification. Brackets must be used to indicate any such changes in quoted material.

Quotations should be introduced logically and gracefully in your text. Make sure that the quoted material either supports or illustrates the point you have just made or the point you are about to make and that your writing remains grammatically correct once the quotation is introduced.

Quotations are an important tool for establishing your claims, but it is important not to overuse them. If you cannot say most of what you want to say in your own words, you probably haven't thought hard enough about what it is you want to say.

Paraphrasing

Paraphrasing involves restating the content of an original source in your own words. It is most useful when the material from your source is too long for your paper, can be made clearer to the reader by rephrasing, or is written in a style markedly different from your own.

A paraphrase should be as true to the original source as you can make it: Do not change the tone or the ideas, or even the order in which the ideas are presented. Take care not to allow your own opinions to creep into your paraphrase of someone else's argument. Your readers should always be aware of which arguments belong to you and which belong to outside sources.

Like a quotation, a paraphrase must *always* include documentation, or you will be guilty of plagiarism. Even though you are using your own words, the ideas in a paraphrase belong to someone else, and that person deserves credit for them. One final caveat: When putting a long passage into your own words, beware of picking up certain expressions and turns of phrase from your source. If you do end up using your source's exact words, make sure to enclose them in quotation marks.

Below is a passage from Shannon Brownlee's "First It Was 'Save the Whales,' Now It's 'Free the Dolphins'" (*Discover* Dec. 1986: 70–72), along with a good paraphrase of the passage and two unacceptable paraphrases.

ORIGINAL PASSAGE:

But are we being good caretakers by holding a dolphin or a sea lion in a tank? Yes, if two conditions are met: that they're given the best treatment possible and, no less important, that they're displayed in a way that educates and informs us. Captive animals must be allowed to serve as ambassadors for their species (Brownlee, 1986, p. 72).

A PARAPHRASE THAT PLAGIARIZES:

In "First It Was 'Save the Whales,' Now It's 'Free the Dolphins,'" Shannon Brownlee (1986) argues that it's all right for people to hold animals in captivity as long as (1) the animals are treated as well as possible, and (2) the animals are displayed in a way that educates the public. Brownlee insists that animals be allowed to serve as "ambassadors for their species" (p. 72).

A PARAPHRASE THAT ALTERS THE MEANING OF THE ORIGINAL PASSAGE:

According to Shannon Brownlee (1986), a captive animal is being treated fairly as long as it's kept alive and its captivity gives people pleasure. In her essay, "First It Was 'Save the Whales,' Now It's 'Free the Dolphins,'" she argues that people who keep animals in cages are responsible to the animals in only two ways: (1) they should treat their captives as well as possible (even if a small tank is all that can be provided), and (2) they should make sure that the spectators enjoy watching them (p. 72).

A GOOD PARAPHRASE:

Shannon Brownlee (1986) holds that two criteria are necessary in order for the captivity of wild animals to be considered worthwhile. First, the animals should be treated as well as possible. Second, their captivity should have educational value for the people who come to look at them. "Captive animals," Brownlee claims, "must be allowed to serve as ambassadors for their species" (p. 72).

Summarizing

A summary is like a paraphrase, but it involves shortening the original passage as well as putting it in your own words. It gives the gist of the passage. Summarizing is useful when the material from your source is too long for the purposes of your paper. As with a paraphrase, a summary should not alter the meaning of the original passage.

In the paper at the end of this chapter, for instance, the statement, "It is generally acknowledged that there is a great deal of difficulty involved in breeding zoo animals" is not a direct quotation, but the idea comes from Jon Luoma's article in *Audubon*. The statement in the paper is both a summary and a paraphrase. Returning to the source makes it clear that neither quoting nor paraphrasing would have been suitable choices in this instance, since for the writer's purposes it was possible to reduce the following passage from Luoma's article to one sentence

> But the successful propagation of entire captive species poses awesome management problems. . . . Sanford Friedman, the Minnesota Zoo's director of biological programs, had explained to me that long-term maintenance of a species in captivity demands solutions to these fundamental problems. "First, we have to learn *how* to breed them. Second, we have to decide *who* to breed. And third, we have to figure out *what* to do with them and their offspring once we've bred them."

This passage is far too long to include in a brief research paper, but it is easily summarized without losing any of its effectiveness.

Avoiding Plagiarism

Plagiarism is the use of someone else's words or ideas without adequate acknowledgment — that is, presenting such words or ideas as your own. Putting something in your own words is not in itself a defense against plagiarism; the source of the ideas must be identified as well. Giving credit to the sources you use serves three important purposes: (1) It reflects your own honesty and seriousness as a researcher; (2) it enables the reader to find the source of the reference and read further, sometimes to verify that the source has been correctly used; and (3) it adds the authority of experts to your argument. Deliberate plagiarism is nothing less than cheating and theft, and it is an offense that deserves serious punishment. Accidental plagiarism can be avoided if you take a little care when researching and writing your papers.

The writer of the zoo paper, for instance, uses and correctly introduces the following direct quotation by James Rachels:

As James Rachels (1976) writes:

> Humans have a right to liberty because they have various
> other interests that will suffer if their freedom is unduly
> restricted. The right to liberty--the right to be free of external
> constraints on one's actions--may then be seen as derived
> from a more basic right not to have one's interests
> needlessly harmed. (p. 210)

If the writer of the zoo paper had chosen to state this idea more briefly, in her own words, the result might have been something like this: "Human beings believe in their fundamental right to liberty because they all agree that they would suffer without it. The right to liberty, then, stems from the right not to suffer unnecessarily." Although the wording has been significantly altered, if this statement appeared as is, undocumented, the author of the paper would be guilty of plagiarism because the ideas are not original. To avoid plagiarism, the author needs to include a reference to James Rachels at the beginning of the summary and a citation of the page number at the end. Taking care to document sources is an obvious way to avoid plagiarism. You should also be careful in taking notes and, when writing your paper, indicating where your ideas end and someone else's ideas begin.

When taking notes, make sure either to quote word-for-word *or* to paraphrase: one or the other, not a little bit of both. If you quote, enclose any language that you borrow from other sources in quotation marks. That way, when you look back at your note cards weeks later, you won't mistakenly assume that the language is your own. If you know that you aren't going to use a particular writer's exact words in your paper, then take the time to summarize that person's ideas right away. That will save you time and trouble later.

When using someone else's ideas in your paper, always let the reader know where that person's ideas begin and end. Here is an example from the zoo paper:

> When zoo animals do mate successfully, the offspring is often
> weakened by inbreeding. According to geneticists, this is because a
> population of 150 breeder animals is necessary in order to "assure
> the more or less permanent survival of a species in captivity"
> (Ehrlich & Ehrlich, 1981, p. 211).

The phrase "according to geneticists" indicates that the material to follow comes from another source, cited parenthetically at the end of the borrowed material. If the student had not included the phrase "according to geneticists," it might look as if she only borrowed the passage in quotation marks, and not the information that precedes that passage.

Material that is considered common knowledge — that is, familiar or at least accessible to the general public — does not have to be documented. The author of *Hamlet,* the date the Declaration of Independence was signed, or the definition of *misfeasance,* while open to dispute (some scholars, for example, claim that William Shakespeare did not write *Hamlet*) are indisputably considered to be common knowledge in our culture. Unfortunately, it is not always clear whether a particular fact *is* common knowledge. Although too much documentation can clutter a paper and distract the reader, it's still better to cite too many sources than to cite too few and risk being accused of dishonesty. In general, if you are unsure whether or not to give your source credit, you should document the material.

Keeping Research under Control

Your preliminary outline provides guideposts for your research. You will need to revise it as you go along to make room for new ideas and evidence and for the questions that come up as you read. Rather than try to fit each new piece of information into your outline, you can use the numbering or lettering system in your outline to cross-reference your notebooks or file cards.

As much as possible, keep all materials related to the same point in the same place. You might do this by making a separate pile of file cards for each point and its support and questions or by reserving several pages in your notebook for information bearing on each point.

How do you know when you have done enough research? If you have kept your outline updated, you have a visual record of your progress. Check this against the guidelines on pages 330–31: Is each point backed by at least two pieces of support? Do your sources represent a range of authors and of types of data? If a large proportion of your support comes from one book, or if most of your references are to newspaper articles, you probably need to keep working. On the other hand, if your notes cite five different authorities making essentially the same point, you may have collected more data than you need. It can be useful to point out that more than one authority holds a given view and to make notes of examples that are notably different from one another. But it is not necessary to take down all the passages or examples expressing the same idea.

To This Point

Before you leave the library or your primary sources for your typewriter, check to make sure your research is complete.

1. Does your working outline show any gaps in your argument?
2. Have you found adequate data to support your claim?

3. Have you identified the warrants linking your claim with data and ensured that these warrants too are adequately documented?

4. If you intend to quote or paraphrase sources in your paper, do your notes include exact copies of all statements you may want to use and complete references?

5. Have you answered all the relevant questions that have come up during your research?

6. Do you have enough information about your sources to document your paper?

MLA SYSTEM FOR CITING PUBLICATIONS

One of the simplest methods of crediting sources is the Modern Language Association (MLA) in-text system, which is used in the research paper on fairy tales in this chapter. In the text of your paper, immediately after any quotation, paraphrase, or anything else you wish to document, simply insert a parenthetical mention of the author's last name and the page number on which the material appeared. You don't need a comma after the author's name or an abbreviation of the word "page." For example, the following sentence appears in the fairy tale paper:

> Famines in the seventeenth century often reduced the peasantry to a diet of "bad black bread, acorns, and roots" (Weber 96).

The parenthetical reference tells the reader that the information in this sentence came from page 96 of the book or article by Eugen Weber that appears in the Works Cited, at the end of the paper. The complete reference on the Works Cited page provides all the information readers need to locate the original source in the library:

> Weber, Eugen. "Fairies and Hard Facts: The Reality of Folktales." Journal of the History of Ideas 42 (1981): 93-113.

If the author's name is mentioned in the same sentence, it is also acceptable to place only the page numbers in parentheses; it is not necessary to repeat the author's name. For example:

> Bettelheim sees symbolic meaning in every motif and element in the story, and assumes that children interpret these symbolically as well (159-66).

The list of works cited includes all material you have used to write your research paper. This list appears at the end of your paper and always starts on a new page. Center the title Works Cited, double-space between the title and the first entry, and begin your list, which should be arranged alphabetically by author. Each entry should start at the left margin; indent all subsequent lines of the entry five spaces. Number each page, and double-space throughout.

Another method of documenting sources is to use notes, either footnotes (at the foot of the page) or endnotes (on a separate page at the end of the paper). The note method is not as commonly used today as the in-text system for two reasons: (1) Reference notes repeat almost all the information already given on the Works Cited page. (2) If footnotes are used, it requires careful calculation during typing to fit them on the page so that there is a consistent bottom margin throughout the paper.

Nevertheless, it is a valid method, so we illustrate it here. Superscript numbers go at the end of the sentence or phrase being referenced:

> Roman authors admit to borrowing frequently from earlier Greek writers for their jokes, although no joke books in the original Greek survive today.[1]

The reference note for this citation would be:

> [1] Alexander Humez and Nicholas Humez, Alpha to Omega (Boston: Godine, 1981) 79.

On the Works Cited page this reference would be:

> Humez, Alexander, and Nicholas Humez. Alpha to Omega. Boston: Godine, 1981.

Notice that the page number for a book citation is given in the note but not the reference, and that the punctuation differs. Otherwise the information is the same. Number the notes consecutively throughout your paper.

One more point: *Content notes,* which provide additional information not readily worked into a research paper, are also indicated by superscript numbers. Susan Middleton's paper on fairy tales features four such notes, included on a Notes page before the list of Works Cited.

Following are examples of the citation forms you are most likely to need as you document your research. In general, for both books and magazines, information should appear in the following order: author, title, and publication information. Each item should be followed by a period. When using as a source an essay that appears in this book, follow the citation model for "Material reprinted from another source," unless your instructor indicates otherwise. Consult the *MLA Handbook for Writers of Research Papers,* Fourth Edition, by Joseph Gibaldi (New York: Modern Language Association of America, 1995) for other documentation models and a list of acceptable shortened forms of publishers.

A BOOK BY A SINGLE AUTHOR

Kinder, Chuck. The Silver Ghost. New York: Harcourt, 1979.

AN ANTHOLOGY OR COMPILATION

Abrahams, William, ed. Prize Stories 1980: The O. Henry Awards. Garden City: Doubleday, 1980.

A BOOK BY TWO AUTHORS

Danzig, Richard, and Peter Szanton. National Service: What Would It Mean? Lexington: Lexington, 1986.

Note: This form is followed even for two authors with the same last name.

Ehrlich, Paul, and Anne Ehrlich. Extinction: The Causes and Consequences of the Disappearance of Species. New York: Random, 1981.

A BOOK BY TWO OR MORE AUTHORS

Heffernan, William A., Mark Johnston, and Frank Hodgins. Literature: Art and Artifact. San Diego: Harcourt, 1987.

If there are more than three authors, name only the first and add: "et al." (and others).

A BOOK BY A CORPORATE AUTHOR

Poets & Writers, Inc. The Writing Business: A Poets & Writers Handbook. New York: Poets & Writers, 1985.

A WORK IN AN ANTHOLOGY

Morton, Eugene S. "The Realities of Reintroducing Species to the Wild." Animal Extinctions: What Everyone Should Know. Ed. J. R. Hoage. National Zoological Park Symposia for the Public Series. Washington: Smithsonian Institution, 1985. 71-95.

AN INTRODUCTION, PREFACE, FOREWORD, OR AFTERWORD

Borges, Jorge Luis. Preface. New Islands. By Maria Luisa Bombal. Trans. Richard and Lucia Cunningham. New York: Farrar, 1982.

MATERIAL REPRINTED FROM ANOTHER SOURCE

Tannen, Deborah. "Talking Up Close." Talking from 9 to 5. New York:
Morrow, 1994. Rpt. in Elements of Argument: A Text and Reader.
Annette T. Rottenberg. 5th ed. Boston: Bedford, 1996. 168.

A MULTIVOLUME WORK

Skotheim, Robert Allen, and Michael McGiffert, eds. Since the Civil
War. Vol. 2 of American Social Thought: Sources and
Interpretations. 2 vols. Reading: Addison, 1972.

AN EDITION OTHER THAN THE FIRST

Cassill, R. V., ed. The Norton Anthology of Short Fiction, 2nd ed. New
York: Norton, 1985.

A TRANSLATION

Allende, Isabel. The House of the Spirits. Trans. Magda Bogin. New
York: Knopf, 1985.

A REPUBLISHED BOOK

Weesner, Theodore. The Car Thief. 1972. New York: Vintage-Random,
1987.

Note: The only information about original publication you need to pro
vide is the publication date, which appears immediately after the title.

A BOOK IN A SERIES

Eady, Cornelius. Victims of the Latest Dance Craze. Omnation Press Dialogues on Dance Series 5. Chicago: Omnation, 1985.

ARTICLE FROM A DAILY NEWSPAPER

Dudar, Helen. "James Earl Jones at Bat." New York Times 22 Mar.
1987, sec. 2: 1+.

ARTICLE FROM A PERIODICAL

O'Brien, Conor Cruise. "God and Man in Nicaragua." Atlantic Monthly
Aug. 1986: 50-72.

UNSIGNED EDITORIAL

"Medium, Message." Editorial. Nation 28 Mar. 1987: 383-84.

ANONYMOUS WORKS

"The March Almanac." Atlantic Mar. 1993: 18.
Citation World Atlas. Maplewood: Hammond, 1987.

**ARTICLE FROM JOURNAL WITH SEPARATE
PAGINATION FOR EACH ISSUE**

Brewer, Derek. "The Battleground of Home: Versions of Fairy Tales."
Encounter 54.4 (1980): 52-61.

**ARTICLE IN A JOURNAL WITH CONTINUOUS
PAGINATION THROUGHOUT VOLUME**

McCafferty, Janey. "The Shadders Go Away." New England Review and
Bread Loaf Quarterly 9 (1987): 332-42.

Note that the issue number is not mentioned here; because the volume has continuous pagination throughout the year, only the volume number (9) is needed.

A REVIEW

Walker, David. Rev. of A Wave, by John Ashbery. Field 32 (1985):
63-71.

AN INTERVIEW

Hines, Gregory. Interview. With D. C. Denison. The Boston Globe Magazine 29 Mar. 1987: 2.

Note: An interview conducted by the author of the paper would be documented as follows:

Hines, Gregory. Personal interview. 29 Mar. 1987.

AN ARTICLE IN A REFERENCE WORK

"Bylina." The Princeton Encyclopedia of Poetry and Poetics. Ed. Alex
Preminger. Enlarged ed. Princeton: Princeton UP, 1974.

GOVERNMENT DOCUMENT

United States. National Endowment for the Arts. 1989 Annual Report.
Washington: Office of Public Affairs, 1990.

Frequently the Government Printing Office (GPO) is the publisher of federal government documents.

COMPUTER SOFTWARE

XyQuest. XyWrite. Vers. III Plus. Computer Software. XyQuest, 1988.
PC-DOS 2.0, 384KB, disk.

Note here that the version is given in roman numerals, since it appears that way in the title; usually software versions are given in decimals (e.g., Vers. 2.1).

DATABASE SOURCE (INFORMATION SERVICE)

Gura, Mark. The Gorgeous Mosaic Project: A Work of Art by the Schoolchildren of the World. Teacher's packet. East Brunswick:
Children's Atelier, 1990. ERIC ED 347 257.

Kassebaum, Peter. Cultural Awareness Training Manual and Study
Guide. ERIC, 1992. ED 347 289.

The ERIC documentation number at the end of the entry indicates
that the reader can obtain this source solely or primarily through
ERIC (Educational Resources Information Center). When no other
publishing information is given, treat ERIC (without a city of publication) as the publisher, as shown in the second entry. ERIC also catalogs many previously published articles with documentation
numbers beginning with EJ rather than ED. Treat these simply as articles in periodicals, not as material from an information service;
that is, omit the EJ number.

NTIS (National Technical Information Service) is another information service.

MATERIAL ACCESSED THROUGH A COMPUTER SERVICE

Boynton, Robert B. "The New Intellectuals." Atlantic Monthly Mar. 1995.
Atlantic Monthly Online. Online. America Online. 3 Mar. 1995.

CD-ROM

Corcoran, Mary B. "Fairy Tale." Grolier Multimedia Encyclopedia. CD-
ROM. Danbury: Grolier, 1995.

UNPUBLISHED MANUSCRIPT

Leahy, Ellen. "An Investigation of the Computerization of Information
Systems in a Family Planning Program." Unpublished master's degree project. Div. of Public Health, U of Massachusetts, Amherst,
1990.

LETTER TO THE EDITOR

Flannery, James W. Letter. New York Times Book Review 28 Feb.
1993: 34.

PERSONAL CORRESPONDENCE

Bennett, David. Letter to the author. 3 Mar. 1993.

LECTURE

Calvino, Italo. "Right and Wrong Political Uses of Literature."
Symposium on European Politics. Amherst College, Amherst. 25
Feb. 1976.

FILM

The Voice of the Khalam. Prod. Loretta Pauker. With Leopold Senghor,
Okara, Birago Diop, Rubadiri, and Francis Parkes. Contemporary
Films/McGraw-Hill, 1971. 16 mm, 29 min.

Other pertinent information to give in film references, if available, is
the writer and director (see model for radio/TV program for style).

TV OR RADIO PROGRAM

The Shakers: Hands to Work, Hearts to God. Narr. David McCullough.
Dir. Ken Burns and Amy Stechler Burns. Writ. Amy Stechler
Burns, Wendy Tilghman, and Tom Lewis. PBS. WGBY, Springfield.
28 Dec. 1992.

VIDEOTAPE

Style Wars! Videotape. Prod. Tony Silver and Henry Chalfont. New Day
Films, 1985. 69 min.

PERFORMANCE

Quilters: A Musical Celebration. By Molly Newman and Barbara
Damashek. Dir. Joyce Devlin. Musical dir. Faith Fung. Mt.
Holyoke Laboratory Theatre, South Hadley, MA. 26 Apr. 1991.
Based on The Quilters: Women and Domestic Art by Patricia
Cooper and Norma Bradley Allen.

CARTOON

Henley, Marian. "Maxine." Cartoon. Valley Advocate 25 Feb. 1993: 39.

Sample Research Paper (MLA Style)

The following paper, prepared in the MLA style, was written for
an advanced composition course. Told to compose a research paper
on a literary topic, Susan Middleton chose to write on fairy tales — a
subject literary enough to satisfy her instructor, yet general enough
to encompass her own interest in developmental psychology. But as
she explored the subject, she found herself reading in a surprising
array of disciplines, including folklore, anthropology, and history.
Although she initially expected to report on the psychological importance of fairy tales, Middleton at last wrote an argument about
the importance of their historical and cultural roots. Her paper, as is
typical for literary papers, anchors its argument in the events and
details of its chosen text, "Hansel and Gretel." But it also makes effective use of sources to help readers understand that there is more
to the tale than a story that sends children happily off to sleep.

When a Fairy Tale Is Not Just a Fairy Tale

By
Susan Middleton

Professor Herrington

English 2A

May 1996

Include a title page if an outline is part of the paper. If no outline is required, include name, instructor's name, course name, and date at the upper left corner of page 1

Writer's name;
page number

Topic outline.
Some instructors
require a thesis
statement under
"Outline" heading
and before the
outline itself.

Middleton   ii

Outline

I. Introduction:

   A. Dictionary definition of "fairy tale"

   B. Thesis: "Hansel and Gretel" has historical roots

II. Origin and distribution of tale

III. Historical basis of motifs

   A. Physical and economic hardship

      1. Fear of the forest

      2. Poverty and starvation

      3. Child abandonment

      4. Fantasies of finding treasure

   B. Cruel stepmother

   C. Wicked witch

      1. Eating meat associated with cannibalism and
         upper classes

      2. Elderly caretaker for unwanted children

      3. Witches in community

      4. Witchcraft as remnant of ancient fertility
         religion

IV. Rebuttals to historical approach

   A. Motivation for telling realistic tales

   B. Psychological interpretations

      1. Fairy tales dreamlike, not literal

      2. Freudian interpretation

V. Conclusion

Middleton   1

When a Fairy Tale Is Not Just a Fairy Tale

"Hansel and Gretel" is a well-known fairy tale, beloved of many children in both Europe and North America.[1] Although it has no fairies in it, it conforms to the definition of "fairy tale" given in Merriam-Webster's Collegiate Dictionary, Tenth Edition: "a story (as for children) involving fantastic forces and beings (as fairies, wizards, and goblins)." As anyone familiar with this tale will remember, Hansel and Gretel are two children on an adventure in the woods, where they encounter a wicked witch in a gingerbread house, who plans to fatten and eat them. Through their ingenuity they outsmart her, burn her up in her own oven, and return home triumphantly with a hoard of riches found in her house.

We think of fairy tales as being lighthearted fantasies that entertain but don't have much relevance to daily life. We often borrow the word to describe a movie with an unlikely plot, or a person not quite grounded in reality: "Oh, he's living in a fairy tale world; he hasn't got his head on his shoulders." In fact, the second definition of "fairy tale" in Webster's is "a made-up story usually designed to mislead."

So what is the meaning of "Hansel and Gretel"? Is it simply a story of make-believe, or something more? Fairy tales are told, read, and heard in the context of a time and place. Today we are exposed to them through illustrated storybooks, cartoons, and film. But in Europe, before technologies in printing made mass publishing possible, folktales were passed on orally. They were told by adults mostly for adult audiences, although people often first heard them as children. They served to entertain and to relieve the boredom of repetitive work in the fields during the day and in the home in the evening (Weber 93, 113). In peasant and aboriginal communities, that is often still the case (Taggart 437).

I believe that "Hansel and Gretel" has historical meaning. Embedded in this simple narrative is a record of the experiences and events once common in the lives of the people who first told and listened to it.

Title centered

Raised, super-script number refers to notes giving information at the end to the paper.

Writer briefly summarizes tale to orient readers.

In-text citation of author and pages; citation appears at the end of the sentence before the period. Thesis with claim of fact that the writer must support

Where did "Hansel and Gretel" come from? We do not know for certain. In oral form this tale shows wide distribution. Different versions have been recorded all over Europe, India, Japan, Africa, the Caribbean, Pacific Islands, and among native North and South Americans ("Hansel and Gretel"). As with all folktales, there is no agreement among folklorists[2] about whether all these versions migrated from one place to another, sprang up independently, or derive from some combination of the two ("Hansel and Gretel"). Most oral versions of it have been recorded in Europe (Aarne 117). This does not prove that the tale originated there--it may simply reflect the eagerness of people in Europe during the nineteenth and twentieth centuries to record their own folk history--but it is the best guideline for now.

The tale may be very ancient, since folktales can be passed on faithfully from one generation to another without change. (The origins of "Cinderella," for example, can be traced back to China in the ninth century [Thompson, Folktale 126].) But we can't know that for sure. So, even though "Hansel and Gretel" may have originated hundreds or even thousands of years ago, it probably is only safe to compare a tale with the historical period when the tale was first recorded. For "Hansel and Gretel" this means Europe in the seventeenth to nineteenth centuries.[3]

Eugen Weber is one historian who sees direct parallels between the characters and motifs in "Hansel and Gretel" (and other Grimms' fairy tales), and the social and economic conditions in Europe during this period. One of the central themes in the tale is poverty and abandonment. Recall how the tale begins: Hansel and Gretel live with their parents near a huge forest; their father is a woodcutter. The family is facing starvation because there is a famine. Twice their parents abandon them in the woods to save themselves. The first time the children are able to find their way home, but the second time they get lost.

As Weber points out, until the middle of the nineteenth century, the forest, especially for northern Europeans, carried the real potential for encountering

Reference to dictionary article — page number not necessary

Square brackets used to represent parentheses within parentheses

Specific support from the tale cited

Consecutive references immediately following an identified source ("Weber") cite only the pages within the source without repeating the source.

Middleton   3

danger in the form of robbers, wild animals, and getting
lost (96-97). Moreover, conditions of poverty, starvation,
early death, and danger from unknown adults were
common throughout Europe for peasants and the working
class (96). The majority of Europeans at the beginning of
the eighteenth century were farmers, and the average life
expectancy was about twenty-five years (Treasure 660,
667). Famines in the seventeenth century often reduced
the peasantry to a diet of "bad black bread, acorns, and
roots" (Weber 96). Hansel and Gretel are treated by the
witch to a dinner of pancakes and sugar, milk, nuts, and
apples (101). This may not sound particularly nourishing
to our ears because we assume a healthy dinner must have
vegetables and/or meat. But when you're starving,
anything is likely to taste good; this would have been a
sumptuous meal for Hansel and Gretel.

> Narrative details linked to histori-cal facts

Childhood was thought of differently then than today.
"Valued as an extra pair of hands or deplored as an extra
mouth to feed, the child belonged to no privileged realm of
play and protection from life's responsibilities" (Treasure
664). Social historian John Boswell estimates that anywhere
from 10 to 40 percent of children in towns and cities were
abandoned during the eighteenth century. Parental
motivation included removing the stigma of illegitimate or
physically deformed children, being unable to support their
children and hoping to give them a better life with strangers,
desiring to promote one child's inheritance over another's,
or simply lacking interest in raising the child (48, 428).

> Source cited after direct quotation

Weber points out that peasants had very little cash
and didn't use banks. Hiding and finding treasure--gold,
silver, and jewelry--was a much more common occurrence
two centuries ago than it is today (101), a kind of lottery
for the poor. In this light, the riches the children find in
the witch's house could reflect the common person's
fantasy of striking it rich.

> Writer's interpre-tation of one as-pect of the story

A central motif in the story is the stepmother who
wants to abandon the children to keep herself and her
husband from starving. (The father, at first reluctant,

Middleton   4

eventually gives in to his wife's plan.) As Weber and others have noted, stepmothers were not unusual in history. The death rate among childbearing women was much higher in past centuries than it is today. When women died in childbirth, there was strong economic motivation for fathers to remarry. In the seventeenth and eighteenth centuries, 20 to 80 percent of widowers remarried within the year of their wife's death. By the mid-nineteenth century, after life expectancy rose, only 15 percent of widowers did so (94, 112).

Reference to a
newspaper

What accounts for the stereotype of the heartless stepmother? Warner argues that mothers, not stepmothers, actually appeared in many of the tales in their original forms, until romantic editors, like the Grimm Brothers, "rebelled against this desecration of motherhood and changed mothers into wicked stepmothers" (D17). Weber suggests that stepmothers were assigned the role of doing evil to children for economic reasons: The family would risk losing its good name and perhaps its land if a biological parent killed a child (107). There is also the issue of inheritance from the stepmother's point of view: If her husband dies, her husband's children, not she, would inherit the land and property. Literary and legal evidence of stepmothers plotting to eliminate stepchildren, especially stepsons, shows up in European literature as far back as two millennia ago (Boswell 128).

Transition to new
topic: witches

Another major theme in "Hansel and Gretel" is the wicked witch, which also shows up in lots of other fairy tales. Were there witches in European history, and if so, where did the reputation for eating children come from?

Weber notes that in fairy tales only evil figures eat meat of any kind, whether animal or human flesh. Before the middle of the nineteenth century the peasantry rarely ate meat, but the aristocracy and bourgeoisie did. This discrepancy may be the origin of the motif in some fairy tales of evil figures of upper-class background wanting to eat children (112, 101). Weber seems to imply that

child-eating witches symbolized to the peasantry either
resentment of or paranoia about the aristocracy.

Although the witch's cottage in "Hansel and Gretel" is
not described as grand or large, there are other allusions to
wealth and comfort. The witch puts the two children to bed
between clean sheets, a luxury for much of the peasantry,
who slept on straw and for whom bed lice were a common
reality (Treasure 661-62). And of course there is the hoard
of coin money and jewelry the children later discover there.
Perhaps more significantly, the witch herself has a lot of
power, just as the aristocracy was perceived to have,
including the power to deceive and take away life.

David Bakan suggests that the historical basis for the
witch is the unmarried elderly woman in the community
who took in unwanted, illegitimate children and was often
paid to do this (66-67). There is also evidence that
witchcraft, ranging from white magic to sorcery (black
magic), was practiced by both individual women and men
among the peasantry during this time. For example, "the
'cunning folk' were at least as numerous in sixteenth-
century England as the parish clergy. Moreover, in their
divinatory, medical, and religious functions they were far
more important in peasant society than were the official
clergy" (Horsley 697). Witches were called on to influence
the weather, provide love potions, find lost objects,
midwife, identify thieves, and heal illnesses (698). Some
services performed by witches were ambiguous: "Apparently some peasants would conjure the storms or weather
spirits to avoid striking their own fields--but to strike someone else's instead," but for the most part the wisewomen
and sorcerers were different people (698).

The idea that an organized witch cult, as portrayed by
the Catholic Church during the Middle Ages, actually
existed is dismissed today by most social historians. Jesse
Nash thinks we should reconsider the possibility that some
of the behavior witches were accused of, including ritual
cannibalism and sexual orgies in the woods, actually

occurred in some form (12). He sees witchcraft as "a surviving remnant of a religion which was concerned with the fertility of crops, animals, humans, and with the alteration of seasons and with the identification of humans with animals" (13). These practices date back to a matriarchal goddess religion which flourished in Europe 5,000 to 7,000 years ago, before invasion of the patriarchal cultures from India (Marija Gimbutas in Nash 12). This religion included human sacrifice and was based on the concept of maintaining balance in the universe: The goddess of life was at the same time the goddess of death. Wood-wives and fairies, who lived in the forest, "were mediators of sacred knowledge to their communities" (16).

> Source within a source cited

Nash suggests that in Europe, although Christianity became the official way of thinking about the world, it did not replace the old beliefs entirely, despite strong attempts by the Church to eliminate them. Religious beliefs and practices can persist hidden for generations if need be.[4] The peasants were able to live with and practice both Christianity and paganism in combination for centuries (25).

So we have seen there is validity to the claim that many of the motifs of "Hansel and Gretel" have historical roots. However, one might well ask why people would want to hear stories so close to their own experiences. If oral tales during this time were meant as entertainment mostly for adults, wouldn't they want something to take their minds off their troubles? Weber suggests a couple of motivations for telling fairy tales. One was to experience "the delights of fear" (97). Fairy tales were told along with ghost stories, gossip, jokes, and fables. I suspect it was similar to the thrill some people get today watching scary movies with happy endings.

> Having supported her major claim, the writer continues by anticipating and addressing possible rebuttals.

Second, fairy tales helped to explain how the world worked. To most people not able to read, the world of cause and effect was mysterious and could only be explained through symbolism and analogy. Folktales had been used in church sermons since the fourteenth century (Weber 110, Zipes 22).

> Two sources cited at once

Middleton   7

But the industrial age ushered in the scientific revolution, and with it came the concept of explaining the
unknown by breaking it down into working parts (Weber
113). Reading became available to large numbers of people.
By this time fairy tales were no longer meaningful ways to
explain the world for ordinary adults, so they became the
province of children's entertainment (113).

Folklorist Alan Dundes thinks it is naive to assume
fairy tales have literal meaning. In recent years he and a
number of other people have looked to psychology to
explain the origin of fairy tales. "Fairy tales are like
dreams--can you find the historic origin of dreams?"
(Dundes). In their structure and characters fairy tales do
have a number of dreamlike aspects: They rarely state the
feelings of the hero directly, and all inner experiences of
the hero are projected outward into objects in nature and
other people (Tatar 91). The other characters seem not to
have separate lives of their own; all their actions and intentions relate to the hero (Brewer 55). Also, magical things
happen: Elements of nature speak, granting favors to the
hero or threatening success or even life. In one version of
"Hansel and Gretel," for example, a white duck talks to the
children and carries them across a lake on their way home.

The symbolic nature of fairy tales, however, doesn't
deny the validity of examining them for historical origins.
As anyone who has recorded their own dreams knows,
people and objects from mundane, daily life show up
regularly in them. Sometimes these elements are disguised
as symbols, but other times they are transparently
realistic. Similarly, the talking duck and the gingerbread
house in "Hansel and Gretel" may be unreal, but other
themes have more literal counterparts in history.

One of the most quoted interpreters of fairy tales is
psychologist Bruno Bettelheim, whose The Uses of Enchantment analyzes fairy tales in Freudian terms. In his view,
"Hansel and Gretel" represents the task each of us as
children must face in coming to terms with anxiety--not
the anxiety of facing starvation and being literally

Competing theo-
ries presented

Telephone inter-
view — no page
numbers

abandoned in the woods, but the ordinary fear of
separating from our parents (especially mother) in the
process of growing up to become independent adults. Bettelheim sees symbolic meaning in every motif and element in
the story, and assumes that children interpret these
symbolically as well (159-66).

Partial validity of
competing theo-
ries acknowl-
edged

Undeniably, there are themes in "Hansel and Gretel"--
as in many of our most common fairy tales--that strike
deep psychological chords with both children and adults.
The wicked stepmother is a good example: Children often
fantasize they are really stepchildren or adopted as a way
to account for feeling victimized and abused by their
parents. "In real life this fantasy occurs among children
with a very high frequency" (Bakan 76).

These themes help to explain the enduring popularity
of fairy tales among middle-class children over the last two
centuries. But we cannot treat fairy tales as if they spring
full-blown from the unconscious and tell us nothing about
the past. For the people who told and heard "Hansel and
Gretel" in the seventeenth to nineteenth centuries in
Europe, the tale was describing events and phenomena that
happened, if not to them, then to someone they knew.
Everyone in rural communities was likely to have been
exposed, whether in person or by hearsay, to some elderly
woman claiming powers to alter weather patterns, heal the
sick, cast spells, midwife, or take in illegitimate babies.
Stepmothers were common, poverty and famine ongoing,
and abandonment and child abuse very real. In addition to
providing entertainment, tales like "Hansel and Gretel"
reassured teller and listener alike that the ordinary
physical hardships, which for most of us today are fictions,
were possible to overcome.

Having qualified
her major claim
in light of other
theories, student
goes on to reiter-
ate the support
of her major
claim in her
conclusion.

Middleton   9

Notes

[1] We in the United States know it primarily in printed form, as it has come to us from Germany. Between 1812 and 1857, the Grimm brothers, Jacob and Wilhelm, published several editions of Kinder und Hausmarchen (Children's and Household Tales) (Zipes 6, 41, 79). In addition to "Hansel and Gretel," this book included over 200 other folktales (though not all of them were fairy tales). The anthology increased in popularity until by the turn of the twentieth century it outsold all other books in Germany except the Bible (Zipes 15). To date it has been translated into some seventy languages (Denecke).

[2] Folklorists collect folktales from around the world and analyze them. Tales are categorized according to type (basic plot line) and motifs (elements within the tale). Two widely used references for folklorists are Antti Aarne's Types of the Folklore and Stith Thompson's Motif-index. "Hansel and Gretel" is type 327A in the Aarne classification.

[3] The Grimms were the first to record tale type 327A in 1812 (see note 1). A related tale about Tom Thumb (tale type 327B) was first recorded by Charles Perrault from France in 1697 (Thompson, Folktale 37, 182).

[4] Consider the example of Sephardic Jews who "converted" to Christianity under duress in Spain in the fifteenth century. Some of them moved to North America, and their descendants continued to practice Christianity openly and Judaism in secret until recently ("Search for the Buried Past").

Content notes appear at the end of the paper, before Works Cited.

Space included between superscript number and beginning of note

Indent five spaces to superscript number; rest of note is flush left.

Works Cited

Sources arranged alphabetically by author's last name

Aarne, Antti. The Types of the Folklore: Classification and Bibliography. Trans. and ed. Stith Thompson. 2nd rev. ed. FF Communications 184. Helsinki: Suomalainen Tiedeakatemia, 1964.

First line flush left in citation, rest indented five spaces

Bakan, David. Slaughter of the Innocents. Toronto: Canadian Broadcasting System, 1971.

Bettelheim, Bruno. The Uses of Enchantment: The Meaning and Importance of Fairy Tales. 1976. New York: Vintage, 1977.

Book

Boswell, John. The Kindness of Strangers: The Abandonment of Children in Western Europe from Late Antiquity to the Renaissance. New York: Pantheon, 1988.

Periodical

Brewer, Derek. "The Battleground of Home: Versions of Fairy Tales." Encounter 54.4 (1980): 52-61.

Encyclopedia article

Denecke, Ludwig. "Grimm, Jacob Ludwig Carl and Wilhelm Carl." Encyclopaedia Britannica: Micropaedia. 1992 ed.

Interview

Dundes, Alan. Telephone interview. 10 Feb. 1993.

"Fairy tale." Merriam-Webster's Collegiate Dictionary. 10th ed. 1993.

"Hansel and Gretel." Funk & Wagnalls Standard Dictionary of Folklore, Mythology, and Legend. Ed. Maria Leach. New York: Funk & Wagnalls, 1949.

Horsley, Richard A. "Who Were the Witches? The Social Roles of the Accused in the European Witch Trials." Journal of Interdisciplinary History 9 (1979): 689-715.

Nash, Jesse. "European Witchcraft: The Hidden Tradition." Human Mosaic 21.1-2 (1987): 10-30.

Radio broadcast

"Search for the Buried Past." The Hidden Jews of New Mexico. Prod. Nan Rubin. WFCR, Amherst, MA. 13 Sept. 1992.

Taggart, James M. " 'Hansel and Gretel' in Spain and Mexico." Journal of American Folklore 99 (1986): 435-60.

Article in an edited anthology

Tatar, Maria. "Folkloristic Phantasies: Grimm's Fairy Tales and Freud's Family Romance." Fairy Tales as Ways of

Middleton   11

Knowing: Essays on Marchen in Psychology, Society
and Literature. Ed. Michael M. Metzger and Katharina
Mommsen. Germanic Studies in America 41. Berne:
Lang, 1981. 75-98.

Thompson, Stith. The Folktale. New York: Holt, 1946.

---. Motif-index of Folk-literature: A Classification of
Narrative Elements in Folktales, Ballads, Myths,
Fables, Mediaeval Romances, Exempla, Fabliaux,
Jest-books, and Local Legends. Rev. ed. 6 vols. plus
index. Bloomington: Indiana UP, 1957.

Treasure, Geoffrey R. R. "European History and Culture:
The Emergence of Modern Europe, 1500-1648." Encyclopaedia Britannica: Macropaedia. 1992 ed. 657-83.

Warner, Marina. "Pity the Stepmother." New York Times.
12 May 1991, late ed.: D17. New York Times Online.
On-line. Dow Jones News Retrieval. 18 Mar. 1996.

Weber, Eugen. "Fairies and Hard Facts: The Reality of Folktales." Journal of the History of Ideas 42 (1981):
93-113.

Zipes, Jack. The Brothers Grimm. From Enchanted Forests
to the Modern World. New York: Routledge, 1900.

Two consecutive
works by the
same author

Volume in a multi-
volume revised
edition

Newspaper
on-line from a
computer service

APA System for Citing Publications

Instructors in the social sciences might prefer the citation system of the American Psychological Association (APA). Like the MLA system, the APA system calls for a parenthetical citation in the text of the paper. Unlike the MLA system, the APA system includes the year of publication in the parenthetical reference. Here is an example:

> Even though many South American countries rely on the drug trade for their economic survival, the majority of South Americans disapprove of drug use (Gorriti, 1989, p. 72).

The complete publication information for Gorriti's article will appear at the end of your paper, on a page titled "References." (Sample citations for the "References" page appear below.)

If your list of references includes more than one work written by the same author in the same year, cite the first work as *a* and the second as *b*. For example, Gorriti's second article of 1989 would be cited in your paper as (Gorriti, 1989b).

Following are examples of the citation forms you are most likely to use. If you need the format for a type of publication not listed here, consult the *Publication Manual of the American Psychological Association,* Fourth Edition (1994).

A BOOK BY A SINGLE AUTHOR

Briggs, J. (1988). Fire in the crucible: The alchemy of creative genius. New York: St. Martin's Press.

AN ANTHOLOGY OR COMPILATION

Gioseffi, D. (Ed.). (1988). Women on war. New York: Simon & Schuster.

A BOOK BY TWO OR MORE AUTHORS OR EDITORS

Atwan, R., & Roberts, J. (Eds.). (1996). Left, right, and center: Voices from across the political spectrum. Boston: Bedford Books.

Note: List the names of *all* the authors or editors, no matter how many.

A BOOK BY A CORPORATE AUTHOR

International Advertising Association. (1977). Controversy advertising: How advertisers present points of view on public affairs. New York: Hastings House.

WORK IN AN ANTHOLOGY

Mukherjee, B. (1988). The colonization of the mind. In Gioseffi, D. (Ed.) Women on war (pp. 140-142). New York: Simon & Schuster.

AN INTRODUCTION, PREFACE, FOREWORD, OR AFTERWORD

Hemenway, R. (1984). Introduction. In Z. N. Hurston, Dust tracks on a
road. Urbana: University of Illinois Press, ix-xxxix.

AN EDITION OTHER THAN THE FIRST

Gumpert, G., & Cathcart, R. (Eds.). (1986). Inter/media: Interpersonal
communication in a media world (3rd ed.). New York: Oxford University Press.

A TRANSLATION

Sartre, J. P. (1962). Literature and existentialism. (B. Frechtman,
Trans.). New York: Citadel Press. (Original work published
1949.)

A REPUBLISHED BOOK

James, W. (1969). The varieties of religious experience: A study in
human nature. London: Collier Books. (Original work published
1961.)

A BOOK IN A SERIES

Berthrong, D. J. (1976). The Cheyenne and Arapaho ordeal:
Reservation and agency life in the Indian territory, 1875-1907.
Vol. 136. The civilization of the American Indian series. Norman:
University of Oklahoma Press.

ARTICLE FROM A DAILY NEWSPAPER

Hottelet, R. C. (1990, March 15). Germany: Why it can't happen again.
Christian Science Monitor, p. 19.

ARTICLE FROM A PERIODICAL

Gorriti, G. A. (1989, July). How to fight the drug war. Atlantic
Monthly, 70-76.

ARTICLE IN A JOURNAL WITH CONTINUOUS PAGINATION THROUGHOUT VOLUME

Cockburn, A. (1989). British justice, Irish victims. The Nation, 249,
554-555.

ARTICLE FROM A JOURNAL WITH SEPARATE PAGINATION FOR EACH ISSUE

Mukerji, C. Visual language in science and the exercise of power: The
case of cartography in early modern Europe. Studies in Visual
Communication, 10(3), 30-45.

GOVERNMENT PUBLICATION

United States Dept. of Health, Education, and Welfare. (1973). Current ethical issues in mental health. Washington, DC: U.S. Government Printing Office.

ABSTRACT

Fritz, M. (1990/1991). A comparison of social interactions using a friendship awareness activity. Education and Training in Mental Retardation, 25, 352-359. (From Psychological Abstracts, 1991, 78, Abstract No. 11474)

When the dates of the original publication and of the abstract differ, give both dates separated by a slash.

ANONYMOUS WORK

The status of women: Different but the same. (1992-1993). Zontian, 73(3), 5.

MULTIPLE WORKS BY THE SAME AUTHOR IN THE SAME YEAR

Gardner, H. (1982a). Art, mind, and brain: A cognitive approach to creativity. New York: Basic.

Gardner, H. (1982b). Developmental psychology: An introduction (2nd ed.). Boston: Little, Brown.

MULTIVOLUME WORK

Mussen, Ph. H. (Ed.). (1983). Handbook of child psychology (4th ed., Vols. 1-4). New York: Wiley.

ARTICLE IN A REFERENCE WORK

Frisby, J. P. (1990). Direct perception. In M. W. Eysenck (Ed.), Blackwell dictionary of cognitive psychology (pp. 95-100). Oxford: Basil Blackwell.

COMPUTER SOFTWARE

UnionSquareware (1987). Squarenote, the ideal librarian [Computer program]. Somerville, MA: Author.

If the primary contributors to developing the program are known, begin the reference with those as the author(s) instead of the corporate author. If you are citing a documentation manual rather than the program itself, add the word "manual" before the closing bracket. If there is additional information needed for retrieving the program (such as report and/or acquisition numbers), add this at the end of the entry, in parentheses after the last period.

DATABASE SOURCE (INFORMATION SERVICE)

LeSourd, S. J. (1992, April). The psychology of perspective consciousness. Paper presented at the annual meeting of the American Educational Research Association, San Francisco. (ERIC Document Reproduction Service No. ED 348 296)

Treat an ERIC document as a database source only if the primary or sole place to find it is from ERIC; if the source was previously published and is readily available in printed form, treat it as a journal article or published book.

MATERIAL ACCESSED THROUGH A COMPUTER SERVICE

Boynton, R. S. (1994, March 3). The new intellectuals [3 parts]. The Atlantic Monthly Online: [On-line serial]. Available America Online: Directory: The Atlantic Monthly Online: Main Menu: Newsstand: Folder: The Atlantic Monthly 40-99669: File: The New Intellectuals: Article: The New Intellectuals Parts 1-3.

REVIEW

Harris, I. M. (1991). [Review of Rediscovering masculinity: Reason, language, and sexuality]. Gender and Society, 5, 259-261.

Give the author of the review, not the author of the book being reviewed. Use this form for a film review also. If the review has a title, place it before the bracketed material, and treat it like an article title.

LETTER TO THE EDITOR

Pritchett, J. T., & Kellner, C. H. (1993). Comment on spontaneous seizure activity [Letter to the editor]. Journal of Nervous and Mental Disease, 181, 138-139.

PERSONAL CORRESPONDENCE

B. Ehrenreich (personal communication, August 7, 1992)

(B. Ehrenreich, personal communication, August 7, 1992)

Cite all personal communications to you (such as letters, memos, and telephone conversations) in text only, *without* listing them among the references. The phrasing of your sentences will determine which of the two above forms to use.

UNPUBLISHED MANUSCRIPT

McIntosh, P. (1988). White privilege and male privilege: A personal account of coming to see correspondences through work in women's studies. Working Paper 189. Unpublished manuscript, Wellesley College, Center for Research on Women, Wellesley, MA.

LECTURE

Kagan, J. (1968, April 30). A theoretical look at child development. Albert F. Blakeslee Lecture, Smith College, Northampton, MA.

PROCEEDINGS OF A MEETING, PUBLISHED

Guerrero, R. (1972/1973). Possible effects of the periodic abstinence method. In W. A. Uricchio & M. K. Williams (Eds.), Proceedings of a Research Conference on Natural Family Planning (pp. 96-105). Washington, DC: Human Life Foundation.

If the date of the symposium or conference is different from the date of publication, give both, separated by a slash. If the proceedings are published annually, treat the reference like a periodical article.

FILM

Golden, G. (Producer). (1975). Changing images: Confronting career stereotypes [Film]. Berkeley: University of California.

VIDEOTAPE

Cambridge Video (Producer). (1987). Setting educational/vocational goals [Video]. Charleston, WV: Cambridge Career Products.

SAMPLE RESEARCH PAPER (APA STYLE)

The following paper urges a change in our attitude toward zoos. Arguing the value claim that it is morally wrong for humans to exploit animals for entertainment, the student combines expert opinion gathered from research with her own interpretations of evidence. She is always careful to anticipate and represent the claims of the opposition before going on to refute them.

The student uses the APA style, modified to suit the preferences of her writing instructor. APA style requires a title page with a centered title, author, affiliation, and a short title that can be used as a "running head" on each page. An abstract page follows the title page and includes a one-paragraph abstract or summary of the article. Amanda Repp was told she could omit the title page and abstract recommended by the APA. A full description of APA publication conventions can be found in the *Publication Manual of the American Psychological Association,* Fourth Edition (1994).

Amanda Repp   Zoos   1

English 102-G

Mr. Kennedy

Fall 1996

Why Zoos Should Be Eliminated

   Zoos have come a long way from their grim beginnings.
Once full of tiny cement-block steel cages, the larger zoos now
boast simulated jungles, veldts, steppes, and rain forests, all
in an attempt to replicate the natural habitats of the incarcerated animals. The attempt, however admirable, is misguided.
It is morally wrong to keep wild animals in captivity, and no
amount of replication, no matter how realistic, can compensate for the freedom these creatures are denied.

   Peter Batten (1976) argues that a wild animal's life "is
spent in finding food, avoiding enemies, sleeping, and in
mating or other family activities. . . . Deprivation of any of
these fundamentals results in irreparable damage to the
individual" (p. 1). The fact that humans may be stronger or
smarter than beasts does not give them the right to ambush
and exploit animals for the purposes of entertainment.

   We humans take our own liberty quite seriously.
Indeed, we consider liberty to be one of our inalienable
rights. But too many of us apparently feel no obligation to
grant the same right to animals, who, because they cannot
defend themselves against our sophisticated methods of
capture and because they do not speak our language,
cannot claim it for themselves.

   But the right to liberty is not based on the ability to
claim it, or even on the ability to understand what it is. As
James Rachels (1976) writes:

>   Humans have a right to liberty because they have
>   various other interests that will suffer if their
>   freedom is unduly restricted. The right to liberty--the
>   right to be free of external constraints on one's
>   actions--may then be seen as derived from a more
>   basic right not to have one's interests needlessly
>   harmed. (p. 210)

Animals, like people, have interests that are harmed if they
are kept in captivity: They are separated from their
families and prevented from behaving according to their

Short title and
page number, per
APA style. Some
instructors may
prefer the stu-
dent's name in-
stead of the short
title as a running
head.

First paragraph
ends with thesis

Citation includes
author, date of
publication, and
page number. El-
lipses (. . .) indi-
cate omitted pas-
sage; period after
ellipses indicates
that the omission
included the end
of a sentence.

Long quotations
of more than 40
words are set off
as block quota-
tions. Start a new
line on a five-
space indented
margin, double
space throughout,
and put the page
number of the
quotations in pa-
rentheses after the
final punctuation.

natural instincts by being removed from the lives they know, which are the lives they were meant to lead.

Some argue that animals' interests are not being harmed when they are kept in zoos or aquariums--that no damage is being done to the individual--but their claims are highly disputable. For example, the Zurich Zoo's Dr. Heini Hediger (1985) protests that it is absurd to attribute human qualities to animals at all, but he nevertheless resorts to a human analogy: "Wild animals in the zoo rather resemble estate owners. Far from desiring to escape and regain their freedom, they are only bent on defending the space they inhabit and keeping it safe from invasion" (p. 9). How can Dr. Hediger explain the actions of the leopards and cheetahs I have seen executing figure eights off the walls and floors of their cages for hours on end? I have watched, spellbound by their grace but also horrified; it is impossible to believe that these animals do not want their freedom. An estate owner would not spend his time running frantically around the perimeters of his property. These cats know they are not lords of any estate. The senseless repetition of their actions suggests that the cats know that they are caged and that there is nothing to defend against, no "estate" to protect.

Shannon Brownlee (1986) also believes that there is no concrete evidence that incarcerated animals are suffering or unhappy, but she weakens her own case in her description of Jackie, a dolphin in captivity who "spends the day in a seeming stupor" and "chews on the mackerel half-heartedly" at feeding time (p. 70). Clearly there <u>is</u> something wrong with Jackie; this becomes apparent when Brownlee contrasts Jackie's lethargic behavior with that of wild dolphins cavorting in the bay. Brownlee points out that Jackie has never tried to escape through a hole in his enclosure, although he knows it is there. But this fact does not necessarily mean that Jackie enjoys captivity. Instead, it may mean that Jackie's spirit has been broken, and that he no longer remembers or cares what his earlier days were like. Granted we have no way of knowing what Jackie

---

Summary of an opposing argument

Writer suggests flaw in comparison.

Refutation of opposing argument based on evidence from personal experience

Writer summarizes, then points out a weakness in, a second opposing argument.

Writer questions an unstated warrant in the argument.

Zoos   3

is really feeling, but does that give us the right to <u>assume</u>
that he is not feeling anything?

To be fair, Brownlee does not go that far. She does
allow Jackie one emotional state, attributing his malaise to
boredom. But perhaps if the author were removed from
members of her family, as well as all other members of her
species, and prevented from engaging in activities that most
mattered to her, she would recognize Jackie's problems as
something more than boredom. In any case, why should we
inflict boredom on Jackie, or any other animal, just because
we happen to have the means to do so?

Having registered these basic objections to zoos--that
keeping any creature in captivity is a fundamental infringement on that creature's right to liberty and dignity--I want
to take a closer look at the zoo as an institution, in order to
assess fairly its goals and how it tries to meet them. Most
zoo professionals today maintain that zoos exist for two
main reasons: to educate humans and to conserve animal
species. These are both admirable goals, certainly, but as
Seal (1985) notes, "none of these [zoo] budgets is allocated
specifically for species preservation. Zoos have been
established primarily as recreational institutions and are
only secondarily developing programs in conservation, education, and research" (p. 74). The fact is most zoos do not
have the money, space, or equipment required to make significant contributions in this area. The bulk of their money
goes to the upkeep of the animals and exhibits--that is, to
put it crudely, to the displays.

On behalf of the education a zoo provides, a common
argument is that there is nothing like seeing the real thing.
But what you see in the zoo is not a real thing at all. Many
zoo and aquarium animals, like Jackie the dolphin, have
been domesticated to the point of lethargy, in part because
they are being exhibited alone or with only one other member of their species, when what they are used to is
traveling in groups and finding their own food, instead of
being fed. Anyone who wants to see the real thing would
be better off watching some of the excellent programming

Writer shifts to
the second half of
her argument.

Clarifying word in
square brackets

Another opposing
argument, with
refutation

Summarizes two
expert opinions
that zoos do not
help endangered
species

about nature and wildlife that appears on public television.

As for conservation, it is clearly a worthwhile effort, but zoos are not effective agents of species preservation. It is generally acknowledged that it is difficult to breed zoo animals (Luoma, 1982, p. 104). Animals often do not reproduce at all--quite possibly because of the artificial, and consequently unsettling, circumstances in which they live. When zoo animals do mate successfully, the offspring is often weakened by inbreeding. According to geneticists, this is because a population of 150 breeder animals is necessary in order to "assure the more or less permanent survival of a species in captivity" (Ehrlich & Ehrlich, 1981, p. 211). Few zoos have the resources to maintain populations that size. When zoos rely on smaller populations for breeding (as many do) the species' gene pool becomes more and more limited, "vigor and fecundity tend to decline" (Ehrlich & Ehrlich, 1981, p. 212), and this can eventually lead to extinction. In other words, we are not doing these animals any favors by trying to conserve them in zoos. Indeed, Wilson (1995) writes that "all the zoos in the world today can sustain a maximum of only 2000 species of mammals, birds, reptiles, and amphibians, out of about 24,000 known to exist" (p. 57). Reserves and preservations, which have room for the larger populations necessary for successful conservation efforts and which can concentrate on breeding animals rather than on displaying them, are much more suitable for these purposes.

For what purposes, then, are zoos suitable? Are they even necessary? At present, they must house the many generations of animals that have been bred there, since these animals have no place else to go. Most animals in captivity cannot go back to the wild for one of two reasons. The first is that the creatures would be unable to survive there, since their instincts for finding their own food and protecting themselves from predators, or even the weather, have been greatly diminished during their time spent in captivity (Morton, 1985, p. 155). Perhaps this

---

Author, date, page cited parenthetically

Source with two authors cited parenthetically

Paraphrase with source cited parenthetically

Zoos   5

is why Jackie the dolphin chooses to remain in his
enclosure.

The other reason animals cannot return to the wild is
an even sadder one: In many cases, their natural habitats
no longer exist. Thanks to deforesting and clearing of land
for homes, highways, factories, and shopping malls--which
are continually being built with no regard for the plant and
animal life around them--ecosystems are destroyed constantly, driving increasing numbers of species from their
homes. Air and water pollution and toxic waste, results of
the ever-increasing urbanization and industrialization
throughout the world, are just some of the agents of this
change. It is a problem I wish to address in closing.

If zoos were to leave breeding programs to more
appropriate organizations and to stop collecting animals,
the zoo as an institution would eventually be phased out.
Animals would cease to be exhibits and could resume being
animals, and the money previously used to run zoos could
be put to much better use. Ideally it could be used to
investigate why endangered species are endangered, and
why so many of the original habitats of these species have
disappeared. Most important, it could be used to explore
how we can change our habits and reorient our behavior,
attitudes, and priorities, so we can begin to address these
issues.

Writer closes by
proposing a solu-
tion of her own.

The problem of endangered species does not exist in a
vacuum; it is a symptom of a much greater predicament.
Humankind is responsible for this predicament, and it is up
to us to recognize this before it is too late. Saving a selected
species here and there will do none of us any good if those
species can exist only in isolated, artificial environments,
where they will eventually breed themselves into extinction. The money that has been concentrated on such efforts
should be devoted instead to educating the public about the
endangered planet--not just its animals--or, like the animals,
none of us will have any place to go.

Zoos   6

References start
a new page

References

Batten, P. (1976). <u>Living trophies</u>. New York: Crowell.

Brownlee, S. (1986, December). First it was "save the
    whales," now it's "free the dolphins." <u>Discover</u>,
    70-72.

A book with two
authors

Ehrlich, P. & Ehrlich, A. (1981). <u>Extinction: The</u>
    <u>causes and consequences of the disappearance of</u>
    <u>species</u>. New York: Random House.

A work in an
anthology

Hediger, H. (1968). From cage to territory. In R.
    Kirchschofer (Ed.), <u>The world of zoos: A survey</u>
    <u>and gazeteer</u> (pp. 9-20). New York: Viking.

An article from a
periodical

Luoma, J. (1982, November). Prison or ark?
    <u>Audubon</u>, 102-109.

Morton, E. S. (1985). The realities of reintroducing
    species to the wild. In J. R. Hoage (Ed.), <u>Animal</u>
    <u>extinctions: What everyone should know</u> (pp.
    147-158). National Zoological Park Symposia for
    the Public series. Washington, DC: Smithsonian
    Institution.

For each refer-
ence, flush left on
first line, then in-
dent three spaces
on subsequent
lines

Rachels, J. (1976). Do animals have a right to
    liberty? In T. Regan & P. Singer (Eds.), <u>Animal</u>
    <u>rights and human obligations</u> (pp. 205-223).
    Englewood Cliffs, NJ: Prentice-Hall.

Seal, U. S. (1985). The realities of preserving species
    in captivity. In J. R. Hoage (Ed.), <u>Animal extinc-</u>
    <u>tions: What everyone should know</u> (pp.
    147-158). National Zoological Park Symposia for
    the Public series. Washington, DC: Smithsonian
    Institution.

An article
on-line from a
computer service

Wilson, E. (1995, October 30). Wildlife: Legions of the
    doomed. [On-line]. <u>Time</u>. pp. 57-62. Nexis
    Library: Mags.

Arguing about Literature

Writing a paper about a work of literature — a novel, a short story, a poem, or a play — is not so different from writing about matters of public policy. In both cases you make a claim about something you have read and demonstrate the validity of that claim by providing support. In papers about literature, support consists primarily of evidence from examples and details in the work itself and your own interpretation of the language, the events, and the characters. In addition, you can introduce expert scholarly opinion and history and biography where they are relevant.

First, a note about the differences between imaginative literature and argumentative essays. Although the strategies for writing papers about them may be similar, strategies for reading and understanding the works under review will be different. Suppose you read an essay by a psychologist who wants to prove that lying to children, even with the best intentions, can have tragic consequences. The claim of the essay will be directly stated, perhaps even in the first sentence. But if an author writes a short story or a play about the same subject, he or she will probably not state the central idea directly but will *show* rather than *tell*. The theme will emerge through a narrative of dramatic events, expressions of thoughts and feelings by the characters, a depiction of relationships, descriptions of a specific setting, and other elements of fiction. In other words, you will derive the idea or the theme indirectly. This is one reason that a work of fiction can lend itself to multiple interpretations. But it is also the reason that literature, with its evocation of the mysteries of real life, exerts a perpetual fascination.

Different kinds of literary works emphasize different elements. In the following discussion the elements of fiction, poetry, and drama are briefly summarized. The discussion will suggest ways of reading imaginative literature for both pleasure and critical analysis.

THE ELEMENTS OF FICTION

The basic elements of imaginative prose — a short story, a novel, or a play — are *theme, conflict,* and *character.* Other elements such as language, plot, point of view, and setting also influence the effectiveness of any work, but without a central idea, a struggle between opposing forces, and interesting people, it's unlikely that the work will hold our attention. (On the other hand, literature is full of exceptions, and you will certainly find examples that defy the rules.)

The theme is the central idea. It answers the question, What is the point of this story or play? Does the author give us some insight into a personal dilemma? Does he or she show how social conditions shape human behavior? Do we learn how certain traits of character can influence a human life? The answers to these questions apply not only to the specific situation and invented characters in a particular story. In the most memorable works the theme — the lesson to be drawn, the truth to be learned — embodies an idea that is much larger than the form the story assumes. For example, in "The Use of Force," the short story by William Carlos Williams at the end of this appendix, the title refers to the *subject* but not the theme. The author wanted to say something *about* the use of force. His theme is a complicated and unwelcome insight into human nature, with implications for all of us, not just the doctor who is the principal actor in the story.

Conflict is present in some form in almost all imaginative writing. It creates suspense and introduces moral dilemmas. External conflicts occur between individuals and between individuals and natural forces. Internal conflicts take place in the minds and hearts of the characters who must make difficult choices between competing goals and values — between right and wrong, pleasure and duty, freedom and responsibility. These two kinds of conflict are not exclusive of each other. A story of war, for example, will include suspenseful physical encounters between opposing forces, but the characters may also be compelled to make painful choices about their actions. In the best works, conflicts are important, not trivial. They may reveal uncommon virtues or shortcomings in the characters, alter their relationships with other people, and even change the course of their lives.

Conflicts exist only because characters — human beings, or in some satires, animals — engage in them. In contests with forces of nature, as in Hemingway's *The Old Man and the Sea,* it is the courage and persistence of a human being that gives meaning to the story.

Memorable fictional characters are not easy to create. As readers we demand that characters be interesting, plausible, consistent, and active, physically and mentally. We must care about them, which is not the same as liking them. To care about characters means retaining enough curiosity about them to keep reading and to regret their departure when the story has come to an end. However different and unfamiliar their activities, we should feel that the characters are real. Even in science fiction we insist that the creatures exhibit human characteristics that we can recognize and identify with. But fictional characters should also be distinguishable from one another. Stereotypes are tiresome and unconvincing.

We learn about characters primarily from their speech and their actions but also from what the author and other characters reveal about them. Remembering that characters often withhold information or conceal their motives, even from themselves, we must often depend on our own knowledge and experience to interpret their behavior and judge their plausibility.

THE ELEMENTS OF DRAMA

Drama shares with fiction the elements we have discussed earlier — theme, conflict, and character. But because a play is meant to be performed, it differs from a written story in significant ways. These differences impose limits on the drama, as opposed to the novel, which can do almost anything.

First, stage action is restricted. Violent action — a war scene, for example — must usually take place offstage, and certain situations — such as the hunt for Moby Dick in Melville's novel — would be hard to reproduce in a theater. This means that a play emphasizes internal rather than external conflict.

Second, the author of a play, unlike the author of a short story or a novel, cannot comment on the action, the characters, or the significance of the setting. (It is true that a narrator sometimes appears on stage as a kind of Greek chorus to offer observation on the action, but this is uncommon.) A much greater burden must therefore rest on what the characters say. They must reveal background, explain offstage events, interpret themselves and others, and move the plot forward largely through speech. If the author of a novel lacks skill in reproducing plausible speech, he can find ways to avoid dialogue, but the playwright has no such privilege. She must have an ear for the rhythms and idioms of language that identify particular characters.

Another element which assumes more importance in a play than in a novel is plot. The dramatist must confine an often complicated and event-filled story to two or three hours on the stage. And, as in any listening experience, the audience must be able to follow the plot without the luxury of going back to review.

As you read a long play, you may find it helpful to keep in mind a simple diagram that explains the development of the plot, whether comedy or tragedy. The Freytag pyramid, created in 1863 by a German critic, shows that almost every three- or five-act play begins in a problem or conflict which sets in motion a series of events, called *the rising action.* At some point there is a *climax,* or turning point, followed by *the falling action,* which reverses the fortunes of the main characters and leads to a conclusion that may be happy or unhappy.

Shakespeare's *Macbeth* is an almost perfect example of the pyramid. The rising action in this tragedy is one of continued success for the main characters. The climax is a crisis on the battlefield, after which the fortunes of Macbeth and Lady Macbeth decline, ending in failure and death. In a comedy, the developments are reversed. The rising action is a series of stumbles and mishaps; then in the climax the hero finds the money or rescues the heroine and the falling action ushers in a number of welcome surprises that culminate in a happy ending. (Think of a Jim Carrey adventure.) Typically the rising action in any play takes longer and thus creates suspense.

Reading a play is not the same as seeing one on stage. Many playwrights, like novelists, describe their settings and their characters in elaborate detail. In *Long Day's Journey Into Night,* Eugene O'Neill's autobiographical play, descriptions of the living-room in which the action occurs and of the mother and father, who appear in the first act, cover more than three pages in small print. When you read, you fill the imaginary stage with your own interpretations of the playwright's descriptions, derived perhaps from places or persons in your own experience. You may forget that the playwright is dependent on directors, set designers, and actors, with other philosophies and approaches to stagecraft, to interpret his or her work. It can come as a surprise to see the stage version of the play you have read and interpreted very differently.

All playwrights want their plays to be performed. Still, the best plays are read far more frequently than they are produced on stage. Fortunately, reading them is a literary experience with its own rewards.

THE ELEMENTS OF POETRY

There are several kinds of poetry, among them epic, dramatic, and lyric. Epic poetry celebrates the heroic adventures of a human or superhuman character in a long, event-filled narrative. Milton's *Paradise Lost* is the preeminent example in English, but you may also be familiar with *The Iliad, The Odyssey,* and *The Aeneid,* the epics of

ancient Greece and Rome. Dramatic poetry also tells a story, sometimes through monologue, as in Robert Browning's "My Last
Duchess," where the Duke recounts the reasons why he murdered
his wife; sometimes through dialogue, as in Robert Frost's "The
Death of the Hired Man." These stories are often told in blank verse,
unrhymed five-beat lines. Playwrights of the past, Shakespeare
among others, adopted this poetic form.

Modern poems are much more likely to be lyrics — poetry derived from song. (The term *lyric* comes from the word for an ancient
musical instrument, the lyre.) The lyric is most frequently an expression of the poet's feeling rather than an account of events. The characteristics that make poetry harder to read than prose are the very
characteristics that define it: compression and metaphor. A lyric
poem is highly concentrated. It focuses on what is essential in an experience, the details that illuminate it vividly against the background of our ordinary lives. Metaphor is a form of figurative
language, a way of saying one thing to mean something else. It is a
simile which omits the "like" or "as": for example, "A mighty fortress
is our God." The poet chooses metaphoric images that appeal to our
senses in order to reinforce the literal meaning. In a famous poem
Thomas Campion compared the beauty of his sweetheart's face to
that of a garden.

> There is a garden in her face
> Where roses and white lilies grow,
> A heavenly paradise is that place,
> Wherein all pleasant fruits do flow.

A poem, like an essay, tries to prove something. Like a short
story, its message is indirect, expressed in the language of
metaphor. It seldom urges a practical course of action. What it tries
to prove is that a feeling or a perception — a response to love or
death, or the sight of a snowy field on a dark night — is true and
real.

The lyric poet's subjects are common ones — love, joy, sorrow,
nature, death — but he or she makes uncommon use of words, imagery, and rhythm. These are the elements you examine as evidence
of the poet's theme and depth of feeling.

Precisely because the poem will condense her experience, the
poet must choose words with immediate impact. For example, in a
poem about an encounter with a snake, Emily Dickinson writes,

> But never met this Fellow
> Attended, or alone
> Without a tighter breathing
> And Zero at the bone —

Although we have never seen this use of "zero" before, it strikes us at once as the perfect choice to suggest a kind of chilling fear.

In the best poems images transform the most commonplace experiences. Here is the first quatrain of Shakespeare's sonnet number 73, about loving deeply what will not live forever.

> That time of year thou mayest in me behold
> When yellow leaves or none or few do hang
> Upon those boughs which shake against the cold
> Bare ruined choirs where late the sweet birds sang.

Nowhere does Shakespeare mention that he is growing old. Instead, here and in subsequent stanzas he creates images of dead or dying things — autumn trees, the coming of night, dying fires — that convey feelings of cold and desolation. The final couplet expresses the theme directly:

> Thus thou perceivs't, which makes thy love more strong,
> To love that well which thou must leave ere long.

It is the imagery, however, that brings the theme to life and enables us to understand and share the poet's feeling.

Rhythm, defined as measured and balanced movement, is almost as important as language. As children, even before we fully understand all the words, we derive pleasure from the sounds of Mother Goose and the Dr. Seuss rhymes. Their sound patterns reflect the musical origin of poetry and the fact that poetry was meant to be chanted rather than read. Listen to the rhythm of these opening lines from Andrew Marvell's "To His Coy Mistress" — "Had we but world enough and time, / This coyness, lady, were no crime" — and hear the lilting four-beat meter that suggests song. If you look through an anthology of poetry written before the twentieth century, you will see even from the appearance of the poems on the page that the cadence or rhythm of most poems creates an orderly pattern. Edgar Allan Poe's "The Raven" is a familiar example of poems in which rhyme and rhythm come together to produce a harmonious design.

Measured movement in poetry is less common today. Free verse breaks with this ancient convention. (The very regularity of "The Raven" is now a subject for parody.) The poet of free verse invents his own rhythms, governed by meaning, free association, and a belief in poetry as a democratic art, one capable of reaching all people. In "Song of Myself," Walt Whitman (1819–1892), one of America's most influential poets, writes in a new voice that resembles the sound of spoken language:

> A child said *What is the grass?* fetching it to me with
>   full hands,

How could I answer the child? I do not know what it is
    any more than he.
I guess it must be the flag of my disposition, out of hopeful
    green stuff woven.

Notice, however, that the phrase "out of hopeful green stuff woven" is the language of poetry, not prose.

Much modern poetry dispenses altogether with both rhyme and formal rhythms, but the lyric remains unmistakably alive. Perhaps you have read poems by William Carlos Williams or e. e. cummings, who have used new rhythms to create their own distinctive versions of the lyric.

THE CULTURAL CONTEXT

Even those works that are presumed to be immortal and universal are products of a particular time in history and a particular social and political context. These works may therefore represent points of view with which we are unsympathetic. Today, for example, some women are uncomfortable with Shakespeare's *The Taming of the Shrew,* which finds comic possibilities in the subjugation of a woman to her husband's will. Jews may be offended by the characterization of Shylock in *The Merchant of Venice* as a Jewish money-lender who shows little mercy to his debtor. Some African Americans have resented the portrayal of Jim, the slave in *Huckle berry Finn.* Even *Peter Pan* has provoked criticism for its depiction of American Indians. In your own reading you may find fault with an author's attitude toward his subject; defending your own point of view against that of the author can be a satisfying literary exercise. To bring fresh, perhaps controversial, interpretations into an analysis may, indeed, enliven discussion and even revive interest in older works that no longer move us. But remember that the evidence will be largely external, based on social and political views that will themselves need explanation.

There is, after all, a danger in allowing our ideas about social and political correctness to take over and to impose our values on those of another time, place, or culture. Literature, like great historical writing, enables us to enter worlds very different from our own. The worlds we read about in novels and plays may be governed by different moral codes, different social conventions, different religious values, many of which we reject or don't understand. Characters in these stories, even those cast as heroes and heroines, sometimes behave in ways we consider ignorant or self-serving. (Russell Baker, the humorist, observed that it was unfortunate that the writers of the past were not so enlightened as we are.) But reading has always offered an experience otherwise unavailable, a ready escape from our own lives into the lives of others, whose ways, however strange, we try to understand, whether or not we approve.

CHOOSING WHAT TO WRITE ABOUT

Your paper can take one of several different approaches. It is worth emphasizing that comedy and tragedy generally share the same literary elements. A tragedy, of course, ends in misfortune or death. A comedy typically ends with a happy resolution of all problems.

1. You may analyze or explain the meaning or theme of a work that is subject to different interpretations. For example, a famous interpretation of *Hamlet* in 1900[1] suggested that Hamlet was unable to avenge his father's murder because of guilt over his own Oedipal love for his mother. Or, having seen a distorted movie version of a familiar book (unfortunately, there are plenty of examples) you can explain what you think is the real theme of the book and how the movie departs from it.

Some stories and plays, although based in reality, seem largely symbolic. "The Lottery," a widely read short story by Shirley Jackson, describes a ritual that hints at other meanings than those usually attributed to lotteries. *Waiting for Godot,* a play by Samuel Beckett, is a work that has inspired a dozen interpretations; the name *Godot,* with the embedded word *God,* suggests several. But exercise caution in writing about symbols. Saul Bellow, the Nobel Prize–winning novelist, has written an essay, "Deep Readers of the World, Beware!" that explains the dangers. He reminds us that "a true symbol is substantial, not accidental. You cannot avoid it, you cannot remove it."

2. You may analyze the conflicts in a story or play. The conflicts that make interesting papers are those that not only challenge our understanding (as with Iago's villainy in *Othello*) but encourage us to reflect on profound moral issues. For example, how does Mark Twain develop the struggle in Huckleberry Finn between his southern prejudices and his respect for Jim's humanity? How does John Proctor, the hero of Arthur Miller's *The Crucible,* resolve the moral dilemmas that lead him to choose death rather than a freedom secured by lies?

3. You may choose to write about an especially vivid or contradictory character, describing his traits in such a way as to make clear why he is worth a detailed examination. The protagonist of *The Stranger* by Albert Camus, for example, is a murderer who, although

---

[1] By Ernest Jones, a Freudian analyst.

he tells us little or nothing about himself and is therefore difficult to understand, eventually earns our sympathy.

4. You may concentrate on the setting if it has special significance for the lives of the characters and what they do, as in Joseph Conrad's *Heart of Darkness* and Tennessee Williams's *A Streetcar Named Desire*. Setting may include time or historical period as well as place. Ask if the story or play would have taken shape in quite the same way in another time and place.

5. You may examine the language or style. No analysis of a poem would be complete without attention to the language, but the style of a prose work can also contribute to the impact on the reader. Hemingway's clean, economical style has often been studied, as has Faulkner's dense, complicated prose, equally powerful but very different. But you should probably not attempt an analysis of style unless you are sure you can discuss the uses of diction, grammar, syntax, and rhythm.

GUIDELINES FOR WRITING THE PAPER

1. Decide on a limited topic as the subject for your paper. The most interesting topics, of course, are those that are not so obvious: original interpretations, for example, that arise from a genuine personal response. Don't be afraid to disagree with a conventional reading of the literary work, but be sure you can find sufficient evidence for your point of view.

2. Before you begin to write, make a brief outline of the points that will support your thesis. You may find that you don't have enough evidence to make a good case to a skeptical reader. Or you may find that you have too much for a short paper and that your thesis, therefore, is too broad.

3. The evidence that you provide can be both internal and external. Internal evidence is found in the work itself: an action that reveals motives and consequences, statements by the characters about themselves and others, comments by the author about her characters, and interpretation of the language. External evidence comes from outside the work: a comment by a literary critic, information about the historical period or the geographical location of the work, or data about the author's life and other works he has written.

If possible, use more than one kind of evidence. The most important proof, however, will come from a careful selection of material from the work itself.

4. One temptation to avoid is using quotations from the work or from a critic so abundantly that your paper consists of a string of quotations and little else. Remember that the importance of your

paper rests on *your* interpretations of the evidence. Your *own* analysis should constitute the major part of the paper. The quotations should be introduced only to support important points.

5. Organize your essay according to the guidelines you have followed for an argumentative essay on a public issue (see Chapter 9, pp. 315–21). Two of the organizational plans that work best are defending the main idea and refuting the opposing view — that is, a literary interpretation with which you disagree. In both cases the simplest method is to state your claim — the thesis you are going to defend — in the first paragraph and then line up evidence point by point in order of importance. If you feel comfortable beginning your paper in a different way, you may start with a paragraph of background: the reasons that you have chosen to explore a particular topic or a description of your personal response to the work — for example, where you first saw a play performed, how a story or poem affected you. (H. L. Mencken, the great American social critic, said discovering *Huckleberry Finn* was "the most stupendous event of my whole life!" What a beginning for an essay!)

It is always useful to look at book or movie reviews in good newspapers and magazines for models of organization and development that suggest a wide range of choices for your own paper.

SAMPLE STORY AND ANALYSIS

Read the following short story and reflect on it for a few moments. Then turn back to the following questions. Were you surprised at the actions of the doctor? What is the author saying about the use of force? Do you agree? What kinds of conflicts has he dramatized? Are some more important than others? How do the characterizations of the people in the story contribute to the theme?

Thinking about the answers to these questions will give you a clearer perspective on the essay written by a student that follows the story. After reading the essay, you may see other elements of fiction that might have been analyzed in a critical paper.

The Use of Force

WILLIAM CARLOS WILLIAMS

They were new patients to me, all I had was the name, Olson. Please come down as soon as you can, my daughter is very sick.

When I arrived I was met by the mother, a big startled looking woman, very clean and apologetic who merely said, Is this the doctor? and let me in. In the back, she added, You must excuse us, doctor, we have her in the kitchen where it is warm. It is very damp here sometimes.

The child was fully dressed and sitting on her father's lap near the kitchen table. He tried to get up, but I motioned for him not to bother, took off my overcoat and started to look things over. I could see that they were all very nervous, eyeing me up and down distrustfully. As often, in such cases, they weren't telling me more than they had to, it was up to me to tell them; that's why they were spending three dollars on me.

The child was fairly eating me up with her cold, steady eyes, and no expression to her face whatever. She did not move and seemed, inwardly, quiet; an unusually attractive little thing, and as strong as a heifer in appearance. But her face was flushed, she was breathing rapidly, and I realized that she had a high fever. She had magnificent blonde hair, in profusion. One of those picture children often reproduced in advertising leaflets and the photogravure sections of the Sunday papers.

She's had a fever for three days, began the father and we don't 5 know what it comes from. My wife has given her things, you know, like people do, but it don't do no good. And there's been a lot of sickness around. So we tho't you'd better look her over and tell us what is the matter.

As doctors often do I took a trial shot at it as a point of departure. Has she had a sore throat?

Both parents answered me together, No . . . No, she says her throat don't hurt her.

Does your throat hurt you? added the mother to the child. But the little girl's expression didn't change nor did she move her eyes from my face.

Have you looked?

I tried to, said the mother, but I couldn't see.   10

As it happens we had been having a number of cases of diphtheria in the school to which this child went during that month and we

---

"The Use of Force," William Carlos Williams, *The Farmers' Daughters* (1938).

were all, quite apparently, thinking of that, though no one had as yet spoken of the thing.

Well, I said, suppose we take a look at the throat first. I smiled in my best professional manner and asking for the child's first name I said, come on, Mathilda, open your mouth and let's take a look at your throat.

Nothing doing.

Aw, come on, I coaxed, just open your mouth wide and let me take a look. Look, I said opening both hands wide. I haven't anything in my hands. Just open up and let me see.

Such a nice man, put in the mother. Look how kind he is to you.   15 Come on, do what he tells you to. He won't hurt you.

At that I ground my teeth in disgust. If only they wouldn't use the word "hurt" I might be able to get somewhere. But I did not allow myself to be hurried or disturbed but speaking quietly and slowly I approached the child again.

As I moved my chair a little nearer suddenly with one cat-like movement both her hands clawed instinctively for my eyes and she almost reached them too. In fact she knocked my glasses flying and they fell, though unbroken, several feet away from me on the kitchen floor.

Both the mother and father almost turned themselves inside out in embarrassment and apology. You bad girl, said the mother, taking her and shaking her by one arm. Look what you've done. The nice man . . .

For heaven's sake, I broke in. Don't call me a nice man to her. I'm here to look at her throat on the chance that she might have diphtheria and possibly die of it. But that's nothing to her. Look here, I said to the child, we're going to look at your throat. You're old enough to understand what I'm saying. Will you open it now by yourself or shall we have to open it for you?

Not a move. Even her expression hadn't changed. Her breaths   20 however were coming faster and faster. Then the battle began. I had to do it. I had to have a throat culture for her own protection. But first I told the parents that it was entirely up to them. I explained the danger but said that I would not insist on a throat examination so long as they would take the responsibility.

If you don't do what the doctor says you'll have to go to the hospital, the mother admonished her severely.

Oh yeah? I had to smile to myself. After all, I had already fallen in love with the savage brat, the parents were contemptible to me. In the ensuing struggle they grew more and more abject, crushed, exhausted while she surely rose to magnificent heights of insane fury of effort bred of her terror of me.

The father tried his best, and he was a big man but the fact that she was his daughter, his shame at her behavior and his dread of hurting her made him release her just at the critical moment several times when I had almost achieved success, till I wanted to kill him. But his dread also that she might have diphtheria made him tell me to go on, go on though he himself was almost fainting, while the mother moved back and forth behind us raising and lowering her hands in an agony of apprehension.

Put her in front of you on your lap, I ordered, and hold both her wrists.

But as soon as he did the child let out a scream. Don't, you're 25 hurting me. Let go of my hands. Let them go I tell you. Then she shrieked terrifyingly, hysterically. Stop it! Stop it! You're killing me!

Do you think she can stand it, doctor! said the mother.

You get out, said the husband to his wife. Do you want her to die of diphtheria?

Come on now, hold her, I said.

Then I grasped the child's head with my left hand and tried to get the wooden tongue depressor between her teeth. She fought, with clenched teeth, desperately! But now I also had grown furious — at a child. I tried to hold myself down but I couldn't. I know how to expose a throat for inspection. And I did my best. When finally I got the wooden spatula behind the last teeth and just the point of it into the mouth cavity, she opened up for an instant, but before I could see anything she came down again and gripping the wooden blade between her molars she reduced it to splinters before I could get it out again.

Aren't you ashamed, the mother yelled at her. Aren't you 30 ashamed to act like that in front of the doctor?

Get me a smooth-handled spoon of some sort, I told the mother. We're going through with this. The child's mouth was already bleeding. Her tongue was cut and she was screaming in wild hysterical shrieks. Perhaps I should have desisted and come back in an hour or more. No doubt it would have been better. But I have seen at least two children lying dead in bed of neglect in such cases, and feeling that I must get a diagnosis now or never I went at it again. But the worst of it was that I too had got beyond reason. I could have torn the child apart in my own fury and enjoyed it. It was a pleasure to attack her. My face was burning with it.

The damned little brat must be protected against her own idiocy, one says to one's self at such times. Others must be protected against her. It is social necessity. And all these things are true. But a blind fury, a feeling of adult shame, bred of a longing for muscular release are the operatives. One goes on to the end.

In a final unreasoning assault I overpowered the child's neck and jaws. I forced the heavy silver spoon back of her teeth and down her throat till she gagged. And there it was — both tonsils covered with membrane. She had fought valiantly to keep me from knowing her secret. She had been hiding that sore throat for three days at least and lying to her parents in order to escape just such an outcome as this.

Now truly she *was* furious. She had been on the defensive before but now she attacked. Tried to get off her father's lap and fly at me while tears of defeat blinded her eyes.

Jennifer Rampolla
Professor Harrington
English 102-C
May 2, 19--

Conflicts in "The Use of Force"

"The Use of Force" tells us something about human nature that probably comes as no surprise: The impulse to use violence against a helpless but defiant opponent can be thrilling and irresistible. But the conflict which produces this insight is not a shoot-out between cops and robbers, not a fight for survival against a dangerous enemy, but a struggle between a grown man and a sick child.

In this story two major conflicts are dramatized, one external or physical, the other internal or psychological. The conflicts seem obvious. Even the blunt, unadorned language means to persuade us that nothing is concealed. But below the surface, some motives remain unacknowledged, and we guess at them only because we know how easily people deceive themselves.

The external conflict is vividly depicted, a physical struggle between doctor and child, complete with weapon-- a metal spoon. The outcome is hardly in doubt; the doctor will win. One critic calls this story primarily "an accomplishment (external conflict) story" (Madden 16). But the internal conflict that accompanies a difficult choice is the real heart of the story. The doctor must decide between waiting for a more opportune time to examine the child or exercising brute force to subdue her now. When he decides on brute force, he seems aware of his motives.

> But the worst of it was that I too had got beyond
> reason. I could have torn the child apart in
> my own fury and enjoyed it. It was a pleasure
> to attack her.

This shocking revelation is not, however, the whole story. <u>Why</u> has he got beyond reason? Why does he take pleasure in attacking a child? The answer lies not only in what we know about the antagonists but in what we can assume about their relationship to each other.

Annotations (right margin):

Title indicates subject

Introduction

The theme

Theme emerges through conflicts

Naming the major conflicts (external and internal)

A concealed conflict (to be explained later)

Body

External conflict developed

Evidence: comment from a critic

Internal conflict developed

Evidence: Quotation

Concealed conflict, based on the characters and their relationship

Rampolla   2

Description
of the child

The child is brilliantly portrayed in a few grim encounters with the doctor. She is strong, stubborn, secretive, and violent. Despite her size and age, she is a match for the doctor, a challenge that at first excites him.

Evidence:
Quotation

I had to smile to myself. After all, I had already fallen in love with the savage brat. . . . In the ensuing struggle . . . she surely rose to magnificent heights of insane fury. . . .

Description
of the doctor

Unexpressed
social conflict

Evidence: External, from history

Evidence:
Quotation

Perhaps another concealed conflict?

The doctor's real motivation

The picture of the doctor is somewhat harder to read. Sixty years ago (when this story was written) the doctor in a working-class community occupied a position of unusual power and authority. He would not be accustomed to challenges at any level. Clearly the differences in social and economic status between the doctor and his clients are another source of conflict that influences his use of force. Like many people in positions of power, the doctor is torn by contradictory emotions toward those below him. On the one hand, he despises those who are deferential to him, in this case the child's parents. On the other hand, it is unthinkable that a child should dare to oppose him, not only in refusing to obey his instructions but in trying, like a desperate small animal, to attack him. It is even more unthinkable that she should prevail in any contest. He confesses to "a feeling of adult shame." If we look for it, there is also a hint of sexual conflict. The child is blond and beautiful; the doctor says he is in love with her. (Would this story have worked in quite the same way if the child had been a boy?) The doctor attempts to rationalize his use of force, but he knows that it is not the child's welfare that finally compels him to overcome her resistance. In the end, reason gives way to pride and vanity.

Conclusion

The reader's mixed reaction

Most of us respond to this story with a mixture of feelings--anger at the pleasure the doctor takes in his use of force, confusion and even fear at the realization that doctors may not always behave like gentle and loving helpers, and pity for the little girl with whom it is easy to identify. The author doesn't spell out the moral implications of the doctor's internal conflict. But perhaps it is significant

Rampolla   3

that the author gives the last words to the little girl: "Tears
of defeat blinded her eyes." I think he has chosen this
ending in order to direct our sympathy to the victim, an
unhappy child who struggled hopelessly to protect herself.
Although we know that the doctor has performed a
necessary and merciful act, we are left to wonder if it
matters that he has done it for the wrong reason.

Sympathy for
the child

Reaction to
the theme

Rampolla   4

Works Cited

Madden, David. Studies in the Short Story. New York: Holt,
       1980.

ACKNOWLEDGMENTS *(continued from page ii)*

Ellen Bravo and Ellen Cassedy, "What Sexual Harassment Is — And Is Not." From *The 9 to 5 Guide to Combatting Sexual Harassment: Candid Advice from 9to5, the National Association of Working Women.* Copyright © 1992 John Wiley & Sons, Inc. Reprinted by permission of John Wiley & Sons, Inc.

Armin A. Brott, "Not All Men Are Sly Foxes." From *Newsweek,* June 1, 1992. Reprinted by permission of the author.

Warren E. Burger, "The Right to Bear Arms." From *Parade,* January 14, 1990. Reprinted with permission from Parade, copyright © 1990, and the author.

Peggy Carlson, "Why We Don't Need Animal Experimentation." From the *Wall Street Journal,* November 7, 1995. Reprinted with permission of The Wall Street Journal © 1995 Dow Jones & Company, Inc. All rights reserved.

Cease Fire advertisement, "A gun in the home is much more likely to kill a family member than to kill an intruder." Reprinted courtesy of Cease Fire, Inc.

John P. Conrad, "Against the Death Penalty." From *Death Penalty: A Debate* by John P. Conrad and Ernest van den Haag. Copyright © 1983 Plenum Publishing Corporation. Reprinted by permission of Plenum Publishing Corporation and the authors.

Louis L. Cregler and Herbert Mark, "Cocaine Is Even Deadlier Than We Thought." From the *New York Times,* July 30, 1986. Reprinted by permission of the authors.

Alan Dershowitz, "The Case for Medicalizing Heroin." From *Contrary to Popular Opinion* by Alan Dershowitz. Copyright © 1992 United Feature Syndicate, Inc. Reprinted by permission of United Feature Syndicate, Inc.

John Patrick Diggins, "The Pursuit of Whining: Affirmative Action circa 1776." From the *New York Times,* September 25, 1995. Copyright © 1995 by The New York Times Co. Reprinted by permission.

Rachel Ehrenfeld, "Selling Syringes: The Swiss Experiment." From the *Wall Street Journal,* September 16, 1995. Reprinted with permission of The Wall Street Journal © 1995 Dow Jones & Company, Inc. All rights reserved.

James Finn Garner, "Jack and the Beanstalk." Reprinted with permission of Macmillan Publishing USA, a Simon & Schuster Macmillan Company, from *Politically Correct Bedtime Stories* by James Finn Garner. Copyright © 1994 by James Finn Garner.

Henry Louis Gates, Jr., "A Liberalism of Heart and Spine." Copyright © 1991 Henry Louis Gates, Jr. First appeared in the *New York Times,* March 27, 1994. Copyright © 1994 by The New York Times Co. Reprinted by permission.

General Electric advertisement, "GE: The initials of a friend." Reprinted by permission of General Electric.

Paul Goodman, "A Proposal to Abolish Grading." Reprinted from *Compulsory Miseducation* by Paul Goodman. Copyright © 1964 Horizon Press, New York. Reprinted by permission.

Francine du Plessix Gray, "Starving Children." Copyright © 1995 by Francine du Plessix Gray. Reprinted by permission of Georges Borchardt, Inc. for the author. Originally appeared in *The New Yorker.*

Adolf Hitler, "On Nation and Race." From *Mein Kampf* by Adolf Hitler, translated by Ralph Manheim. Copyright © 1943, © renewed 1971 by Houghton Mifflin Co. Reprinted by permission of Houghton Mifflin Co., the Estate of Adolf Hitler, the Estate of Ralph Manheim, and Hutchinson.

Philip K. Howard, "A Nation of Enemies." From *The Death of Common Sense* by Philip K. Howard. Copyright © 1994 by Philip K. Howard. Reprinted by permission of Random House, Inc.

Joshua B. Janoff, "A Gen-X Rip Van Winkle." From *Newsweek,* March 27, 1995. All rights reserved. Reprinted by permission.

William Severini Kowinski, "Kids in the Mall: Growing Up Controlled." From *The Malling of America* by William Severini Kowinski. Copyright © 1985 by William Severini Kowinski. Reprinted by permission of William Morrow & Co.

Land's End advertisement, "Numbers don't lie." Reprinted courtesy of Land's End Direct Merchants.

Michael Levin, "The Case for Torture." Reprinted by permission of the author.

John E. Mack, "UFO Abductions: An Introduction." Reprinted with the permission of Scribner, a Division of Simon & Schuster from *Abduction: Human Encounters with Aliens* by John E. Mack. Copyright © 1994 by John E. Mack, M.D.

Metropolitan Energy Council advertisement, "Gas heat makes me nervous." Reprinted by permission of the Metropolitan Energy Council.

Jacob Neusner, "The Speech the Graduates Didn't Hear." Copyright © 1983 by Jacob Neusner. Reprinted from the Brown *Daily Herald,* June 12, 1983. Used by permission of the author.

Tony Parker and Hank Sullivan, "People Like Me." From *The Violence of Our Lives: Interviews with American Murderers* edited by Tony Parker. Copyright © 1995 by Tony Parker. Reprinted by permission of Henry Holt and Co., Inc.

Curtis Peebles, "Abductions and Abductionists." Reprinted from *Watch the Skies! A Chronicle of the Flying Saucer Myth* by Curtis Peebles (Washington, DC: Smithsonian Institution Press), pages ix–x, 234–41, by permission of the publisher. Copyright 1994.

Stanton Peele, "Addiction Is Not a Disease." Reprinted with permission from *Diseasing of America: Addiction Treatment Out of Control* by Stanton Peele. Copyright © 1989 Stanton Peele. First published by Lexington Books. All correspondence should be sent to Jossey-Bass Inc., Publishers, San Francisco. All rights reserved.

"Plastic That Goes to Waste," pie chart. From the *Wall Street Journal,* February 2, 1990. Reprinted by permission of The Wall Street Journal © 1990 Dow Jones & Company, Inc. All rights reserved worldwide.

David Rakoff, "A Former Smoker Cheers." From the *New York Times,* April 14, 1995. Copyright © 1995 by The New York Times Co. Reprinted by permission.

William Rathje and Cullen Murphy, "The Landfill Excavations." From *Rubbish! The Archaeology of Garbage* by William Rathje and Cullen Murphy. Copyright © 1992 by William Rathje and Cullen Murphy. Reprinted by permission of HarperCollins Publishers, Inc.

Heloisa Sabin, "Animal Research Saves Human Lives." From the *Wall Street Journal,* October 18, 1995. Reprinted with permission of The Wall Street Journal © 1995 Dow Jones & Company, Inc., all rights reserved, and by permission of Americans for Medical Progress Educational Foundation.

Saturn advertisement, "Cheryl Silas had a highway collision, was hit twice from behind, and then sold three cars for us." Reprinted by permission of the Saturn Corporation.

Lisa Schiffren, "Penalize the Unwed Dad? Fat Chance." From the *New York Times,* August 10, 1995. Copyright © 1995 by The New York Times Co. Reprinted by permission.

Albert Shanker, "The Real Victims." Copyright © 1995 by Albert Shanker and reprinted with his permission.

Joseph P. Shapiro and Andrea R. Wright, "Sins of the Fathers." From *U.S. News & World Report,* August 14, 1995. Copyright, Aug. 14, 1995, U.S. News & World Report.

Deborah Tannen, "Talking Up Close." From *Talking 9 to 5* by Deborah Tannen, Ph.D. Copyright © 1994 by Deborah Tannen, Ph.D. By permission of William Morrow & Co.

Kathleen Kennedy Townsend, "Not Just Read and Write, but Right and Wrong." From *The Washington Monthly,* January 1990. Reprinted with permission from *The Washington Monthly.* Copyright by The Washington Monthly Company, 1611 Connecticut Ave., N.W., Washington, D.C., 20009 (202) 462-0128.

Abigail Trafford, "Advice for the Anti-Smokers: Take a Message from Garcia." Taken from her "Second Opinion" column. Copyright © 1995. Reprinted with permission of Universal Press Syndicate. All rights reserved.

Ernest van den Haag, "For the Death Penalty." From *Death Penalty: A Debate* by John P. Conrad and Ernest van den Haag. Copyright © 1983 Plenum Publishing Corporation. Reprinted by permission of Plenum Publishing Corporation and the authors.

Alexander Volokh, "Kessler's a Drag." Reprinted with permission from the August 1995 issue of *Reason* magazine. Copyright 1995 by the Reason Foundation, 3415 S. Sepulveda Blvd., Suite 400, Los Angeles, CA 90034. This article appeared in the *Wall Street Journal,* August 8, 1995.

The *Wall Street Journal*, "Green Eggs and Ham," editorial, April 27, 1992. Reprinted with permission of The Wall Street Journal © 1992 Dow Jones & Company, Inc. All rights reserved.

"Want to Bet?" bar graph. From the *New York Times,* May 28, 1989. Copyright © 1989 by The New York Times Co. Reprinted by permission.

Waterman Pen Co. advertisement. Courtesy, Waterman Pen Company.

Claudius E. Watts III, "Single-Sex Education Benefits Men Too." The *Wall Street Journal,* May 3, 1995. Reprinted with permission of The Wall Street Journal © 1995 Dow Jones & Company, Inc. All rights reserved.

William Carlos Williams, "The Use of Force." From *Doctor Stories* by William Carlos Williams. Copyright © 1938 by William Carlos Williams. Reprinted by permission of New Directions Publishing Corp.

James Q. Wilson, "Bring Back the Orphanage." The *Wall Street Journal,* August 22, 1994. Reprinted with permission of The Wall Street Journal © 1994 Dow Jones & Company, Inc. All rights reserved.

Glossary and
Index of Terms

Abstract language: language expressing a quality apart from a specific object or event; opposite of *concrete language* *223–27*

Ad hominem: "against the man"; attacking the arguer rather than the *argument* or issue *267–68*

Ad populum: "to the people"; playing on the prejudices of the *audience* *271*

Appeal to tradition: a proposal that something should continue because it has traditionally existed or been done that way *271–72*

Argument: a process of reasoning and advancing proof about issues on which conflicting views may be held; also, a statement or statements providing *support* for a *claim* *3–24*

Audience: those who will hear an *argument;* more generally, those to whom a communication is addressed *13–14*

Authoritative warrant: a *warrant* based on the credibility or trustworthiness of the source *186*

Backing: the assurances upon which a *warrant* or assumption is based *180–81*

Begging the question: making a statement that assumes that the issue being argued has already been decided *269–70*

Claim: the conclusion of an argument; what the arguer is trying to prove *10–11*

Claim of fact: a *claim* that asserts something exists, has existed, or will exist, based on data that the audience will accept as objectively verifiable *10, 47–53*

Claim of policy: a *claim* asserting that specific courses of action should be instituted as solutions to problems *11, 62–72*

Claim of value: a *claim* that asserts some things are more or less desirable than others *10, 54–62*

Cliché: a worn-out expression or idea, no longer capable of producing a visual image or provoking thought about a subject   *227–30*

Concrete language: language that describes specific, generally observable, persons, places, or things; in contrast to *abstract language*   *223–27*

Connotation: the overtones that adhere to a word through long usage   *215–18*

Credibility: the audience's belief in the arguer's trustworthiness; see also *ethos*   *14–17*

Data: see *evidence*

Deduction: reasoning by which we establish that a conclusion must be true because the statements on which it is based are true; see also *syllogism*   *253–58*

Definition: an explanation of the meaning of a term, concept, or experience; may be used for clarification, especially of a *claim,* or as a means of developing an *argument*   *13, 94–105*

Definition by negation: defining a thing by saying what it is not   *100–01*

Enthymeme: a *syllogism* in which one of the premises is implicit   *256*

Ethos: the qualities of character, intelligence, and goodwill in an arguer that contribute to an *audience's* acceptance of the *claim*   *14*

Euphemism: a pleasant or flattering expression used in place of one that is less agreeable but possibly more accurate   *216*

Evidence: *facts* or opinions that support an issue or *claim;* may consist of *statistics,* reports of personal experience, or views of experts   *140–54*

Extended definition: a *definition* that uses several different methods of development   *102–03*

Fact: something that is believed to have objective reality; a piece of information regarded as verifiable   *50–51*

Factual evidence: *support* consisting of *data* that is considered objectively verifiable by the audience   *140–42, 146–48*

Fallacy: an error of reasoning based on faulty use of *evidence* or incorrect *inference*   *248*

False analogy: assuming without sufficient proof that if objects or processes are similar in some ways, then they are similar in other ways as well   *266–67*

False dilemma: simplifying a complex problem into an either/or dichotomy   *268*

Faulty emotional appeals: basing an argument on feelings, especially pity or fear—often to draw attention away from the real issues or conceal another purpose   *272–73*

Faulty use of authority: failing to acknowledge disagreement among experts or otherwise misrepresenting the trustworthiness of sources   *264*

Substantive warrant: a *warrant* based on beliefs about the reliability of *factual evidence*   *186–87*

Support: any material that serves to prove an issue or *claim;* in addition to *evidence,* it includes appeals to the *needs* and *values* of the *audience*   *11, 138–60*

Syllogism: a formula of deductive *argument* consisting of three propositions: a major premise, a minor premise, and a conclusion   *254–58*

Thesis: the main idea of an essay   *261–63*

Toulmin model: a conceptual system of argument devised by the philosopher Stephen Toulmin; the terms *claim, support, warrant, backing, qualifier,* and *reservation* are adapted from this system   *261–63*

Two wrongs make a right: diverting attention from the issue by introducing a new point, e.g., by responding to an accusation with a counteraccusation that makes no attempt to refute the first accusation   *270–71*

Values: conceptions or ideas that act as standards for judging what is right or wrong, worthwhile or worthless, beautiful or ugly, good or bad   *158–60*

Warrant: a general principle or assumption that establishes a connection between the *support* and the *claim*   *11–13, 179–87*

Index of Authors
and Titles